The
ACADEMY
IN CRISIS

The
ACADEMY
IN CRISIS

The Political Economy
of Higher Education

Edited by
JOHN W. SOMMER
Foreword by Nathan Glazer

Transaction Publishers
New Brunswick (U.S.A.) and London (U.K.)

This book is printed on acid-free paper that meets the American National Standard for Permanence of Paper for Printed Library Materials.

Library of Congress Catalog Number: 94-9271
ISBN: 1-56000-182-8 (cloth); 1-56000-801-6 (paper)
Printed in the United States of America

Library of Congress Cataloging-in-Publication Data

The Academy in Crisis : the political economy of higher education / edited by John W. Sommer ; foreword by Nathan Glazer.
   p. cm.
Includes bibliographical references and index.
Contents: Higher education / John W. Sommer—The evolution of American higher education / Roger Meiners—In service to the state / Joel Spring—Federal student aid and institutional support programs / C. Ronald Kimberling—Higher education, the individual, and the humane sciences / Antony Flew—The economics of higher education / E.G. West—Economics of fundamental research / Stephen Dresch—Property rights in academe / Roger Meiners—Normative and positive models of scientific research / Peter Aranson—Science and technology for economic ends / Joseph Martino—Universities and training of scientists / Cotton M. Lindsay.
   ISBN 1-56000-182-8
   1. Higher education and state—United States. 2. Federal aid to higher education—United States. 3. University autonomy—United States. 4. Federal aid to research—United States. 5. Education, Higher—Economic aspects—United States. I. Sommer, John W., 1938-   . II. Glazer, Nathan.
LC173.A48 1994
379'.0973—dc20   94-9271
                                                     CIP

Contents

The **INDEPENDENT INSTITUTE**

THE INDEPENDENT INSTITUTE is a non-profit, scholarly research and educational organization which sponsors comprehensive studies on the political economy of critical social and economic problems.

The politicization of decision-making in society has largely confined debate to the narrow reconsideration of existing policies, the prevailing influence of partisan interests, and a stagnation of social innovation. In order to understand both the nature of and possible solutions to major public issues, the Independent Institute's studies adhere to the highest standards of independent inquiry and are pursued regardless of prevailing political or social biases and conventions. The resulting studies are widely distributed as books and other publications, and are publicly debated through numerous conference and media programs.

Through this uncommon independence, depth, and clarity, the Independent Institute pushes at the frontiers of our knowledge, redefines the debate over public issues, and fosters new and effective directions for government reform.

For further information and a catalog of publications, please contact:
THE INDEPENDENT INSTITUTE
134 Ninety-Eighth Avenue, Oakland, CA 94603
(510) 632-1366   FAX: (510) 568-6040

Foreword

The structure of American higher education is unique. While higher education in the great European nations is almost entirely in the hands of government, with either a nonexistent private sector or one limited to a few Catholic institutions or business schools, half the institutions of higher education in the United States are private and one-fifth of our students attend private institutions. In addition, our most distinguished research universities and our most selective colleges are in large part private. The only nations that, in some degree, approach our system of higher education are those that have fallen (in large measure and at key points in their development) under American influence: Japan, Korea, and the Philippines. But even in these nations, the most distinguished and prestigious institutions are public, not private.

Is it owing to this distinctive role of the private sector that American higher education remains one of the few areas of American life in which American predominance and advantage are so marked? Many might think so: Henry Rosovsky, the former dean of the Faculty of Arts and Sciences of Harvard University, has often pointed to this predominance of American institutions among the leading universities of the world. And it stands to reason that the remarkable flow of private funds—individual, corporate, and foundation—to American colleges and universities can be attributed to a direct link between these institutions and students, communities, and donors.

But, while it is still meaningful to make use of the public-private dichotomy in American higher education, in increasing measure all institutions of higher education are dependent upon public support, state or federal. In even greater measure, all institutions of higher education fall under some degree of public control and regulation, a degree that grew alarmingly during the 1970s, a decade in which public support, particularly in the form of student loans and grants, grew enormously.

The consequences to American higher education is the central theme of *The Academy in Crisis.* The findings of this excellent book are in favor of the private sector, in favor of an institutional pattern that links those who seek advantage in their personal lives and economic opportunities directly with the institutions that provide it. In this way the process is left as much as possible to the workings of a market of free choice and free provision, in which the effect of competition, of choice among alternatives, is unimpeded. It is safe to infer that most of the contributors to this book come to the conclusion that institutions should be as free of government control as possible, even though the writers take a variety of positions on the question of just how government control and support adversely affects institutions of higher education.

This is a markedly minority but increasingly influential view in American higher education. The leaders of American higher education, public and private, university and college, are as eager for as much government support as they can get—for student tuition, for research, for the maintenance of libraries, for the building of dormitories, and indeed for whatever other function regarding which they may be able to justify public support. However, these same administrators are agitated by the degree of public control that comes with these funds. They are concerned by the cost of implementing regulations for women, for minorities, for the handicapped, and so on. Such regulations have increasingly established their legitimacy quite independently of the fact that government may provide funds to these institutions.

In recent years, we have also seen a surprising amount of governmental intervention into the conduct of research, which has been very alarming to scientists, the chief beneficiaries of the cornucopia of government grants. Universities have lost their claim to a superior level of morality, despite the fact that they are nonprofit institutions: they are now viewed as suspiciously by some congressmen and by parts of the mass media as are private firms working on government arms contracts, and these watchdogs leap to the charges of whistle-blowers in universities as eagerly as they do to the charges of those who expose screw-drivers that cost $600 apiece or unimaginably expensive toilet seats.

But, whatever the complaints about government regulation, universities and colleges do not see how they can escape substantial dependence on public funds and the interventions and intrusions that come with them, and, as we have pointed out, today come even without them. Our courts have defined beneficiaries so expansively that any aid from government accepted by a student (and how can students or anyone else be realistically expected to forego the funds that legislation makes available to them?) makes the institution they attend a government contractor, or a beneficiary of public aid, strengthening the power to place more and more areas of college and university activities under the power of government agents.

This expansion of the interconnection of higher education and government seems to grow inexorably. In the late 1970s, the level of government regulation reached a peak. One of the most egregious forms of governmental intervention was legislation and regulations for the "protection of human subjects" in research. This had started with the understandable desire to protect human subjects in medical research but soon spread into a bureaucratic nightmare as humans involved in any kind of research (even public opinion surveys, researchers began to fear) would have to be asked to sign waivers. But rather more serious, undoubtedly, was the steady expansion of protection for women and the handicapped, which required a substantial expense in making buildings available and in providing the same sports facilities for women as for men. It also, for religious institutions, meant that local rules that defended an institutional view of the proper relations between the sexes had to be abandoned.

Even those educational leaders whose general political outlook was liberal and rights-oriented began to complain. Using a particularly vivid image, Kingman Brewster, president of Yale University, protested: "Use of the leverage of the government dollar to accomplish objectives which have nothing to do with the purposes for which the dollar is given has become dangerously fashionable.... It might be called the 'now that I have bought the button, I have the right to design the coat' approach."[1] But Congress (not to mention the Federal bureaucracy) was unyielding. To quote Senator Claiborne Pell: "The more federal assistance you get, of course, the more federal control of your institution there is, because there is a great deal of truth in the old adage 'He who pays the piper calls the tune.'"[2]

Institutions of higher education hoped for relief when President Reagan replaced President Carter—after all, here was a president who insisted the problem was government and that there should be less of it. But higher education certainly wasn't ready to make the deal that Senator Pell's remarks suggested: yes, we'll take less money, for less regulation. In any case, the state of constitutional law, with its wide reach to protect rights regardless of federal support, would have made such a deal improbable. Institutions of higher education still sought more federal money, in all the forms and for all the functions for which it is available, and expanded their staffs of lawyers and administrators to manage the work required to get the aid and to comply with the regulations and requirements that accompany such aid.

The Academy in Crisis explores with remarkable ingenuity the arguments so commonly taken for granted reagarding the reasons institutions of higher education need and should have government aid. For instance, the chapter by the redoubtable E. G. West pursues the argument for public support in all its various forms. He challenges the idea of high social returns to education and finds inefficiencies not often noted by advocates of more public investment (for example, the "use of education in the socially wasteful practices of job-market signalling and occupational licensure.") The high private rates of return suggest that tuition "could be raised significantly without large effects on enrollment." (American experience would certainly support this finding.) He points to the "inevitability of the 'crowding out' of private by public academic institutions." Again, American experience supports this. Public choice theory "reminds us that the political process that advocates rely upon to pursue external benefits, equity, etc., does not, in practice, respect the preferences of a wide and undifferentiated electorate but tends to allow particular interest groups...to exploit asymmetric political power." A free and competitive system based on student choice (and the paying for that choice by those benefitting from it) would, to his mind, lose nothing.

The argument is exemplary, and perhaps the main counter-argument is that of "externalities," the things society might need that the individual or firms will not pay for, in particular research. Here there is a particularly rich group of chapters. Stephen Dresch analyzes the arguments for support of fundamental research, something that is hardly challenged. Those of us without experience in fundamental research will learn much, and some of what we learn can be tested by our own experiences. As Dresch points out, the nature of the distribution of talents means that ever more research will attract ever more mediocre researchers, a finding that could be supported by any of us who have experience in the distribution of grants in the social sciences and humanities. And, whatever the benefits from fundamental research, the inevitable pressure from public funders of such research will be to demand justification in terms of measurable achievements that fundamental research cannot supply. Roger Meiners and Robert Staaf point out that the pattern of rewards for administrators, trustees, and faculty from research and teaching means an inevitable underinvestment in teaching. And the further chapters by Peter Aranson, Joseph Martino, and Cotton Lindsay raise questions on the public support of scientific research and the training of scientists, questions that rarely come up in public discussion, where really all one hears, as the theory of public choice would tell us, is "more."

This book does not and cannot be expected to exhaustively raise all the issues one might want to raise in considering the costs and benefits of various kinds of public support for higher education and its various functions. I confess that there are public costs for which I would argue without knowing how the various arguments deployed in this book might come out, and without knowing how the costs might be justified: for example, the maintenance of our great university and other public libraries. I do not know how to justify the maintenance of collections rarely consulted, collections that simply reflect our past experience, and perhaps mostly our past errors. The kind of argument with which the contributors to this volume are most at home would not, I think, be able to justify expenditures that are rising at a frightening rate (perhaps, they might say, they rise at such a rate because the producers know there will be funds available, mostly public, to pay them).

A second question is the issue of competition in international prestige. Falling behind other developed nations in a number of spheres, Americans pride themselves on the fact that they attract so many students from abroad and that their universities are still in the first rank. However, here contributing author Cotton Lindsay asks, what is wrong with importing skilled scientists and engineers and doctors? Let other countries train them! We, being economically more rational, would benefit from *their* irrational decisions. This is a rather startling suggestion and leads us to ask ourselves not only what value we place on our primacy in research but what our moral obligations are in contributing to the world's stock of trained personnel, and how, then, we can morally justify drawing them from poorer countries.

The Academy in Crisis does not wish to prescribe a specific program for the reduction of the public role in higher education. Instead, we have presented a series of very learned and challenging arguments and considerations, many raising new and perhaps unpopular points, but which might lead us to raise a skeptical eyebrow when we hear the ever-present cry, "more!" from students, parents, scientists, faculty members, and administrators. They will have to consider the various arguments presented in this book, arguments that suggest not "more" but "less" to be the answer.

Nathan Glazer
Professor of Education and Sociology,
Harvard University

Notes

1. Chester E. Finn, Jr., *Scholars, Dollars, and Bureaucrats* (Washington D. C.: Brookings Institution, 1978) p. 139.
2. Ibid., p. 139.

Acknowledgments

The writing of a book is a complicated process, made less so by the effort and support of special individuals and institutions who have touched us along the way. When there are many contributing authors the list of those who should be acknowledged is so extraordinary as to make it impracticable, if not impossible. I shall assert the editor's prerogative and make my own statement.

To the contributing authors, I thank you for your forbearance in a much drawn out journey to publication: your contributions have worn the trip very well.

To the Independent Institute, the sponsor of this book, and its president, David Theroux, we congratulate you on your endurance as well as good taste, both in literature and in employees, especially Mrs. Theresa Navarro, who put so much of herself into this book. Thank you Theresa, from all of the contributors.

To Dartmouth College, I extend my thanks for the education it permitted me in the 1950s and the inspiration that it has provided me since the mid-seventies to publish these thoughts.

Lastly, I thank an old and dear friend who also was a founding member of the Board of Advisors for the Independent Institute, now harrumphing with the angels, for his advice and criticism: Thank you Aaron Wildavsky even though you are nodding your head vigorously and affirmatively over my final acknowledgment, that the errors contained herein are entirely my responsibility!

Introduction

American Higher Education: State of the Art or Art of the State?

John W. Sommer

Prologue

What comes to mind when your child or young acquaintance announces an acceptance for admission to college? For some adults it is the thought of prolonged tranquility, punctuated only by vacations that dot the academic calendar. For others it is either triumph or failure of status achievement to be celebrated or justified, as the case may be. For virtually everyone it is the astronomical and escalating price of tuition and fees of private colleges and universities, and the not inconsequential expenses associated with many state supported schools. Lately, it is often the character of the campus experience to which one is willing to subject a young person. Thanks to a spate of books critical of higher education—for example, Bartley's *Unfathomed Knowledge*, Bloom's *Closing of the American Mind*, Meiner and Amacher's, *Federal Support of Higher Education*, Smith's *The Killing Spirit*, D'Souza's *Illiberal Education*, Anderson's *Imposters in the Temple* and Sykes's two books, *Profscam* and *The Hollow Men*—more families are asking what they get for their investment.[1] In *The Hollow Men*, Charles Sykes delivers an incisive critique of the "politically correct thinking," or "PC" phenomenon, describing its various interest group manifestations, and identifying, in particular, the fundamental nihilism that has invaded the feminist didacticism on campuses.[2] In college after college these activated special interest groups have had their way with educational standards as administrators and faculty looked on.

For the majority of students and their parents the reality of political correctness has been a nuisance or a source of embarrassment, but increasingly it is realized that to contend with demands for fealty to the dicta of special interest organizations or cliques on campus diminishes the value of the investment in college. The "college experience" is thereby transformed into something

1

more like a gauntlet of insults than a refuge for reflective thought and the realization of cherished dreams of advancement through education.

Has the seeming acceptance of, or spearheading, of PC thinking by faculty destroyed the credibility of university faculty as the responsible agents for higher education? The answer is probably—no more so than the variety of other contra-academic denigrations institutions of higher education have visited upon themselves in recent years, as the "treasons of the clerks," described in this book by Antony Flew, has progressed. Unfortunately, trustees, boards of directors, and regents have assigned too little blame to those administrators of higher education who used the power of their offices, the purses of the institutions, and the hard-earned reputational capital to assuage their moments of decision at times of confrontation instead of confronting students and faculty alike over their responsibilities to learn and to teach. In that sense, the governance of higher education, discussed so cogently from a property rights perspective by Staaff and Meiners in this volume, must be regarded as one of the most important questions for the nineties.

But this brief and lamentable summary of current events is more symptomatic of a larger retreat from responsibility by the officers of institutions of higher learning rather than it is causative of a decline. In other aspects of university affairs one can witness the "lowering" of "higher" education: the transformation of amateur athletics at universities into a professional business in violation of the code of ethics to which each institution nominally subscribed; the expansion of study abroad programs, whose dual advantage to many colleges is merely to increase enrollment without additional building of classrooms, labs, and dormitories and to increase tuition revenues without hiring new faculty; the time-honored "bait and switch" technique of advertising a famous faculty member as the instructor of record whose actual role in the classroom is dwarfed by that of a graduate student or adjunct faculty member; the enormous expansion of part-time faculty, where one finds institutions of higher education trading off accumulated academic reputation for cash flow by employment of adjunct faculty whose rates of pay are a mere shadow of those of full-time faculty and who are usually only casually acquainted with the institution's core faculty and its students.

The education of students, particularly undergraduate students, is the casualty in this transformation because the lack of commitment to the enterprise of the mind at all levels of the institution is transparent, and the articulation of the university by its administrators as a collection of cost centers is transcendent.

To echo a question from a well-known protest song of the sixties, "where have all the educators gone"? In fact, most have retreated to their homes or laboratories to do the required business of publishing, hoping to write their way into tenured positions, and once having achieved this protected status, to continue to write their way out of the undergraduate classroom and the unenviable committee assignments. If an undergraduate teaching assignment is required of the faculty member it is common for him or her to treat it as an opportunity to winnow out those students who do not show promise in the technical proficiency of the faculty member's discipline. This practice of "professionalization" places a premium on rote acceptance of "training," over the open-ended exploration of ideas characteristic of quality education. So pervasive has the rejection of undergraduate education become among the professoriate that at many universities receipt of an award for teaching excellence virtually dooms an untenured faculty member, whereas a mediocre article in a recognized journal is tallied in the plus column for the advancement of a career. A "double plus" is entered in the ledger for one who receives a research grant, not because there is the promise of erudite articles to follow, but because it brings both tangible evidence for university administrators seeking to justify their programs and support for the growing staff in offices of sponsored projects from indirect cost recovery. One important consequence of this process is that those who aspire to research recognition have displaced the teacher in the positions of authority in the departments and in so doing have established the equation of "good teaching equals pandering to students." Supporting this change, unintended to be sure, is the federal government, the principal source of the research funds.

Some may ask what this prologue has to do with the state. Fair enough—that is what the remainder of this introduction is about and, more importantly, what the contributing authors to this volume have labored to describe.

State of the Art or Art of the State?

My chief contention is that American institutions of higher education have undergone a major transformation during the last half century and that governments, state and federal, have been instrumental in provoking that change. Furthermore, the direction of change has been one in which the colleges and universities have turned away from instruction of students in favor of a federally financed research mission and have, thereby, increasingly become creatures of the state rather than self-sustaining, independent bases of thought and criticism. We have ended a decade in which the national political order was nominally committed to diminished government influence in American life, yet state-crafted higher education continues to grow. This transformation is both willful and woeful.

To some, this may appear to be an extravagant claim, but fifty years of enhanced federal funding of universities has guided the growth of the general framework of higher education, redirected the efforts of faculty, diminished the capacity for independent action by administrators, and has likely promoted disciplinary ossification and nurtured rank utilitarianism in place of the search for the fundamentals of critical inquiry. Federal support for research outweighs all other sources, and dependency of faculty and institutions on these funds has developed over time. Support of certain fields of study over others, directly by the grants system and indirectly through the purchase of services, has stimulated this trend and has introduced a kind of "intellectual policy" equivalent to the recognizably bankrupt "industrial policy" that some pundits have sought to foist on the nation in recent years.

It is not that the state has never been involved in higher education, nor that many Americans, particularly university-based research grant recipients, would urge that government should reduce its role. Rather, what is important is to document that role, its direction of change over time, and to ask questions that those uncritical of government intervention either avoid or do not recognize. That is what this book does. Roger Meiners reminds us in this volume that from colonial days the state, often theocratic, supported education, and that this process continued through the founding of the Republic, subsequently building momentum during the nineteenth century through acts of Congress. Even Mr. Thomas Jefferson, American patriarch of ideals closely held by most of the contributors to this volume, was a clear supporter of contributions from collective resources to the education of citizens. Joel Spring's chapter introduces evidence of the continuation of this graduated involvement in the twentieth century, such that by the late 1930s the federal government was poised to enter into a greatly expanded relationship with American higher education. The degree to which that potential has been met is amply discussed in the chapter by Ron Kimberling, who served as assistant secretary for higher education in the last years of the Reagan administration.

This book does not argue for the abandonment of public support for higher education, although contemplation of the moral hazards associated with such support might lead some to embrace that view. Nor should these remarks be construed as an attack on university research, because nothing could be farther from their intent. Instead, the greater part of the chapters that follow aim to review the role of the state in higher education from a "zero-based" standpoint; that is, they do not accept the inevitability of the continued growth of this role. Indeed, the authors point out some possible pathologies that follow from the increasingly bureaucratized and centralized decision making of a state-dominated enterprise. I think it fair to claim that the authors aim to improve higher education in America by identifying systemic processes, and the habits of mind developed to accommodate these, that have invaded the universities and are unlikely to sustain a citizenry of strong independent judgment.

One may fully acknowledge that, in many respects, American higher education, especially technical education, is state of the art; otherwise it would be difficult to explain the magnetic quality it has for students from all over the world. Even discounting the sanctuary attraction of coming to America from more troubled countries or the contact system a foreign student can build in a massively affluent market, there remains a capacity for excellence in technical education that is unsurpassed. Moreover, when one examines that part of higher education most influenced by the state—the sciences and technology—it is impossible not to indicate, as several of these chapters do, that these fields are the greatest attractors of the world's students. Recently, Martin-Rovet, a policy analyst with the Centre Nationale de la Recherche Scientifique, has written on the reasons French scientists come to the United States to do advanced study, and she is unequivocal about their motivation to work in the most advanced situations.[3] In some major fields, particularly in engineering and the sciences, the majority of the graduate students are from foreign countries. One may take this as recognition of superiority of the educational experience offerred by American universities; alternatively, it may indicate something about the preparation of students in American secondary schools.

Even with this superior national capability there is ample room for critique and warning because a priori there are few readers (and none of the contributing authors) who would urge that higher education in America should become the art of the state. A vision of higher education that promotes the forging of views of students in the foundries of the state, the crafting of a cadre of highly trained workers to execute the designs of government agents, and the fusing of minds to missions of national purpose is precisely the ethic many Americans have fought against and died to prevent when governments, fascist and socialist alike, have imposed it on their own people. Much of the moral authority that permits politicians to make the words "Free World" reverberate when comparing America to other countries rests on an independent-minded and educated citizenry. By contrast, a citizenry "trained" to supply specialized labor to those public or private enterprises deemed valuable by agents of government inexorably will become hostage to those agents by virtue of their specialization. Why this subtle *corvee* should be resisted abroad but accepted in the United States is another important question to consider as the Orwellian decade has come to a close.

In the areas of science and technology, there exist some of the greatest tensions between education and training because it is here, not in music or literature, that today's technocrat prefers to invest public wealth. This admits of a materialist program that exalts the production of items over ideas and rests on the misguided premise that society is enriched chiefly by things rather than by thoughts. Yet, it is precisely this social engineering style of thinking that provokes calls for "greater coordination" of effort to counter the "challenge of Japanese competitive genius." It is worth rereading and reflecting upon Jean-Jacques Servan-Schreiber's book from the late 1960s, *The Ameri-*

can Challenge, to recall how shallow and opportunistic are these arguments.[4] Ironically, the application of such social engineering programs in the past may have contributed substantially to the diminished capacity of the American science and engineering community to address the applications side of technological development today.

In a 1981 study of the impact of federally sponsored research and development on leading research institutions, Bowering and Sheehan found that federal funding from the mid- to late 1970s was instrumental "in attracting and keeping graduate students (particularly Ph.D's) **against** the attractions of industry and business incentives.... and...even greater infusions of federal monies may be needed, perhaps specifically focused to have maximum effect on students and faculty, to maintain current levels of influence in the future."[5] This practice would appear simultaneously to withhold talented labor from productive pursuits and to induce individuals of relatively diminished capabilities to enter graduate studies programs at academic institutions.

Is this merely a philosopher's complaint? Hardly! The genius of American society has been its open competition of ideas, springing from the brains of individuals whose education permits the forging of new combinations of mind and matter into goods and services for consumers. This process also requires training and the development of specific skills, but these are often best recognized and provided on-site, where propinquity to production promotes pertinence in the individual's investment to acquire knowledge. That is why many firms support training programs at an enormous expense. That is also why, as C.M. Lindsay outlines in his chapter, government programs to "produce" a supply of scientists are likely to fail, a fact of life widely understood by those in the scientific and engineering communities.[6]

For the reader who is not close to the workings of institutions of higher education, it may be surprising to see the emphasis on science and technology in a third of the chapters of this book, but it is directly in these areas that the federal government has made its greatest impact on the colleges and universities of America, shaping the development of a system of research universities differentiated from the teaching colleges and promoting a pecking order within and among them. That it is a system full of feedback paths and interconnections is important to comprehend because at different levels interest groups have formed to ensure sustentation of the arrangement by those in Congress who control the federal purse strings. Peter Aranson, in his brilliant chapter, has analyzed the political economy of this development and offers both positive and normative models that aid one to understand better the motivations of individual actors in different parts of the system. It is hardly surprising after reading Aranson to understand that a half-century of concerted federal funding would have contributed substantially to the development of a self-justifying enterprise that is dependent upon this funding.

Before relinquishing the reader to the subsequent chapters, it will serve this discussion to trace the course of the transformation of higher education.

A Half Century of Federal Research Support

By the beginning of the United States involvement in WWII the federal government had begun to consider how to harness university research to meet "national needs." In 1938 a federally sponsored committee report, "Research—A National Resource," stated: "Most research workers and administrators are so concerned with their own immediate interests in research that they do not consider enough the work as a whole or sufficiently relate their work to the entire research enterprise of the country."[7] This report had, among its several objectives, the aim of showing "the particular research activities of the universities that are of concern to the Government, and to point out the chief contribution which the universities make to the research program of the Nation."[8]

Research was defined broadly for this report, taking into account arts and humanities and social sciences, but it clearly focused on the physical sciences as "particular research activities of the universities that are of concern to government." Such fundamental utilitarianism supported the Morrill Act of 1862 and its focus on agricultural improvements, just as it undergirded the National Cancer Institute Act of 1937 and the National Science Foundation Act of 1950. According to a report on education by the Office of Technology Assessment, the Higher Education Act of 1965 was the first major national legislation for higher education that was not limited to a specific goal like agriculture, health, or defense.[9]

From 1935 to 1936, research at universities totaled $50 million, of which federal grants supported 10 percent; state government, 28 percent; private foundations, 16 percent; industry, 12 percent; and university sources, 34 percent.[10] By contrast, in 1986 the proportions were: federal government, 62 percent; state government, 8 percent; foundations, 7 percent; industry, 6 percent; and university sources, 17 percent.[11] Strict comparisons are elusive for many reasons, not the least of which are the differences in the content of the categories, but there is no question concerning the vast augmentation of the federal role in academic research support, such that it was dominant by the early 1950s. The salient feature of the change over this period is that the proportional contributions from state government and from university resources were more than halved, and those of foundations and industry significantly diminished in the face of the immense increase in the federal support brought on by WWII. Postwar sustentation of scientific research was justified on the basis of future preparedness for national emergencies and for economic ends, as Joe Martino so amply demonstrates in his contribution to this book. It seemed to have been lost on the policy-makers of the era that the widely hailed success of scientists in the war effort was founded on a situation characterized by diversity and independence, not one that had required huge government expenditures; however, the political-bureaucratic logic of fixing something that is not broken has prevailed.

Using expenditures of research performers in 1935–36 as a yardstick, universities did about 20 percent of the research in the United States, while government accounted for 35 percent, and industry for 45 percent.[12] Fifty years later the proportions were: universities, 33 percent; government, 14 percent; industry, 48 percent; and nonprofit institutions (not recorded in 1935–36), 5 percent.[13] In many respects universities have increasingly adjusted to the role of executors of indirectly defined research programs supported by the federal government or of directly defined programs, as is the case with FFRDC's (federally funded research and development corporations like APL, the Applied Physics Laboratory at Johns Hopkins University). By "indirectly defined," I mean the canonization of certain fields that, as the 1938 Science Committee report indicated, "are of concern to the Government." These favored fields are candidates for federal support, whereas others are not. Scions of these fields harbor the favored faculty who, in turn, become the next generation of academia's chief decision makers. This is "intellectual policy" at incubation stage.

There were 1,450 institutions of higher education in the United States in 1935–36, according to the 1938 National Resources Planning Board report. The top 150 of these universities, as defined by research expenditures, had a combined budget of $265 million, of which $50 million, or a little under 20 percent, was spent on research. The remaining 1,300 institutions had a combined budget of $155 million, of which a little more than $1 million was for research.[14] Citing a study made at the University of Chicago, already a leading research university in 1929–30, it was noted that 32.5 percent of the university budget and 26.9 percent of faculty time was spent on research, and at the University of California during 1928–29 the figures were 25 percent of the budget and 27 percent of faculty time.[15]

From 1985 to 1986 there were 3,301 institutions of higher education in the United States. The combined budget of the top 150 (defined by research expenditures) was about $33 billion, of which $9 billion, or about 27.3 percent was spent on research; the remaining 3,150 institutions had a combined budget of $45 billion, of which about $1 billion was for research.[16] The mean percentage of time spent on research by a faculty member at a major research institution today must exceed that recorded in the earlier study.

These data, and particularly those used in interperiod comparisons, cannot be regarded as exact, but the general direction of change is clear: vast federal involvement has dramatically impacted higher education. Whereas, the 1938 study could unblinkingly report "research" expenditures by higher education institutions in terms of physical sciences, social sciences, and humanities in roughly 40:30:30 proportions, by 1988 one is hard pressed to find information on "research" expenditures in the humanities, and it rarely ever appears in connection with reports on research expenditure in the physical and social sciences.[17] In 1935–36 private foundation support for research at universities was proportionally greater by more than half again that of the federal government, and much of that support was for the social sciences.[18] By 1985–86 the federal government contribution to academic research dwarfed that of private foundations by a factor of 9:1, and the proportion awarded for physical sciences, social sciences, and humanities was closer to 90:5:5![19]

Thus, the transformation of the education system in the United States over the past half-century can be characterized by its expansion in the number of institutions and the emergence of research as an activity dominant in status relative to teaching. Both of these trends have been fueled by federal sources of support, and in so doing the nature of research conducted at universities has been reoriented toward the sciences and engineering fields, which "are of concern to the government." Geiger, in his study of the growth of American research universities, points out that the trend had been building from the early 1900s and that the progress of concentration of research in a limited number of institutions was manifest by the beginning of WWII, but he also concludes:

> The growing federal contribution to university research consequently mingled in complex ways with the continued provision of private resources. The federal presence may have modified university behavior at times, as had been predicted, but it did not become so overbearing as to smother those manifold linkages between the research universities and American society. The stature of the research universities in the postwar world has derived in no small measure from this deeply rooted pluralism. Thus, the diverse social linkages that the research universities forged during the first four decades of the century have served to safeguard their independent initiative and to enhance their continued development during the succeeding era of federally funded university research.[20]

To the contrary and by virtue of this revised support system, the universities and colleges in the United States, public and private, are strongly tied to the federal government and have forfeited much freedom of action in their internal affairs. Significant loss of budget control derives from a dramatic increase in the ratio of administrators to faculty, much of which is due to demands to meet federal reporting requirements thrust upon institutions in receipt of federal funds.

The loss that looms largest, so large indeed that it is hard to distinguish its boundaries, is the loss of control of the content of intellectual directions at the university. A manifestation of this condition is the "hardening of the categories," as George Reynolds, a Princeton physicist, has described it. One major effect of federal funding has been to support the development of cadres of individuals committed to certain fields of study, or disciplines, and to exclude others, thereby slowing a process of intellectual exchange and transformation. Most of these disciplines have formed associations and some have joined consortia to lobby on behalf of their memberships. Success is gauged by whether or not "official representation" in the funding programs of the federal research bureaucracy has been achieved, or whether the professional label of the discipline has been placed on a scheduled status at the Office of Personnel Management of the federal government. The supply of resources to these groups through formal and informal "peer review" procedures virtually guarantees that new, challenging, and contending ideas will be suppressed by those with orthodox views. Given the reward structure of universities already described, there is a tendency to retain the orthodox researchers who are funded to pursue the research programs sanctioned by the federal government and to dismiss those who do not receive support.

Dramatic evidence of the widespread recognition of the effects of this system are provided in a massive survey of scientists conducted by Sigma Xi, the Scientific Research Society, a venerable century-old honor society for research scientists. During 1988 scientists were asked to rank the two chief concerns they have with respect to the use of peer review in the grant awarding process. They could specify an unlisted choice of their own, indicate that they thought peer review worked well (and less than 8 percent did), or choose from among seven other responses on the list. The top two concerns were: "Reviews are marred by cronyism, old boy networks, and insider politics," chosen by 31 percent, and "Original, nonmainstream ideas are unlikely to be funded," chosen by 25 percent.[21] Because the survey was administered to a random sample of 10,000 research scientists nationwide, and representing all fields of science, the indictment of the peer review system is as wide as it is deep.

One must step back from the higher educational system in the United States to discover that its current outlines include the following dimensions: 1) increased emphasis on research relative to teaching, resulting in the advancement to senior positions of those who accept and excel in research; 2) reliance on federal support for research (there are ten "private" universities among the top twenty institutions in receipt of federal research funds, and these twenty universities account for 40 percent of *all* federal research dollars spent at universities); 3) research programs are largely defined in utilitarian terms by government by virtue of government's control of the purse strings; 4) disciplinary interest groups lobby successfully for support of their brand of truth; 5) a research grant award system widely thought by its main participants, research scientists, to be cronyistic and supportive of orthodox ideas over creative frontiers of thought. It seems that a system has developed that is internally consistent and survives by importing resources from the general public.

Whether one believes in a world of affirmative government in which those in charge somehow "get it right" by sheer good intentions more often than would market forces pure and simple, or one views government as a powerful set of predatory forces against which the wealth and well-being of independent citizens must be protected, there is no question that the growth of government influence upon higher education has become great during the past half-century. Most of these gains have come through loan programs and subsidies to students for education, like the GI Bill, but apart from their role in inflating the system these programs were relatively neutral concerning the state of the art of higher education. It has been through support for research, principally in the sciences, that the art of the state has been insinuated into the fabric of higher education.

It would be absurd to argue that scientific achievements made with public support would necessarily have occurred in its absence, but it is equally absurd to ignore public investments in researches that have yielded nothing, or more ominously, that have had negative consequences. Among these negative consequences is the superenrichment of some fields of study over others and the subsequent torquing of the leadership and curricula of higher-education institutions in those directions desired by government elites.

To some this may be a distinction cut too fine, and to others, particularly those who have built brilliant careers around state guided research, it is virtually impossible to think that it was not only worthwhile but ordained, because of the importance of the lines of inquiry they pursued. That is human nature, and each of us is guilty in this regard. This chapter, and those that follow, do not demand the Academy to don sack cloth and ashes to signal repentance for being participants in the changes that have influenced higher education. Rather, the call from these authors is for recognition that ideas have consequences, and the ideas imported by governments into higher education, along with substantial tax dollars, particularly over the past half-century, have done much to transform higher education into an artful composition of state design. It is for the reader to determine if this is "public art" they will continue to support, and it is for university leadership to consider the implications of its continuance with care.

Notes

1. W.W. Bartley, *Unfathomed Knowledge* LaSalle, IL: Open Court, 1990; Allan Bloom, *The Closing of the American Mind: How Higher Education Has Failed Democracy and Impoverished the Souls of Today's Students* (New York: Simon & Schuster, 1987); Roger E. Meiners and Ryan C. Amacher, eds., *Federal Sup-*

port of Higher Education: The Growing Challenge to Intellectual Freedom (New York: Paragon House, 1989); Page Smith, *The Killing Spirit: Higher Education in America* (New York: Viking Press, 1990); Dinesh D'Souza, *Illiberal Education: The Politics of Race and Sex on Campus* New York: The Free Press, 1991; Martin Anderson, *Imposters in the Temple* New York: Simon & Schuster, 1992; Charles J. Sykes, *ProfScam: Professors and the Demise of Higher Education* (Washington, D.C.: Regenery Gateway, 1988), and *The Hollow Men: Politics and Corruption in Higher Education* (Washington, D.C.: Regenery Gateway, 1990).

2. Sykes, *Hollow Men*, pp. 36–45.
3. Dominique Martin-Rovet, *The Young French Scientists in the United States*. Centre National de la Recherche Scientifique, Paris, 1988.
4. Jean-Jacques Servan-Schreiber, *The American Challenge* (New York: Athenaeum, 1968), and in French, *Le Defi Americain* (Paris: Editions Denoel, 1967).
5. David J. Bowering and John K. Sheehan, *Research Study of the Direct and Indirect Effects of Federally-Sponsored R&D in Science and Engineering at Leading Research Institutions* (Executive Summary. Final Report to the National Science Foundation of grant number #SRS-8018112, November 16, 1981), p.28. Added emphasis mine.
6. A survey of scientists conducted by a scientific society addressed a number of questions but did not publish all of the results; among these were three concerning the most efficacious agency to steer students into careers in science. Government agency was regarded as the least efficacious by a margin as large as market resources were regarded as most efficacious (Sigma Xi, *A New Agenda For Science* [New Haven, Conn.: Sigma Xi, 1987], p. 110).
7. National Resources Planning Board, *Research-A National Resource*, Washington, D.C., 1938, p. 167.
8. Ibid.
9. U.S. Office of Technology Assessment, *Educating Scientists and Engineers: Grade School to Grad School*, Washington, D.C., 1988, p.84.
10. *Research-A National Resource*, p. 178.
11. National Science Board, *Science and Engineering Indicators-1987*, Appendix Table 4-10 (Washington, D.C.: Science Resource Studies, 1987), p. 243.
12. *Research-A National Resource*, p. 178.
13. Percentages derived from consideration of basic and applied research, but not development (*Science and Engineering Indicators-1987*, appendix 4-7, p. 241).
14. *Research-A National Resource*, p. 177.
15. Ibid.
16. National Science Foundation, *Federal Support to Universities, Colleges, and Selected Non-Profit Institutions, FY 1986* (Washington, D.C.: Science Resource Studies, 1986).
17. *Science and Engineering Indicators-1987*, Appendix 4-20, p.254.
18. *Research-A National Resource*, p. 180.
19. Of $10,718,402,000 R&D expenditures at universities and colleges in 1986 only $459,303,000 was for social sciences, and 63.7 percent of those funds were from nonfederal sources, whereas $10,259,000,000 of R&D expenditures at universities were for other sciences and engineering, and nonfederal sources accounted for 40 percent. Figures for humanities research at universities was imputed to be the same as social sciences, although that is undoubtedly a significantly high

estimate, but the point is made that the federal government has made an all-out effort to support at least nominally utilitarian science and technology programs at universities (*Science and Engineering Indicators,* Appendix 4-20, p. 254).

20. Roger L. Geiger, *To Advance Knowledge: The Growth of American Research Universities, 1900–1940* (New York: OUP, 1986), p. 267.

21. Jack Sommer and Deborah Seltzer, *Sketches of the American Scientist* (New Haven, Conn.: Sigma Xi, 1988).

I

The Politicization of
Higher Learning

Introduction to Part I

John W. Sommer

The introductory chapter of this book expressed both angst and anger that the officers (faculty and administrators) of many higher-education institutions are failing their students and themselves by substituting safe bureaucratic responses for the courageous exercise of wisdom in the stewardship of higher learning. The direction of those responses, be they in the admission of students, the choices of curriculum, the conduct of courses, or the certification of student achievement, are made with reference to forces outside the academy— chiefly those emanating from public agency. Officers at private colleges and universities are less exposed than are those at state institutions, which must be more attuned to legislative directives, but those in both settings are responsible for the defense of the central mission of the institution. Those missions, usually stated in the beginning pages of the institution's catalogue, are uniformly high-minded paeans to the education of students, a fact that makes the difference between goals and achievement that much more difficult to endure.

It is possible that the capacity for exercising wise choice has diminished significantly over the past four decades as the university officer has been confronted by the requirement to make many more decisions that have the potential to reduce flexibility of choice later, e.g. the acceptance, in the face of curricular initiatives that cut across disciplines, of the categories of the HEGIS code (Higher Education General Information Survey) upon which state formulas for funding, regional agencies for accreditation, and federal agencies requiring information for a variety of classification purposes base decisions. This example is cited because it appears to be innocuous, indeed even reasonable for accounting purposes, but this labeling becomes the plat that provides the boundaries for subsequent decision-making. To redraft such a plat, or to violate it by not using those categories, restrains the wise officer and places a premium on his or her knowledge of the exogenous agency rules rather than on understanding the desires of the students. State and federal concerns for assessment of the outcomes of education, i.e., value-added by the institution, are likely to lead to mandated measurement of student achievement, thereby creating a nightmare of bureaucratic formulas that entirely miss the point that educational institutions are only partially engaged in "training." Officers of institutions of higher learning who are unable to distinguish between education and training are unlikely to make cogent arguments to legislators, trustees, or to the general public.

The four chapters that make up this section on the politicization of higher education take more precise aim at the course of higher learning and each, in turn, articulate different features of the system. Common to all four authors is a concern that higher learning has ceded much of its independence to external agency, although Meiners observes that this attentiveness to external, usually political, forces has been with us since colonial days when church and state were not separate. This observation is not meant as a justification for continuity in practice but as a caution that retreat from this arrangement would not be easy. Spring, in his chapter, also documents the historical context of the increasing federal role and the drive for instrumental outcomes chronicled in the legislation of the past one hundred years.

A second common theme is that the increasing politicization of higher learning subjects it to the inconstant whims of the political process: Kimberling, in particular, notes that changing federal student aid rules under different administrations has led to complexity and confusion.

Flew points out the other side of the adjustment process, citing that when the college age population shrunk in 1977 (and institutions were faced with the prospect of reduced flow of federal funds) there was great pressure to find "other bodies" to populate courses and this led to a dramatic increase in the number of students taking remedial mathematics, reading, and writing courses. Flew adds a comment that chills the heart of any who would argue for increased federal funding for education when he points out that the United States has made enormous investments in education in the past but seems to have reaped a crisis from those efforts. Why invest more?

Spring develops the theme of the disruptiveness of federal intervention in labor markets, as universities have become the instruments of *dirigiste* plans to supply firms with skilled labor: the problem comes when one administration's favored sector is not that of the next and individuals who have been "trained" for one must adjust abruptly to another. I am sure that there are many who would not conclude as strongly as does Spring:

> These conditions are a logical result of a university system that was originally organized to serve the state and a professorate that professionalized in a climate of service. Ones thinking should not be confused by the myth that during some previous period of time professors and universities pursued truth for its own sake. The university and the professorate were and are for sale to the highest bidder. Unfortunately, the state is the bidder with the most power and money.

But, the challenge Spring poses and his documentation of the growth of government's role in higher learning must be recognized.

A third theme, developed principally by Meiners, Spring, and Kimberling, is that the politicization of higher learning has brought with it wealth transfers from lower-income individuals to higher-income individuals, be it through the simple fact that the better off are better informed about the availability of public funding for higher learning and have more resources at their disposal to deploy in sorting through the complexities of how those funds are secured, or whether it is written into the legislation, as Kimberling observes of the Federal Supplemental Loan Program. Meiners again gives us the historical perspective when he cites the governor of Kentucky railing against state support for Transylvania College in 1825 on the basis that "The State has lavished her money for the benefit of the rich, to the exclusion of the poor...the only result is to add to the aristocracy of the wealth[y], the advantage of superior knowledge."

The authors of the first four chapters set out the historical and developmental characteristics of the increasing influence of politics on higher learning, and in doing so begin to unfold some of the difficult conditions under which decisions in and about the institutions that purport to offer higher learning will be made. The literature about higher education of the 1980s is replete with the description of one pathology after another, some focusing on students, others on the professoriate, and still others on the their administration. Is something wrong? The answer is a thunderous "Yes" from all quarters, but the solutions vary dramatically. A compendium of statements from a variety of authors, such as is the composition of this work, does not lend itself to the easy advancement of a unique solution [as if there could be a unique solution], but beginning with the chapters by Meiners, Spring, Kimberling, and Flew and continuing throughout the work there is a clear suggestion that the nexus of interaction between the state and the institutions of higher learning is an important first place to search for answers.

1

The Evolution of American Higher Education

Roger E. Meiners

The discipline of colleges and universities is, in general, contrived not for the benefit of the students but for the interest, or more properly speaking, for the ease of the masters. Its object is, in all cases, to maintain the authority of the master, and whether he neglects or performs his duty, to oblige the students in all cases to behave toward him as if he performed it with the greatest diligence and ability.[1]

Introduction

The history of higher education reminds us that, although institutions change, the state of the world today is in many ways not unlike the world of the past. Adam Smith's discussion of higher education in *The Wealth of Nations* provides as insightful a view of the behavior of college teachers and students as any that has ever been written. The American system of higher education is the same in some fundamental ways as that observed by Smith over two centuries ago. For anyone who thinks that higher education has reached some new low with respect to the diligence of faculty and students, remember what Smith told us:

> If the teacher happens to be a man of sense, it must be an unpleasant thing to him to be conscious, while he is lecturing his students, that he is either speaking or reading nonsense, or what is very little better than nonsense. It must too be unpleasant to him to observe that the greater part of his students desert his lectures; or perhaps attend upon them with plain enough marks of neglect, contempt, and derision.... The teacher, instead of explaining to his pupils himself, the science in which he proposes to instruct them, may read some book upon it; and if this book is written in a foreign and dead language, by interpreting it to them into their own; or, what would give him still less trouble, by making them interpret it to him, and by now and then making an occasional remark upon it, he may flatter himself that he is giving a lecture.[2]

21

This chapter is intended to increase the reader's understanding of why higher education operates as it does today. Although the size and scope of the institutions are different in twentieth century America from those found in eighteenth century Great Britain, the incentives of the participants in the market for higher education have not changed in many important ways. The nonprofit structure of our colleges and universities denies us many of the benefits visited upon private organizations by competitive forces.

The chapter begins with an overview of the structure and development of American higher education from colonial times to the present. Special attention is given to the primary sources of subsidies for colleges: churches, foundations, and governments. Some remarks are then made concerning the role of the modern university and the issue of academic freedom.

Support for Higher Education in Colonial Times

Beginning with Harvard College, nominally founded in 1636, and for decades afterwards all new colleges were sectarian and quasipublic. Each college was a corporation chartered by the respective colonial assembly, and was clearly a state-church college. Since nine of the thirteen colonies had established religions, the assemblies were not interested in allowing dissenting sects to found colleges.[3] Most colleges founded during the colonial period received government support. For example, the General Court of Massachusetts appropriated £400 in 1636 toward the founding of Harvard College, which was under the control of the Congregational Church.[4]

As the list in table 1.1 illustrates, many colleges were quasimonopolies because many assemblies would not grant more than one college charter. When the states chartered a second college, usually to be controlled by another church, it indicated a shift in the power of religious groups within the colony. Although the nature of colleges has changed drastically over time, many of the premier institutions undoubtedly benefited by their long stature as the only college in a state. Harvard had no competition in Massachusetts until Williams College was chartered in 1793, and Yale had no competition in Connecticut until 1823 when Trinity College was chartered. Yale and Harvard did offer one another competition, but high transportation costs limited such efforts. Restriction on entry into higher education in many of the older colonies resulted in fewer colleges being established and in a relatively high survival rate. On the other hand, a few of the original colonies and some of the newer states, such as Pennsylvania, New York, and Virginia, allowed numerous colleges to be formed. There was active competition in many states to establish colleges as a way of demonstrating the growth and vitality of new towns.[6] For instance, in Missouri eighty-five colleges were established before the Civil

TABLE 1.1
Chronology of College Formation in Colonial Times[5]

College	Colony	Religion	Charter Year
Harvard University	Massachusetts	Congregational	1636
College of William and Mary	Virginia	Episcopal	1693
Yale University	Connecticut	Congregational	1701
Princeton University	New Jersey	Presbyterian	1746
Columbia University	New York	Episcopal	1754
University of Pennsylvania	Pennsylvania	Episcopal	1755
Brown University	Rhode Island	Baptist	1765
Rutgers University	New Jersey	Dutch Reformed	1766
Dartmouth College	New Hampshire	Congregational	1769
Washington College	Maryland	Episcopal	1782
Washington and Lee University	Virginia	Presbyterian	1782
Hampden-Sidney College	Virginia	Presbyterian	1783
Transylvania College	Kentucky	Presbyterian	1783
Dickinson College	Pennsylvania	Presbyterian	1783

War, but only eight still existed in 1861. College mortality in states that were not restrictive about college formation was usually around 90 percent before the Civil War.

Although colleges in the seventeenth and eighteenth centuries were primarily schools for training ministers, they received state support. In 1652 and 1653 the General Court of Massachusetts donated 2,000 acres of land to support Harvard and ordered a tax levy of £100 for its support. Harvard was also assigned the Charlestown Ferry revenues, a support that lasted for 200 years. The charter of William and Mary College provided for a tax on tobacco to support the school and placed the state functions of land control in the Virginia colony into the hands of a collegiate land office. George Washington received his commission as a surveyor from the president of the college. At various times the school was awarded the receipts from a tax on skins and furs, and in 1759 it received the revenues from a tax on peddlers.[7] The legislature in Connecticut relieved students attending Yale from paying taxes and from having to serve in the military. Other financial support, such as the revenue from the sale of a captured French ship in the eighteenth century, was given to the school. Hence, through colonial times it is not possible to distinguish between public and private colleges. The effective establishment of state churches meant little division between the interest of the colleges and those of the state.

The Growth of Colleges in the Early 1800s

During the settling of the Midwest, scores of colleges were formed in the new states and territories. Most of these colleges were small, often having only one teacher. To call them colleges seems a misnomer. Most frontier colleges were created with a religious motive because the boom towns in the frontier areas wished to convey an aura of success and sophistication. Hence also the creation of towns with names like Athens and Oxford. Unlike the established Eastern colleges, which were generally protected from competition, the Western states had few or no controls on entry, and colleges had a high mortality rate.[8]

State support of private colleges continued after the founding of the Republic. The Commonwealth of Massachusetts granted Harvard $10,000 a year from 1814 to 1823. Bowdoin and Williams colleges each received $30,000 during the same time, and the state guaranteed the solvency of the institutions.[9] In the late 1700s Columbia was given $140,000 and the University of Pennsylvania was given $287,000 by their respective states. Princeton was given permission to operate lotteries in New Jersey, Pennsylvania, and Connecticut to support itself. Dartmouth and other colleges were granted public lands to sell in order to support themselves. Such gifts to private schools became less common as the nineteenth century progressed, but Williams College received $75,000 from the state in 1868, Dartmouth received $200,000 from the state between 1893 and 1921, and as late as 1926 several state legislatures still provided support for private colleges.[10]

The Dartmouth College case of 1819,[11] which assured the right of private colleges to be free from legislative interference even though their charter was issued by the legislature, was, for colleges, generally irrelevant. Dartmouth, like most private colleges, pressed the state legislature for assistance. During the nineteenth century such assistance appears to have been important to the survival of many colleges. Such institutions were more financially independent than are modern state universities, but it would be a mistake to believe that at some point there was a golden age of private higher education. However, the religious nature of most colleges, and perhaps the desire to avoid the expense of a public university, makes it appear that state support for colleges was essentially charitable.

The state universities established in the first half of the nineteenth century had strong religious requirements. The state of South Carolina decreed that at its state university "...a religion 'pure and undefiled' was to be preached to the youth of the State; and from the College, as from a fountain, were to go forth the waters of salvation...Christian doctrine was to be taught from the pulpit, and from the Professor's chair..."[12] Many state universities' boards of trustees were dominated by representatives from the ministries of particular religions. Even Mr. Jefferson's University of Virginia took on the character of a religious institution during the mid-1800s.[13]

The cost of attending college has always been heavily subsidized. Numerous colleges in the nineteenth century charged no tuition. Brown University and others were often unable to collect tuition from students, yet allowed them to remain in attendance. Colleges have consistently campaigned for scholarship funds to help increase the quantity and quality of students.[14] Hence, competition for students among subsidized private universities was sufficient to keep tuition rates substantially below cost even before public universities existed.[15]

The suspicion that public support for higher education has generally served to redistribute income to persons of higher-than-average wealth has existed since the inception of public universities. The governor of Kentucky denounced state support of Transylvania College in 1825, claiming, "The State has lavished her money for the benefit of the rich, to the exclusion of the poor...the only result is to add to the aristocracy of the wealth, the advantage of superior knowledge."[16] Similar observations about the redistributive effects of higher education were noted in Georgia, South Carolina, and Missouri.

The Development of the Modern University

Until the turn of this century, although there were many colleges, enrollments were small. It was 1860 before Harvard had a graduating class with 100 students. That same year in Ohio the average enrollment in 22 colleges was 85 students.[17] Before the Civil War colleges were small institutions where the faculty (masters) lived in residence with the students. Most faculty members were ministers or men of independent wealth who did not rely on their college salary to subsist. The education was mostly religious and "classical." There was no effort to train students for careers, other than for the ministry. Through the mid-1800s, although the population grew rapidly and wealth increased, the percentage of the college-age population that attended college declined until 1890. Except for the ministry, the primary purpose of attending college was to maintain or achieve social status.

College graduates were generally disdained by businessmen, and the value of college status may be evidenced by the decline in the percentage of congressmen in the late 1800s who were college graduates.[18] Andrew Carnegie, one of the greatest benefactors of education, commented in 1889 that the knowledge obtained by college students "seems adapted for life upon another planet.... College education as it exists is fatal to success in that [business] domain."[19]

Around 1890 the fortunes of colleges began to improve. Several benefactors provided major funding for private colleges. Land-grant universities (mostly state colleges) benefited from the legislation passed in 1890 that provided them direct federal funding. During this time the academic culture as we know it today began to develop. The social sciences grew, faculty began to form professional associations, scientific journals appeared, and universities began to compete for faculty members based on their scholarly productivity.

The ties between the church and state gradually disintegrated. Religious requirements, such as mandatory chapel attendance at state colleges, were eliminated early in the twentieth century. Radical political activity by academics increased, although active socialists, such as economist Richard T. Ely, were careful to call themselves Christian socialists. The political radicalism of many of the new social scientists did not seem to dampen enthusiasm for expanded public support of colleges.

During this time there was considerable experimentation with education programs. Some of the most novel approaches were tried at private universities. However, despite the creation, and the sometimes lengthy control, of private universities by conservative donors who may have had a particular mission in mind, the history of American colleges, as I read it, does not indicate a difference in the political orientation of faculty members at private universities compared to that of faculty at state universities. Despite the absence of tenure, as we know it today, faculty members were rarely fired for espousing radical notions. [20]

Faculty members at the turn of the century frequently had a view of universities quite similar to that of today. "A university is a body of mature scholars and scientists, the 'faculty'—with whatever plant and other equipment may incidentally serve as appliances for their work."[21] Veblen's view, written about 1910, fails to mention either the existence of administration or of students in a university. The university exists primarily for faculty members to do research. While Veblen's view may have been extreme, there is no question that at about the turn of the century there was a drive at leading universities to achieve recognition through faculty publications. Although Stanford University and other institutions were established with undergraduate education foremost in mind, they quickly deviated from the ideas of the benefactors and became like other institutions, the faculty of which did not claim to concern themselves primarily with such education. Major universities competed with one another through the quality of their graduate programs. More resources were devoted to the production of Ph.D.'s, a degree that was becoming mandatory for faculty status by the turn of the century. At least in the leading universities, "by 1910 research had almost fully gained the position of dominance which it was to keep thereafter."[22]

The 1890s was a boom market for professors. Between 1889 and 1892 the University of Chicago, Stanford University, and Clark University opened with substantial endowments. Existing private universities, especially Harvard and Columbia, expanded at the same time, and numerous state universities were opening and growing. New Ph.D.'s found themselves being promoted quickly to full professors as academic salaries jumped rapidly.

At the same time that the academic profession began to develop more as we know it, the quality and seriousness of college students appeared to increase. Around 1900 the Ivy League schools were essentially social centers for the sons of the wealthy. There appeared to be little concern with academics; most colleges were little more than large fraternities.

There would be noisiness and open defiance of the teacher; beans, paper wads, and lighted firecrackers might be hurled at a young instructor when he turned to face the blackboard. At Columbia rhythmic stamping, collective groans, and sarcastic laughter were in vogue. At Princeton in the nineties, fifty students surreptitiously brought as many alarm clocks into the lecture hall, setting them to sound at short intervals during the hour. After the turn of the century new riots broke out at Stanford, Michigan, and elsewhere, usually when the administration seriously threatened to interfere with aspects of the "good life" enjoyed by the students.[23]

Historians report that student rebellions, of one form or another, were not uncommon in the nineteenth century. Student riots and strikes, generally set off by some internal university policy disliked by the students, occurred at Princeton, Harvard, Yale, Dartmouth, Amherst, Brown, Williams, and at many other institutions.

Contrary to those who harken to olden days of serious students clamoring for wisdom from faculty, one would seem hard-pressed to show that the quality of undergraduate education, even at leading universities, has deteriorated during the twentieth century. Around 1910, faculty teaching loads were ten to fifteen hours a week at the best universities and as high as twenty-two hours at smaller colleges. Large lecture sections were frequently used, and graduate students at Harvard and Columbia taught "quiz sections" that had forty to fifty students each.[24] The equivalent of grade inflation appeared to exist in Ivy League institutions at the turn of the century. It was rare that a student flunked out of the university, and the "gentlemen's C" was common. The work required of undergraduates and graduate students appears to have been low by today's standards.

Academic publishing as the primary criterion for monitoring faculty performance, for determining rewards, and as a way for faculty members to establish their reputations became dominant in the late 1800s. Johns Hopkins led the way with the founding of *The American Journal of Mathematics* in

1877. Journals in all disciplines quickly emerged at several universities. Journals printed at the University of Chicago totaled 150,000 copies a year by 1898. By 1904, thirty-five journals were being edited by faculty at Columbia.[25] The number of journals grew quickly as many universities decided that respectability required the subsidization of academic journal publication. During the late 1800s many professional associations, specific by discipline, were formed. There was considerable discussion about the fact that the quality of teaching was not important to academic success. This tradition emerged before formal tenure existed and before state universities emerged as a leading factor in the structure of higher education.

The active marketing of universities began about the turn of the century, with such devices as pamphlets designed to attract desired students and to influence public opinion. Advertisements emphasized the financial advantages that would accrue to the college graduate. Fund-raising activities became more professional. Universities began to operate publicity bureaus that released news stories about the accomplishments of the university, including faculty research, student facilities, and the performance of football teams. At least in advertising, the changes in universities seemed to follow developments that first occurred in private corporations.

Despite the emulation of some business practices, by the turn of the century there was considerable concern by faculty that businessmen, particularly the great benefactors, would have too much influence over the operations of universities. Professors then, as now, frequently espoused the idea that they should be given large sums of money to spend at their discretion.[26] Private universities, which had been dominated by various churches since inception, had their boards of trustees change from a majority of clergymen to businessmen and other men from nonacademic professions. As today, men of high esteem were sought to serve on boards, particularly those who might be benefactors to the university. Traditionally, the trustees of private and public universities have been quite passive. Only at a few colleges did they play an active role in the selection of faculty and curriculum. Such colleges were not considered attractive places of employment (nor in general are they now) and were held in low regard.[27]

Despite the conservatism of donors and trustees, and despite the lack of formal tenure to protect most faculty, there were few attempts to control the selection of faculty based on political persuasions or to control the political activities of faculty members. While one can find accounts of professors being driven from their positions because of their radical political activities, a few instances have been repeatedly recounted. In most of these cases, even faculty who sympathized with the "persecuted" faculty member recognized that the behavior was extreme by any standard.[28] Often the faculty member forced a confrontation with university leaders that led to his dismissal, faculty committees playing little or no role in such decisions. The professors usually obtained subsequent employment at another institution of similar or higher reputation. At both private and public universities, notably Nebraska, Wisconsin, and Cornell, radical faculty members found havens. There is not much evidence that the lack of formal tenure led to significant loss of academic freedom or that it encouraged trustees or administrators to control the political actions of faculty members.

The Development of Direct Federal Involvement in Higher Education

The federal government has been involved in higher education, at private and public colleges, since the founding of the Republic. In 1785 the Congress ordered that one thirty-sixth of the land in each new state (the territorial lands beyond the thirteen original states) be set aside for the maintenance of public schools. Congress also mandated that two townships be reserved in Ohio for the support of a university. Townships in Ohio, Indiana, Illinois, and Michigan were set aside to be sold to support a seminary. Such support of religious organizations continued until the 1820s.

The federal government and the states battled to determine which level of government would have control over certain activities. Presidents Washington, Adams, Jefferson, and Madison lobbied for the establishment of a national university. The Congress was not as interested in that scheme, preferring to devote some federal resources to support existing colleges or to help establish state colleges. The exception to this was the creation of the U.S. Military Academy at West Point in 1802. Congressmen made sure that admission to the institution was in their hands.

During the first half of the nineteenth century, Congress was pressed by various interest groups to endow agricultural schools or other institutions of higher learning in the states. There were repeated attempts to have federal lands turned over to the states to be sold for the support of various institutions. President Pierce vetoed a bill in 1854 granting federal lands to the states to subsidize insane asylums. Similarly, in 1857, a bill was introduced to grant to each state, for the maintenance of agricultural schools, federal lands equal to 20,000 acres for each senator and representative in Congress. The federal government would pay an amount to a state equal to the value of the land if there were insufficient federal lands within the state. The proceeds of the land sale were to be invested in "safe stocks," yielding at least 5 percent interest. The income of the fund was to be used to support colleges. Each state was required to establish at least one college that would include the study of agriculture and mechanical arts. Despite opposition by Southern representatives, the bill passed in February 1859 but was vetoed by President Buchanan. The bill became law in 1862 (when Southern opposition was moot), but the grant of land had been raised to 30,000 acres for each member of Congress.

The Morrill Act of 1862 did not represent the first instance of federal support for higher education. After the formation of the union, twenty-one new states were admitted to the union before the Civil War (and before the Morrill Act). Except for Vermont, Kentucky, Maine, and Texas, all of these states were recipients of land grants by Congress to support the founding of universities. Among the grants to fund an agricultural college were: Ohio, 630,000 acres; Indiana, 390,000 acres; Illinois, 480,000 acres; Michigan, 240,000 acres; and Wisconsin, 240,000 acres. As one might have predicted, the granted lands that were sold by state officials did not raise the revenues expected. The lands were sold for less than their value (the lands frequently were quickly resold at high profits by the original purchasers), and the proceeds were reduced by poor investments and by embezzlement.[29] These lands, combined with the 17,430,000 acres given to the states under the Morrill Act, resulted in the distribution of about 30,000 square miles of federal lands to the states for the support of universities. This is a land area equal in size to Maine or South Carolina.[30]

Only 10 percent of the funds raised by the Morrill Act land sales could be used to help establish a college; the remainder of the fund was to be a perpetual endowment. While the majority of the seventy land-grant colleges that exist today have been founded since the time of the legislation, eight existing state universities (in Michigan, Pennsylvania, Maryland, Iowa, Wisconsin, Minnesota, North Carolina, and Missouri) were given the endowment and became land-grant institutions. Six states arranged for existing private colleges (including Dartmouth and Brown) to provide the agricultural and mechanical education required by law. Cornell and Purdue were both established by joining the federal grant with a private gift to establish a new college. [31]

After the establishment of land-grant colleges, a number of states founded agricultural experiment stations to supplement agricultural research. The Hatch Act in 1887 gave federal aid to support state agricultural experiment stations.[32] Funds for these are still dispensed annually through the Department of Agriculture. Although some members of Congress wanted to establish a system of federal experiment stations, Congress voted instead to dispense the money directly to the state colleges. The Second Morrill Act was passed in 1890, granting additional funds to land-grant colleges for instruction (this appropriation was increased in 1907). While the payments were to be derived from the proceeds of the sale of federal lands, this turned out to be a formality, as annual payments came to be paid out of general revenues.[33] Funds provided by the two Morrill Acts and by the Hatch Act were restricted to certain teaching and research programs, which helped to define the agenda of land-grant colleges.

The Morrill Act of 1862 motivated the states to spend money on higher education. The Second Morrill Act of 1890 helped induce states to spend a certain amount on their colleges by establishing the matching grant principle. Under the act, the colleges were required to meet specific standards or to be ineligible for the federal money.[34] This move, especially with respect to land-grant colleges, was also spurred by Hatch Act subsidies for agricultural research; by the Smith-Lever Act of 1914, which provided federal support for extension services; and by the Smith-Hughes Act of 1917, which provided federal support for vocational education and home economics at land-grant colleges. Federal support for land-grant colleges, which especially stimulated the growth of state universities, seemed to be motivated less from a desire to support higher education than from a need to respond to political pressure from agricultural interests.[35] Funding for such programs reached $23 million a year by 1930. Although few politicians ever questioned the legitimacy of the federal role in higher education, President Hoover's Advisory Commission on Education assured him that there are thirty-one provisions in the Constitution under which the federal government can find authority to support higher education.[36]

One of the earliest examples of federal regulation of college activities that did not bear directly on the subject matter being supported occurred under the second Morrill Act in 1890. It required that the colleges must not deny admission on the basis of race unless there were separate but equal facilities. Seventeen states were stimulated to create separate colleges for the instruction of blacks.[37] The onset of World War I produced an immediate 20 percent decline in college enrollment. The combination of the colleges' alarm at the loss of student population and the government's desire to have numerous training facilities led to the establishment of the Student Army Training Corps. By the fall of 1918 the draft age had been lowered to eighteen, which provided an extra incentive for young men to attend college and serve in the Student Army Training Corps, as some 140,000 men in 525 colleges did in 1918. The war ended on November 11, 1918, and the students were discharged in December. The facilities built by the federal government to house the students and other aspects of the program were turned over to the colleges.[38]

World War I also produced the first federal research contracts to universities. MIT was awarded $800 in 1915 by the National Advisory Committee for Aeronautics. From 1915 to 1918 that agency supported university research with funds totaling $12,000.[39] The National Academy of Sciences, a private organization chartered by Congress, created a National Research Council in 1916 to help coordinate research relating to national defense. The NRC was composed of government personnel and scientists from educational institutions and from industry. It initially operated on funds provided by the Rockefeller and Carnegie Foundations. By the end of World War I federal funding for research had become institutionalized, although on a trivial scale when compared to more recent years. Numerous federal programs created during the Great Depression provided direct or indirect assistance for colleges and universities. During the years 1935–43 about 620,000 students were employed in work programs at the college or graduate level and earned a total of $93 million. The average monthly employment during this period was over 110,000. In addition, various federal construction programs (WPA) during the depression provided new facilities for many colleges.

All but a few hundred thousand of the millions of federal dollars allocated for research in 1940 was distributed by the Department of Agriculture. Much of the subsequent increase in research expenditures is attributed to the rapid rise in government spending on military research during World War II. By 1950 over $150 million a year was being spent by at least fourteen federal agencies on research by higher education. Over two-thirds of all budgeted university research came from federal money. Approximately 90 percent of all research money for the natural sciences was dependent on federal support. Most of the funds were for defense-related projects, agriculture, and public health. As has always been true of federal support, this money was distributed mostly to the larger and more prestigious universities.[41]

The social sciences soon benefited from the explosion of federal research funds. Much of the initial funding for social science research came through the Department of Defense. The Office of Naval Research sponsored research in the fields of human relations, manpower, psychophysiology, and personnel and training. The Air Force, through the RAND Corporation and the Human Resources Research Institute, sponsored studies on topics such as group motivation and morale, role conflict, leadership, and social structure in the military community.[42] This research support, combined with federal support for veterans of World War II and of the Korean War (the GI Bill), helped boost the higher-education industry.

At its peak in 1947, over one million veterans were enrolled under the GI Bill. This support, which is like a voucher system, averaged $1,000 a year to each veteran in college and subsidized a large portion of the doubling of college enrollments from 1.3 million to 2.6 million from 1938 to 1946. To help handle the rapid increase in enrollment after World War II, numerous colleges were given land and government buildings (that had often been constructed during World War II for military purposes and were adjacent to a campus). Property valued by the government at $43 million, but probably worth double that amount, was turned over to 153 colleges for only $1.5 million.[43] Some

700 colleges were provided 75,000 dormitory units and 53,000 family units by the Public Housing Administration. Many units constructed during the war were no longer used by the military and were given to college campuses.[44] By 1948, the U.S. Office of Education dispensed $150 million in federal properties to colleges to provide land and buildings for instruction purposes.[45] Colleges and universities have been loaned billions of dollars at below-market interest rates since the Korean War under the College Housing Loan Program for the construction of dormitories and other revenue-producing facilities.[46]

The National Science Foundation was created in 1950. Congress allocated $3.5 million to the NSF for fiscal 1951. At about the same time, federal funding for hundreds of graduate fellowships was initiated from sources such as the Atomic Energy Commission, the Public Health Service, the Reserve Officer's Training Corps, and the National Science Foundation. Federal support for graduate and post-graduate study has expanded to fund thousands of students each year. The Public Health Service, Veterans Administration, and other federal agencies began to underwrite the cost of operating medical schools. Such funds have turned many medical schools into research institutes, the research interests often determined by the funding source.[47]

Through the 1950s federal support of higher education was tied to defense spending. Because defense accounted for the majority of direct federal expenditures, it is not surprising that federal involvement in higher education came through this avenue. The National Defense Student Loan program, initiated in 1958, spurred by the Sputnik scare, declares:

> The present emergency demands that additional and more adequate educational opportunities be made available....This requires programs that will give assurance that no student of ability will be denied an opportunity for higher education because of financial need....[48]

This loan program was designed to provide support on a need basis for students interested in science, math, and foreign languages. This was followed in the late 1960s and early 1970s with various guaranteed loan programs, which, by the mid-1980s required $7 billion in federal authorizations. Other federal grant programs, such as Pell grants, which are usually income based, required another $4 billion in federal support. Veterans' assistance, which had risen to over $4 billion per year in the mid-1970s declined to about $1 billion per year in the mid-1980s.

The National Defense Education Act (1958, with amendments in 1964) required that students receiving benefits swear an oath of loyalty to the United States and disclaim membership or belief in subversive organizations. Educators asserted that these were McCarthy-era tactics and that they constituted a restriction on academic freedom. The loyalty oath has since been discontinued, but the potential constraints that federal funding might impose on colleges were made clear at that time. Although the federal role in higher education has grown substantially in the last few decades as social agencies expanded, the incentives of federal bureaucrats with respect to public and private institutions of higher learning are essentially the same, whether the agency is concerned with agriculture, defense, or social programs.

Pell grants and other federal grant and guaranteed loan programs for students initiated in the early 1970s emphasized that colleges were subject to all federal regulations and required states to establish central commissions of higher education to work with the Department of Education, rather than have state colleges work individually for such general support. Many states established central authorities in response to this legislation. Presumably, within a state this has served to "cartelize" certain aspects of public colleges' activities, reducing incentives to compete with one another before the legislature. More importantly, since the 1970s it has become clear that colleges, public or private, must fulfill many federal regulatory requirements to remain eligible for federal support directly or for students to be able to receive federal grants or loans.

The costs of complying with rules imposed by the Civil Rights Act of 1964, the Equal Employment Opportunity Act of 1972, Executive Order 11246 (affirmative action), and a host of other federal requirements became quickly obvious to college administrators. By the 1974–75 school year, the cost of implementing federally mandated social programs was costing institutions between 1 and 4 percent of their operating budgets.[49] Because regulations have multiplied since that estimate, the cost must be even greater today in terms of direct expenses.

Private Foundations and Higher Education

Andrew Carnegie chartered the Carnegie Institute of Pittsburgh in 1896. This was the first of twenty-two charitable foundations he would found before his death in 1919.[50] Before that time the number of foundations that existed and the value of their assets were so small as to be insignificant.

While wealthy individuals had endowed universities such as Chicago and Stanford in the late 1800s, the growth of giant foundations began in the early 1900s. John Rockefeller established the General Education Board in 1903 with resources of $46 million. His Rockefeller Foundation was established in 1913 with resources of $154 million. The Carnegie Foundation was endowed in 1906 with $31 million, and the Carnegie Corporation was funded with $151 million. These foundations generally required matching grants, providing strong incentives for university presidents to become fundraisers. There seems to be little doubt that in the early part of the twentieth century the foundations played a large role in homogenizing American higher education and in encouraging the organization of the academic community along certain lines.

The letter announcing a gift of $10 million from Rockefeller to create the General Education Board in 1905 (written by Frederick Gates, who ran the Board) stated that the purpose of the contribution was to reduce "higher education to something like an orderly and comprehensive *system,* to discourage unnecessary duplication and waste, and to encourage economy and efficiency."[51] Studies were undertaken to determine the structure of higher education in the United States, so the foundation could move to change the "absurdity of the situation," that is, the existence of too many low-quality colleges.[52] Gates wanted to establish a comprehensive system of higher education with a nationwide system of strong universities.[53] This attitude was illustrated in 1908 when Gates recommended to the trustees that no funds be given to the "nine so-called Christian colleges" in Nebraska; their existence was "destructive of higher education."[54] Both foundations worked to eliminate "tottering, feeble, or superfluous institutions" that were being kept alive by "denominational pride, vanity, or self-interest."[55]

The Carnegie Foundation and the General Education Board refused to make grants to church colleges. This helped to accelerate the division of private colleges from their religious origins. Bowdoin, Wesleyan, Rochester, Drake, Coe, Hanover, and Occidental colleges all dispensed with their denominational connections to obtain foundation money.[56] A grant application had to demonstrate that the university had or would make certain reforms to qualify for Carnegie assistance. Church colleges could no longer require that their faculty be chosen so that the members of one church would have a majority. The colleges could not appeal to their denominations for support and could not allow their names to be used in connection with any church. The president or trustees of a college could not be required to be "in doctrinal sympathy" with a specified denomination.[57]

Before the active involvement of the foundations in college structure, beginning about 1905, most state and private colleges had adopted a certification system to control the quality of college entrants. Various accrediting associations, the National Education Association, and the College Entrance Examination Board offered to measure the quality of potential entrants for colleges. The Carnegie Foundation and the General Education Board worked to standardize admission to college. To be eligible for Carnegie funds, a college had to have an admission requirement "not less than four years of academic or high school preparation, or its equivalent."[58] The Carnegie Foundation required that all affiliated institutions maintain a four-year curriculum and be staffed by at least six full professors. In practice this meant that the minimum size of the American liberal arts college would be at least six or eight departments.[59] The foundation required that all department heads hold a Ph.D. Private colleges were required to have an untouched productive endowment of at least $200,000, and state universities were required to have an annual income of at least $100,000.

The trusts established by Carnegie and John D. Rockefeller had a large impact. In the decade of the 1920s, $136 million was granted to higher education by the 100 largest foundations.[60] Although many more foundations were established, the trusts set up by Carnegie and Rockefeller before 1915 contained over three-fourths of the known assets of foundations in the mid-1930s.[61] Seven Rockefeller and Carnegie trusts provided about two-thirds of the total foundation disbursements in 1934.

The General Education Board had donated over $4 million by 1915 to the endowment of thirty-five colleges that were admitted to the Carnegie pension system. The Carnegie Foundation paid $30 million in pensions and allowances to college faculty from 1906 to 1935, and assumed pension obligations totaling $70 million.[62] Rockefeller gave $50 million in 1919 to the General Education Board to be "specifically devoted to the increase of teachers' salaries."[63] This gift, distributed in five years, helped raise salaries at leading universities and created rewarding positions for senior faculty members. The funds distributed required matching grants from private or public sources. For example, to receive a grant from the Board, the North Carolina legislature doubled its previous appropriation for the university and voted $1.5 million for new buildings.[64] These grants helped to produce additions to endowments of over $120 million.[65]

Originally the Carnegie Foundation had hoped to provide all of the funding necessary to provide pensions for any professor who had served twenty-five years. By 1910, seventy-one colleges with several thousand professors were affiliated, although professors at Harvard, Yale, Columbia, and Cornell fared best (those institutions received one-third of the money). Ten institutions received over half of the funds. By 1915, it was clear that the foundation would be bankrupt under its operating conditions. The foundation then helped to establish the Teachers Insurance and Annuity Association (TIAA). Professors who had expected to receive a free pension bitterly opposed the idea of contributing toward their retirement.[66] The Carnegie Corporation gave the TIAA $1 million to start issuing contracts in 1919, and by 1936 had given over $10 million to TIAA.[67] The American Association of University Professors censured the foundation in 1918 because it had not included faculty on its board. Although some faculty members were upset that the TIAA was going to be the monopoly provider of faculty pensions and thought that free choice of company selection should be allowed, TIAA won AAUP acceptance by adopting some of their proposals, such as including faculty in TIAA decision making. [68]

To imagine the impact of the foundations, one must realize that in 1900 the total revenue of higher education was $31.7 million and that endowment income supplied only 20 percent of the total from endowments worth $165 million.[69] Between 1902 and 1934 the major Rockefeller and Carnegie foundations distributed over one-third of a billion dollars to colleges and universities. The matching basis used for many of those grants was supposed to have generated hundreds of millions more in endowments, the primary basis of endowment growth at that time.[70]

Foundations and Research Trends

Much like the distribution of federal dollars to higher education today, foundation money in the first part of the century was concentrated at the elite schools. Only 20 universities received one-quarter of a billion dollars—approximately three-fourths of all foundation grants between 1902 and 1934. The remaining one-fourth was distributed among 300 other institutions, excluding another 700 colleges from foundation largess.[71] The grants from the General Education Board and the Carnegie Corporation alone accounted for approximately one-fifth of the total budgets of all the colleges and universities in the years before World War I.[72]

Foundations supported the development of education as a profession, including the fields of educational administration, educational methods, and educational psychology.[73] The Peabody Education Fund was dissolved in 1914; its assets of $2 million were distributed to fifteen schools of education. The General Education Board distributed about $10 million at the same time to colleges of education at various universities.[74] In total, major foundations provided over $30 million for newly developing schools of education in the first decades of this century.

Other institutions, such as the American Law Institute, the Brookings Institution, the American Political Science Association, and the National Bureau of Economic Research, were started by the generosity of the major foundations. The Rockefeller Foundation appointed a committee of economists in 1914, chaired by Edwin Gay of Harvard, to select "problems of economic importance which could be advantageously studied."[75] The foundation then created the Institute of Government Research, which was later merged with the Brookings Institution. Beardsley Ruml, a young psychologist, was hired in 1923 to run the new Laura Spelman Rockefeller Memorial that was endowed with $74 million. He guided over $40 million in novel research in the social sciences over the next six years. Funds were given to Chicago to study its urban community, to Harvard and Radcliffe for economic and legal research in international relations, to Wisconsin for studies in rural tenancy and land ownership, and to social scientists at other leading universities.[76] The foundation provided substantial support for the founding of schools of social work at five universities. Because the federal government did not actively support the social sciences until years later, Chancellor Hutchins of the University of Chicago was probably correct when he claimed that the "Memorial in its brief but brilliant career did more than any other agency to promote the social sciences in the United States."[77]

The Memorial was merged into the Rockefeller Foundation in 1929. The foundation spent $11 million over three decades to finance the development of the field of public administration at leading universities, to help train students for government service.[78] The Spelman Fund, another Rockefeller foundation, was used to create and finance the Public Administration Clearing House, designed to bring together twenty-one organizations of public officials representing all aspects of government functions. It also supported research by organizations such as the Municipal Finance Officers Association and the American Public Works Association.[79]

Some of the social science research sponsored by the Rockefeller Foundation was put into practice during World War II. Scholars working in the Treasury Department studied war-bond buying practices. This led "to the emphasis which was so successfully placed on payroll deduction plans and other schemes utilizing personal solicitation and group pressure."[80] Other scholars working for the Army employed social science methodology to study troop activities and factors that affected morale. They helped to design various veterans' aid programs.[81] In a quarter of a century the Rockefeller foundations had underwritten the social sciences with at least $100 million.

Law schools traditionally had little support from foundations until the 1920s, when the Rockefeller Foundation and Carnegie Corporation made large grants to the American Law Institute (ALI) to finance the production of the Restatement of the Law. Over the years, the ALI, supported by numerous foundations, has produced many Restatements, model codes, and has underwritten the development of the Uniform Commercial Code.[82] Regardless of the view one has of the value of such works, there is little question that they have played a substantive role in the development of law in America. Various foundations have, in recent years, supported many other projects in law schools, such as the Ford Foundation's National Legal Aid and Defender Association.

Reviewing foundation gifts and the economics profession, George Stigler observed several points that may be generally applicable to all disciplines. The foundations tend to support work in statistical economics. Basic theoretical research tends to be done by a single scholar, and that does not require extensive clerical assistance. Foundations have been a major funding source for large quantitative research projects, such as Leontief's input-output tables and Harvard's business cycle project. The foundations have supported "the

dominant position of the relatively few major universities and research institutes in economic research."[83] Stigler notes that the penchant of the foundations for large programs, and to support the most distinguished scholars, leads
them to concentrate most of their grant money in a few major universities.
This has helped to prevent the diffusion of capable scholars to a larger number
of universities. Stigler also notes that foundations tend to increase the homo-
geneity of research projects. There are fashions in scientific research that tend
to be reinforced by foundation grants. He attributes the popularity of economic studies of underdeveloped economies in the 1950s and 1960s to the
generous support of the Ford and Rockefeller foundations.

Academic Freedom and Government Support

As Table 1.2 illustrates, no matter how it is measured, college education is
heavily subsidized by government. Federal subsidization of higher education
has become increasingly important in the past forty-five years, but may have
hit its watermark, in relative terms, right after World War II. State governments concurrently provide the bulk of the support for higher education. This
support has the effect of redistributing income in general from lower income
families to higher income families.[84] Because our political economy produces
a complex redistribution of income via a complex series of taxation and expenditure measures, it is not particularly useful to claim that the redistribution
that occurs by higher education expenditures at the various levels of government is "unfair." It is simply part of a larger redistribution scheme, so it cannot realistically be analyzed outside that context. This does not mean that
economists cannot or should not make efficiency evaluations about the financing and provision of higher education, but such studies are likely to have
little impact.[85] There is no reason to predict a change in the system unless
there is a shift in electoral support or a change in the composition of the electorate. Regardless of one's perception about the desirability of governmental
support for higher education, governmental support of higher education necessarily poses a threat to academic freedom. Only a trivial number of colleges
have divorced themselves from all governmental ties.

Private colleges are an important part of the maintenance of academic freedom. Some worry that private colleges will be unable to compete with state
colleges. It is difficult for subsidized private colleges to compete with state
colleges that are even more subsidized, yet the political system may be generating an odd balance in this regard. In 1983, 26.8 percent of all full-time college students were in private institutions. Private colleges received 44 percent
of the federal dollars spent on higher education. Hence, the federal subsidy
per student at private colleges is greater than it is for students in public col-

TABLE 1.2
Government Support of Institutions of Higher Education

	% Current Fund Revenue		% All Revenue
Year	Federal	All Government	All Government
1920	6.4	37.3	31.8
1930	3.7	30.9	28.9
1940	5.4	30.0	31.2
1950	22.1	45.4	46.1
1960	18.0	44.3	37.2
1970	12.5	43.0	(*)
1980	15.2	49.3	50.4
1982	13.3	46.2	47.8

Source: Table 137, *Digest of Education Statistics, 1985–86*. U.S. Department of Education, 1986.
*Believe it or not: "Data not collected."

leges. According to one study, the subsidy was $1,670 in 1976–77 compared to $1,160 per student at public colleges (state support was $290 and $2,660 per student respectively).[86] This result may emerge, one might speculate, because private colleges have greater incentive to lobby for federal dollars. In any event, the result is for the federal government to somewhat ameliorate the competitive disadvantage faced by private colleges relative to state colleges (although the bulk of the federal funds goes to support the prestige private universities).

The fact that public universities are mostly state rather than federal institutions is, arguably, beneficial to academic freedom. There is no national monopoly provider of higher education. Some states provide relatively little support for higher education (New Hampshire, Connecticut, and Massachusetts were the lowest in 1982). Other states devote two to three times as much of state income to higher education (Alaska, Arizona, Hawaii, Mississippi, New Mexico, North Carolina, and Utah being the highest in 1982).[87] Such diversity in amount and origin of support will produce more alternatives than would exist under a federal regime of universities, although not as many as there would be in a system of completely private universities.

Notes

1. Adam Smith, *An Inquiry into the Nature and Causes of the Wealth of Nations* (Indianapolis: Liberty Classics, 1981), p. 764.
2. Ibid., p. 763.
3. Donald G. Tewksbury, *The Founding of American Colleges and Universities Before the Civil War* (New York: Columbia University, 1932), p. 63.

4. Richard G. Axt, *The Federal Government and Financing Higher Education* (New York: Columbia University Press, 1952), p. 16.
5. Tewksbury, *Founding of American Colleges*, pp. 32–34.
6. Daniel Boorstin, *The Americans: The Democratic Experience* (New York: Vintage Books, 1973), p. 120. For an entertaining fictional account of a frontier boomtown college, see Garrison Keillor, *Lake Wobegon Days* (New York: Viking Press, 1985), pp. 24–63.
7. Frederick Rudolph, *The American College and University* (New York: Alfred A. Knopf, 1962), pp. 13–14.
8. Tewksbury, *Founding of American Colleges*, p. 28.
9. Rudolph, *American College*, p. 185.
10. It is interesting to note that the state of New Hampshire aids Dartmouth today in the form of tax-free bonds to be used for student loans (Ibid., p. 189).
11. Trustees of Dartmouth College v. Woodward, 17 U.S. (4 Wheat.) 518 (1819).
12. Tewksbury, *Founding of American Colleges*, p. 179.
13. Ibid., p. 182.
14. Rudolph, *American College*, p. 199.
15. An interesting note is that in pre-Jacksonian times students attending college at less than full tuition were called charity students. This term was considered derisive and was changed to scholarship students. This euphemism has applied to students whether the scholarship was awarded on the basis of "need" or of "merit" (Ibid., p. 205).
16. Ibid., p. 206.
17. Ibid., p. 219.
18. Laurence R. Veysey, *The Emergence of the American University* (Chicago: University of Chicago Press, 1965), p. 4.
19. Ibid., p. 14.
20. No one has adequately explained why faculty members tend to be socialist in orientation. It may be that education as a career attracts certain personality types, especially those who might otherwise be ministers or politicians. It may also be partly due to envy of those without as much education as academicians, yet who have achieved more wealth and stature in society. Whatever the reason, the social radicalism of faculty has been prevalent in American academics for almost a century.
21. Thorstein Veblen, *The Higher Learning in America* (New York: Hill and Wang, 1957), p. 13.
22. Veysey, *Emergence of American University*, p. 177.
23. Ibid., p. 277.
24. Ibid., p. 358.
25. Rudolph, *American College*, p. 405.
26. Veysey, *Emergence of American University*, p. 347.
27. Ibid., p. 303.
28. Ibid., p. 416.
29. George W. Knight, History and Management of Land Grants for Education in the Northwest Territory, papers of the American Historical Association, vol. 1, no. 3, 1885.
30. Why the federal government was willing to give away such an asset to the states for the support of their universities is an interesting question. 1 would speculate that the reason had to do with the method of electing senators during the nine-

teenth century. Members of the Senate had to be very responsive to the demands of their state legislatures because these alone were their constituencies. Since there was little federal money to dispense, senators dispensed the next best thing. Before the Civil War such attempts to dispense federal lands were blocked by several presidents. Because the president was less responsive to the wishes of state legislatures than were members of Congress, it is natural that he would have been less interested in disposing of federal assets for the benefit of state governments.

31. Rudolph, *American College*, p. 253.
32. Axt, *Federal Government Financing Higher Education*, p. 50.
33. Such legislation was passed instead of the perennial proposal to establish one or more national universities (Ibid., p. 56).
34. John S. Brubacher and Willis Rudy, *Higher Education in Transition* (New York: Harper and Brothers Publishers, 1958), p. 225.
35. Homer D. Babbidge, Jr. and Robert M. Rosenzweig, *The Federal Interest in Higher Education* (New York: McGraw-Hill, 1962), p. 10.
36. Ibid., p. 17.
37. This does not imply that the federal regulation was not beneficial to higher education opportunities for blacks (Rudolph, *American College*, p. 254).
38. Axt, *Federal Government Financing Higher Education*, pp. 74–6.
39. Ibid., p. 78.
40. Ibid., pp. 85–7.
41. Ibid., pp. 93–4.
42. Ibid., pp. 112–13.
43. Ibid., p. 136.
44. Ibid., pp. 136–37.
45. Ibid., p. 137.
46. Babbidge and Rosenzweig, *Federal Interest in Higher Education*, p. 62.
47. Axt, *Federal Government Financing Higher Education*, Chap. 8.
48. Title 1, National Defense Education Act.
49. The Costs of Implementing Federally Mandated Social Programs at Colleges and Universities, Washington, D.C.: American Council on Education, 1976.
50. Ernest V. Hollis, *Philanthropic Foundations and Higher Education* (New York: Columbia University Press, 1938), p. 22.
51. Raymond B. Fosdick, *Adventure in Giving* (New York: Harper and Row, 1962), p. 129.
52. General Education Board, The General Education Board: An Accounting of Its Activities 1902–1914, New York, 1915, p. 109.
53. General Education Board, Review and Final Report 1902–1964, New York, 1964, p. 29.
54. Fosdick, *Adventure in Giving*, p. 131.
55. Hollis, *Philanthropic Foundations*, p. 139.
56. Rudolph, *American College*, pp. 431–33.
57. Hollis, *Philanthropic Foundations*, p. 55.
58. Ibid., p. 130.
59. Ibid., p. 137.
60. Ibid., p. 125.
61. Ibid., p. 121.
62. Ibid., p. 190.

63. General Education Board, Review and Final Report, p. 31.
64. Fosdick, *Adventure in Giving*, p. 147.
65. Hollis, *Philanthropic Foundations*, p. 191.
66. Ibid., p. 195.
67. Ibid.
68. Savage, William W. Savage, *Interpersonal and Group Relations in Educational Administration* (1968), pp. 138–40.
69. Hollis, *Philanthropic Foundations*, p. 200.
70. Ibid., pp. 269–76.
71. Ibid., p. 44.
72. Warren Weaver, ed., *U.S. Philanthropic Foundations* (New York: Harper and Row, 1967), p.168.
73. Hollis, *Philanthropic Foundations*, p. 230.
74. Ibid., p. 228.
75. Fosdick, *Adventure in Giving*, p. 193.
76. Ibid., p. 196.
77. Ibid., p. 200.
78. Ibid., p. 205.
79. Ibid.
80. Ibid., p. 234.
81. Ibid., p. 235.
82. Erwin N. Griswold, "Philanthropic Foundations and the Law," in *U.S. Philanthropic Foundations*, ed. Warren Weaver, p. 289.
83. George J. Stigler, "The Foundation and Economics" in Ibid., p. 280.
84. W. Lee Hansen and Burton A. Weisbrod, *Benefits, Costs, and Finance of Public Higher Education, 1969* (Chicago: Markham Pub. Co., 1969); and Douglas Windham, *Education, Equality and Income Redistribution* (Lexington, MA: Lexington Books, 1970).
85. George Stigler makes a similar point in "Economists and Public Policy," in *Regulation*, May/June, 1982, p. 13.
86. *The Carnegie Council on Policy Studies in Higher Education* (San Francisco: Jossey-Bass Pub., 1980), p. 119. Whether private colleges are really on the decline is a matter of perception. In 1929–30, private colleges had 49.87 percent of FTE student enrollment (out of 8,560,000 students). Hence, while total enrollment increased 9.6 times, private college enrollment increased 4.6 times over that time period (Howard Bowen, *The Costs of Higher Education* [San Francisco:Josey-Bass Pub., 1980], Table 41).
87. U.S. Department of Education, Digest of Education Statistics, 1985–86, 1986, Table 147.

2

In Service to the State: The Political Context of Higher Education in the United States

Joel H. Spring

From the time of the Morrill Act of 1862 to the present, the federal government influenced higher educational policies in the direction of serving the needs of the labor market and creating knowledge in service to political objectives. In the twentieth century, federal influence resulted in continual change and chaos in higher education. Rather than solving economic problems, higher education, under the influence of the federal government, might have contributed to problems in productivity.

Initially, the Morrill Act provided land for establishing state universities to serve the needs of agriculture and industry. During World War I and the Depression, the federal government tried to use the educational system to manage the economy and humanpower. This trend accelerated after World War II when federal legislation made higher education part of Cold War policies. During the 1970s, federal efforts resulted in the establishment of clear labor market objectives for higher education. In addition, the increase in federal student aid in combination with clear labor market objectives made higher education a central institution for selecting, training, and certifying the labor force. In the 1980s, changes in federal tax policies stimulated closer relations between business and higher education. The result was a finer tuning of higher education's service to the labor market.

Through the years, federal influence occurred in the context of differing beliefs about the social role of higher education and the academic profession. The major difference is between the conferring of social status through a liberal education, as represented by English universities and American colleges in the nineteenth century, and higher education in service to the state, as represented by nineteenth century German universities.

The tension between the liberal and service ideal was reflected in the academic profession. In the traditional American college, the professor was primarily a transmitter of knowledge and not a creator of new knowledge. In the American university based on the German model, the emphasis was on faculty research and consulting to government and industry. The German model opened the opportunity for increased status, economic rewards, and professional independence for American professors. Therefore, federal policies, which moved higher education in the direction of the service ideal, were often supported by the academic community.

A conflict over the meaning of academic freedom and the role of the professor as a critical thinker resulted from the acceptance of the German model and the professors' desire for professional independence. In the German tradition, complete freedom for the faculty to teach and to do research was considered necessary for the advancement of knowledge. In turn, the advancement of knowledge, it was assumed, would serve the interests of the state. In this context, academic freedom was considered a constructive force toward the advancement of the interests of the state.

Obviously, there is a potential conflict between the ideals of academic freedom and service to the state. A myth created by the German model of academic freedom is that of the scholar, who, free of worldly concerns and political pressures, pursues knowledge for its own sake. This myth receives support within the academic community because it idealizes the scholar and justifies professional independence. In fact, as will be discussed later in this chapter, there is little in the history of higher education in the United States to support the myth of the American professor as a critical and independent scholar.

When the federal government used higher education for political goals, academic freedom was tolerated as long as it served the interests of the state. Some critical thinking was tolerated, and defended by professors, because the ideal of academic freedom was central to the ideological justification of the profession.

The following sections of this chapter describe the effect of relationships between higher education and the federal government on the tension between the liberal and service ideals, on academic freedom and the social role of the American professor, and on the preparation of students for the labor market.

The College and the University

The future direction of federal policy in higher education was foreshadowed in the Morrill Act's title, "An Act Donating Public Lands To The Several States And Territories Which May Provide Colleges For The Benefit Of Agriculture And Mechanic Arts." After an earlier veto by President Buchanan in 1859, the act passed Congress in 1862 under the sponsorship of Representative Justin Morrill of Vermont.[1]

The goals of the Morrill Act were a sharp departure from the traditional aims of the American college, which were to prepare students for professions and to confer status as a gentleman. These two social functions were served by a curriculum centered on Latin and Greek. Latin was the traditional education for the ministry, and the study of Greek was part of the Renaissance ideal for the education of the gentleman ruler.[2] During early colonial years, colleges reflected these social goals. In the eighteenth century, these goals were challenged by an interest in science and an emphasis on the use of reason. In *Academic Freedom in the Age of the University,* Richard Hofstadter writes, "During the last three or four decades of the eighteenth century the American colleges had achieved a notable degree of freedom, vitality, and public usefulness and seemed to have set their feet firmly on the path to further progress."[3]

This early glimmer of the modern concept of the university quickly faded during the college boom of the early nineteenth century, when religious denominations competed in the construction of small colleges. The number of colleges in the United States increased in number from 12 prior to the Revolutionary War to approximately 262 by the time of the Civil War. Of the approximately 250 colleges established between the two wars, 182 survived into the twentieth century.[4]

The guiding philosophy of these early nineteenth century colleges, as represented by the Yale Report of 1828, was quite different from the educational philosophy that created the Morrill Act. Historian Theodore Crane writes, "For decades after 1828 the Yale Report sustained traditionalists. Its assumptions seemed to reflect a realistic appraisal of the role played by American colleges and of the expectations of the public."[5] Frederick Rudolph argues that the report satisfied established elites because it withstood demands for reforms that would have given American colleges a more practical and popular curriculum: "The religious, the very pious, the privileged—were the people who ran the colleges, people who also knew that the American college was running on a shoestring and that the old course of study, while the best, was also the cheapest."[6]

Rejecting pressures to provide a practical and career-oriented education, the Yale Report advocated a liberal education designed to develop character and mental abilities. The report stated:

> The great object of a collegiate education, preparatory to the study of a profession, is to give that expansion and balance of the mental powers, those liberal comprehensive views, and those fine proportions of character, which are not to be found in him whose ideas are always confined to one particular channel.[7]

The report advocated a collegiate education that would provide a general background of knowledge and an exercise of mental powers so that the graduate would be able to participate in a wide range of intellectual activities. In the words of the report, "Wherever he [the college graduate] goes, into whatever company he falls, he has those general views, on every topic of interest, which will enable him to understand, to digest, and to form a correct opinion, on the statements and discussions he hears."[8]

The report reasoned that a collegiate education should, through exercise, balance mental faculties in order to assure a balanced character. This objective, it argued, could be achieved through general studies. Each subject matter would contribute to the exercise of a set of mental faculties and, therefore, to the formation of a balanced character. For instance, the report claims that mathematics would teach demonstrative reasoning, physical sciences would teach inductive reasoning, ancient literature would provide finished models of taste, English reading would teach speaking and writing, philosophy would teach thinking, and rhetoric and oratory would teach the art of speaking.

One result of this type of collegiate education is to provide graduates with the cultural capital necessary to set them apart from the rest of society. For those born into the middle or upper classes, this form of education confirms their status. For those wishing to enter those classes, this type of education confers status.

In discussions leading up to the Morrill Act, distinctions were made between a higher education serving the needs of the upper classes and one serving the needs of the majority of the population. Jonathan Turner, the principal lobbyist for the Illinois Industrial League, drew up a plan for an industrial university for Illinois that was endorsed by the state legislature in 1853. The legislature's endorsement contained a request for public land as endowment. This request was answered by the Morrill Act. In his plan, Turner stated that society was divided into two social classes, which he labeled professional and industrial. In his words, "Probably, in no case would society ever need more than five men out of one hundred in the professional class, leaving ninety-five in every hundred in the industrial...." For Turner, the liberal education of the nineteenth century college was appropriate for the professional class. What the industrial class required was a higher education adapted to their life pursuits or, as Turner phrased it, "their life-business."[9]

Therefore, within the context of Turner's argument, adding vocational aims to higher education meant adding social class distinctions. Liberal education would continue for those destined for the "professional class," while vocational-oriented education would be provided for the industrial class.

The Morrill Act gave a vocational orientation to higher education and endorsed the German concept of the role of the university. Henry Tappan, one of the foremost reformers of higher education in the 1850s and an advocate of the principles in the Morrill Act, embraced the model of the German university. He was a critic of the Yale Report and, as president of the University of Michigan between 1852 and 1863, gave new direction to higher education. In his 1852 inaugural address at Michigan, he supported the model of the German university and proclaimed the university as a major center for the creation and expansion of national wealth: "In demanding the highest institutions of learning.... [we are] creating not only, important and indispensable commodities in trade, but providing also, the very springs of all industry and trade, of all civilization and human improvement." Following what he called the Prussian model, Tappan proposed the establishment of a scientific course of study that would parallel the classical curriculum. Accepting the types of distinctions made by Turner, he argued that both the classical and the scientific curricula were equally good and equally responsive to students' needs, and, in an example indicating the direction in which Tappan wanted the university to move, he stated, "A farmer may find Chemistry very closely connected with his calling but what can he do with Latin and Greek and the higher mathematics."[10]

The Morrill Act of 1862 specifically dealt with the issue of educating the industrial classes. The legislation stated that the money derived from lands granted under the act would be used "to teach such branches of learning as are related to agriculture and the mechanic arts, in such manner as the legislatures of the States may respectively prescribe, in order to promote the liberal and practical education of the industrial classes in the several pursuits and professions in life."[11] The Morrill Act gave to each state 30,000 acres of public land per senator and representative. Because the Civil War was in progress at the time, the teaching of military tactics was included in the legislation. By the beginning of World War I, this provision, along with legislation passed in 1916, would result in the establishment of 115 Reserve Officers Training Corps (ROTC) on college campuses.[12]

In this way the Morrill Act provided the financial means for the establishment and expansion of a system of public higher education that emphasized vocational goals. In addition, the model of the German university, with its emphasis on research and service, was gaining in popularity as more and more American scholars studied abroad. Before 1850, roughly 200 American students had made the trip, but after the Civil War, the numbers increased rapidly, and during the decade of the 1880s, almost 2,000 made the journey.

The model of the German university promised to increase the prestige of higher education and of the professor in American life. The model was part of a general view of the instrumental nature of knowledge in modern society. Knowledge was to be the guiding factor in the operation of government, business, agriculture, labor organizations, social institutions, and in personal relationships. Within this context, the source of knowledge was to be the university. The university was to create new knowledge through research, to distribute knowledge through the education of students, and to guide institutions and people through expert advice. The expert armed with knowledge gained through research was to lead the progressive evolution of society.[13]

This vision of higher education guided the establishment of graduate schools, complete with research seminars and armies of graduate students digging into every possible area of scholarship. Professors gained income and prestige as they gave expert advice to government and business and claimed that their research would improve interpersonal relationships, the raising of children, and the organization of the family. The Wisconsin Idea represented the grandest notion of the university, with its claim that the boundaries of the university are the boundaries of the state.

Also, the service model of higher education received support from the new industrial enterprises of the late nineteenth century. In 1865, Ezra Cornell, having earned a fortune in the telegraph business and in public lands, endowed Cornell University, which was to serve the industrial classes and was to be a model research institution. In 1867, Johns Hopkins, who had gained a considerable fortune through commerce, endowed Johns Hopkins University as primarily a graduate institution. As the twentieth century approached, the list of donors and new universities increased: Jonas Clark founded Clark University as a graduate center in 1887, Leland Stanford founded Stanford University in 1885, and John D. Rockefeller established the University of Chicago in 1890.

Large-scale corporate wealth believed the university would be a source of research to serve industry and to maintain social stability. In *America by Design: Science, Technology, and the Rise of Corporate Capitalism,* David Noble writes, "The growing need within industries for scientific research, and the drive toward cooperation with educational institutions to secure it, paralleled the development of research with the universities." Noble argues that the new universities, like the public schools, were given the task of educating individuals to meet the needs of the industrial system:

> While the primary mission of the university within the industrial system was the "efficient production of human material" according to "industrial specifications"—which made not only the building of universities, but education itself an industry—the role of universities as centers of research for industry was also a vital one.[14]

Throughout the twentieth century, the American university has been plagued by contradictory elements. Foremost is the conflict between the ideal of service and that of academic freedom. Inevitably, scholarship in service to industry and government causes restraints on intellectual freedom.

The various meanings given to academic freedom resulted in conflict. On the one hand, academic freedom was considered a necessary condition for conducting research in service to industry and government. On the other hand, academic freedom was used by the professorate as job protection and justification for professional independence. The confusion over these two uses of academic freedom would lead some professors, who were enamored of the vision of the noble scholar in pursuit of truth, to accuse their colleagues of violating this vision by working for government or industry.

In Germany, academic freedom was based on certain assumptions about the inevitable progress of knowledge. Based on the idea that the pursuit of truth requires freedom to conduct research, the ideal of *Lehrfreiheit* gave university professors freedom to lecture and report on their research, and freedom to conduct any type of research. But this concept was based on the assumption that pure scientific research would lead to a refined support of the German concept of an organic society ruled by the authority of the state. For instance, as Jurgen Herbst points out, American historians had difficulty dealing with the "scientific" history produced by German universities because it emphasized the importance of the evolution of the power of the state, it denied natural rights, and it claimed Aryan superiority. Within this context, academic freedom was supported as instrumental in the pursuit of a particular type of truth.[15]

In the United States, academic freedom was the key concept in the professional organization of the American professorate. One of the first acts by the newly organized American Association of University Professors (AAUP) in 1915 was the issuance of a "Declaration of Principles on Academic Freedom and Tenure." Under this declaration senior professors were granted the right to pursue research, to discuss controversial ideas with graduate students, and to speak freely outside the university on subjects of professional competence. Sheila Slaughter argues, "This definition of academic freedom was designed primarily to ensure that established professors giving scientific advice to government, foundations, and private sector organizations would not suffer reprisals."[16]

While academic freedom was justified as necessary for the progress of knowledge, it also served to project the image of the cloistered scholar, free of political and social pressures, pursuing truth for its own sake. This provided a noble, if not largely mythological, picture of the American professor. At the second annual meeting of the AAUP, the president declared:

> The truth is that we are a single profession—the most responsible branch of that profession which Fichte forever exalted with his inspired essay on "The Nature of the Scholar." And, to adapt a phrase of his from "The Vocation of Man," "It is the vocation of our profession to unite itself into one single body, all the parts of which shall be thoroughly known to each other and all possessed of similar intellectual standards."[17]

When the United States entered World War I, universities and professors raced to provide service to the state. As Carol Gruber describes in *Mars and*

Minerva, debate on campuses was quickly stifled as universities rallied around the flag.[18] The quickness with which debate ended was surprising given the controversial nature of the United States' involvement and the recent assertions by faculties on the value of academic freedom.

Even the AAUP was quick to assure the loyalty of its professors. Rather than promoting open discussion over the ends and methods of the war, the AAUP favored closing debate and firing professors who were critical of the war effort. Shortly after intervention in the war, Frank Thilly, president of the AAUP, began to receive complaints of pressure being placed on faculty members because of statements about the war. Almost immediately, the AAUP issued a report on the meaning of academic freedom during wartime. The report states that during wartime there were legitimate reasons for dismissing outspoken faculty members.

Specifically, the report declares, "members of college or university faculties should...be required by their institutions to refrain from propaganda designed, or unmistakably tending, to cause others to resist or evade the compulsory service law or the regulations of the military authorities...." As punishment, it was recommended that faculty members "may be, and should be, dismissed, even before any action has been taken against them by the law-officers of the state."[19]

The AAUP sounded the death note to critical debate by American professors with the statement that, in proving a speech to be "unmistakably tending," it was not "necessary that a speech or other public utterance should contain, in so many words, an exhortation to disobey the law." The demand for complete loyalty to the official word of the government was made abundantly clear: "If, for instance," the report attempts to clarify, a speaker should declare that "all participation in war is immoral, or should praise the example of the Russian troops who deserted their posts and betrayed their allies, or should assert that the payment of war taxes is contrary to sound ethical principles—such a speaker may be presumed to know that the *natural tendency* of his words is to stir up hostility to the law and to induce such of his hearers as are influenced by him to refuse to perform certain of the obligations of citizenship."[20]

In addition, the AAUP recommended dismissal for faculty members who tried to persuade others from providing voluntary assistance to the war effort, including the buying of war bonds and the support of war charities. American academics clung to the ideal of the noble scholar in pursuit of truth, while their professional organization supported only a limited definition of academic freedom. In keeping with the defense of academic freedom as a condition instrumental in the pursuit of knowledge, its application was confined to situations within universities. Therefore, it provided no protection for faculty members who engaged in controversial activities outside of their respective universities. In the 1930s, faculty members were fired for engaging in radical activities outside the context of the academic world, but they were not fired for participating in discussions about radicalism in classrooms or in academic journals.

In fact, in 1940 the AAUP agreed with the Association of American Colleges to a statement of principles on academic freedom that actually placed limitations on the exercise of a professor's political rights. The statement argues that faculty members should realize their special position within communities and that they "should at all times be accurate, should exercise appropriate restraint, should show respect for the opinions of others, and should make every effort to indicate that...[they are] not an institutional spokesman."[21] In addition, faculty members agreed to live exemplary lives and to allow "moral turpitude" to be used as grounds for dismissal.

In return for these limitations on academic freedom, the American Association for American Colleges agreed to a tenure system, where permanent tenure was to be granted by peer review after a maximum probationary period of seven years. Once granted tenure, professors were guaranteed lifelong employment unless dismissed for "adequate cause."

While adequate cause was not clearly defined, Sheila Slaughter writes, "the interpretation appended to the 1940 document specifically states that the exercise of a professor's political rights as a citizen might legitimately be considered sufficient."[22]

In other words, the American professorate, as represented by the AAUP, agreed to limitations on freedom outside the academy in return for job security. William Van Alstyne, a past president of the AAUP and a law professor, states, "the trade-off that the AAUP appeared to have accepted with the Association of American Colleges in 1940...is substantially more inhibiting of a faculty member's civil freedom of speech than any standard that government is constitutionally privileged to impose in respect to...other kinds of public employees." This agreement, in Van Alstyne's words, was "namely, to cultivate public confidence in the profession by laying down a professionally taxing standard of institutional accountability for all utterances of a public character made by a member of the profession."[23]

Since civil liberties were not included in the agreement on academic freedom, the AAUP did little between 1945 and 1955 in cases involving approximately seventy-five dismissals of faculty members for participation in allegedly radical politics. Since the 1950s, the major protection for the civil liberties of faculty members has been court interpretations of the Fourteenth Amendment to the Constitution.[24]

In conclusion, what is important to understand is that criticisms of universities or of professors for serving the interests of the state completely miss the mark. In fact, it was the goal in the organization of the modern university and of the professorial profession to provide that type of service. Complaints about universities and professors serving the state are often based on a vision, which is mainly mythological, of the noble and independent scholar.

Therefore, higher education in the twentieth century is a mixture of conflicting goals and beliefs. The tradition of the liberal arts college of the nineteenth century continues in the midst of the modern university. Higher education continues to confirm and to confer status, and to serve government and society. Colleges and universities organize to train students for specific careers, while there continues to be a cry for a general liberal arts education. Professors complain about violations of academic freedom when job security is threatened, but they provide little help when a colleague is fired for political activity outside the university. And, as the federal government helps to make higher education a central institution for gaining access to the job market, students, particularly disadvantaged and minority students, demand equal opportunity to gain access to higher education.

In Service to the State

The following generalizations can be made about the effect of government actions and policies on higher education in the twentieth century: 1) It undercut the role of the scholar as critical thinker; 2) It influenced the acceptance of vocational goals for higher education; 3) It promoted the role of universities and of scholars as managers of human resources; 4) It reinforced the certifying role of universities and colleges by increasing access for youth cohort groups.

For instance, during World War I critical discussion about the most important events of the day disappeared from college campuses, and professors were recruited into writing war-related propaganda. Historians and social scientists joined the government's Division of Civic and Educational Publications of the Committee on Public Information and organized, under the leadership of Guy Stanton Ford, into a National Board of Historical Service. Ford played a leading role in justifying to fellow academics their participation in propaganda warfare. He declared that the "fight for public opinion" was part of modern war. The military, Ford argued, required support from the whole country. Therefore, the "morale of the nation itself becomes of military importance."[25]

Frequently called the Creel Committee after its chairperson, George Creel, the Committee of Public Information was officially organized in 1917. The Creel Committee bombarded the civilian population with posters, public speakers, and pamphlets on the correctness of the allied cause and on the barbarity of German power. In addition, professors were called on to analyze foreign-language newspapers for possible subversive statements. Involved in these activities were some of the leading American scholars of the time, including Charles Beard, Carl Becker, and John R. Commons.

Carol Gruber maintains that the American scholars who served on the National Board of Historical Service and on the Creel Committee "thought that intellect derived its social legitimacy from demonstrably 'useful service.' They did not bother to explore the complexities surrounding the relationship of intellect to power."[26]

Also, academics across the country participated in designing a college course on war issues for the new Student Army Training Corps (SATC) organized in 1918. The full summaries of the lectures that remain from the University of Michigan's War Issues Course contain such objective titles as "How Autocracy Drills Its Subjects," "Dreams of World Power," "Superman," and "A State Without Moral Obligations."[27]

Besides providing an opportunity for academics to teach in service to the state, the SATC provided much-needed financial support to universities and colleges that were suffering from shrinking student enrollments as a result of the war. In fact, for many institutions, the awarding of an SATC contract was essential for economic survival.

The war not only stifled open debate and brought ideas into service to the state, it also had a profound effect on the nature of academic scholarship. This was particularly true for the academic field of psychology, which for many years had been trying to establish itself as a legitimate field of study in American colleges and universities. The war provided the opportunity to prove the usefulness of psychologists to society.

What is important about the effect of the war on the development of psychology is the interrelationship that existed between the war's influence on psychological research, psychologists' acceptance of a military model for social organization, and the use of psychological methods to manage human resources. In fact, it was World War I's influence on the development of psychology that provided the tools for linking the goals of higher education to the needs of the labor market.

The field of psychology provides a good example of the effect of service to the state. The war made "measurement" the central focus for the professionalization of psychology. During and after the war, the majority of articles appearing in psychological journals were devoted to measurement. The concept of psychological measurement was linked to a vision of a scientifically organized society managed by academic experts.[28]

During the war, the government funded a team of psychologists to develop a test for classifying human resources for the military. Based on earlier work by French psychologist Alfred Binet, the team developed the first intelligence tests designed to be given to large groups for the purpose of general classification of human resources. The original Binet test was designed to determine whether or not individuals needed special education. Meeting in 1917, the psychologists spent little time debating the meaning of intelligence as they quickly designed the Alpha test for literate soldiers and the Beta Test for illiterate soldiers. By the end of World War I, the tests had been given to 1,726,966 members of the army.

The development of these tests had a direct influence on elementary, secondary, and higher education. After the 1918 armistice, the government flooded the market with unused test booklets, which educators immediately utilized. Guy M. Whipple, a leading psychologist, reported in 1922 that the army Alpha test was most widely used in colleges, both because it was the first test constructed by a team of well-known psychologists to be tried on large numbers of men in the army and because "the test blanks were procurable for several months after the armistice at prices far below what other tests could be produced."[29]

The psychologists involved in the development of the tests were aware of the implications for the organization of society. The head of the United States Army psychological team, Robert Yerkes, wrote, "Great will be our good fortune if the lesson in human engineering which the war has taught is carried over directly and effectively into our civil institutions and activities." The psychologists believed that the army was the ideal form of modern social organization because it embodied what was considered to be the proper classification of labor power. Expressing great hope for the future, Yerkes stated, "Before the war mental engineering was a dream; today it exists and its effective development is amply assured."[30]

Psychologists envisioned a society where intelligence (academic experts) would rule and students would be scientifically selected and educated for their proper places in the social organism. It was hoped that testing would enable schools to fulfill a dream of providing fair and objective equality of opportunity through scientific selection. Tests were considered the key to a socially efficient society.

One member of the army's psychological team, Henry Herbert Goddard, captured this vision in a lecture published in 1920: "[It] is not so much a question of the absolute numbers of persons of high and low intelligence as it is whether each grade of intelligence is assigned a part, in the whole organization, that is within its capacity." Goddard went on to suggest that humans could learn from the busy bee how to achieve "the perfect organization of the hive." "Perhaps," he stated, "it would be wiser for us to emulate the bee's social organization more and his supposed industry less."[31]

Between World War I and World War II, standardized testing had the greatest impact on the classification of students within elementary and secondary schools. It was after World War II that the federal government brought higher education into a national system for the classification and management of human resources. Besides influencing the social uses of psychology, World War I demonstrated that there was no conflict between academic freedom and service to the state as long as academic freedom was limited to an instrumental role in the pursuit of knowledge designed to serve the state.

War again set the stage for government involvement in higher education. World War II and the following Cold War with the Soviet Union established lasting connections between government policies and higher education. Not only was research influenced in the direction of military needs, but higher education was shaped to meet the needs of the labor market. As a result of strong links with government policies, higher education was directly affected by changes in the political world.

Two important events during World War II set the stage for government influence over higher education. One was the passage of the Servicemen's Readjustment Act of 1944, which provided veterans with tuition, books, and living expenses. Against the background of the Depression, a major purpose of the legislation was to avoid any massive unemployment that might occur after the war. The effect was to make higher education accessible to larger numbers of the population. In 1945, 1,012,00 veterans attended college, doubling the existing college population. In the seven years in which benefits were provided, 7.8 million veterans received some form of postsecondary education.

Concurrently with expanding the enrollments of higher education, the federal government established policies that were designed to influence college students to study science, mathematics, and engineering. This approach was a direct use of higher education to solve what were considered national humanpower shortages.[32]

During World War II, President Roosevelt requested that Vannevar Bush, the head of research for the federal government, establish priorities for postwar science policies. In *Science—the Endless Frontier*, Bush recommended the expansion of scientific capital by improving science and mathematics curricula in elementary and secondary schools, by encouraging college students to study mathematics and science, and by funding basic scientific research. Based on these recommendations, Congress finally (in 1950) passed legislation for the establishment of the National Science Foundation (NSF). The NSF provided money for fellowships, basic research, and curriculum planning.[33]

Concern with the increasing supply of mathematicians, scientists, and engineers would eventually become part of a larger discussion about using higher education to plan national humanpower objectives. Since the Depression years there had been a concern with youth unemployment and with humanpower planning. During the Depression youth were the last hired and the first fired.

President Roosevelt rejected the idea of using the schools as custodial institutions to keep young people out of the labor market because of his basic dislike of professional educators. This distrust between federal officials and professional educators would have an important impact on postwar educational policies. But, during the Depression it resulted in the federal government's creating a paramilitary Civilian Conservation Corps (CCC) to work primarily in national forests. Roosevelt was enamored with the idea of the CCC and contemplated making it into a national year of service for all American males. When World War II broke out the youth problem was solved, but discussion continued about some form of national service.[34]

The resolution of the call for a national year of service had a profound effect on the role of higher education in American society. After Roosevelt's death, President Truman continued to plan for a national year of service which, in the context of his fears about a postwar threat from the Soviet Union, became a plan for compulsory military service. Truman favored a national year of military service for all males, including those with physical handicaps. In his plan, a national year of military service would provide national health care (through health examinations and the medical treatment of all recruits), a national remediation program (through testing and instruction), and a national humanpower plan (through compulsory vocational guidance). After World War II, Truman's plan was criticized by the Defense Department, by universities and colleges, and by the military-defense industry. The Defense Department wanted national military service but did not want to be a remediation service for educational and health problems. Colleges and universities feared a loss of students. The military-defense industry, which included the scientists that had backed Bush's report, wanted the best students to be deferred for higher education in mathematics, science, and engineering.[35]

After several years of debate, the legislative compromise in 1951 was to continue the selective service system of World War II, with deferments from service being granted, not only for those employed in jobs considered to be in the national interest, but also for college attendance. This revolutionary concept provided another major boost to college enrollments as men avoided military service by enrolling in colleges and other institutions of higher learning.

As a result of the need to monitor attendance, there was federal support for the creation of what was to become the national gatekeeper to higher education, the Educational Testing Service (ETS). The Selective Service decided to use grades and performance on a Selective Service Qualification Test to determine eligibility for deferment. The contract for the test was granted to the newly organized ETS. One of the founders of ETS, James Conant, was a leading scientist-politician who, like his friend Vannevar Bush, wanted national humanpower planning to increase scientific capital. ETS merged the previously existing College Entrance Examination Board and Scholastic Aptitude Test.[36]

Selective service was a very rough tool for national humanpower planning. It primarily persuaded men to attend institutions for higher education. It was assumed that an increase in college graduates would be of general benefit to the economy. It was hoped that general improvement in the public school science and mathematics programs, plus financial aid from the NSF, would persuade many college students to major in engineering, science, and mathematics.

Federal policies regarding higher education were more closely tied to national defense policies after the Soviet launching of Sputnik in 1957. Congress responded with passage of the National Defense Education Act of 1958 and by allocating more money to the NSF. It is important to note that the major supporters of the NDEA were from the military-defense industry and from the new breed of political scientists. Professional educators wanted general aid from the federal government so that they could determine how it would be used in educational institutions. Those supporting the NDEA objected to general aid because they claimed that professional educators could not be trusted. The result was federal categorical aid that only provided support in the areas of science, mathematics, foreign languages, and teacher training.[37]

This major revolution in federal involvement in higher education in the 1950s occurred under a Republican administration. In fact, President Eisenhower was very much in favor of national humanpower planning to meet military and scientific needs.[38] But, as this revolution was occurring, a massive civil rights movement was building that would reach its peak in the 1960s. Most of those in the civil rights movement were considered to be part of the constituency of the Democratic Party. The Democratic Party was a strange and conflicting mixture of white Southerners, Catholics, urban blue-collar workers, and ethnic and minority groups. Since the Republican Party in the 1950s made education an important part of federal policies, it was logical for the Democratic Party to formulate educational policies to meet the needs of its constituency. When John F. Kennedy was elected in 1960 the civil rights movement appeared to be heading in the direction of a general poor people's campaign. A demand within the Democratic Party was for federal action to protect civil rights and to end poverty. The actions of the Republican Party in the 1950s and those of the Democratic Party in the 1960s made educational policies an important part of national politics. Democratic action in the Kennedy and Johnson administrations was based on a human capital theory that proved faulty by the end of the 1960s. This theory assumed that investment in education would increase productivity which, in turn, would cause economic growth. Economic growth, it was assumed, would create new jobs for high school and college graduates. In addition, the Kennedy and Johnson administrations believed that lack of educational opportunities caused a continuation of poverty. Therefore, it was assumed that federal investment in education combined with efforts to increase educational opportunities would pay for itself by sparking economic growth and by eliminating poverty.[39]

These economic theories provided arguments for supporting a variety of educational legislation during the Kennedy and Johnson years. The Higher Education Act of 1965 was designed to increase the educational opportunities for disadvantaged groups by providing equal opportunity grants and federal scholarships for undergraduate students. In addition, it provided a wide array of funding for community service programs, college library assistance, teacher training programs, instructional equipment, and insured student loans.[40]

Like the NDEA, the Higher Education Act of 1965 was primarily the result of political concerns. According to Senator Daniel Moynihan, who had been involved in educational planning in the Kennedy and Johnson administrations, higher education in the 1950s and 1960s accepted federal aid that it had never lobbied for and did not have the power to demand. In reference to the Higher Education Act of 1965, Moynihan writes:

> Once again higher education policy was deployed by the national government to serve external political needs, in this case to press further to fill out a central theme of the Kennedy and Johnson administration[s]—that of equality.... Higher education was a means of obtaining goals elsewhere in the political system.[41]

In the late 1960s, federal policies crumbled with the onset of educational inflation, campus demonstrations against the Viet Nam War, and resistance to selective service. As educational inflation occurred, college graduates were forced to take employment that was below their educational qualifications. Ph.D.'s were driving cabs, and many B.A.'s were doing office work that had previously been done by high school graduates. The assumption that education would increase productivity and expand opportunities in the labor market proved false. The number of college graduates expanded at a rate faster than did the creation of new jobs requiring college degrees. In addition, criticisms appeared about the assumption that education increased productivity. In *The Great Training Robbery*, Ivar Berg argued that in some cases increased education reduced productivity because it caused worker dissatisfaction. This was particularly true when a person's educational qualifications were greater than the requirements of his or her job.[42] Also, selective service as a system of humanpower planning was brought into question by critics of campus antiwar demonstrations.

Campus disruptions and educational inflation created a new context for consideration of federal higher education policies. In 1968, President Richard Nixon was elected on a law and order platform that included restoring law and order to college campuses. In addition, the Republican Party, because it lacked a large minority constituency, was not as interested as was the Democratic Party in extending equality of educational opportunity.

The Nixon Administration did not reject the general idea of linking higher education policies with the needs of the labor market. The failure of previous policies, it was argued, resulted from failure to establish tighter links between educational programs and the needs of the labor market. Increases in college attendance did not guarantee increased employment opportunities or economic growth. What was required, according to Nixon's educational planners, was educational training for specific careers. This meant an expansion of vocational and technical schools, and college curricula directed toward training for specific career opportunities.

Ironically, considering the emphasis in the 1980s on a general liberal arts education, Nixon's Commissioner of Education, Sidney Marland, identified general education courses as the primary cause of educational inflation and campus disruption. He believed that a combination of career education and curricula linked to specific careers would end campus disruptions and drug usage. By linking education to a specific career, he argued, students would find their schooling more meaningful and more relevant.[43]

Also, the Nixon Administration believed that too many students were channeled into colleges and universities. The solution was to reduce the number of students attending traditional institutions of higher education by increasing opportunities to attend junior colleges, community colleges, and postsecondary vocational schools.[44]

These career policies found their place in the Education Amendments of 1972. The amendments gave a new meaning to higher education by including under that term trade and technical schools, and "other postsecondary institutions." The Amendments of 1972 extended financial assistance to students attending schools under this broadened definition of higher education. The result was to encourage all institutions of higher education to emphasize career curricula.[45]

Writing in the mid-1970s for the Center for the Study of Higher Education, Bette Hamilton and Martin Laufer described the effect of these changes in federal policy. They wrote, "The new priorities given to career education are challenging the supremacy of liberal and graduate (traditional) education and are thus causing consternation within certain corners of the higher education community." These challenges and the basic need to survive, they stated, "has tempted many traditional institutions of higher education to offer career education programs in competition with vocational-oriented institutions."[46]

The policies of the Nixon Administration were in keeping with the general trend of federal involvement since the time of the Morrill Act. By creating closer links between higher education and careers, federal policies turned higher education into a major certifying institution for a large part of the labor market. This process was aided by the extension of financial aid to middle-class students. Reflecting on the vocational trends in higher education and on the importance of higher education in the certifying process, Theodore White wrote, in 1982, about the previous decade: "College became the avenue to any career beyond that of blue-collar worker or supermarket clerk."[47]

The expansion of student aid programs in the 1970s provided support for children of middle-income families. Essentially, this represented the expansion of the welfare system to the middle class. The Education Amendments of 1972 authorized the Basic Educational Opportunity Grants (Pell grants). During the Carter administration, student aid programs were expanded to the middle class with the passage of the Middle Income Student Assistance Act of 1978. Aid to middle-class students was again expanded in 1980 with new amendments to the Higher Education Act. Table 2.1 shows the type of federal assistance programs and the rapid expansion of federal student assistance between 1970 and 1980.

In the 1980s, federal education policies continued to be tied to the needs of the economy. During this period, the major political parties became more sharply divided over specific educational issues. In part, this was a result of the alignment of educational interest groups in the 1970s. In 1976, the National Education Association (NEA) decided, for the first time in its history, to back a candidate for the presidency of the United States. In exchange for this support, Jimmy Carter promised to get Congress to approve the establishment of a department of education, with its own secretary participating in cabinet meetings. The American Federation of Teachers (AFT), the smaller of the two teachers' unions, also agreed to support Carter. Carter's election and the establishment of the Department of Education guaranteed, at least for the time, continued NEA and AFT support of the Democratic Party.[49]

By the 1980 national elections, the Republican Party faced the problem of the two major teachers' unions being in the Democratic camp. By this time, educational issues were of such importance in national politics that Republicans were forced to identify their own educational constituency. During the 1980 election the Republicans formed a loose-knit educational constituency composed of supporters of private schools, critics of the moral standards of public schools, and advocates of federal deregulation. The most vocal of these groups were the Protestant fundamentalists, who charged the public schools with teaching secular humanism and demanded either establishment of private Christian schools or greater influence over public schools. To this coalition of educational interests, Ronald Reagan promised to support a school prayer amendment, tuition tax credits, federal deregulation, and abolition of the recently established Department of Education.[50]

Ultimately, economic concerns were to dominate discussions of educational policy during the Reagan administration. Rather than abandon the vocational

TABLE 2.1[48]
Federal Student Assistance (In Millions of Dollars)

Department of Education Programs	1970–71	1975–76	1980–81
Pell Grants	—	936	2,607
Supplemental Grants	134	201	366
State Incentive Grants	—	20	76
College Work-Study	277	295	658
National Direct Loans	240	460	695
Guaranteed Student Loans	1,015	1,267	6,204
Total	1,616	3,179	10,607

thrust of higher education policy, the Reagan administration changed the emphasis to accommodate new economic issues. These were most clearly stated in the administration's report on education in 1983, *A Nation at Risk*. The report declared international trade to be America's primary economic problem and blamed the schools for the declining rates of productivity relative to Japan and West Germany.[51]

Ironically, the blame for international trade problems was placed on the vocational emphasis that had dominated educational policy in the 1970s. *A Nation at Risk*, as did many other reports of the period, bewailed the decline of academic studies in public schools and called for increased academic requirements. Like the 1950s, there was a new call for the schools to produce more scientists and engineers. And, contrary to the career emphasis in higher education in the 1970s, there was a call for strengthening liberal arts programs.

Due to the Carter adminstration's disastrous impact on the economy, President Reagan was able to establish even closer links between higher education and the needs of the labor market. The key strategy was to support tax policies that would favor partnerships between business and higher education. In other words, as the Reagan administration reduced federal spending for education, incentives were given for direct business support of higher education. These incentives were given in the Economic Recovery Tax Act of 1981.[52]

Given these tax benefits, the American Council on Education organized the Business-Higher Education Forum which issued in 1983 its major report, "America's Compelling Challenge: The Need for a National Response." The Business-Higher Education Forum clearly defined international trade issues as the major concern for higher education in the 1980s. The report states:

The central objective of the United States for the remainder of the decade must be to improve the ability of American industry and American workers to compete in markets at home and abroad. The new economic realities of global competition demand a broadly based national effort to make this possible.[53]

Sparked by tax incentives, business-higher education partnerships reached 300, according to a directory published by the American Council on Education in the mid-1980s. These partnerships were primarily concerned with strengthening university programs that would serve economic goals which, at this point in time, included liberal arts programs.[54]

While aiding the development of business-higher education partnerships, the Reagan administration sought reductions in student aid programs. According to one analysis, the shifts in aid programs tended to favor middle-class students over disadvantaged students. Under the Omnibus Budget Reconciliation Act of 1981, limits were placed on Guaranteed Student Loans and on Pell Grants, and Social Security education benefits were ended.[55]

In keeping with the idea of a limited federal role in education, Reagan's second Secretary of Education, William Bennett, announced that he would use his office as a "bully pulpit." His hope was to use rhetoric to bring about changes in higher education. One of his major goals was to emphasize the importance of a strong core liberal arts curriculum. As mentioned previously, while this goal was contrary to the federal emphasis in the 1970s on a career-oriented curriculum, it was part of the new drive in education for excellence to meet the economic challenges of Japan and West Germany.

Also, a core liberal arts curriculum was supported by those members of the educational constituency of the Republican Party who wanted the teaching of values restored to the curriculum. Discussions of a core curriculum increased the politicalization of higher education by creating a debate between the Republican administration and organized ethnic groups within the Democratic Party. Differences over the core liberal arts curriculum appeared during Secretary Bennett's confirmation hearings before the United States Senate. In a letter to the closed hearings, Arnold S. Torres, National Executive Director, League of United Latin American Citizens (LULAC), questioned Bennett's statement that, "We are a part and a product of Western civilization. The core of the American college curriculum—its heart and soul—should be the civilization of the West, source of the most powerful and pervasive influences on America and all of its people."[56]

From LULAC's perspective, Bennett's proposed core curriculum contained a strong cultural bias. Torres responded to this bias, saying, "Yet Western Europe is merely one continent on the globe; the melting pot of North America also has its roots in the cultures of the East, of Africa, of the Pacific, and finally of the rest of the Western Hemisphere—Central and Latin America."[57]

The very process of Secretary Bennett's appointment moved education to new political heights. During the confirmation hearings, he was asked by Senator Lowell Weicker about having received approval, before being appointed by President Reagan, from a conservative group called the Committee for the Survival of a Free Congress. The Committee for the Survival of a Free Congress is an umbrella group representing approximately thirty conservative organizations, including the Moral Majority, the Eagle Forum, and the Heritage Foundation. In his response, Secretary Bennett admitted that before his appointment by President Reagan he received two telephone requests from Connie Marschner of the Committee for the Survival of a Free Congress to meet with the group. Bennett said he initially refused to meet with the group because of the possible affects on his being considered for the position. But, Bennett stated, he then received a third telephone call from Ms. Lynn Ross Wood of the Office of Presidential Personnel. Bennett then told the Senate Committee: "The advice to me was to attend the meeting, that they requested that I should attend this meeting."[58] Senator Weicker then quoted from an article entitled "Finally a Friend in Education," published in a Moral Majority report: "Bennett talked with conservatives consistently during the decision-making process and even met with more than thirty conservative organizations."[59]

The process of Bennett's appointment highlights the increased politicalization of education at the federal level. As higher education was brought into service to the federal government, it was brought into the web of national politics. Inevitably, the creation of a Department of Education in the late 1970s would lead to the types of political pressures as those evident in Bennett's appointment. While service to the state meant that higher education would primarily serve the needs of the economy, it would also mean that it would have to serve the politicians in power and their interpretation of economic needs. Whether liberal or conservative, Republican or Democrat, service to the state meant service to a particular political ideology.

Conclusion

Ironically, the attempt by government to use higher education to meet economic needs might be self-defeating. There is often a time lag between particular economic needs, the expression of those needs through government, and the changing of policies in higher education to meet those needs. By the time policy changes go through each of these stages, the nation has moved on to a new economic crisis. For instance, the problems of unemployment and stagflation in the 1970s were quickly replaced with concerns about international trade in the 1980s. A student educated to meet one set of economic concerns might graduate in a world with different economic priorities.

Adding to the chaos in educational policies caused by government attempts to relate education to economic problems are the changes in educational policies resulting from changes in political control. The two major national parties have differing educational objectives. In the last decade, the effect of these differences was made evident in the newly created position of Secretary of Education. Each new political administration appoints a Secretary who reflects the political values of the party in control of the administration. This creates the possibility of dramatic changes in higher-education policies with each new national administration.

Therefore, political and economic transitions will keep higher-education policy in a constant state of change and turbulence. This will probably result in the loss of money, as higher educational institutions continually adapt to each new swing in the economic and political cycle. In addition, university and college graduates might be continually frustrated as they find their education out of sync with the economic cycle and when they discover that they have been developed as human resources in the interest of national policy objectives.

These conditions are a logical result of a university system that was originally organized to serve the state and a professorate that became professional in a climate of service. One's thinking should not be confused by the myth that during some previous period of time professors and universities pursued truth for its own sake. The university and the professorate were and are for sale to the highest bidder. Unfortunately, the state is the bidder with the most power and money.

Notes

1. The Morrill Act (1862), in *The Colleges and the Public 1787-1862*, ed. Theodore Rawson Crane (New York: Teachers College Press, 1963), pp. 190-94. For a discussion of liberal versus vocational education in land-grant colleges established under the Morrill Act see David Madsen, "The Land-Grant University: Myth and Reality," in *Land-Grant Universities and Their Continuing Challenge* (East Lansing: Michigan State University Press, 1976).
2. For a history of the development of this liberal curriculum see Lawrence Cremin's, *American Education: The Colonial Experience 1607-1783* (New York: Harper & Row, 1970), pp. 58-79.
3. Richard Hofstadter, *Academic Freedom in the Age of the College*, (New York: Columbia University Press, 1955), p. 209.
4. Frederick Rudolph, *The American College and University* (New York: Alfred A. Knopf, 1962), pp. 48-9.
5. Crane, *Colleges and the Public*, pp. 17-8.
6. Rudolph, *American College*, p. 135.
7. Yale Report (1828), in Crane, *Colleges and the Public*, p. 88.
8. Ibid.

9. Jonathan Baldwin Turner, "Plan for an Industrial University for the State of Illinois (1851)," in Crane, *Colleges and the Public,* pp. 172–89.

10. Henry Philip Tappan, "Inaugural Discourse (1852)" in Crane, *Colleges and the Public,* pp. 147–71.

11. Ibid., p. 192.

12. Carol S. Gruber, *Mars and Minerva: World War I and the Uses of the Higher Learning in America* (Baton Rouge: Louisiana University Press, 1975). pp. 223–25.

13. For a general discussion of the influence of the German university see Rudolph, *American College*; Walter Metsger, *Academic Freedom in the Age of the University* (New York: Columbia University Press, 1955); and Lawrence R. Veysey, *Emergence of the American University* (Chicago: University of Chicago Press, 1965).

14. David F. Noble, *America by Design: Science, Technology, and the Rise of Corporate Capitalism* (New York: Alfred A. Knopf, 1977), pp. 131, 147.

15. Jurgen Herbst, *The German Historical School in American Scholarship: A Study in the Transfer of Culture* (Ithaca, N.Y.: Cornell University Press, 1965), Chap. 5.

16. Sheila Slaughter, "Political Action, Faculty Autonomy and Retrenchment: A Decade of Academic Freedom, 1970-1980," in *Higher Education in American Society,* eds. Philip G. Altbach and Robert O. Berdahl (Buffalo, N.Y.: Prometheus Books, 1981), pp. 75–6.

17. Quoted in Gruber, *Mars and Minerva,* pp. 16–7.

18. Ibid., Chap. 3.

19. Quoted in Ibid., p. 167.

20. Ibid.

21. Quoted in Slaughter, "Political Action," p. 77.

22. Ibid.

23. Ibid.

24. Ibid., pp. 77–93.

25. Gruber, *Mars and Minerva,* pp. 138–39.

26. Ibid., p. 158.

27. Ibid., p. 240.

28. For a general discussion of the development of the field of measurement see Clarence Karier, *Shaping the American Educational State: 1900 to the Present* (New York: Free Press, 1975). For a discussion of the development of testing in the context of World War I see Joel Spring, "Psychologists and the War," *History of Education Quarterly* 12 (Spring 1972).

29. Guy M. Whipple, "Intelligence Tests in Colleges and Universities," *National Society for the Study of Education Yearbook* 21 (1922), pp. 254–60.

30. Quoted in Spring, "Psychologists and the War," p. 3.

31. Henry Herbert Goddard, *Human Efficiency and Levels of Intelligence* (Princeton, N.J.: Princeton University Press, 1920), pp. 35, 62.

32. See Joel Spring, *The Sorting Machine: National Educational Policy Since 1945* (New York: David McKay, 1976).

33. Vannevar Bush, *Science—The Endless Frontier* (Washington, D.C: Government Printing Office, 1945).

34. See David Tyack, Robert Lowe, and Elisabeth Hansot, *Public Schools in Hard Times: The Great Depression and Recent Years* (Cambridge, Mass: Harvard University Press, 1984).

35. These various proposals were discussed in hearings before the U.S. Congress, Senate Committee on Armed Services, *Universal Military Training and Service Act of 1951—Hearings before the Preparedness Subcommittee of the Committee on Armed Services*, 82d Cong., 1st. sess., 10 January-2 February 1951.
36. Spring, *The Sorting Machine*.
37. See testimony in U. S. Congress, Senate Committee on Labor and Public Welfare, *Science and Education for National Defense: Hearings before the Committee on Labor and Public Welfare*, 85th Cong., 2d sess., 1958.
38. See Dwight D. Eisenhower, "Our Future Security" and "Message from the President of the United States Transmitting Recommendations Relative to Our Educational System," reprinted in Ibid., pp. 239-62 and 1357-59.
39. "The Problem of Poverty in America," in *The Annual Report of the Council of Economic Advisors* (Washington, D.C.: Government Printing Office, 1964).
40. See William V. Mayville, *Federal Influence on Higher Education Curricula* (Washington, D.C.: American Association of Higher Education, 1980), pp. 16-7.
41. Ibid., p. l6.
42. Ivar Berg, *Education and Jobs; The Great Training Robbery* (New York, published for The Center for Urban Education by Praeger Publishers, 1970).
43. See "Quoting Marland," *American Education* 7 (January-February 1971); pp. 3-4, Sidney Marland, Jr., "The Condition of Education in the Nation," *American Education* 7 (April 1971) pp. 3-5, and Sidney Marland, "The School's Role in Career Development," *Educational Leadership* (30 December 1972) 203-205.
44. See Ira Shor, *Culture Wars: School and Society in the Conservative Restoration: 1969–1984* (Boston: Routledge & Kegan Paul, 1986), pp. 30-59.
45. Mayville, *Federal Influence*, pp. 13-4.
46. Ibid., p. 19.
47. Quoted in Terry Hartle, "Federal Student Aid: Where We Have Been, Where We Are," in *Impact and Challenges of a Changing Federal Role*, ed. Virginia Ann Hodgkinson (San Francisco: Jossey-Bass Inc., 1985), p. l0.
48. Adapted from Hartle, "Federal Student Aid," p. 15.
49. See Joel Spring, *American Education: An Introduction to Social and Political Aspects*, 3rd ed. (White Plains, New York: Longman Inc., 1985), pp. 197-205.
50. Ibid., pp. 198-202.
51. The National Commission on Excellence in Education, *A Nation at Risk* (Washington, D.C: U.S. Government Printing Office, 1983).
52. Alan H. Magazine and Michael Usdan, "Business and Higher Education: New Partnerships for a New Era," in Hodgkinson, *Impact of a Changing Federal Role*, p. 51.
53. Ibid., p. 46.
54. Ibid., p. 48.
55. Hartle, "Federal Student Aid," pp. 21-4.
56. U. S. Congress, Senate, *Hearing Before the Committee on Labor and Human Resources*, 97th Cong., 1st sess., on William J. Bennett, of North Carolina, To Be Secretary, Department of Education, 28 January 1985, p. 187.
57. Ibid., p. 188.
58. Ibid., p. 61.
59. Ibid.

3

Federal Student Aid:
A History and Critical Analysis

C. Ronald Kimberling

The largest category of federal financial support to higher education is student aid, amounting to $10.3 billion or 47.4 percent of *total* federal postsecondary education expenditures in fiscal year 1985.[1] This figure primarily includes appropriations for U.S. Department of Education (ED) programs as well as expenditures for veterans benefits, ROTC scholarships, science and engineering fellowships, and miscellaneous other forms of federal student aid. An additional 46.2 percent of the total fiscal year 1985 federal funds was available for college and university research and development. Finally, 6.4 percent of the total was provided for non-R & D institutional support, including the U.S. service academies and facilities construction and renovation at public and private higher-education institutions.

Clearly, student aid has overshadowed traditional forms of federal government financial support to higher education. This point is further underscored when one notes that the appropriation for Guaranteed Student Loans (GSLs) covers only subsidy costs, not the actual volume of loans generated in any given year. In fiscal year 1990, for example, the GSL appropriation was $3.9 billion, although the actual loan volume was considerably higher, at some $11 billion. In addition, some of the Education Department student aid programs require matching funds from states or institutions of higher education. The total amount of student aid, leveraged by Education Department appropriations of $9.9 billion for fiscal year 1990, was $18 billion.[2]

All this grew from a seed planted in the National Defense Education Act of 1958, and the enactment of the National Defense Student Loan program (NDSL), modest efforts to provide low-interest loans to low-income students that began with a few million dollars in appropriations in fiscal year 1959. The NDEA was passed, despite misgivings on the part of the Eisenhower administration, largely because of the Soviet launch of the Sputnik satellite in

1957. This event was used as a rallying point by members of Congress, who argued that the United States was falling behind in technological development, therefore investment of federal dollars would be required in certain targeted activities to improve education and, by extension, competitiveness. The $31 million NDSL appropriation, incidentally, provided 24,831 students with loans averaging $383. By academic year 1990–91, student aid had grown 32,097 percent, to $9.95 billion in appropriated dollars, which in turn provided 9,905,000 grants, loans, and subsidized work-study jobs.[3]

The watershed for student aid came in 1965 with the passage of the Higher Education Act, President Johnson's Great Society program for college and university support. The Higher Education Act (HEA), together with its companion, the Elementary and Secondary Education Act (ESEA), also enacted in 1965, were the cornerstones of the contemporary federal role in education. In a typically expansive mood, President Johnson remarked at the November 8, 1965, signing ceremony for the HEA, that "the first session of the 89th Congress...did more for the wonderful cause of education in America than all the previous 176 regular sessions of Congress put together..."[4]

The Higher Education Act brought together the two main pieces of federal non-R & D higher education program legislation, the NDEA of 1958 and the Facilities Act of 1963. It also incorporated and extended the College Work-Study Program begun the previous year by LBJ's famous Office of Economic Opportunity. Two new student aid programs were enacted, Basic Educational Opportunity Grants (BEOGs) and Guaranteed Student Loans (referred to in the 1965 HEA as "Federal, State and Private Programs of Low-Interest Insured Loans to Students in Institutions of Higher Education"). Several institutional aid programs were also authorized, including the Title III Strengthening Developing Institutions program, designed primarily to assist historically black colleges and universities and the Title I Community Service and Continuing Education programs.

The rationale for the expanded federal role under the HEA was significantly broader than that provided for the National Defense Education Act. In 1950, a modest expansion of federal support could only be justified by linking NDEA programs to national security and defense. By 1965, LBJ's War on Poverty was ready to claim higher education as part of the battleground. Congressional hearings focused on the question of access to higher education, and the Senate Committee report of September 1965 observed: "Information delineating the continuing upward spiral of the cost of education beyond the high school, the rapidly mounting size of high school graduating classes...and the aggravated plight of students who do not have the means to acquire education, demonstrates in clear terms the extent and depth of the problem."[5] Although the post-World War II Baby-Boom generation has long ago passed through America's colleges and universities, making the mid-1960s concern for an impending enrollment boom anachronistic, the underlying rationale for student aid as an investment in access and opportunity for low-income students has remained a fundamental part of the political debate to the present day.

The growth of student aid programs during the Johnson Administration was a natural outgrowth of the passage of the Higher Education Act. From its modest beginnings in 1958–59, the National Defense Student Loan Program had become a $122 million program in 1964–65, providing loans to nearly a quarter of a million students, ten times the number receiving loans in 1958–59. In fiscal year 1966, the first full budget year after passage of the HEA, student aid appropriations in the Office of Education totaled $348.8 million, generating 940,000 awards of grants, loans, and work-study jobs. By fiscal year 1969, the last budget year of the Johnson Administration, appropriations totaled $529.5 million, and awards totaled nearly $2 million. Thus, during the half-decade of the Great Society, student aid appropriations grew more than fourfold and awards by eightfold. During that same period, tuition, room, and board charges at public colleges rose 27 percent, 33 percent at private colleges.[6]

Although the student aid programs were dramatically expanded under the Higher Education Act, it was by no means certain that they would become the focus of the federal role. Activists argued among themselves about whether the proper form of support should be the financing of expenses or of people. Former Congressional Budget Office Director Alice M. Rivlin succinctly summarizes the two camps:

> The advocates of institutional aid envisioned a major, federal, formula-grant program that would give general support to all institutions of higher education. This position was popular among public institutions; many saw it as a first step toward universal, free, public, higher education, financed, at least partly, by the federal government. Another group—deemed quite pernicious by the first—stressed the desirability of a student aid approach. They regarded funding of students as a more efficient mechanism for equalizing opportunities in higher education...as well as a superior way to enhance the quality of higher education through harnessing market forces....[7]

The original Higher Education Act of 1965 can be seen as a compromise between the two positions. Of the $1.1 billion in spending authorized by the HEA, 68 percent was set aside for institutional aid programs and only 32 percent for student financial assistance. The largest single authorization in the 1965 bill was $460 million for undergraduate academic facilities grants.

By 1972, however, the dominance of student aid was permanently established with the enactment of a new, portable, voucher-like grant for needy students. This grant program was originally called the Basic Educational Opportunity Grant (the 1965 BEOG was renamed the Federal Supplemental Educational Opportunity Grant, or FSEOG), although since 1980 it has been known as the Federal Pell Grant Program after Senator Claiborne Pell of Rhode Island. (To prevent confusion, I shall refer to this program hereafter by its current name, Federal Pell Grant.) The Federal Pell Grant program was the Nixon Administration's major contribution to the expansion of student aid.

The Federal Pell Grant operates as a quasientitlement voucher. Applicants must meet a means test that assembles information concerning a student's family income and assets, excludable liabilities, household size, number of dependents enrolled in postsecondary education, and the cost of attendance at the college or university chosen by the student. This information is centrally processed by the U.S. Department of Education, and a "student aid report" is made available to the student and to the institution of higher education. Payment is rendered upon enrollment.

The major difference between the Federal Pell Grant program and the Federal Supplemental Educational Opportunity Grant program is that funds for the latter are distributed in a lump sum to colleges and universities, which in turn are given discretion to "package" the aid in various modes to needy students. Individual campuses have latitude to concentrate funds on the very poor or to spread out smaller grants among more recipients. Campus-based FSEOG funds are not portable; if a student transfers to another school, the FSEOG funds remain on the original campus, while the voucher-like Federal Pell Grant migrates with the student. Proponents of Federal Pell Grants have traditionally touted two features: the uniformity of its award rules and the greater choice of institutions provided to students. Critics of the program are opposed to grant aid on general principles; they prefer that any form of public support to students require some sort of payback, either directly (as is the case with loans), or in the form of "sweat equity" (as is the case with Federal Work-Study).

During its first year of operation, 1973–74, 176,000 Federal Pell Grants were awarded from $122 million in appropriations. Initial funding for Federal Pell Grants came from a restructuring of the student aid budget. Work-study was cut from $426.6 million in fiscal year 1972 to $270.2 million in fiscal year 1973, and a smaller reduction of $23.6 million was made in the NDSL program. The savings from these cuts provided the $122 million for Federal Pell Grants and underwrote most of the $83 million in increased costs for the Guaranteed Student Loan program, which had been steadily increasing in size since fiscal year 1966. All in all, student aid appropriations in 1973–74 grew only $15 million from the $1.17 billion appropriated the previous year. By the end of the Nixon-Ford era, however, in fiscal year 1977, the student aid budget was nearly $3.3 billion, thanks primarily to a whopping 1,559 percent increase in Federal Pell Grant appropriations, which in fiscal year 1977 totaled $1.9 billion.

During the mid-1970s other changes were occurring to Higher Education Act programs. The late 1960s boom in academic facilities construction turned to bust as the postsecondary infrastructure became complete and enrollment growth slowed. By 1973, the once hyperactive academic facilities program had ground to a halt, and the college housing program (operated by HUD until its transfer to the new Department of Education in 1981) was shut down completely from 1973 to 1977. A few institutional support programs were brought into the HEA, however, notably the so-called TRIO programs (Talent Search, Upward Bound, and Special Services), designed to provide nonacademic counseling and remedial services for low-income and first-generation college students. Upward Bound, the oldest of the TRIO programs, was originally part of the Office of Economic Opportunity. Upward Bound was melded with its newly authorized mates in 1972, as part of the Nixon administration's effort to close down the OEO.

In 1976, major surgery was also performed to rescue the troubled Guaranteed Student Loan program. Since their beginning in 1965, GSLs have always contained three major subsidy components: 1) an in-school interest subsidy to borrowers whereby interest is paid directly to private lending institutions during periods of enrollment plus a post-graduation grace period; 2) a 100 percent guarantee to lenders against loss from default, death, or permanent disability; and 3) a partial interest subsidy to lenders during the repayment period (normally 10 years) to cover the difference between the borrower's lower rate of interest and a higher rate, designed to guarantee a reasonable profit to lenders.

Originally, the lenders rate was fixed by statute. By the mid-1970s, however, increases in the general interest rate structure were beginning to make it unprofitable for private banks, savings and loan companies, and other lenders to participate in the Federal GSL program. The 1976 amendments provided a variable rate of return based upon current market conditions. The borrower's rate remained fixed at 7 percent (this later increased to 9 percent in the Carter administration and dropped to 8 percent in the Reagan administration), while lenders were guaranteed 3.5 percent above the average three-month T-Bill rate of the preceding quarter. The quarterly rate adjustments assured lenders that their profit margins would always keep current with changing market conditions, and they quickly jumped back into the program.

Another shift in the GSL program brought about by the 1976 amendments to the HEA was the movement away from direct federal lender guarantees (Federally Insured Student Loans, or FISLs) toward a system of indirect subsidies via state and national guarantee agencies. Although seventeen states had guarantee agencies prior to passage of the 1965 HEA, all states quickly established them afterward. However, the 1965 legislation provided only an 80 percent federal guarantee for agency-insured loans. Consequently, the vast majority of loans through the mid-1970s were made under the FISL and not through the intermediate mechanism of state guarantors.

The 1976 amendments provided for a full 100 percent reinsurance on loans guaranteed by state agencies, while $150 million in new reserve advances was appropriated. Other subsidies to state agencies were also enacted, including an administrative cost allowance of 1 percent of annual loan originations. Part of the reason for expanding the role of guarantee agencies was a belief that more local lenders would be attracted to the program if they could work under agreements with state entities rather than with a monolithic federal bureaucracy. More importantly, there was an ideological tilt toward a decentralized, neofederalist model that envisioned the states as potential partners in the operation of the, by then, large GSL program. As will become apparent later in this chapter, the complex structure set up in the latter days of the Ford administration contributed to a general crisis in the GSL program.

A sweeping change in philosophy came with passage of the Middle Income Student Assistance Act (MISAA) in 1978. MISAA was the result of a political decision made by the Carter administration during a period when Congress was seriously contemplating enactment of tuition tax credit legislation. The House of Representatives had passed a bill providing tuition tax credits for elementary and secondary school fees, while the Senate, spurred on by Senator Daniel Patrick Moynihan, had enacted legislation providing tax credits for higher education tuition. The two houses appeared hopelessly deadlocked, and the Carter administration, bolstered by support from the higher-education lobby, entered into the fray with a completely different alternative—a proposal to open up the student aid programs, formerly targeted at low-income groups, to middle-class families. With inflation and interest rates shooting through the roof, Congress jumped at the chance to secure more political support for student aid.

MISAA called for no new student aid programs, but it made two shrewd changes in the existing GSL and Federal Pell Grant programs. For years, borrower eligibility had been sharply limited in the GSL program. From 1965–76, borrowing was limited to individuals from families earning less than $15,000 in adjusted gross income. In 1976, this cap was moved up to $25,000. Under MISAA, the cap was completely eliminated. Every college student in America became eligible for a federally subsidized, low-interest student loan. As a result, annual loan volume jumped from $1.9 billion in fiscal year 1978 to $7.8 billion in 1981, while annual subsidy appropriations increased during the same period, from $480 million to $2.5 billion. In short, if the Nixon-Ford years could be called the "era of grants," the Carter period could be termed the "era of loans."

The second change made under MISAA was more technical and more subtle. In essence, a few hundred thousand middle-income students were made eligible for Federal Pell Grants through a set of technical changes in the means test formula. So-called "discretionary" income—the amount left over after standard household expenses were deducted from a family's adjusted gross income—was subjected to a lower assessment rate in determining a family's expected contribution toward higher education expenses. If a family was expected to contribute less, students from marginally higher-income households could qualify for federal grant support. The end result of these changes shows up not so much in budget increases, but rather in the total number of Federal Pell Grant awards, since many of the newly eligible middle-class recipients received only the minimum $200 grants. Thus, while total Federal Pell Grant appropriations increased only 21 percent between 1978 and 1981 (from $2.2 billion to $2.6 billion), total awards increased 151 percent, from 1,261,293 to 3,164,965. Before MISAA, approximately one of every ten American college students received a Federal Pell Grant; after MISAA, one in every four did.

The final chapter of the Carter administration included a fairly unexciting reauthorization of the Higher Education Act completed in October 1980, just before the presidential election. Perhaps the most significant change wrought by the 1980 amendments was the elimination of a provision limiting the number of years a student was eligible to receive Federal Pell Grant awards. Other than this change, however, and aside from some tinkering with the distribution formula for Campus-Based Programs (NDSL loans, Federal FSEOGs, and the Federal Work-Study Program) and minor changes to other student aid programs, the most significant aspect of the 1980 amendments was a major restructuring of the Title III program for developing institutions. Congress expressed the view that too much money had been spent "developing" the same group of historically black colleges and struggling liberal arts institutions since 1965. In general, the "new" Title III stressed eventual "graduation" from dependency on direct federal support. In a sense, the restructuring of Title III seemed a signal that the battle over institutional aid versus student aid was, once and for all, over. By the 1980 reauthorization of the HEA, about 90 percent of appropriated funds went to student aid.

The Reagan Era

Establishment Washington seemed braced for the worst on January 21, 1981, as Ronald Wilson Reagan took the oath of office, becoming the fortieth president of the United States. Reagan was a different sort of political animal for the nation's capital, a city that one poet has deemed "neither Rome nor home." Members of Congress and higher education lobbyists were well aware of the fact that the 1980 Republican Party platform had called for the abolition of the Department of Education, which had just begun life as a Cabinet department on May 4, 1980. Many assumed that the new president also advocated complete elimination of the programs administered by ED, including student aid and institutional support programs authorized by the Higher Education Act.

These assumptions proved wrong, although the perception that the Reagan administration favored complete elimination of student aid continued to the end. In fact, no Reagan budget ever proposed elimination of the two major student aid programs, Federal Pell Grants and Guaranteed Student Loans, and funding for the Federal Work-Study program was sought in every Reagan budget save one. To be sure, almost every Executive Branch budget submitted to the Congress between fiscal year 1982 (the first real Reagan budget year) and fiscal year 1988 proposed significant reductions in annual appropriations for student aid. But some of the reductions represented cutbacks or eliminations of subsidies, as opposed to real reductions in aid to students. The fact of the matter is that the basic policy of the most conservative administration since the 1920s was to change the mix of student aid, not to eliminate it.

Like nearly every administration, the Reagan era was marked by some inconsistencies from year to year in its policy proposals, as reflected by its budget submissions. The Federal Work-Study program, for example, was marked by vast swings in policy, ranging from a proposed increase of some $350 million in the fiscal year 1984 Reagan budget to zero-funding in the fiscal year 1988 budget. Likewise, the Reagan administration vacillated in offering support to the New GI Bill during the mid-1980s. Tax-free earnings on individual Education Savings Accounts were proposed from 1982–86 and then dropped, as the administration began pushing tax code simplification.

Notwithstanding these inconsistencies, the Reagan administration undeviatingly pushed for changes in eight major areas of student aid program policy:

1.   Reverse the decline in the share of college costs contributed directly by students and their families.
2.   Extend some form of means testing to all borrowers of subsidized Guaranteed Student Loans (preferably the standard "need analysis" used to determine student eligibility for Campus-Based aid).
3.   Reduce the scope of GSL subsidies—to borrowers, guarantee agencies, and lenders.
4.   Crack down on student loan defaults, both in the GSL and NDSL programs.
5.   Target grant aid on the lowest income individuals, generally by reversing the financial eligibility formula changes enacted under the Middle Income Student Assistance Act.
6.   Tighten up on so-called "ability to benefit" rules permitting students lacking high school degrees or GED diplomas to enroll in postsecondary edu-

cational institutions (including private career schools) and to receive federal student aid.

7. Restore a reasonable limit on the numbers of years of eligibility for Federal Pell Grant assistance.

8. Eliminate the State Student Incentive Grant (SSIG) program, begun in 1974 to provide matching federal dollars as an incentive for states to start up their own grant programs.

The results were mixed, although the Reagan policies, over time, won full or partial victories in seven of the eight policy areas (the sole exception being the elimination of SSIG). Some victories occurred during the Reagan years, while others took longer. For example, complete means testing for all recipients of subsidized GSLs was finally enacted in the 1986 reauthorization of the Higher Education Act, after having been endorsed by the National Association of Student Financial Aid Administrators on general equity principles. Likewise, Federal Pell Grant eligibility was limited to five years for four-year bachelor degrees and six years for five-year undergraduate degree programs as part of the 1986 amendments to the HEA. The family share of contributing to college costs has also risen slightly, after declining during the Carter administration, but this may be due primarily to the fact that the price of a college education has increased far faster than have either inflation or available student aid from all sources.

While the restoration of means-testing GSLs represented a partial reversal of the policies enacted under MISAA, the Reagan administration clearly lost the battle with regard to Federal Pell Grants. Not only has the Congress refused to increase assessment rates on discretionary income back to pre-1978 levels, but it has also added new elements to the formula to make even more applicants eligible for awards. In the 1986 amendments, all individuals over twenty-four years of age were defined as "independent" students. This meant that even if such individuals received parental financial support, it could not be taken into consideration in calculating award eligibility. Additionally, Congress determined that state and local taxes would be deducted from the gross income figure used for purposes of determining Federal Pell Grant eligibility. The Reagan administration objected vociferously, arguing that the provision was counter-progressive, since poor people paid little or no state or local taxes. By the administration's count, this single change added $243 million to program costs in fiscal year 1988, with most of the new money going to middle-income grant recipients. Despite these arguments, Congress held firm. Additional middle-class eligibility for Federal Pell Grants came about as a result of the 1992 HEA reauthorization. Home equity was permanently excluded from means testing, as were significant amounts of farm and family business assets.

One area in which the Reagan administration established a successful theme was in the crackdown on student loan defaults. Indeed, it is remarkable to reflect upon the fact that prior to passage of the administration-backed Debt Collection Act of 1982, it was actually forbidden to report student loan default information to commercial credit bureaus! During the Reagan years, the Department of Education had collected nearly $804 million on defaulted student loans from the start of fiscal year 1982 through the end of fiscal year 1987, compared to $205.5 million collected from 1959 through the end of fiscal year 1981.[8] Default collections by ED have skyrocketed since fiscal year 1985, largely through implementation of a statutory provision permitting offset against income-tax refunds. Education Department offset collections totaled $193 million in fiscal year 1986 (the first year of the offset program), and jumped to $293 million by fiscal year 1987.

While some civil libertarians have expressed concern about the IRS tax offset program, the structure seems designed to protect against unwarranted intrusion by Big Brother. Debts must be certified by the agencies owed money, not by the IRS, and the certifying agencies must attest that other, reasonable means have been attempted to collect the debt. Debtors are given sixty days written notice to enter into repayment agreements before any information is transferred to the IRS. Even when the offset is triggered, the IRS receives only minimal data through tape transfer. The original loan records remain with the creditor agency, while tapes and any permanent record of the offset are destroyed once the offset is made. Thus, no taxpayer's IRS file contains information concerning past refund offsets. Finally, creditor agencies are required to promptly resolve disputes and make refunds when appropriate.

The offset provision was but one of many debt collection tools devised by the Reagan administration. Others include the widespread use of private collection agencies, salary offsets for federal employees, and referral of hard-core default claims to U.S. attorneys in the Justice Department. In the NDSL program, collections are handled by participating colleges and universities for the most part, although rights to defaulting accounts can be permanently assigned to the Department of Education. In order to encourage better collection by postsecondary institutions, the Education Department promulgated new regulations in 1982, providing that no new federal capital contributions to the NDSL fund would be made for any campus with gross default rates above 25 percent. Federal capital would be proportionately reduced for campuses with default rates between 15 and 25 percent. By 1986, the Reagan administration was able to convince the Congress to put this provision into the Higher Education Act and to lower the threshold figures to 10 and 20 percent, respectively.

In terms of budget appropriations, the Reagan era was one of slow growth for the student aid programs authorized under the Higher Education Act. In current dollars, student aid appropriations increased from $6.34 billion in fiscal year 1981 (the last Carter budget year) to $8.2 billion in fiscal year 1987. In constant 1982 dollars, there was still an increase, from $6.88 billion in 1981 to $7.04 billion in 1987.[9] To get a better picture, one ought to separate out the appropriation for Guaranteed Student Loans, since annual subsidy costs bear no direct correlation with annual loan volume, reflecting instead current market interest rates and default costs. Thus, appropriations for Federal Pell Grants, Campus-Based aid, and the State Student Incentive Grant program increased from $4.13 billion in fiscal year 1981 to $4.71 billion in fiscal year 1987, as measured by constant 1982 dollars.

If this is indeed the case, why, then, is there the common misperception that student aid was actually cut during the Reagan administration? And if Federal Pell Grant funding actually increased during the Reagan years, why does one constantly hear assertions that loans virtually overtook grants as the major form of student financial assistance? The answers to these questions are complex, but at least some of the following facts can help explain the mismatch between perception and reality:

1. During nearly every year of the Reagan administration, the White House proposed reductions in student aid funding. This generally triggered howls of outrage on the part of college and university presidents, the higher education lobby, and numerous members of Congress. By the time the president signed a final appropriation bill, the budget generally reflected increases in funding. But the memory of proposed cuts tends to linger.
2. Increases in the prices charged by colleges and universities for tuition, room, and board went up faster than did the rate of increase in student aid. In constant 1986–87 dollars, college prices increased 21 percent at public institutions and 30 percent at private institutions during the period 1981–82 through 1986–87.[10] These increases, which have continued since the late 1980s, especially for public institutions, no doubt add to the perception that less money is available to meet higher-education expenses.
3. Some disingenuous arguments have been put forth by those lamenting the "decline" of grants. Typically, means-tested grants, such as Federal Pell Grants and FSEOGs, are lumped together with entitlement benefits, such as GI Bill grants and Social Security survivor benefits. The latter are not what the public usually thinks of when it talks about student aid. Yet, since such aid dramatically declined in the 1980s (due to the expiration of GI Bill eligibility for Vietnam-era veterans and the abolition of nonmeans-tested Social Security survivor benefits in 1981), the mixing of apples and oranges makes it appear to less observant eyes that the major student aid programs under the Higher Education Act were actually cut back during the Reagan years.

The Bush Years, Part I

Crisis in the Guaranteed Student Loan Program

Almost immediately after the 1986 Higher Education Act reauthorization, a number of events stimulated considerable reform-minded discussion concerning the Guaranteed Student Loan program. Soaring annual default costs, reaching $1.6 billion or 46 percent of the total GSL appropriation in fiscal year 1988, prompted concern within the higher-education community, the Reagan administration, and the Congress. Additional concerns were expressed as the general subsidy structure of the GSL program became more widely scrutinized in light of the federal budget deficit and a growing interest on the part of public policy researchers, the Office of Management and Budget, and congressional budget committees in the broader issue of reforming federal credit programs. The convergence of these interests made it possible for major changes in the GSL program to be enacted during the Bush administration.

The GSL default picture is complex. A GSL loan goes into default when no payment has been made for at least 180 days after a scheduled payment date. This follows standard commercial practice. Historically, the Education Department defined the default rate as the percent of matured paper (loans that have reached the stage where repayment begins) in default. Between fiscal year 1980 and fiscal year 1983, the default rate declined from 12.5 percent to 10.8 percent. Between fiscal year 1983 and fiscal year 1986, however, the rate increased again to 12.6 percent. In other words, no real progress was made in lowering the default rate during the Reagan administration, despite the administration's outstanding record of collecting on defaulted loans.

Annual default costs are represented in terms of claims paid out by the Education Department. These costs are a function of both the default rate and cumulative matured paper, since a GSL can go into default at any time during the repayment period, normally ten years. The explosive growth of loan volume between fiscal year 1978 and fiscal year 1981 created a surge in matured paper during the early 1980s. Annual loan volume increases slowed during the Reagan administration, ranging from $7.8 billion in fiscal year 1981 to more than $9 billion in fiscal year 1987. Nevertheless, total matured paper at the end of fiscal year 1987 exceeded $44 million, more than four times the amount of matured paper at the start of the Reagan administration. This risk exposure contributed to an explosive growth in annual federal default costs, which rose from a few hundred million dollars in the early 1980s to $1.6 billion in fiscal year 1988. By that year, default claims represented the third largest category of expenditure in the Department of Education, behind the Chapter One Compensatory Education program for elementary and secondary school students and Federal Pell Grants.

As one might imagine, this situation triggered strong political rhetoric and prescriptions of strong medicine. In 1987, Education Secretary William J. Bennett called the situation "disgraceful" and proposed a number of remedies, the most controversial was initiating action to limit, suspend, or terminate GSL program eligibility, starting in 1990, against institutions failing to hold the annual "cohort" default rate of graduates below 20 percent. The new "cohort rate" concept involved looking at the default percentage of an institution's student borrowers within the first year or two of loan repayment. Democratic Senator Claiborne Pell, chairman of the Education Subcommittee of the Senate Labor and Human Resources Committee, followed suit by holding two oversight hearings on the default problem in 1988. Separate bills were submitted that year in the Senate by Republican Dan Quayle and a trio of Democrats—Senators Kennedy, Simon, and Dodd. In the House, Postsecondary Education Subcommittee Chairman Pat Williams of Montana convened a summit meeting of bankers, guarantee agency officials, higher-education representatives, and federal officials to hammer out a "consensus agenda" of solutions. Perhaps the most extreme proposal was the introduction of a bill by Representative William Ford of Michigan, one of the original sponsors of the 1965 Higher Education Act, to provide grants only to first- and second-year students and loans only to upper-division undergraduates.

Clearly, something had to be done. But the 20 percent cutoff proposed by Secretary Bennett was viewed as too draconian by the higher-education community. When Lauro Cavazos was appointed education secretary in the waning months of the Reagan administration, he struck a deal with Congress for a moratorium on both legislation and the regulations proposed by his predecessor.

After several months of study, the Cavazos team rolled out new final regulations, effective in June 1989, which took a "tiered" approach to high default institutions. At the lowest tier of enforcement, schools with cohort default rates above 20 percent for a given year would have to devise "default management plans" and submit them for ED's approval. At higher rates, institutions would have to delay disbursements of loan proceeds and implement modified *pro rata* student refund policies. At the highest tier (60 percent initially, but dropping to 40 percent over time), schools would face loss of eligibility for student aid programs.

The Cavazos plan was well received, but budget deficit woes forced Congress to go beyond these strictures and pass, in late 1989, the first in a series of legislative amendments to use an institution's cohort default rate as a device for rationing GSL funds. As part of that year's budget reconciliation package, it was mandated that schools with cohort default rates above 30 percent for the most recent reporting year would immediately lose eligibility for federal SLS loans, loans which were subject to federal default guarantees but not interest subsidy. This measure was influenced, not only by the growing bipartisan acceptance of the high-default-rate-equals-bad-school equation originally voiced by Bennett, but also because the volume of SLS loans began to soar in 1988 and early 1989, largely due to their growing popularity with private career and technical schools.

For several months in 1990, one of the biggest sideshows in Washington was a series of special GSL oversight hearings held by Senator Sam Nunn's (D.-Ga.) Subcommittee on Investigations of the Senate Governmental Affairs Committee. In the wake of the much larger scandal concerning federally insured savings and loan institutions, the Nunn Committee saw an opportunity to probe serious weaknesses in the student loan program. Testimony and reports identified a host of villains, from a failed California "nonbank" lender, to a defunct loan servicer that had experienced a computer programming meltdown, and to the Education Department itself, which was excoriated for lax monitoring and poor record-keeping.

The combination of the political need to take immediate action to address the Nunn Committee's concerns and the pressure to find additional spending cuts in domestic entitlement programs prompted Congress to take a second whack at the GSL program in its 1990 budget reconciliation bill. The new measure provided that any institution with cohort default rates above 35 percent each year for the most recent three fiscal years would lose eligibility for the highly subsidized Stafford loan program (the largest program within the GSL family). In a bow to due process, and in recognition of various reports suggesting that loan default data provided by the various loan guarantee agencies were occasionally suspect, Congress provided rights of appeal based on default rate errors and nebulously defined mitigating circumstances, such as serving a high number of low-income students.

The implementation of the two statutes, cutting off institutional eligibility for SLS and Stafford loans, created certain administrative problems throughout the Bush administration. The equation of high default rates with poor quality education persisted as official Washington dogma, despite the evidence of a growing number of studies that pointed to various borrower characteristics (family income, sex, ethnicity, employment status, etc.) as being more relevant to defaults than type of institution or educational program. Accordingly, the Education Department bureaucracy, prompted by pressures from Congress; the Office of Inspector General; and even some lobbying groups representing traditional colleges and universities began shifting from its historical client-centered mission (to "do good" with student aid monies) to a compliance oriented mode of punishing "bad" schools—mostly proprietary institutions—with loss of loan eligibility.

This change in orientation sometimes caused pressured ED officials to act too hastily in trying to terminate program eligibility. The Reagan-Bush transition and the hasty departure of Secretary Cavazos in late 1989 also contributed to confusion and high turnover in leadership at the sub-Cabinet level. Between March 1988 and the end of the Bush administration in January 1993, five different political appointees served as assistant secretary for postsecondary education. A new appointee had no real time to learn the complexities of the student aid programs before he or she departed office. Consequently, key decisions had to be made by the senior civil servants, individuals who felt they were given a mandate to combat program abuse, but with few specific guidelines on carrying out the mandate.

As a result, a number of lawsuits were filed in the early 1990s, challenging the Education Department's methods for applying the statutory eligibility cutoffs. The first challenge came in a federal court action filed in 1991 by the accrediting commission representing cosmetology schools. The cosmetologists argued that ED erred in implementing the 1990 Stafford loan cutoff in 1991, based on cohort default rates from earlier years (for technical reasons, the rates always lag by two years). In this case, the court ruled that ED properly interpreted the statute by using the most recently available default data.

But in May 1992, ED lost the first in a series of a dozen or so lawsuits brought by individual colleges and trade schools. In this case, *Atlanta College of Medical and Dental Careers, et al. v. Alexander*, a proprietary health careers college, argued that ED improperly failed to consider data on loan servicing errors independently compiled by the college's outside accounting firm, relying instead on decisions by the guarantee agencies to accept or reject the alleged errors.[11] The Atlanta plaintiffs pointed out that guarantors have a vested economic interest in minimizing loan servicing error claims, since they might be subjected by ED to having to repurchase defaulted loans previously submitted for federal reinsurance. The Atlanta college won rights in U.S. District Court to an independent review, and these due process rights were later upheld and expanded to include rights to obtain loan servicing records from guarantors when the case went before the U.S. Court of Appeals.

A flurry of litigation followed, mostly from proprietary institutions facing business failure from loss of loan program eligibility. Through 1992 and into 1993, federal courts in several districts granted injunctions and summary judgments, forcing ED to suspend cohort rates and to establish new posttermination appeal rights for schools facing loss of SLS loan eligibility.

Meanwhile, nothing seemed effective in stemming the student loan default tide. In 1990, the nation's largest student loan guarantor, the Higher Education Assistance Foundation (HEAF) financially collapsed. The cost of the ensuing takeover by ED, just to manage an orderly dissolution of HEAF, escalated in three years from an original estimate of $30 million to well over $200 million. Not surprisingly, a disproportionate share of HEAF-guaranteed loans went into default. Subsequent to the HEAF collapse, officials of one of the nation's largest student loan lenders, Florida Federal Savings, were indicted and convicted on charges of fraud involving loan servicing. Also, the tiny Kansas Bank of Horton, which almost overnight had grown to become one of the top volume student loan lenders, collapsed and fell into FDIC receivership.

The loan default issue surfaced at a time when other questions were being raised about the GSL program. By 1990, most higher education policy specialists observed that virtually all short-term cost savings gambits had been exhausted, and in light of continued concern about the federal deficit, they began looking at the long-term picture. A number of analysts questioned whether the partial interest rate subsidy to borrowers should continue through the full ten years of loan repayment, long after the average person has entered the workforce. Requiring borrowers to pay market rate interest, beginning with the third or fourth year of repayment, was one suggestion.

Similar questions surrounded the interest subsidy paid to lenders, which from 1986 through 1993 was 3.25 percent above the three-month Treasury rate, adjusted quarterly. In times of low interest, this subsidy costs little. Through most of 1987, for example, the three-month Treasury rate ranged between 5.5 and 6.0 percent, providing lenders with a yield of 8.75 to 9.25 percent on GSLs. Since the borrower's rate was 8.0 percent, the net cost to the taxpayer in 1987 averaged about 1 percent.

In times of higher interest rates, however, the GSL interest subsidy could shoot through the roof. For every 1 percent increase in the three-month Treasury rate, annual GSL program costs climb $500,000,000. If the high interest rates of 1981–82 were to reappear quite suddenly, the cost of the GSL program could jump as much as $5–6 billion annually.

This scenario began to reveal a fundamental structural flaw in the GSL program. By basing the interest subsidy on short-term rates, the framers of the GSL program left the taxpayers completely exposed to all downside risks. Contracts for loans already made are binding. Therefore, any upward pressure on GSL costs would represent an uncontrollable entitlement expenditure. Further, fluctuations in short-term interest rates cannot be predicted over the average life of a GSL with any great certainty. Put another way, the full subsidy costs of a student loan could never be accurately known at the time of loan origination. As we shall see later, these subsidy costs played an important role in the 1992 HEA reauthorization and the 1993 Student Loan Reform Act.

The uncertain multiyear costs of Guaranteed Student Loans is a feature common to many federally guaranteed loans, even though most programs, unlike GSL, have fixed rates of interest paid to lenders. Barry P. Bosworth of the Brookings Institution observes in *The Economics of Federal Credit Programs* that the fundamental problem rests with the federal budget system: "Most benefit-cost analyses of government programs involve some ambiguity because the benefits are often elusive and difficult to quantify. For loan subsidies, however, the situation is even worse because the costs are also elusive."[12]

At least half the problem lay in the unusual rules of accounting then in use in federal budgeting. In the case of direct loans, the loan amount was scored as an outlay during the fiscal year in which the loan was made, while payments were counted as "negative outlays" as received. The immediate asset value of the loan was not taken into account, nor was the present value of the stream of payments over the life cycle of the loan. In short, direct loans were undervalued. Guaranteed loans, in comparison, were even more vexing. No expenditure of funds was recorded at the time a loan guarantee was made. Outlays were recorded only as default claims were paid or other subsidy costs were incurred. Put in plain English, the federal budget system of the 1970s and 1980s made direct loans look more expensive at the time of loan origination than they really were, and it made guaranteed loans look dirt cheap, when they really may have been quite expensive.

The Reagan administration, in March 1987, submitted a proposed credit Reform Act designed to address these problems. Among other things, the act required computation of the market value of most direct loans at the time of origination by selling them to private investors. Loan sales would not have been required in the case of certain politically sensitive loans. Congress would have appropriated funds to cover only the difference between the face value of direct loans and the market value. The difference would represent the subsidy value of such loans.

For guaranteed loans, the present value of all estimated subsidies, both short- and long-term, would be appropriated in the year a loan was originated. Subsidy payments would be made from the appropriation over the life of the loan, as directed by the cognizant program agency. If the subsidy estimates were high, surplus funds would be returned to the Treasury. If the estimates were low, the program agency would be responsible for providing additional funds or for seeking a supplemental appropriation. Additionally, in a number of guaranteed loan programs, the 1987 act would have required purchase of private insurance policies to cover default, death, and disability costs. This provision would allow for determination of true market costs of providing guarantees.

Although many aspects of the administration's bill received favorable treatment in the Congress, it was not enacted in 1987. The private insurance program prompted considerable criticism, and the administration appeared to back away from it as it failed to draw expected support from the insurance industry. Nevertheless, the legislation was modified and resubmitted in 1988 and again, by the Bush administration, in 1989.

Finally, in 1990, credit reform was enacted as part of the "pay as you go" provisions of the 1990 budget bill. This reform was adopted for three reasons:

1) it had support from both major political parties and from both liberals and conservatives; 2) it set a level playing field within the budget for computing true costs of different credit programs, a feature that attracted supporters at a time when the large federal deficit put the squeeze on all expenditures; and 3) it was a "good government" measure. Importantly, in the student loan arena, this reform set the stage for a truer cost comparison between direct and guaranteed loans.

As the 1980s wound down and the Bush administration came to power, the crisis in the GSL program prompted many reformers to look for a radical solution. Beginning in 1989, Charles Kolb, a senior White House advisor on domestic policy, began a quiet campaign to build support for a complete changeover to a direct loan program. Under Kolb's plan, the middle layers of lenders and guarantee agencies would be completely eliminated. New student loan capital would be raised through the sale of federal Treasury securities, and loans would be disbursed directly to students via their colleges and universities, in the same manner as Federal Pell Grants. Servicing and collection would be conducted by a limited number of private sector firms under contract to ED or, possibly, through the federal income tax withholding system.

In late 1989, word began to leak out that the direct loan concept was being considered for inclusion in the Bush administration's 1990 budget. Almost immediately, OMB Director Richard Darman and other administration officials opposed to direct loans began clamping down on the initiative. With Cavazos's sudden exit from the Cabinet, it was decided to let incoming Secretary Lamar Alexander have time to review the proposal. Not surprisingly, Alexander decided that ED lacked the administrative capability to launch such a bold new program. Additionally, a number of administration officials were concerned about converting a program that relied on private sector capital (albeit heavily leveraged with attractive subsidies) to one using public funds. Consequently, by the end of 1990, it became clear that the administration would not follow through on Kolb's idea.

The Bush Years, Part II

The 1992 Reauthorization of the Higher Education Act

As the 1990s began, Congress and the administration turned toward the task of reauthorizing the Higher Education Act. It was widely accepted that the crisis in the GSL program warranted a keen look at the loan component of student aid. The publication of the Nunn Committee report created a political imperative for Congress to go beyond minor tinkering and to examine whether a completely different approach to student loans should be tried.

Other issues moved into sharp focus in the early 1990s as hearings and debates on reauthorization began. Within the community of student aid administrators, program simplification was a dominant theme. The 1986 amendments had created a dual system of needs analysis (student aid means testing) that set forth different criteria for awarding Federal Pell Grants and other forms of student aid. On the margins, therefore, a student could qualify for a Federal Pell Grant but not a Stafford Loan, or vice versa. Also, a considerable amount of data were required from students and parents. By 1991, the information required by law to determine if a student was dependent upon parental support or was independent required an entire page on the student aid application form. No wonder researchers were beginning to note that student aid paperwork was now the second most complicated set of federal forms, just behind the IRS tax forms. Some noted that the sheer complexity of student aid created a threshold barrier to participation by significant numbers of low-income individuals, precisely the population historically targeted for federal assistance.

Another issue related to the explosive growth of private career schools (so-called "proprietary" schools) in the 1970s and 1980s. By the late 1980s, some 5,000 private career schools participated in at least one of the federal student aid programs. The share of Federal Pell Grant funds committed to students in private career schools increased from 12 percent in 1980 to nearly 25 percent by the end of that decade, reflecting to some extent the swings that can occur in the educational marketplace with the kind of voucher-like funding provided by Federal Pell Grants.

This situation led to envy and strong criticism of the proprietary sector by traditional public and nonprofit colleges and universities. The National Association of Independent Colleges and Universities, representing traditional nonprofit colleges, began advocating in the late 1980s that support for proprietary institutions be shifted to the Labor Department, since the majority of such institutions provide short-term, vocationally oriented instruction.

The key criticisms of the proprietary sector focused on two themes: 1) that some owners of proprietary institutions engaged in aggressive, even unfair marketing techniques designed to maximize profits, and 2) that many proprietary schools had excessively high student loan default rates. The schools responded to such criticisms by pointing out that many programs at traditional colleges are vocationally oriented (law, medicine, architecture, journalism, engineering, etc.) and that it would be elitist to separate out "high- and low-prestige" occupations. They also noted that many proprietary schools serve "high risk" populations—largely minorities—whose propensities to default on student loans are independent of the type of institution the student has attended. The main lobbying group for the proprietary sector, the Career College Association, also noted a number of internal reforms taken within the sector.

As the reauthorization debate moved into clearer focus in 1991, it became evident that most members of the congressional authorizing committees were persuaded that proprietary institutions played an important role in the postsecondary spectrum and that banishment to the Labor Department would not be the solution. At the same time, there was a growing consensus that amendments were needed to ensure better monitoring of institutional quality. The two traditional mechanisms for such oversight, private accreditation and state licensing, came under sharp attack. Accrediting bodies were criticized during reauthorization for being too collegial, too slow to react to reports of abuse, too weak in protecting student consumers, and not at all focused on financial stability and regulatory compliance. State licensing agencies were criticized for being understaffed and underfunded. Weak licensing statutes and dispersion of licensing authority among multiple state agencies were also noted. A particularly influential report on "The Methods and Effectiveness of State Licensing of Proprietary Institutions" was issued in September 1991 by the State Higher Education Executive Officers.[13]

These criticisms resulted in considerable debate over the historical purpose of the Higher Education Act. The bywords of the 1965 legislation were "access" and "choice." Historically, this meant that portable student aid was designed to give the individual student consumer access to postsecondary educational opportunities (especially for the financially needy student) and a choice of institution and academic program. Budgetary limitations in the 1980s had already limited choice to some extent, though the majority in Congress remained committed to the concept that qualified students should be able to choose to become trained as an electronics technician or as an M.D. As to access, the new skeptics were beginning to insert the concept of educational effectiveness by asking the question, "Access to what?" The implication clearly was that federal funds should be limited to those institutions and programs that could demonstrate effective educational outcomes.

The House reauthorization bill, passed in late 1991, created a greater sense of urgency in this debate by incorporating the radical solution of completely eliminating the role of accreditation as an element in determining an institution's eligibility for federal program funds, a role that had existed since the inception of the student aid programs. This proposal awakened the interest of the regional accrediting agencies representing most traditional higher-education institutions. Hitherto, these agencies had believed that the debate over accreditation was limited to the proprietary sector. The House bill, however, revealed that congressional concerns over quality went beyond the proprietary sector.

The more moderate Senate bill, passed in early 1992, preserved a role for accreditation while incorporating certain reforms such as a requirement that accrediting bodies be organizationally separated from advocacy groups. During the ensuing conference in the summer of 1992, House and Senate conferees hammered out a compromise that appeared in the final legislation, which was signed by President Bush on July 23, 1992. The compromise consisted of two elements. First, the statute embodied certain existing ED regulations regarding the recognition of accrediting agencies by the secretary of education and also expanded the secretary's authority to set stricter recognition criteria. The intent was to force accreditors to include in their criteria stronger standards of financial review and consumer protection. The second element was the creation of a new federal mandate to the states to create State Postsecondary Review Entities (SPREs), new state agencies whose mission would be to conduct in-depth, accreditation-like reviews of those institutions identified by ED as having potentially troublesome characteristics, characteristics such as high default rates, prior federal compliance problems, relative inexperience in federal student aid programs, and so on.

The SPREs would stand in addition to whatever licensing bodies had already been created by the states, and they would be given absolute authority to determine whether an institution should retain eligibility for federal programs. Federal funds were authorized to help support the SPRE function, but any state that chose not to conduct SPRE activities would be faced with the sanction of having all its institutions, including public universities, become ineligible for participation in student aid programs. In essence, the SPRE concept married the Washington "belt-and-suspenders" approach to politically sticky problems with a neofederalist relegation of program oversight in the states. In the wake of the 1992 reauthorization, all postsecondary institutions, not just the proprietary schools, would face four overlapping layers of oversight: the U.S. Department of Education, private accreditation, state licensure, and SPRE review.

A number of other changes came about in the 1992 reauthorization. The simplification agenda was evident as Congress combined the two separate needs analysis systems enacted in 1986 into a single system. Additionally, uniform student loan applications and related forms and reports became a requirement under the new law. On the other hand, parts of the system became more complex. For example, pro ration of all Title IV student aid programs was required for students with less than one full academic year of studies remaining. A new definition of the term academic year set a minimum duration of thirty weeks, with additional pro ration required for schools with shorter academic calendars. The combination of both types of pro ration has made precise calculation of student aid awards more difficult. Also, a multiplicity of effective dates and borrower interest rates were implemented for the GSL program (renamed Federal Family Education Loan program or FFEL under the new legislation), and as a result, the work of student loan counselors was made considerably more complex. In short, the gains made by simplification in some aspects of student aid administration were at least offset by new layers of complexity in other areas.

The GSL (now FFEL) crisis described earlier in this chapter had a major impact on the reauthorization. Subsidies were trimmed for all beneficiaries (students, lenders, and guarantors), and the temporary default rate cutoffs previously included in budget reconciliation acts were made permanent. Most significantly, despite the Bush administration's short-lived courtship with direct loans, members of Congress on both sides of the aisle championed the concept's advantages. The House bill went so far as to mandate a complete six year transition to direct loans, while the Senate bill simply established a modest direct loan pilot program. Faced with, by then, stiff opposition from the Bush administration, conferees settled on a somewhat broadened pilot program that would begin with the 1994–95 student aid award year. House Education and Labor Chairman William Ford (D.-Mi.), however, suggested that he would be ready to revisit the direct loan concept at an earlier date if sufficient support were to grow for the concept.

New Directions Under Clinton

With the inauguration of President Clinton in January 1993, a chance for Chairman Ford's "revisit" came about. The Clinton platform contained two major initiatives in postsecondary education, enactment of a permanent direct loan program designed to replace FFEL and passage of a national and community service bill to provide college aid to those who volunteered for specified community service duty. During President Clinton's first year in office, both programs passed handily. Interestingly, support for both Clinton initiatives came through a somewhat unexpected source; the February 1993 final report of the National Commission on Responsibilities for Financing Postsecondary Education, a congressionally chartered panel whose members were all appointed by President Bush, endorsed both direct loans and community service programs.[14]

The Student Loan Reform Act of 1993, enacted in August 1993, converted the direct loan pilot into a permanent program. Beginning in July 1994, 5 percent of total student loan volume would fall under the direct loan model. The program would then grow by leaps and bounds, jumping to 40 percent of loan volume in 1995 and 60 percent by 1997. At that juncture, the new legislation called for a pause to allow Congress to decide whether to proceed with a full phase-out of the old FFEL program or to permit both programs to coexist. Despite this last-minute bow to private lenders, it seemed evident that the

Clinton administration and most members of Congress had already decided in favor of direct loans. The Student Loan Reform Act, for example, also contained even further curtailments of subsidies to lenders and guarantors, with the sharpest hits coming just as the direct loan program was scheduled to move up to 40 percent of total volume. A key question preying on many minds was whether these cuts would drive off lenders too quickly, leaving a politically embarrassing loan access gap for ED to fill just before the direct loan model could prove itself. Expanded "lender of last resort" amendments were designed to fill such a gap, but by early 1994 the Education Department had not moved effectively to implement such provisions.

The National and Community Service Act was also passed by Congress in 1993. After a short honeymoon in Washington, however, the concept of student aid for voluntary service lost considerable support when members of Congress looked at the price tag and realized that the total per-student cost of providing minimum wage subsistence salaries for community service jobs, coupled with the subsequent package of student educational assistance, was more expensive than the existing student aid programs. Consequently, the final legislation was considerably watered down, and the program as finally enacted will operate on a much smaller scale than President Clinton originally envisioned.

What Lies in Store?

With the reauthorization of 1992 and the Clinton administration legislation of 1993 now behind us, we can begin to see the shape of student aid through the end of the century. Some issues, such as legislative adjustments for unforeseen kinks in the process of transitioning to a direct loan program will undoubtedly arise over the next few years, but overall, since the next reauthorization will not likely take place before 1998, the die is already cast.

While the structure of the programs is generally known, their size in terms of the federal budget will be more difficult to predict. Significant external forces, of which the most significant is the mounting federal debt, will have an impact even greater than that witnessed in the past decade. Even if President Clinton, responding to the political will of the American electorate, finds himself signing a Balanced Budget Amendment in 1994 or 1995, the United States will be left with a vast, unpaid, historical debt. The compound interest effect of this debt is bound to eat up a large percentage of annual federal budgets for years to come.

Support for higher education, along with all other federal programs, is bound to receive continued close scrutiny. The poor image created by athletic scandals, the controversial "political correctness" movement, and recent price hikes leave higher education somewhat damaged. It seems unlikely that the reauthorization of 1992 will provide politicians with the necessary level of comfort. Certainly the ambitious funding authorization levels for Federal Pell Grants and other student aid programs are unlikely to be reached through the annual appropriations process.

On the other hand, both educators and many business leaders have been relatively successful in making the case for higher-education funding as part of a human capital resource development strategy. Therefore, barring any great swings in ideology, educational funding support will almost certainly outlast support for tobacco subsidies, Small Business Administration loans, and many other domestic programs. Those cuts that are likely to be made in student aid will most likely be incurred by the smaller programs such as Perkins Loans or State Student Incentive Grants.

On a larger scale, academic administrators must begin to ponder the issue of how dependence on federal student aid monies has opened the door for significant federal regulation of academic and administrative matters hitherto the province of individual institutions. Critics of the 1958 National Defense Education Act, who warned of creeping federal intrusion into higher education, were scorned. Yet now, thirty-five years later, we find the federal government tying together federal funding with the issues of how many weeks a college's academic calendar will be or whether a college has established a policy for providing counseling services to students and staff who may have substance abuse problems. With the onset of the State Postsecondary Review Entities and discussion reportedly taking place among Clinton education officials about potential price controls for higher education, it remains to be seen whether there will be any limits to omnipresent government.

Notes

1. L.E. Gladieux and G.L. Lewis, *The Federal Government and Higher Education: Traditions, Trends, Stakes, and Issues* (New York: College Board, October,1987), p. 5.
2. U.S. Department of Education. *The FY 1991 Budget* (Washington, D.C.: U.S. Department of Education, January 1990), p. 37.
3. Ibid., pp. 37–8.
4. See *New York Times.* November 9, 1965, p. 28.
5. See *H.R. Report No. 673*, Washington, D.C.: 89th Congress, 1st Session, 35, 1965.
6. Center for Education Statistics. *Facts on Education. 1*(4), Washington, D.C.: U.S. Department of Education, 1987, p. 34.
7. Alice M. Rivlin, "Reflections on Twenty Years of Higher Education Policy," in *Educational Access and Achievement in America* (New York: College Entrance Examination Board, 1987), p. 5.
8. Office of Postsecondary Education. *Program Summary Book for 1985–86* (Washington, D.C.: U.S. Department of Education, 1987), p. 134.

9. College Entrance Examination Board. *Trends in Student Aid: 1980 to 1987* (New York: College Entrance Examination Board, 1987), p. 8.

10. Center for Education Statistics, *Facts on Education*, p. 34.

11. Atlanta College of Medical and Dental Carrers, Inc., *et. al.* v. Lamar Alexander, Secretary of Education. *792 F. Supp.* 14 (D.D.C. 1992).

12. B.P. Bosworth, A.S. Carron, and E.H. Rhyne,*The Economies of Federal Credit Programs* (Washington, D.C.: The Brookings Institution, 1987), p. 19.

13. State Higher Education Executive Officers. *The Methods and Effectiveness of State Licensing of Proprietary Institutions* (Denver: State Higher Education Executive Officers, 1991).

14. National Commission on Responsibilities for Financing Postsecondary Education. *Making College Affordable Again* (Washington, D.C.: National Commission on Responsibilities for Financing Postsecondary Education, 1993).

4

Higher Education, the Individual, and the Humane Sciences

Antony Flew

It is a fundamental and universal fact, as notorious as it is uncomfortable, that everything human will always and most naturally degenerate, save insofar as well-directed efforts are continually being exerted to prevent such degeneration.

The physically minded might care to formulate this most important of practical truths as a Second Law of Human Dynamics—describing the universal tendency of everything to go downhill, unless checked by some countervailing force. Others will prefer some demythologized version—along the lines of the ninth article of religion in the Church of England, in which the church by law established: "...man is far gone from original righteousness and is of his own nature inclined to evil.... This infection of nature doth remain, yea in them that are regenerated." Yea, it doth remain also in them that are tenured faculty, and even unto retirement, and among the professores emeriti.

Applied to our institutions of tertiary education and to their personnel, the never-to-be-forgotten moral is that the price of sound standards and realized ideals is eternal vigilance. Although it is so often hard to suggest measures that might be effective in preventing the degeneration or in undoing the corruption, certainly the first step always is to recognize what has been and what is going wrong.

Presuppositions of Humane and Liberal Education

Although the present chapter is being written before the writer has had an opportunity to read its conference predecessors, it is, nevertheless, safe to assume that much will have been said about the causes of the behavior both of academics and of academic institutions. It therefore becomes of the last importance to insist that there are causes and causes.

To highlight this assertion, note how the author of a recent, remarkably realistic review of criminological studies rightly repudiates assertions that "the individual who is confronted with a choice among kinds of opportunities, does not *choose*, he 'learns deviant values' from the 'social structure of the slum.'"[1] Yet the same author has argued earlier that, "if causal theories explain why a criminal acts as he does, they also explain why he *must* act as he does."[2]

The crucial distinctions needed here are: a distinction between two fundamentally different senses of the word "cause"; a corollary distinction between two correspondingly different senses of the word "determinism."[3] In one sense causes necessitate the occurrence of their effects. So what is determined by causes—in this first, physical sense of "cause"—must be necessitated: determination—in the corresponding physical sense of "determination"—therefore and necessarily, is physically necessitating. But all this most emphatically is not true of causes of the second, moral or personal sort and of their corresponding kind of determination. Certainly, given the total cause of an eclipse, or of the explosion of a bomb, or indeed of any event other than a human action, that event will inevitably follow as the naturally necessitated effect of that cause. There is nothing that anyone can now do to stop it. This, however, is precisely not true of the causes of those events that are human actions. Suppose that, by bearing splendid news, I give you cause to celebrate. Then I do not, thereby, force you to celebrate willy-nilly. Instead I do something that you yourself may or may not choose to make your own reason for throwing a party.

For all those either working in or using materials produced by the social sciences, these crucial and fundamental distinctions between different senses of the words "cause" and "determinism," and of all their logical associates, ought to be, yet in fact most deplorably and most manifestly are not, unforgettable commonplaces. Furthermore, although it is equally obvious that these are distinctions that ought to be developed and heavily labored over in every introduction to the philosophy of the social sciences, again the truth is that usually they are not even so much as mentioned. Indeed the sole exception known to me is Flew 1985, which is also unique in containing consequent consideration of whether there could be natural laws (necessarily) determining human actions (advertisement).[4]

Adequately equipped with these essential distinctions, we become able to see that the inference quoted from J.Q. Wilson rests upon an equivocation. For, if the "causal theories" that "explain why a criminal acts as he does" are "causal theories" in the second, moral or personal sense of "cause"—as indeed they must be if the criminal truly was an agent acting—then those theories will explain, not why he behaved as he did behave and why things could not have been other than they were, but why he acted as in fact he did act, notwithstanding that he could have acted otherwise. Had he recognized the invalidity of that inference, J.Q. Wilson could have developed a properly compelling rationale for his commonsensical and quasiinstinctive rejection of the claim that "the individual who is confronted with a choice among kinds of opportunities, does not choose, he 'learns deviant values' from the 'social structure of the slum.'"

The causes found in the world of natural science are all physical, and hence physically necessitating. But when criminologists and other psychological and social scientists report, say, either that poverty is a cause of (blue collar) crime, or else that various design faults common in public housing result in an increase in (tenant) vandalism, then the causes that they believe they have discovered are not, and could not be, physically necessitating. Too often the researchers themselves fail to appreciate such fundamental differences between the human and the natural sciences. Among the publicizers of the supposed findings of the former, this failure is well-nigh universal. Yet there are among the researchers golden exceptions. For instance, although they never spell out any of the crucial distinctions, the authors of *Utopia on Trial: Vision and Reality in Planned Housing* earn top marks for not putting a foot wrong as they detail their compelling conclusions.[5]

One practically important consequence is that, although the discoveries that psychological and social scientists do actually make about the causes of various kinds of delinquent conduct will often extenuate these several delinquencies, such findings cannot serve as always and completely sufficient excuses. For what, typically, the social scientists will have discovered are some specific environmental conditions—environmental conditions that made it tempting for certain persons to act in the particular ways in which most (but almost never all) of them did in fact act—specific environmental conditions that, perhaps, made it measurably likely that in the event they would so act. Yet there is a world of difference between showing this and showing that these same conditions were physical causes, inexorably necessitating these persons to behave in the ways in which they severally did behave—showing, that is, that literally they had no choice, showing therefore, that they were, on the relevant occasions, patients rather than agents.[6]

All this has a double relevance to our present concerns. In the first place it helps to bring out that many of the external causes of what some of us rate as academic degeneration and academic corruption are not physical but moral. Often we shall be inclined to say that the persons affected by and reacting to such moral causes "had no choice" and "could not have done other than they did." In those cases we would not have expected them—in either the prescriptive or the descriptive sense of the word "expect"—to have adopted and pursued any different course of conduct.[7]

When, however, we say that someone "had no choices" and "could not have done otherwise," these expressions must not be taken "at the foot of the letter." For, in more literal and more fundamental senses they surely did have a choice and they could have done otherwise. What and all we are asserting when we seem to be denying such obvious truths is that, although there were alternatives, there was none that the agent could reasonably have been expected to choose. Yet, prescriptive expectations always can and often ought to be revised.

The second sort of relevance is, to us, even more important. For, in insisting that people can and cannot but make choices, we are rejecting a view of the nature of man that is certainly inconsistent with the very idea of humane and liberal education. It is also one that, arguably, must involve a denial of the possibility of knowledge. This view is often assumed, and sometimes asserted, to be a presupposition of psychological and social science.

Yet, it is not only those who more or less reluctantly perceive this as something that their academic trades require them to presuppose, it is also the more forthright and aggressive advocates who find that it is a position that they are unable consistently to maintain. They can all, with comparative ease, pretend that the subjects of laboratory experiments, convicted criminals safely confined in penitentiaries, and other emotionally remote objects of professionally detached study, are really automata, wholly necessitated in their every movement. But it is quite another thing to hold to the same assumptions in dealing with yourself, your colleagues and, still more, your political and personal opponents. Here you cannot but recognize the systematically rejected truth that there actually are people—indeed a majority, or at least a plurality of the voters—who, subject to no inexorable physical necessitation, chose the abominable Ronald Reagan and the hated Margaret Thatcher.

The whole project of a humane and liberal education presupposes, and in its progress proves, a conception of man as the distinctively rational animal.[8] Bertrand Russell, who knew and should have done better, loved to make cheap fun of this Aristotelian definition. But, of course, only a kind of creature that is rational as opposed to nonrational—that is, that is to spead, capable of commendable rationality—can sensibly be described as either creditably rational or discreditably irrational.

The rationality of Aristotelian man takes two forms. On the one hand, there is that of the thinker, concerned with reasons for believing. On the other hand, there is that of the agent, who can have reasons for acting in this way rather than that. These two sorts of reasons can be distinguished as evidencing and motivating. It is a distinction best fixed in mind by reference to the Wager Argument of Pascal.[9] Alone among the traditional arguments for the existence of the theist God, this deploys motivating reasons for self-persuasion, even perhaps for self-delusion, rather than evidencing reasons for believing that the commended existential is in fact true.

Given that any project for a humane and liberal education must presuppose such an Aristotelian conception of the nature of man, a contemporary review of internal and endemic threats to such projects has to include at least some outline indication of how offensives launched in the name of the psychological and social sciences are to be repulsed. In his self-revelatory vision *Walden Two,* a mouthpiece for the author, B.F. Skinner, asserts: "I deny that freedom exists at all. I must deny it—or my programme would be absurd. You can't have a science about a subject matter which hops capriciously about."[10] Later, the same author developed this theme in a widely circulated work entitled, chillingly, *Beyond Freedom and Dignity.*[11] Since what we have here is a project for the development of a science based upon a denial of the most peculiar and distinctive fact about its human subject matter, there could scarcely be a comment more apt than the oft-quoted words of Groucho Marx: "It looks absurd. But don't be misled. It *is* absurd."

For, it is a most familiar fact about people, and the most important difference between people and the rest of the furniture of the universe, that they are agents as well as patients. When agents act, it must be true, in a profound and crucial sense, that they always could do other than they do. Agents, as such, can, and cannot but, make choices. These choices are sometimes free and sometimes not. But, whether free or under some constraint, agents acting are always and necessarily making choices between alternatives—the alternatives that have to be open to them precisely insofar as and because they are agents.

So, consider Luther before the Diet of Worms: "Here I stand. I can no other. So help me God." Or, at a somewhat less elevated level, consider the unfortunate businessperson receiving from The Godfather "an offer that he cannot refuse." Both when we agree with Luther that he could not have done other than he did, and when we allow that the businessperson had no choice but to yield to the extortionist Mafioso, we speak in ways which, though perfectly correct and idiomatic, are very misleading. For it would be quite wrong to apply either of these idioms if we were not certain that the two agents in question, in more profound senses, both could have done otherwise and did have a choice. It is not as the victim of a sudden general paralysis that Luther deserves to be admired as the archetypal Protestant hero; while the businessperson does in fact choose (and who will cast the first stone?) to sign rather than to be shot.

In order both to better appreciate what those more profound senses are, and to bring out the way in which we can know, as agents, that we cannot be physically necessitated to act in whatever ways we in the event actually do act, let us contemplate two contrasting passages from the great chapter "Of

Power" in Locke's *Essay Concerning Human Understanding*.[12] This chapter (II(xxi)) is especially interesting and relevant since Hume certainly had it in the front of his mind, if not actually open before him, when he argued—powerfully, influentially, yet mistakenly—that we have and can have neither idea nor experience of physical necessity.[13] Be warned, however, first, that Locke sees himself as spelling out what is meant by 'a free agent' rather than, correctly and more fundamentally, by either 'an agent' or—tautologically—'a choosing agent'; and, second, that the three Latin words mean St. Vitus dance:

> 1. This, at least, I think evident: we find in ourselves a power to begin or forbear, continue or end several actions...the doing or not doing of a particular action.

> 2. We have instances enough, and often more than enough in our own bodies. A man's heart beats, and the blood circulates, which 'tis not in his Power...to stop; and therefore in respect of these motions, where rest depends not on his choice, he is not a free agent. Convulsive motions agitate his legs so that, though he wills it ever so much, he cannot...stop their motion (as in that odd disease called chorea Sancti Viti), but he is perpetually dancing. He is...under as much necessity of moving as is a stone that falls or a tennis ball that is struck with a racket. On the other side, a palsie or the stocks hinder his legs....

Suppose now that, taking our cue from Locke, we distinguish two categories of bodily movements. Going with, rather than against, the grain of common usage, let us call those movements in which persons are agents (active and doing) "movings," applying the word "motions" only to those movements in which persons are patients (passive and suffering). Certainly it is obvious that, as with most other distinctions of the greatest human interest and importance, there are plenty of marginal cases. Nevertheless, so long as there are plenty—indeed far, far more—that fall unequivocally upon one side or the other, we must resolutely and stubbornly refuse to be prevented from insisting on an absolutely fundamental and humanly vital distinction by any such diversionary appeals to the existence of marginal cases.

By thus establishing a contrast between the movings, the doings, of agents and the necessitated motions of patients, and by also indicating how we can then go on to provide ostensive (showing) definitions of the terms employed to mark the differences between members of these two categories of bodily movements, we take up a position impregnable to all necessitarian determinist onslaughts. For, no one could even understand what is meant by contrasting necessitated with chosen behavior unless they had themselves had abundant experience of both kinds. It therefore becomes paradoxical to the point of incoherence to suggest either that all human behavior is necessitated or that it is all chosen.

Suppose now that either Skinner himself or one of his disciples still wants to insist that—science teaches—every movement of every single body in the universe, a body animate as well as a body inanimate, is causally necessitated to occur exactly as it does occur, and in no way otherwise. Then we have to put to it an immediate counter-challenge: Is this a denial that there are both movings and motions and that there actually is the difference in terms of which the two have been defined as opposites? Since persons denying these manifest truths can scarcely avoid provoking doubts either about their sincerity or about their claims to membership of our species, the only resort would seem to be a desperate adversative: "Nevertheless, really, ultimately, and in the last analysis, all ostensible movings are and must be motions."

But when, by whom, to whom, and with what inexpungeable authority has it been revealed that all human movements, as well as and just as much as all the movements of all other objects both animate and inanimate, are with an equal and universal necessity determined to occur? The truth, surely, is that there is no "are" and "must be" about it; or, rather, that all the "are's" and "must be's" are the other way round? For, as we have just seen, the key pairs of contrasting expressions "could or could not do otherwise" and "is or is not physically necessitated" have been—and, it would seem, can only be—defined and explained by reference to two fundamentally different categories of universally experienced realities, namely, movings and motions. So, to be able even to understand the contention that there are no such creatures as agents choosing between alternative courses of action one has to be in a position to know that this same contention is false. What, after all, is it for outcomes to be ineluctably necessitated if not that no one can by any means prevent their occurrence? Yet, by definition, this is precisely not true of those many human bodily movements that are movings.

Before proceeding to Part II of this chapter, it is worth mentioning a further argument which, if sound, exhibits: first, that the view of the nature of man presupposed by every project for humane and liberal education is also presupposed by every claim actually to know anything at all; and, hence, that the necessitarian determinist cannot consistently claim truly to know that his necessitarian determinism, or indeed anything else, is the truth. A revised and strengthened version of this further argument has recently been deployed in what some of Sir Karl Popper's more mischievous admirers nickname his "Concluding Scientific Postscript":

> It is the assertion that, if 'scientific' determinism is true, we cannot in a rational manner, know that it is true; we believe it, or disbelieve it, but not because we freely judge the in its favor to be sound, but because we happen to be so determined (so brainwashed) as to believe it, or even to believe that we judge it, and accept it, rationally.[14]

Here the heart of the matter becomes, not, as in most earlier versions, whether our beliefs are caused by evidencing reasons rather than by chemical processes in our brains, but, instead, whether we could by any means have believed other than we did. Unless we could have believed other than we did, we cannot take credit for having, as rational beings, judged that these beliefs and not others, are true. Popper proceeds to add an important, certainly correct comment:

> This somewhat strange argument does not, of course, refute the doctrine of 'scientific' determinism. Even if it is accepted as valid, the world may still be as described by 'scientific' determinism.[15]

If we want not merely to discredit the necessitarian determinist but also to prove that the human world is not in fact as such determinists allege that it is, then we shall have to resort to some development of the ideas sketched immediately above. One reinforcing consideration, which deserves to be pondered much more than it has been, is that the necessitarian account of human behavior becomes less believable the nearer we stand to the individuals to whom it is alleged to apply. Has anyone ever sincerely and consistently believed it—could anyone ever believe it—about themselves?

Academic Standards and Academic Nature

So far we have taken care to write always "a humane and liberal education" rather than just "a liberal education." The point was to remind us that the preponderant part of any syllabus for a liberal education, and of any liberalizing element introduced into courses of more specialist occupational training, must always be drawn from the humanities and from the moral sciences. There is a parallel purpose in reviving the expression "moral sciences." Long before Whewell sponsored the introduction of the modern sense of the word "science," making it refer primarily to the natural sciences, Hume and other leaders of the Scottish enlightenment distinguished moral from physical subjects. For them the expression "moral subjects" embraced all studies of human beings. So, for us, "moral sciences" will include human psychology as well as such necessarily social studies as anthropology and sociology.

Because human studies must play the preponderant part in any syllabus for a liberal education, it becomes essential to dismiss from the beginning all radically depreciating views of the nature of man. Certainly man is a part of nature, inasmuch as to make this claim is to insist that the origin of our species has to be explained without recourse to particular supernatural intervention. But to maintain that man is, in this understanding, a part of nature is by no means to deny the many massive differences between this particular privileged part and all the rest. There is an important sense in which, with us and in us, nature has become progressively self-aware and even self-controlling. For, through the blind and undirected process of the evolution of species, there has emerged on planet earth the species Homo sapiens: the species of which some members are acquiring theoretical knowledge of the workings of the universe; and the species that collectively, in effect if not by intention, is coming to control the future of that process.[16]

In this perspective we are bound to recognize, as the most grotesque features of an egregiously preposterous methodological manifesto, the contention that an authentic science of man must eschew all peculiarly anthropomorphic notions. B. F. Skinner's work *Beyond Freedom and Dignity* begins by observing: "We have used the instruments of science; we have counted and measured and compared; but something essential to scientific practice is missing in almost all current discussions of human behaviour."[17] It soon appears that what is missing is, a shade awkwardly and most perversely, the absence of all such peculiarly anthropomorphic and hence especially appropriate notions. For, Skinner goes on, "Although physics soon stopped personifying things...it continued for a long time to speak as if they had wills, impulses, feelings, purposes and other fragmentary attributes of an indwelling agent. All this was eventually abandoned, and to good effect...." Nevertheless, deplorably, what should be "the behavioural sciences still appeal to comparable internal states..."[18] We are, therefore, supposed to regret that: "Almost everyone who is concerned with human affairs—as political scientist, philosopher, man of letters, economist, psychologist, linguist, sociologist, theologian, educator, or psychotherapist—continues to talk about human behaviour in this prescientific way."[19]

It is characteristic of all or almost all work in both the humanities and the moral sciences that it is most naturally assessed by reference to letter grades rather than to percentages. This makes it extremely difficult, if not impossible, to establish and maintain what, in the jargon of educationists, are called, not norm-related, but criteria-related standards. An examination system is said to be norm-related: when the performance of each candidate is compared with that of all other members of the peer group, and where the upshot is that roughly the same proportions of the candidates from every successive cohort are rated according to A's, B's, C's, or whatever. If, and to the extent that any system of assessment is in fact norm- rather than criteria-related, then direct year-on-year comparisons of performance must be invalid. To attempt them is like trying to compare the caliber of sports teams from different generations—say Aston Villa 1939 with Manchester United 1950.

The opposite is true of criteria-related systems. Here the whole object is to set a steady standard such that year-on-year comparisons will be valid. In this case the sporting analogy is with field and track athletics: a four-minute mile is a four-minute mile whenever and wherever it is achieved. Of course no actual criteria-related system either is or ever will be perfect in this respect, or indeed in any other. But, while all are, no doubt, capable of improvement, albeit sometimes only at an unacceptable cost, some certainly do approach ideal perfection more closely than do others. None of this, however, makes it any less true that (to the extent that the assessment of any operation is norm-related rather than criteria-related) it becomes excessively difficult to know whether things are looking up, are getting worse, or still remain the same.

The dangers are greater in the humanities and the moral sciences than they are in specialist professional schools. For, changes in the quality of those graduating from the latter are much more likely to be noticed outside the academy and to give rise as appropriate either to countervailing pressures or to incentive pulls. This being so, all those teaching and testing in these danger areas ought always to make greater efforts than they usually do make to push things from the norm-related to the criteria-related end of the scale.

On a rather different occasion, or in another country, I might have added some relevant comparisons between course unit systems, under which those who teach a course do all the grading of the work done by pupils taking that course, and final examination systems, under which work is graded partly, primarily, or even exclusively by those who have not taught the material to the pupils. But here and now I prefer to proceed to a matter that is quite certainly better ordered in the U.S. than it is in the U.K.

Back in the early sixties, at the beginning of the comprehensive revolution in British state secondary education, the boards running A-level examinations—taken by all those aspiring to proceed to tertiary institutions—were officially urged to follow (what, perhaps, had not yet been christened) norm-related rather than criteria-related principles. Those who, having been to school with Cicero, ask the Roman lawyer's question *"Cui bono?"* will conclude, I believe correctly, that the object was to conceal the catastrophic costs of that revolution of destruction. But in the U.S., despite the worst efforts of Ralph Nader and his associates, there exist what are misleadingly called Scholastic Aptitude Tests. Since these certainly are criteria-related, and since they in fact measure the educational achievement of high school graduates rather than their innate abilities, the almost continuous downward slide of the average scores achieved constitutes a true index of the performance of those students.

Where, in Britain we have to scratch around for the evidence showing only that a huge increase in resource input has quite certainly not been rewarded with any corresponding improvements in educational output, in the U.S. it is possible, from compellingly clear and hard evidence, to know that a similarly vast increase in expenditure has yielded not just no improvement at all but a quite disastrous decline. Everyone will recall the conclusions of *A Nation at Risk*, the 1983 report of the National Commission on Excellence in Education: "The educational foundations of our society are presently being eroded by a rising tide of mediocrity that threatens our very future as a nation and as a people." To this the commission added an even more sobering comment: "If an unfriendly foreign power had attempted to impose on America the mediocre educational performance that exists today, we might well have viewed it as an act of war. As it stands, we have allowed this to happen to ourselves."

No doubt both conclusion and comment refer primarily, perhaps exclusively, to performance at the primary and secondary levels. But changes in the quality of the output from the high schools cannot but affect proceedings at the tertiary level. And here we do come to a case where the actual reactions of the institutions and of those who staff them can be said to have been caused by the actions of government and, in particular, of the Congress. But this has been a nonnecessitating causing, a moral as opposed to physical, if not perhaps a moral as opposed to immoral causing. For, the tertiary institutions and those who staff them certainly could have done other than they did, even if it would not have been reasonable either to predict that they would or to prescribe that they should.

What they in fact did, and are doing, is made very clear by a recent leading article in the *Wall Street Journal*. The article begins most aptly with a simple multiple choice question:

> Identify which of the following budget items has experienced the largest percentage increase in outlays since 1970: a) defense; b) farm subsidies; c) student aid. If you answered 'a' or 'b,' you flunk. Outlays for student aid have increased by more than 1,005 since 1970, far outstripping increases in outlays for national defense, farm-income stabilization and most other budget items.[20]

After recounting how administration proposals to reduce this item in the federal budget had run into total, bipartisan opposition in the Congress, the *Journal* continued:

> Somehow over the past two decades student aid has come to be perceived as a universal entitlement. Yearly increases in student aid have consistently run about 2 1/2 times the rate of inflation. Meanwhile, the college-age population has dropped by 12% since 1977 and is expected to drop by another 10% by the end of the decade. Pressed to find other bodies to keep federal student aid flowing, many colleges have admitted larger numbers of under-qualified students. An Education Department report revealed that in the 1983–1984 academic year 25% of college freshmen were enrolled in remedial math, 21% in remedial writing and 16% in remedial reading.[21]

It is salutary to identify the nature and source of this pressure "to find other bodies to keep federal student aid flowing...." For, it is not, of course, compulsion by government. This pressure is entirely internal to the tertiary insti tutions and to those who staff them. And it comes from what, in the first and greatest masterpiece of development economics, Adam Smith recognized as the dynamic of growth—the strong and nearly universal drive to better the condition of ourselves and our families or, at least, to maintain it. Though much inclined to vilify and despise the world of commerce and material production, academics are surely no less disposed than are other people to strive to maximize, or at least to maintain, their own utilities.

Yet, this said, we should remember what Smith himself never forgot, that this natural drive ought at all times to be restrained by various legal and moral inhibitions. When, in the middle sixties, the long decline in average SAT scores began, then all concerned could and surely should have held firm to previous admission standards, accepting the pains of what, given that response, might have been strictly temporary contractions. The result of their not doing so seems to have been an actual acceleration of the decline. A recent article in the "Insight" supplement to the *Washington Times* entitled "Freshmen: A Study in Unreadiness" quotes Education Secretary Bennett recalling:

> …how it used to be said that if Johnny or Mary didn't study in high school they wouldn't be able to go to college. One really can't say that with a straight face anymore because we know that very, very few of our institutions of "higher education" are selective in any reasonable meaning of the term.[22]

He went on to predict that "informally, if not formally" what will happen is that, without any institution openly declaring itself to be "a remedial college, as opposed to another kind of college, the marketplace will somehow sort this out, and certain schools will have reputations of being slightly advanced high schools and others will maintain their reputations as colleges and universities."[23]

Whatever adjustments were or were not to be made in either general admission or general graduation standards at the tertiary level, once it had become obvious that the decline in SAT scores was not just a brief hiccup but a secular tendency, then very sharp questions should have been raised about the standards, the direction, and the effectiveness of colleges, departments, and programs for the training of teachers. There is much to be said most of the time in favor of live-and-let-live noninterference. But departmental sovereignty, like state sovereignty, can be a cover for all manner of festering evils. "Education," as Thomas Sowell has wickedly remarked, "is a notoriously undemanding field of study", and the value of teacher training qualifications has to be estimated in the light of the equally notorious fact that almost no one flunks.[24] Certainly, too, all those who have both to pay the salaries of, and to expose their children to, the products of these training operations have a right to press intrusive questions: what requirements are being demanded; what is being taught; what and how much is actually being learned; and, above all, how effective are those products when they eventually get on the job. It is much too often forgotten that for colleges, schools, departments, and institutes of education, as for all other institutions of professional training, that last intrusive question must be the bottom line.

Inquiries Inhibited by Interests

Nor is this the only sort of intrusive question in need of being pressed. For, all universities and most other tertiary institutions profess a commitment both to teaching and to research. So we need to ask also, and perhaps even more urgently, what efforts are being made there to discover both why things have gone so wrong and how the situation might be righted. I do not pretend to know what the answers to these further questions would be in the U.S. But in Britain it is remarkable how little policy-related research is in fact done within the academy. In Britain, everyone in what Tom Lehrer would have us call Edbiz speaks of teacher/pupil ratios as improving when the average size of the class taught by each teacher goes down. It seems never to occur to proponents of this viewpoint that in any other industry a higher ratio in such a relationship would be construed as revealing not improvement but inefficiency and overmanning. When challenged to produce the evidence that small classes do in fact make for more or better learning no one is able to cite any British research, and almost no one is willing to attend to what has been done in the U.S. and in other countries.[25]

Both the lack of such work in Britain and the widespread British reluctance to attend to what has been achieved elsewhere cannot but provoke some embarrassing allusion to certain strong and rather obvious distracting interests. Of course, distracting interests constitute at most a temptation. And anyone can, and many people do, overcome temptations. Of course, too, considerations of individual and family interest are usually reinforced by other pulls and pushes—such as ties of friendship with and loyalty to fellow members of some further social set with which the persons in question have been long and closely associated. (Social sets are not necessarily social classes, whatever those may be: by Cantor's Axiom for Sets the sole essential feature of a set is that its members have at least one common characteristic, any kind of characteristic.)

Certainly it is less discreditable pulls and pushes such as these rather than the more sordid temptations of immediate and manifestly material interest that do most to explain why some people remain inseparably attached to movements and parties long after they have become totally disillusioned about the direction, aims, and achievements of these movements and parties.[26] Nevertheless, in the academic world as elsewhere, we do always need to recognize not only all the distracting interests but every other corrupting temptation as well.

In respect of one particular present distracting interest, many perhaps illuminating parallels can be drawn between, on the one hand, departments, schools, and institutes of education and, on the other hand, departments, schools, and institutes of social work. The faculty in these would seem to be the obvious, even the appointed people to research, respectively: the effectiveness of teacher training and the results achieved by different educational methods and policies; and the effectiveness of both social work training and actual social work. So, their almost total failure to do these jobs, and the often lamentable quality of what little work is done, are to be explained, surely, in some part—however small a part—by reference to an entirely understandable, albeit still scandalous, fact. This fact is that those making comfortable livings out of training teachers or social workers are naturally reluctant "to foul their own nests" and "to work themselves out of jobs" by perhaps discovering: either that an entirely different and even less expensive and extensive training would be more effective or that considerably fewer teachers or social workers are really required in order to do the same or even a better job.

There is, perhaps, an even greater reluctance to produce, or even to attend to, materials suggesting that better educational results might be achieved if only we could break *The Public School Monopoly*.[27] It is significant that in Britain the first revisionist history of education, showing how much was achieved before and without the establishment of that monopoly, was produced not by a professional educationist but by an academic economist;[28] while the major work revealing the wretched educational results of abolishing selection within that system has since been done by three people, none of whom either is or ever has been employed in any college, department, school, or institute of education.[29]

But, the most striking example of reluctance, indeed refusal, to pursue policy-related research to unwelcome conclusions, and to reveal embarrassing findings, comes not from Edbiz but from the world of social work. For a depressing, because full and critical, review of social work and social work training in Britain, we have to refer to Brewer and Lait, 1980.[30] But for present purposes it is enough to consider how, and to ask ourselves why, a great research opportunity was recently wasted. Our story begins when 275 social workers at the London Borough of Tower Hamlets went on strike. Unlike most, this particular strike seems not to have greatly inconvenienced anyone. Certainly, I saw no TV news flashes of desperate clients fighting their way through howling picket lines to secure the services of whatever social workers were still working. (Could it have been that there simply were no "scabs" or "blacklegs" from the ranks of these famously compassionate professional "carers"?)

At the end of the day the Department of Health and Social Security directed the London Region of Social Work Service to launch the inquiry that was eventually published as *The Effect on Clients of Industrial Action in the London Borough of Tower Hamlets: An Investigation*. It is as significant as it is typical that the outfit charged with initiating this inquiry is part of the social-work establishment. The minister appears to have been as innocent as was the otherwise so proudly adversarial media of the difficulties of "separating the expert knowledge of any group of specialists from the special interests of that group."[31] American readers may also need to be warned that "industrial action" is—*lucus a non lucendo*—a British labor union euphemism for "strike."

This whole affair had provided a rare and splendid research opportunity. "Clients" abandoned during the ten months of the strike constituted a perfect control group to set against an experimental group of those not so neglected in some subsequent ten months. It would not be callous researchers who were proposing to deprive that control group of what might or might not be valuable services; but, instead, those professedly "caring" social workers who had already done so. The wasting of this precious research opportunity deserves to become, and has indeed been made, a textbook example.[32]

The report, apparently accepted without protest either from the minister himself or from the concerned department or from the specialist press, should leave the alert reader in no doubts about the general quality of the investigation. As for the specialist press, the treatment of such matters in *New Society* and the *Times Educational Supplement* ought to remind us that G.K. Chesterton once defined "journalism" as "writing on the backs of advertisements." Much insight into the editorial policies of each of these two journals can be gained by studying the Situations Vacant notices on the other sides of the pages.

One single feature of this particular investigation was, however, totally discrediting. For, the two professing social scientists appointed by the London Region of Social Work Service—who "individualize and personalize" themselves by adding both their signatures in facsimile at the end—were asked to discover the effects *on the clients*. Believe it or not, they do not so much as claim to have asked for the views of even one client.[33] So who truly wants to know?

A writer recently commenting on the corruptions afflicting the moral sciences complained of "the common tendency to foster international studies not for the sake of finding the truth but for the purpose of cultivating the foreigners' goodwill by writing nice things about them."[34] It is all much worse when we are dealing with a particular lot of foreigners suffering an authoritarian or totalitarian regime, and when many of the academics involved in this particular field at home share to a greater or lesser extent the ideological commitments of that regime.

Steven Mosher is an American who speaks fluent Cantonese. He was able to spend a full year, starting in March, 1979, studying life in a Guandong village. He thus became the first foreigner to see and report on the harsh realities of the all-out birth control program. He was also led to doubt the truth of the stock excuse cherished by Committees of Concerned Asian Scholars and their like—the claim that, whatever else might be said against the Communist Revolution ("the Liberation"), at least from the beginning it produced a much better life for the vast peasant majority. To no one's surprise such revelations distressed the Chinese authorities. So they made it clear to Stanford University that, unless Mosher was penalized to their satisfaction, Stanford people could not in future expect to get permission to work in China; and, further, to supply Stanford with excuses for action, they charged that Mosher had during his stay broken some strands of Communist red tape.

From that point on the story is long, complicated, and controverted. Suffice it to say two things only. First, at no stage has Stanford University taken the properly firm and principled stand of insisting that, whatever the merits or demerits of this individual case, permissions conditional on not discovering and telling unwelcome truths are simply not acceptable; and that, if permissions are obtainable only upon this unacceptable condition, then the researchers will have to do the best they can do at home. Second, Stanford has effectively deprived Mosher of the chance of receiving a very well-deserved doctorate for what was and remains a uniquely valuable study of a Chinese village thirty years after "Liberation."[35] In these credentialist days this deprivation is likely to bar him from academic employment.

So, unless another institution comes to his rescue, his case should serve as an unforgettable warning to generations of ambitious sinologues—not to discover or to tell any truths uncongenial to the powers that be, whether in China or nearer home.

Up to this point, the inhibiting interests we've examined were primarily intradepartmental; although in all the particular cases cited there would appear to have been some ideological reinforcement. A still more formidable, because more general, threat comes from the guidelines adopted by many institutions to prevent research when it is feared that its findings "may place the reputation or status of a social group or an institution in jeopardy." The words just quoted, like the two further elucidatory passages below came from a policy statement by Chancellor Albert H. Bowker of the University of California at Berkeley. I myself copied them out of a letter from Sidney Hook, published in *Encounter:*

a) Procedures designed to measure the characteristics of easily defined sub-groups of a culture may entail risk if the qualities measured are ones which have positive or negative value in the eyes of the group.

b) Likewise, an institution, such as a church, a university, or a prison, must be guarded against derogation, for many people may be affiliated with or employed by the institution, and pejorative information about it would injure their reputations and self-esteem.[36]

How widely such guidelines have been adopted in the U.S., and to what extent their theoretically universal application has in practice been confined to certain privileged social sets, I have myself no means of knowing. (It is perhaps hard to believe that such guidelines either will in fact affect, or are indeed even intended effectively to protect, privately owned corporations: Ralph Nader has, surely, no cause for alarm.) So, let us conclude by merely mentioning that on 31 March 1985 the Biological and Physical Sections of the Sub-Department of Anthropology in the British Museum were shut down. The stated reason was that the work of those sections is no longer regarded as being appropriate to the museum. "Since that work was the study of genetically determined human differences, a word will no doubt be sufficient to the wise."[37]

Defections from liberality

The first part of this chapter considered and indicated how we should refute a false view of the nature of man: a view that, it is often thought, is both presupposed and confirmed by the moral sciences; but that is certainly incompatible with any project for a humane and liberal education. This false view—precisely because it is, however mistakenly, thought to be both presupposed and confirmed by the moral sciences—constitutes an internal threat. The section of the chapter that follows proceeded to take note of similarly internal threats arising from the fact that academics are no less inclined than are other persons to strive for, at least to maintain, and hopefully to improve the condition of themselves, and of their families—to say nothing of all those others with whom they identify. It is this, surely, that has been the main cause of grade inflation. The third section went on to notice various ways in which inquiry may be, and has been, inhibited by various kinds of interest, variously located. Continuing to attend primarily to internal rather than to external threats to the academy, I want now to notice some important defections from liberality. This is not the place to try to spell out all of what should be meant by the expression "a liberal education." Instead, it must here be sufficient to mention one or two paradigm programs, observing those principles that were realized in these but which in recent times have elsewhere proved to have the most precarious hold. My paradigm programs are the Great Books course at the University of Chicago, of which I know only by repute, and "Greats"! (*Literae Humaniores*) at Stanford, in which I graduated myself. To these we might add for comparison, if only because I happen to have had teaching experience in all three: the humanities degree programs of the four ancient Scottish universities; those traditionally insisted upon by American liberal arts colleges such as Swarthmore; and that demanded, at least for its first twenty-five years, by their nearest U.K. equivalent, the University of Keele. (All of these three programs, of course, required that their students should at least dip into some natural science. But that is another story.)

All these paradigm programs are strictly nonvocational, inasmuch as they are not intended to equip their alumni for one particular occupation. Yet "Greats" was for a century or more, and perhaps still is, recognized as a valuable if not a sufficient qualification for any occupation putting some premium on a capacity for and an inclination to critical thinking. (Educational theorists never should but sometimes do forget that capacity and inclination are not the same thing and that here capacities without inclinations, or with only closely limited, tightly inhibited inclinations, are of very doubtful value.) Apart from "critical" two other key words here are "broad" and "detached." Typically any project for a liberal education must be philosophical, in the sense in which Plato defined the philosopher as a spectator of all time and all existence.

It is, however, equally typical of contemporary defections from the ideal of liberality in education that they are promoted as both relevant and critical, as being elements that any suitably broad program must include. This promotion is based upon misunderstandings of both these key concepts. Far too many people, not only students and outsiders but faculty also, make the mistake of thinking that to manifest a critical approach it is both necessary and sufficient to offer some reason for rejecting whatever is under review. But, if this were true, then there could be no such thing as critical as opposed to uncritical acceptance; while to qualify as a Shakespearean critic it would be not only necessary but also sufficient simply to conclude that even the best of his plays are no good. We should also have to say that, when Sir Winston Churchill maintained that the only merit of democracy is its superiority to all actual alternatives, his commitment was uncritical. This provides what is always welcome—an occasion to quote the most acerbic of textual critics, commenting on the oversight of a fellow scholar: "Three minutes thought would suffice to find this out, but thought is irksome, and three minutes is a long time."[38]

With regard to relevance the misunderstanding is a shade more subtle. Just as the evidence of one's own eyes—actually seeing something oneself—is not really evidence but, because more direct, better than evidence, so what is relevant to this must be other than this and not this itself. In studying the history of Greece in the fifth century B.C.—and attending directly, as would not be possible with more recent periods, to all the original sources—"Greats" pupils are detached from the hurly-burly of our contemporary crises. Nevertheless that study is by no means irrelevant to a critical consideration of those crises. For it essentially involves a reading of Thucydides. And, as his first

English translator insisted, the supremely tough-minded and detached Thucydides had, and still has, a claim to be "accounted the most politic historiographer that ever writ."[39] It is, furthermore, much easier to grasp general and perhaps universal principles in detachment from the particular cases in which at the time the passions are most strongly engaged.

To bring all this out more vividly, let us treat ourselves to two illustrations. What, for one, could be more relevant to any consideration of the preinvasion confrontation of Soviet with Czechoslovak representatives at Cierna and Tisou in 1968 than the Melian Dialogue of Thucydides, referring to events of 416 B.C.?[40] Both the Melians and the Czechoslovaks tried to appeal to moral ideals—justice and "socialism with a human face," respectively. But both the Athenians and the Soviets, disclaiming any reference to their services in their respective Great Patriotic Wars, instead insisted on talking of the interests of a great power within its own sphere of domination. Or again, what could be more relevant to all the great ideological conflicts of our time than the comments of Thucydides upon class conflict and civil war in Corcyra (Corfu): "They altered the accepted usage of words in relation to deeds as they thought fit."[41] In the week in which I first read those two chapters a collective despotism, describing itself as devoted to the principles of "democratic centralism," denounced Switzerland as "fascist."

In my own undergraduate days—before Noah's Flood—we rarely knew the political opinions of our teachers. When we did it was normally because we had heard tell of some extramural activity of theirs, not because they had themselves intruded those opinions into lectures and tutorials with us (their "student contact hours"). Since then and most intensively since 1968—The Year of Student Revolutions—all this has changed. The change has surely been greatest, and certainly best documented, in the U.S.[42]

Politicization in the academy takes two forms: one afflicts preestablished and previously nonpoliticized subject areas; the other involves the introduction of new, politically motivated programs. Both involve more or less serious defections from the ideal of a humane and liberal education. Necessarily and by intent both abandon the attempt to be academically detached. Perhaps less necessarily, but often just as intentionally, both promote indoctrination rather than critical teaching. What, after all, is the point of such political interventions by persons enjoying pulpit privileges if it is not to persuade students either to accept political positions that they might not otherwise have adopted or else to continue to hold political positions that they might otherwise have abandoned?

It is also, surely, beyond dispute that in the U.S. the drive to politicize the academy comes overwhelmingly from the left, if only because, as successive Carrnegie Commission studies have shown, the political center of gravity of the academic elite, like that of the media elite and the intelligentsia as a whole, is far to the left of that of the general population.[43] Most leftists like to see themselves as opposing some sort of establishment. So, if they are at all inclined to confuse a critical with a rejectionist approach, they may well congratulate themselves and all their fellow leftists on being, as such and by this very opposition, commendably critical.

To anyone concerned to defend the ideals and institutions of liberal education this leftist predominance is important in two ways: it affects the quality of the education presently provided; and it makes reform more difficult. If only what we had was more of a hubbub and less of a chorus, then, whatever the intentions of the various partisans in this battle of ideas, the actual effect upon the students might have been salutary. For it might have stimulated them to critical inquiry; although any such effect would presumably have been weakened by a course-unit system, under which the students' access to every subject subarea is controlled by a single instructor. Again, if only that progressive politicization of recent decades had resulted in a more or less equally balanced hubbub of contrary opinions, then it would have been comparatively easy to induce all participants to agree to a ceasefire. But, as things are, and when everything is so obviously and so decisively going their way, why ever should the dominant left agree to anything of the sort? Conservatives can appeal only to a shared commitment to the ideal of a liberal education, a commitment that is in too many cases clearly wanting.

Politicization by the introduction of fresh programs should, in principle, be easier to remedy. Since all were originally introduced by administrative fiat, someone might be so naive as to believe that it would be similarly easy and simple to reverse those fiats. Yet, abundant experience should have taught us that, in academia as well as in Washington and Whitehall, once something has been allowed to start it very soon becomes excessively difficult if not impossible to stop. Arguably the most unrealistic, the most delusive, and the most grotesquely preposterous proposition ever put forward as a prediction of social science was the claim that the coercive machinery of the state, having lost its original function, must "wither away."[44]

Most of these newly introduced and always aggressively partisan programs start by picking out some supposedly undervalued objective or some previously underappreciated social set and then proceed to make allegiance to that aim or to that social set the uniting principle of an embryonic academic discipline. It is this frighteningly fertile procedure that has produced Black Studies, Peace Studies, Women's Studies, (Third) World Studies, and next, no doubt, Chicano Studies. In England it has been frivolously suggested that the importance in so many spheres of human life of holes ought to be acknowledged by the introduction of programs of Hole Studies. But the first serious objection is that the proposed uniting principles are of a quite unsuitable kind. For they collect together heaps of heterogeneous material the mastery of which belongs to various established disciplines and demands the many different forms of preparation appropriate to those various disciplines. (This same objection also holds against the abortion of Science Studies, which includes just about everything else but science and is offered as a soft substitute for something felt to be too demanding, real science.)

For us here there are two further, very disparate things to be said. The first is that, so far as I know, none of these new programs for So-and-So Studies has, in either the U.S. or the U.K., indeed in any other NATO country, been forcibly imposed on any tertiary institution by central government. If and insofar as such programs are in any way academically obnoxious, then the entire blame must fall inside not outside the academy. Here we have had, and have, not surrenders to superior force but rather—in the perhaps overdramatic words of my chosen title—"Treasons of the Clerks."

It has been different, but not completely different, at the secondary (high school) level. There J.S. Mill's fears that, if the state not only provided the funds for universal public education but also established and ran the schools, then all these schools would inevitably be used for indoctrination, might for a long time have been thought exaggerated, at any rate in countries with strong traditions of Protestant individualism. Perhaps in part because those traditions have weakened, in Britain this is quite certainly no longer true. Since at least 1980, whenever the hard left Labour Party has won control of any Local Education Authority (a local public school monopoly equivalent to a U.S. school district), it has hastened to introduce "Peace Studies," and this with very little pretense that these are anything but propaganda for its own policies of defenselessness.[45] But here again many schoolteachers—especially members of the NUT, the British equivalent of the NEA—were, before any directives arrived from above, already propagandizing for this Soviet cause in their individual classrooms.[46]

The second thing that we need to say here is that all these programs, both more or less frankly reject the ideal of academic detachment and claim to be critical only in the vulgar sense in which criticism always and necessarily means opposition. Sometimes the rejection of detachment goes far beyond any merely verbal encouragement, by actually giving academic credit for approved forms of political activism.[47] The uncritical, indoctrinative approach common to the promoters and professors of all such programs is made most manifest by the fact that egregiously questionable conclusions are regularly to be found among the unquestioned assumptions of the whole enterprise. Sometimes these presuppositions are so questionable that the very fact of their being assumed or asserted at all is itself a demonstration that they have not been, and are not intended to be, critically examined. Sometimes, too, the promoters and professors make no bones about their lack of interest in truth: "Philosophers have interpreted the world, the task is to change it."

Two illustrations must suffice. The first comes from a chapter on "The Creation of the Third World" in a widely used introductory textbook of *Cultural Anthropology*. Here we have revealed the chief presupposition of (Third) World Studies, that European expansion and colonialism:

> created the underdevelopment of the Third World...a constant drain of wealth... has produced incredible poverty and has not only hampered but systematically destroyed indigenous economic development.[48]

A complementary illustration comes from the world of Women's Studies:

> In other words, feminist theory cannot be accurately regarded as a *competing* or rival account, diverging from patriarchal texts over what its as true. It is not a true discourse, nor a more objective or scientific account. It could be appropriately seen, rather, as a *strategy*, a local, specific intervention with definite political, even if provisional, aims and goals.... [I]t seeks effective forms of intervention into systems of power in order to subvert them and replace them with others more preferable.... It aims to render patriarchal systems, methods and presumptions unable to function, unable to retain their dominance and power.[49]

No Hope or Bad Faith

It will, perhaps, be at least temporarily useful to distinguish two sorts of source of academic failures persistently to pursue truth: one is the fear or the conviction that truth is, perhaps only ultimately, unattainable; the other is the absence of any desire to attain it, or even a positive longing not to. Signs of that fear or that conviction can in our time be detected in many academic areas, and they become an ever ready excuse for shoddy and dishonest work. The absence of such a desire is revealed by the refusal to subject various preferred and privileged candidate propositions to thorough critical examination.

There are two main modern developments which, combining with ancient arguments for various relativistic conclusions, often produce a demoralized defeatism. One is in the philosophy of natural science, and in particular the philosophy of physics. ("In science," as Lord Rutherford was saying in the Cambridge of my boyhood, "there is only physics; and stamp-collecting!") The other is the sociology of belief, miscalled the sociology of knowledge, but then perversely misinterpreted as showing that there neither is nor can be any true beliefs justifiably awarded the diploma title knowledge."

In *Counter Course: A Handbook for Course Criticism* and in a similarly radical collection of essays entitled *Ideology in Social Science* we find professional historians referring to what is supposed to have been established by this new philosophy. In the first of these professing historians tells us: "It is now generally realized that the claim to record facts and reconstruct the past 'as it happened' is not tenable...'facts' are defined as worth recording at all, in terms of some model in the historian's mind."[50]

The editor of the latter promises that a contributor soon to be tenured at an elite school, Gareth Stedman Jones, will show that "the assumption that there exists a realm of acts independent of theories which establish their meaning is fundamentally unscientific."[51] Jones himself writes: "Carr attacked the notion that 'facts' and 'interpretation' are rigidly separable. Pointing out that all writing of history involves a selection from the sum of facts available, he demonstrated that any selection of facts obeys an implicit evaluative criterion. 'Facts' are thus inseparable from 'interpretations', which in turn are determined by 'values.'"[52]

Again, in a collection widely adopted as a textbook of the sociology of education, we find one contributor asking, in high Kantian style: "How is sociology possible?" It is, he concludes:

> ...easy to see that the methodical character of marriage, war and suicide is only seen, recognized and made possible through the organized practices of sociology. These regularities do not exist 'out there' in [a] pristine form to which sociologists functionally respond, but rather, they acquire their character of regularities and their features as describable objects only through the grace of sociological imputation. Thus, it is not an objectively discernible purely existing external world which accounts for sociology; it is the methods and procedures of Sociology which create and sustain that world.

The discoveries of social science, we may be discouraged to learn, simply consist in "the negotiated understandings of sociologists."[53]

It is a black day for scholarship when professional historians dare thus slightingly to dismiss the great Leopold von Ranke. For he it was who claimed, famously and truly, that his and their proper professional business was to discover and to tell, *"wie es eigentlich gewesen"* [how it really was]. Anyone who truly believes that it is, necessarily and in all cases, impossible "to reconstruct the past 'as it happened,'" and who nevertheless accepts employment as a historian should ask himself, and tell us, what honest claim he has to draw his compensation, and what reason we now have left for believing anything he chooses to say about the past.

Nor is it compatible with any sort of science, whether social or other, much less required by it, to deny "that there exists a realm of facts independent of theories." For if it was not possible—as of course it is—to describe experimental and other data in ways logically independent of rival theories offered to explain such data, then no one could ever show that any theories are inconsistent with the facts, and, therefore, false. There is, surely, some give-away significance in the fact that Jones covers his embarrassment over the finding that real wages rose between 1790 and 1850 with bluster, sneering, and abuse.[54] For, to demonstrate the falsity of one of its main logical consequences, the "Immiseration Thesis," is, necessarily, to falsify the cherished theory of *Capital*. (It is, by the way, worth remarking that this Immiseration Thesis, which by 1867 at latest Marx himself certainly knew to be false, has since World War II acquired a fresh lease of life in a transmogrified form as the basic presupposition of both World Studies and of Third Worldism generally.)

In the sense in which the word "criticism" has been used in the present chapter, the only sense in which criticism can have any claim to be self-evidently good, it necessarily involves appraisal and questioning whether that which is criticized truly is what it pretends to be. To bring out the reason refusal to criticize or to attend to criticism is a mark of academic bad faith we need to show the logical links between the concepts of sincerity, of rationality, and of monitoring. Sincerity in any purpose whatsoever absolutely presupposes a strong concern to discover whether and how far that cherished purpose has been or is being achieved. Furthermore, if and insofar as the agent becomes aware that it has not been or is not being achieved, we cannot, unless there is a readiness to attempt alternative tactics, truly say that that purpose continues to be sincerely cherished.

Rationality comes into the picture since, not Descartes only, but all the rest of us also preferred, or prefer, to estimate the actual intentions and the sincere beliefs of other people, and even of ourselves, by looking to what is done, or not done, rather than to what—with whatever appearances of impeccable integrity—is merely said. Indeed, it is impossible to identify a particular belief as having whatever particular content it does have unless we attribute some minimal rationality to the behavior of the believer.

Let us suppose that someone proclaims a Quest for the Holy Grail. And suppose then that, almost before the fanfares have died, they settle for the first antique-seeming mug offered by the first fluent rogue in the local bazaar. We surely have to say that this neglect of any systematic inquiry, this total lack of interest either in the true history of the purchase put in the place of honor on the mantelpiece or in the evidence that perhaps the real thing does survive somewhere, all conspire together to show that, whatever else they may have been after, it certainly was not to unearth and acquire the vessel actually employed in the original Last Supper.

Again, since many find it hard to accept that such a down-to-earth point can be enforced by an illustration so far-fetched, consider two more pedestrian alternatives. Suppose someone professes to be in business in order, no doubt among other things, to turn a profit; or suppose that the captain of a cricket team says that he is playing, no doubt again among other things, in order to win. Then, what credence could we give to these professions if there is not care to keep, in the one case, accounts and, in the other, the score?

The next step is to relate the logical linkages displayed above to the main methodological recommendations of Sir Karl Popper. He makes proposals, which are of course close kin the one to the other, for the spheres of both theoretical science and practical policy. In each case Popperian methodology can be seen as the direct and necessary outcome of sincerity in the appropriate purposes. It is the more worthwhile to represent these recommendations in this way inasmuch as Popper himself seems never to have done so. His apparent reluctance, and the consequent failure to deploy what is perhaps the most powerful supporting argument, are probably to be explained by reference to a characteristically generous yet very unrealistic reluctance to recognize in any of his academic opponents either discreditable distractions or even sheer bad faith.

The aim of theoretical inquiry is, I dare to insist, truth. Given this aim then the critical approach must follow. The person who truly wants the truth, like the knight who, with pure heart and single mind, seeks the Holy Grail, cannot and will not embrace unexamined candidates. He must and will be ever ready to test, and test, and test again. But in this present context testing for truth is precisely what criticism is.

Where the single aim of theoretical inquiry is truth, the purposes of practical policies, and of the institutions established for the implementation of those policies and the fulfillment of those purposes, are as multifarious as human desires. Yet, parallel considerations apply here too. If, therefore, you want to claim that it was in order to secure some particular reliefs of man's estate that the policy was originally introduced, and that it is with those objectives that it is still sustained, then you have to show that both those who first introduced and those who now support and sustain that policy and those institutions were, and are, eager to monitor their success or failure by that stated standard. Indeed the originators would have been well advised to make sure that the policy itself embraced provisions both for monitoring and for adjustment in response to consequent discoveries; while those manning the institution, insofar as they are individually devoted to its official collective aims, are likely to find themselves doing a deal of detailed and informal monitoring every day of their working lives.

The argument presented above may now seem to have been laboring the obvious. Its implications are, nevertheless, explosive. For it provides a simple, easy to use, devastatingly effective, diagnostic tool. It is a tool that should be in constant employment both within academia and outside. Here and now let us simply make that suggestion and explain how it needs to be applied to some of the products of "the Long March through the institutions," in particular to those of the fiercer members of *The Left Academy.*[55]

In considering this Long March we should never forget: first, that, like the eponymous original, it is, and is by all the marchers themselves seen as, a struggle for power; and, second, that for Leninists, as a matter of principle, power is something to be seized for keeps, irremovably. Recently a leading American academic was frank in revealing the name of the game: "Marxists . . . work to place themselves in strategic positions where their theory can shape events; at the same time, they seek to prevent others . . . from capturing influential positions. The contest between theories is thus accompanied by a more or less visible struggle among different theorists to control social positions, to co-opt resources, or to influence social movements."[56]

As soon as we begin to apply our new tool to Long March material, it appears that the entire tradition stemming from Marx and Engels has, from the beginning, been rotted by both academic and political bad faith. The academic bad faith is revealed first in a sustained reluctance to formulate clear and unequivocally falsifiable theses, and thereafter in an equally sustained reluctance to attend to criticism showing that most, if not all, the Marxist theses that have been so formulated are in fact false. This reluctance began with the Founding Fathers, and in them too these faults were sometimes compounded into that of continuing to assert crucial propositions already known to be false. Dr. Johnson was no doubt right to insist that in a lapidary inscription no man is on oath. It is, nevertheless, instructive to examine the contention of Engels, in the address at the graveside of his lifelong friend, that the achievement of Marx in social science was comparable with that of Darwin in biology.[57]

Notice for a start that—unless you count the *Communist Manifesto*, which is scarcely composed as a theoretical document directed toward scientific colleagues—neither Marx nor Engels ever produced a crisp, clear-cut, and unambiguous statement of exactly what it was that, in their correspondence, they always referred to as "our view," or "our theory," or the like. By contrast, many years before he ventured to publish anything about evolution by natural selection, Darwin wrote for his private, purely scientific purposes a "sketch of my species theory"; a sketch that was intended to force him to recognize the difficulties which, if they could not be overcome, would demand the abandonment of that theory. When finally he did publish *The Origin of Species* there was, of course, no attempt to deny or to evade those difficulties. Now, can anyone point to any passages in all the massed volumes of MEGA in which Marx accepted that anything at all constituted even a serious difficulty for "our view"?

Again, can anyone point to any reiteration of a known falsehood, however trivial, in Darwin? Yet Marx frequently reiterated fundamentals he knew to be untrue. Thus, the Immiseration Thesis, as restated in *Capital,* is that: "The accumulation of wealth at one pole is...at the same time the accumulation of misery, the torment of labour, slavery, ignorance, brutalization at the other...." Faced with falsification Marx simply suppressed the data. Hence, in the first edition, various available British statistics are given up to 1865 or 1866, but those for the movement of wages stop at 1850. In the second edition all the other runs are brought up to date, but that of wage movements still stops at 1850.[58] Then, in his Inaugural Address to the First International, Marx supported this same, crucial, false contention by misquoting W.E. Gladstone as having said in his 1863 budget speech the diametric opposite of what, with perfect clarity and truth, he actually did say. *"So war dieser Mann der Wissenschaft"* [Thus was this man of science].[59]

The same powerful instrument can and must be employed to reveal similar bad faith over issues of alternative policies and their alleged and actual effects. Thus, in the *Communist Manifesto* proletarian revolution is presented as the means to realize utopia—an atheist analogue of the Kingdom of God on Earth, in which "the free development of each will be the condition of the free development of all." The most damning evidence on this count is that of the consistent and persistent refusal of Marx to make any serious attempt to answer those critics who argued that the enforcement of full socialism, Marxist style, would inevitably result, as in fact it has, in a vastly intensified and more universally repressive form of oriental despotism; or of "the Asiatic mode of production," as it is euphemistically labeled by Marxists. The fact that Marx so swiftly abandoned his studies of that phenomenon is doubly significant: first, because it could not be encompassed within, and therefore constituted a falsification of, "our view" of a progressive, unilinear, historical development; and, second, because it provided the best available evidence of the likely political and social effects of establishing a totally centralized command economy.

Criticism on these lines in fact began very early, even before the first publication of the *Manifesto*. Already in 1844 Arnold Ruge, who was "still a democratic, not a socialist revolutionary," protested that the realization of such socialist dreams would be "a police and slave state."[60] In the year of the *Manifesto*, when Engels explained its ideas to the vice-president of Louis Blanc's party, that luminary responded: "You are leaning towards despotism."[61] The fullest contemporary development was to come in 1873, in Bakunin's *Statehood and Anarchy*. The only known response ever made by either Marx or Engels to any of this criticism consists in a few unpublished marginal notes by Marx in his copy of *Statehood and Anarchy*. What conclusion can we draw, other than that it was the revolution itself for which they were hoping and striving, and that they either did not care what the consequences would be, or even looked forward to being, themselves, despots? How right Engels was in his second main claim at the graveside, that Marx was before all else a revolutionary.

The same cruelly effective instrument for uncovering both academic and political bad faith needs to be applied now to the militants of that "Marxist cultural revolution," which the editors of *The Left Academy* assure us "is taking place today in American universities."[62] We have to challenge, and to persist in challenging, the sincerity of academic purpose—the commitment, that is, to the pursuit of truth—of all those shown to be indifferent to evidence that their favorite and foundational assertions are in fact false. The offense becomes the more gross when those thus revealed as being, about these most cherished contentions, paradigmatically uncritical, then have the effrontery to make "critical" a code word for "Marxist"; proceeding to preen themselves on being—so unlike their detested and despised liberal opponents—critical sociologists or critical whatever else it is that they are paid to be.

Such indifference appears to be typical rather than exceptional. Thus, the author of a recent series of studies of fourteen *Thinkers of the New Left* first lists the names of several of the most powerful critics of Marx, from Weber to Popper, and then asks himself a rueful question: Since all these "have made *no impact whatsoever* on the fundamental items of left-wing belief," and have apparently failed "even to *attract the attention* of those whom they have sought to persuade"; then "how can *he* hope to make an impact?"[63] He goes on to give case after case of that refusal even to attend. Thus, "Althusser praises the labour theory [of value] and purports to be persuaded by it."[64] So, what does the prophet Althusser make of the overwhelming critical literature—from the early marginalists, on through such giants of the Austrian school as Eugen von Bohm-Bawerk and Ludwig von Mises?

Nothing. All profane pagans are silently ignored. Althusser is perhaps egregiously scandalous as he certainly was a demented figure. By contrast, several contributors to the *Dictionary of Marxist Thought*, edited by Tom Bottomore, do take rather more notice of objections. Yet, even at their best they too still choose to emasculate or ignore the most powerful. Nor do they ever so much as entertain the thought that the whole system ought to be abandoned utterly rather than here and there amended. Thus, in their entry "Critics of Marxism," the editors manage to mention Popper but not *The Open Society*, only *The Poverty of Historicism*, his feeblest work. Again, the article "Lenin" takes care not to mention Sidney Hook or any of the others maintaining that the success of the October coup in the Russian Empire falsifies a characteristic and surely fundamental claim in *A Contribution to the Critique of Political Economy*: "...no social order ever disappears before all the productive forces for which there is room in it have been developed...."

The editors conclude with two genuflections, both to "the distinctive explanatory power of Marxist thought...notwithstanding some [unspecified] unresolved problems", and to "its capacity to generate not a religion, but a body of rational norms for a socialist society...." What can this second be but an absurdly exaggerated devotion toward *A Critique of the Gotha Programme*? Certainly all the earlier writings are full of denunciations of those who would ask for or provide such "cookbooks for the future." Furthermore, in thus disclaiming the religious description, do they not protest too much? For, to compile such a dictionary of the thought, on every subject under the sun, of one man and his devotees is itself more a religious than a scientific enterprise; while to introduce courses in Marxist economics into departments of economics is like nothing so much as to allow "equal time", to Creation science.

In deference, perhaps, to the Marxist "unity of theory and practice" the political bad faith is often closely integrated with the academic. Consider, for instance, those radical criminologists who say or suggest that delinquency and its mistreatment are the characteristic and ineradicable consequences of a predominantly private and intentionally pluralist form of economic organization, and that the only hope and panacea lies in a total and absolute collectivism; yet all the time they do not attend for one moment to the experience of the now numerous more or less fully socialist countries. We might, perhaps, ask how these people continue never to hear of the Gulag Archipelago, were it not for the nasty but not arbitrary suspicion that it is precisely their awareness of the nightmare realities of Soviet power that makes them thus careful to eschew what Mill christened the Method of Agreement and Difference.

Such academically faithless eschewals are typical of the disillusioned decades since the Twentieth Congress. In the thirties and forties every Marxist onslaught on the actual or alleged faults of nonsocialist societies used to be complemented by contentions that in these respects everything was different and better in "the socialist sixth of the world." A prize specimen of the more modern mode comes from *Schooling in Capitalist America*, which offers total socialism only obliquely as the panacea alternative to a system uniquely responsible for "drugs, suicide, mental instability, personal insecurity, predatory sexuality, depression, loneliness, bigotry and hatred...."[65]

Again, how can we possibly accept, either as honest colleagues in scholarship or as sharers of our own sincere ecological and environmental concerns, Marxists insisting that capitalism is the cause of all or almost all the trouble, while refusing to notice pullulating pollution scandals in the now all too numerous countries of "actually existing socialism." It would be easy to multiply such examples of radical academic and political bad faith ad nauseam and beyond. But I will end, at too long last, by quoting a prize passage from one of the works of a man who has both made a successful academic career for himself and done his full share as a comrade in the cause of imposing irremovable despotisms upon the whole human race. His chosen instrument for both purposes has been plotting the supposedly sinister role of *The State in Capitalist Society*—with never a glance at its enormously more oppressive and conspicuously unwithering role in either Leninist theory or Leninist practice. Our sample sentence is gratifyingly short: "Social control is a social process occurring continuously within capitalist society, and is a product of the class antagonisms of that society." *Pravda* and Soviet German papers, please copy!

Notes

1. J.Q. Wilson, *Thinking about Crime* (New York: Vintage, 1977), p. 63.
2. Ibid, p. 58.
3. A.G.N. Flew, *David Hume: Philosopher of Moral Science* (Oxford: Blackwell, 1986), chap. 8.
4. A.G.N. Flew, *Thinking about Social Thinking* (Oxford: Blackwell, 1985).
5. Alice Coleman, et. al., *Utopia on Trial: Vision and Reality in Planned Housing* (London: Shipman, 1985).
6. A.G.N. Flew and G. Vesey, *Agency and Necessity* (Oxford: Blackwell, 1987).
7. A.G.N. Flew, *Thinking Straight* (Buffalo, NY: Prometheus, 1975), sections 5.9 and 6.11.
8. A.G.N. Flew, *A Rational Animal* (Oxford: Clarendon, 1978).
9. A.G.N. Flew, *An Introduction to Western Philosophy* (Indianapolis, IN: Thames and Hudson, and Bobbs-Merrill, 1971), pp. 218–21.
10. B.F. Skinner, *Walden Two* (New York: Macmillan, 1948), chap. 29.
11. B.F. Skinner, *Beyond Freedom and Dignity* (New York: Knopf, and Cape, 1971).
12. J. Locke, *An Essay Concerning Human Understanding*, ed. P.H. Nidditch. (Oxford: Clarendon, 1975).
13. Flew, *David Hume*, op. cit., chapters 5 and 8.
14. K.R. Popper, *The Open Universe: An Argument for Indeterminism* (London: Hutchinson, 1982), pp. 92–3.
15. Ibid., p. 93.
16. Flew, *David Hume*, op. cit., chapter 4.
17. Skinner, *Freedom and Dignity*, op. cit., p. 7.
18. Ibid., p. 8.
19. Ibid., p. 9; and compare Flew, *A Rational Animal*, op. cit., chapter 7.
20. *Wall Street Journal*, January 16, 1987.
21. Ibid.
22. *Washington Times*, January 19, 1987.
23. Ibid.
24. Thomas Sowell, *The Economics and Politics of Race* (New York: Morrow, 1983), p. 160.
25. R.A. Freeman, "The Income and Outcome in Education" in Freeman, *The Wayward Welfare State* (Stanford, CA: Hoover Institution, 1982); but compare also G.V. Glass, L.S. Cohen, M.L. Smith and N.K. Filby, *School Class Size* (Beverly Hills, CA: Sage, 1982).
26. For one topical example, see S. Lukes, *Marxism and Morality* (Oxford: OUP, 1986), and compare Flew, *David Hume*, op. cit.
27. R.B. Everhart, ed., *The Public School Monopoly* (San Francisco: Pacific Institute for Public Policy Research, 1982).

28. E.G. West, *Education and the State*, 2nd Ed. (London: Institute of Economic Affairs, 1970).
29. See J. Marks, C. Cox and M. Pomian-Srzednicki, *Standards in English Schools* (London: National Council for Educational Standards, 1983), J. Marks, C. Cox and M. Pomian-Srzednicki, *Standards in English Schools: Second* (London: National Council for Educational Standards, 1985), and J. Marks, C. Cox and M. Pomian-Srzednicki *Examination Performance of Secondary Schools in ILEA* (London: National Council for Educational Standards, 1986).
30. C. Brewer and J. Lait, *Can Social Work Survive?* (London: Temple Smith, 1980).
31. G. Williams, "The Missing Bottom Line," in G.C. Moodie, *Standards and Criteria in Higher Education* (London: NFER-Nelson, 1986), p. 35.
32. Flew, *Thinking About Social Thinking*, op. cit., pp. 202–03.
33. Compare S. Lait, "Central Government's ineptitude in monitoring local welfare," in A. Seldon, ed., *Town Hall Power or Whitehall Pawn* (London: Institute of Economic Affairs, 1980), pp. 63–8.
34. S. Andreski, *Social Sciences as Sorcery* (London: Deutsch, 1972), p. 56.
35. S. Mosher, *Broken Earth: The Rural Chinese* (New York: The Free Press, 1983).
36. Personal correspondence from Sidney Hook to Antony Flew.
37. B. Halstead, "The New Left's Assault on Science," in *The Salisbury Review* (London, January 1987).
38. A.E. Housman, *Juvenalis Saturae* (Cambridge: CUP, 1931), p. xi.
39. T. Hobbes [1629], Translation of "History of the Peloponnesian War," in Thucydides, *Works*, W. Molesworth, ed., (London: Bohn, 1839–1845), p. vii.
40. Ibid., V 89–90.
41. Ibid., III 82–3.
42. See, for instance, J. Epstein, "A Case of Academic Freedom," in *Commentary* (September, 1986); see also journals such as *Commentary* and *Quadrant*, passim.
43. S.R. Lichter, S. Rothman and L.S. Richter, *The Media Elite* (New York: Adler and Adler, 1986); and S. Rothman, "American Intellectuals," in *The World and I* (January, 1987).
44. F. Engles (1878), *Anti-Duhrig*, C.P Dutt, ed., (London: Laurence and Wishart, 1934), p. 309.
45. A.G.N. Flew, "Peace, 'Peace Movements', and Peace Studies," in L. Grob, ed., *Educating for Peace: Testimonies of Spirit* (New York: Orbis, 1987); for the U.S. compare A. Ryerson, "The Scandal of Peace Education," in *Commentary* (June, 1986), and J. Adelson and C.E. Finn, "Terrorizing Children," in *Commentary* (April, 1985).
46. American readers will be able to assure themselves that this is not an unfair account of the objects of the exercise by reading Andre Reyerson's letter in *Commentary*, February 1987, pp. 12–3.
47. S.H. Balch and J.I. London, "The Tenured Left," in *Commentary* (November, 1986).
48. Quoted in R. Sandall, "The Rise of the Anthropologue," in *Encounter* (December, 1986), p. 71.
49. Noted in D. Stove, "A Farewell to Arts," in *Quadrant* (May, 1986), p. 9.
50. T. Pateman, ed., *Counter Course: A Handbook for Course Criticism* (Harmondsworth: Penguin, 1972), p. 284.
51. R. Blackburn, ed., *Ideology in Social Science* (London: Collins Fontana, 1972), p. 10.

52. Garreth Stedman Jones in Blackburn, op. cit., p. 113.
53. M.F.D. Young, ed., *Knowledge and Control* (London: Collier Macmillan, 1971), p. 131.
54. Jones, in Blackburn, op. cit., pp. 107-09.
55. B. Ollman and E. Vernoff, eds., *The Left Academy* (New York: McGraw Hill, 1982); and compare Balch and London, op. cit.).
56. A. Gouldner, *Against Fragmentation* (New York: OUP, 1985), p. 89.
57. A.G.N. Flew, *Darwinian Evolution* (London: Granada Paladin, 1984), p. 3.
58. B. Wolfe, *Marxism: One Hundred Years of a Doctrine* (London: Chapman and Hall, 1967) pp. 322-23 and passim.
59. D. Felix, *Marx as a Politician* (Carbondale, IL: Southern Illinois University Press, 1983), pp. 161-12.
60. L. Schwartzschild, *The Red Prussian* (London: Pickwick, 1986), p. 80.
61. Ibid., p. 154.
62. Ollman and Vernoff, op. cit., p. 1.
63. R. Scruton, *Thinkers of the New Left* (London: Longman, 1986), p. 5: italics in original.
64. Ibid., p. 89.
65. S. Bowles and H. Gintis, *Schooling in Capitalist America* (New York: Basic Books, 1976), p. 276.

II

The Political Economy of Higher Learning

Introduction to Part II

John W. Sommer

A full treatment of the political economy of higher learning would include among its topics such fascinating subjects as real estate development, television sports entertainment contracts, medical treatment facilities, endowment management, and a host of other income generating activities virtually unknown to colleges and universities a century ago. It would also include discussion of accreditation organizations, association memberships, lobbying firms, government-industry-university compacts, and collective bargaining agreements with faculty and staff as part of the many political arrangements of the modern university.

The advent of major public universities, and other universities devoted to research (both public and private), ushered in an era of change from a relatively simple and coherent institutional framework to a more complex organizational structure characterized by vast diversification of functions. For many university officers the emphasis has shifted from oversight of the classroom instruction of youngsters to corporate management of extensive assets and an incessant search for financial resources from alumnae and friends of academe.

The economics and politics of higher learning have become exceedingly complex as the economic and political relationships of the modern college and university have multiplied, interwoven, and extended into society more broadly. The section that follows makes no pretense to offer a comprehensive review of the many features of this political economic complexity, yet each chapter in its own right offers some extraordinarily useful generalizations that can aid our understanding of higher learning in America.

In their turn, the authors treat such fundamental topics as the social return on public investment in higher learning (West), the rationale for public support of pure (basic or fundamental) research, which is principally undertaken at universities (Dresch), and a property rights perspective applied to several activities of universities: administration, teaching, and research (Meiners and Staaf). Taken together these three chapters prepare us to question the role of the state (federal, state, provincial, or local) in the affairs of higher learning.

Professor West, utilizing three different economic analyses and his vast experience in Canada, systematically decomposes arguments for state intervention in higher education: public finance (welfare economics), organization theory, and public choice theory are applied to the conventional arguments for public support and each argument is found wanting.

If West's analyses were nothing else they would be methodical—but they are also subtle and relentless. He first considers efficiency arguments through the lens of public finance, deploying standard benefit/cost analysis to derive rates of return from education to compare with rates from noneducation investments. Following basic, unheroic assumptions, and identifying some of the important foibles of these kinds of analyses along the way, West concludes that private real rates of return on investment in higher education exceed social rates.

He then observes that the main justification for public support for higher education rests on a market failure argument concerning externalities: higher education is said to benefit society in ways individual investors in such activity cannot fully capitalize upon, therefore the private demand for education will be less than the social demand, resulting in its undersupply. West points again to the frailties of benefit/cost analysis and shows that there are also important dead weight losses due to taxes lost from those who have been induced by public subsidy into schooling they would not otherwise have chosen. On the basis of his analysis West concludes that even if positive marginal external benefits from higher education could be demonstrated it is unclear that government education could capture them. Moreover, when he considers one form of public support, scholarships, he suggests that most college students in the United States would undertake higher learning without such subsidies.

When he examines what it is that governments can do more efficiently than the private sector with respect to higher education, West suggests that the "administrative convenience" of using the tax system to collect student loans (misguided though those may be) is a contender because the government possesses monopoly access to machinery unavailable to the private sector. However, its demonstrated failure to deploy its advantageous position in the face of high loan default rates suggests there is no case for government to continue in the student loan business.

West then applies an organization theoretic framework to higher education and concludes that the universities are oversupplied with public funds and that economic arguments to justify government intervention have been based on assertion rather than on evidence. Significant educational output expansion after intervention has never been demonstrated, and he suggests that it is time that the way is cleared for proprietary educational institutions to develop under the healthy discipline of consumer choices.

Finally, public choice theory permits West to remind us that political processes relied upon by the advocates of external benefits tend to concentrate

the benefits rather than to disperse them widely, thereby vitiating equity considerations. As West sees it (and he is not alone), the main beneficiaries are
politicians, bureaucrats, teachers, and middle-class students because they have
the information and the capability to exploit asymmetric political power. Thus,
the main arguments for government intervention on grounds of either equity
or efficiency are regarded as vacuous.

While West's treatment focuses principally on the relationship between
government and university in education broadly writ, Dresch follows with an
examination of another important interaction, research.

In his treatment of the economics of fundamental research Dresch brings
forth issues at the heart of the relationship between academe and the state. He
asks what it is society derives from public investment in fundamental research
(most often associated with scientific research due to the overwhelming funding of science relative to the arts or humanities).

He identifies two "social warrants" that are part of the contemporary literature of justification. First, fundamental research is regarded as possessing inherent social utility, that is, it expands the domain of thought and by so doing
it contributes to the expansion of culture. This view of fundamental research
(chiefly scientific research) is "ideational" and is "indistinguishable from those
of other classes of ideas [philosophical, religious, and so on]." Fundamental
research, conceived in this way, may have future applications to be sure, but it
is not justified on that basis: it is, instead, a form of "social consumption comparable to the building of monuments..."

This view is juxtaposed with an "instrumental" justification of fundamental research as an investment in the development of a stock of useful knowledge which, after technological transformation, yields direct benefits to society.

Dresch asserts that the "ideational" view is being supplanted by the "instrumental" view, but the pace of that replacement is ultimately slowed by
recognition of the reality that benefits flowing from the radically uncertain
process of fundamental research cannot be known *ex ante,* therefore the instrumental arguments for public investment in fundamental research must rest
to some degree on faith (ideational) that such investment will translate into
useful items sometime in the future.

Dresch marks the moral hazard of superinvestment in fundamental research
when he points out that because scientific or artistic talents are not uniformly
distributed across individuals increased public allocations will call forth increasingly marginal practitioners, implying diminishing marginal social utility. This is hardly what the science lobby in Washington wishes to learn.

An important observation is made by Dresch concerning the nonlinear nature of the transformation of fundamental research into societal benefits. The
standard model that fundamental research first yields the discovery of laws

followed by applications of these laws that result in beneficial products is badly flawed and often contravened by historical evidence. For example, the steam engine was in use before the fundamental physical principles behind its operation were understood. In other words, there is no unidirectional flow from theory to application (and there is clear evidence of reciprocal flows), and there exists no *ex ante* measure of what might be the payoff for an investment in fundamental research.

Naturally, these ideas pose serious difficulty for those who ask for more and more funds for fundamental research, namely the many institutions of higher learning. If the chief provider of those funds is the public treasury, and the prevailing rationale for their provision is an instrumental argument that benefits will flow from this research, it must be expected that public agency will increasingly demand accountability and measurement of the payoffs. Except in the most trivial sense, that is impossible. Universities, the principal "houses" of pure research, will increasingly face the choice of scaling back research operations or replacing pure research by research that takes its direction from government agents whose responsibility it is to insure a flow of benefits to the supporting public. The choice for university administrators is not enviable but is likely to continue to be made in support of the trend toward service to the state unless an alternative justification for its locus at universities can be advanced.

Dresch resurrects a third justification for public investment in fundamental research that is, in fact, returning to vogue—that pure research in its own right is an important "educational" exercise, the societal payoff of which is a stock of individuals whose education and training may become important as exigencies occur in the future. Its value, Dresch argues, is that "[T]o exploit knowledge one must contribute to the creation of knowledge."

In a clever way he points out the irony that the desire to appropriate the knowledge of others motivates contribution to the aggregate stock of knowledge, thereby turning the classic "free rider" problem on its head. What Dresch has done is to provide important support for a long understood characteristic of universities: prospecting on knowledge frontiers by faculty contributes to the "alertness" of the faculty, and student participation in that process, in turn, contributes to their education.

One is compelled to observe that this process can only be true where the researcher and the faculty member are one, and linked in a common learning enterprise with the student, otherwise fundamental research becomes a bauble for the researcher and the university and a consumption item for society. More ominously, if researcher and teacher are functionally separated the education of students tends to take the form of training, and the research units at universities are inexorably driven toward a likeness of federal laboratories where research follows the dictates of state-defined problems.

Whether one will conclude that the "human capital" argument for public support of fundamental research is sufficient to warrant public funding is another matter and remains unanswered; at least Dresch has put the debate on a course that may be welcomed by all of those who have a stake in the higher education community.

Who does have a direct stake in the university and what does that mean? Meiners and Staaf have sought, in their chapter, to explain the distributional and allocative consequences of higher education decision making in three areas: governance and administration, teaching, and research. That most colleges and universities are not-for-profit organizations means that the "owners" (trustees) of the institution cannot lay claim to the difference between revenues and costs, therefore their attentions are diverted from efficient resource use and their behavior differs from that which would characterize their behavior in the board rooms of businesses. This is taken to be true for both public and private colleges and universities and to characterize the "management" of these institutions (administrators). Both owners and administrators are asserted to use criteria such as "prestige" or "quality" of students and faculty to mark progress, and to diffuse responsibility for decision making to committees.

Faculty, as officers of the institutions, often play a major role in its administration by virtue of the fact that they participate in decision making (faculty recruitment, advancement, and rewards), but they are not subject to strict monitoring and therefore they are not fully accountable. This, according to Meiners and Staaf, results in a "median faculty" at those colleges and universities with more democratic than autocratic department structures, and they offer evidence from salary votes and other resource allocations to support their view. They conclude that higher education institutions are much like worker managed firms and proceed to describe the rights and obligations associated with teaching and research. In so doing they raise some provocative issues, including the joint-production of learning, which requires both student and faculty inputs and that highlights some differences between public and private schools. At larger public institutions, where less discrimination has been exercised in the admission of students and where class sizes are larger, there is greater tendency for students and faculty to shirk and for neither to monitor the other's performance closely. Conversely, at private institutions, which advertise smaller classes and that tout faculty instructional quality (and at which the price per hour of instruction is much higher) there is greater mutual monitoring of performance by faculty and students.

Under any circumstances, public or private, the teacher is unable to capture much of the benefit for having taught well and the penalties for not teaching well are slight, there being no liability for malpractice in academe. An important consequence of this situation is underinvestment in teaching by faculty and a greater investment in research, the output of which is more broadly and immediately recognizable. Such recognition is revenue enhancing by virtue of the increased bargaining power of the faculty member for positions elsewhere. Meiners and Staaf observe that administrators also are able to capture some gains by hiring faculty who excel in research because of the ability of such faculty to attract extramural revenues to the institution, thereby increasing the institutional budget during the administrator's tenure.

There are a number of other putative benefits for research pursuits, over teaching pursuits and whether or not all of these are realized by even the median faculty member, it is clear that Meiners and Staaf, along with Dresch, have identified an important and, in some respects, deleterious dynamic in the modern university. What comes through from each of the chapters is a picture of an institutional structure largely insulated from the discipline of market forces and more likely suffering from superfluity than from scarcity.

5

The Economics of Higher Education

Edwin G. West

The following investigation of postsecondary education will proceed via three subdisciplines of modern economic analysis: first, by way of well-known techniques used in the study of public finance (welfare economics); second, through models connected with the economic theory of organization; and third, through the approach of "public choice" (the economics of politics). There are important areas of actual or potential conflict arising from these different approaches, and these will be illustrated. The first part will begin with the traditional public finance approach, the second will apply the theory of economic organization, and the third part will deal with public choice. The final section will offer the chapter's main conclusions.

Public Finance

This branch of economics, as applied to higher education, contains both normative analysis of the relationship between higher education and "equality of opportunity" or "equity" and a separate investigation, using mainly positive analysis of matters concerning efficiency. We will begin with the latter issue.

Benefit/Cost Analysis

A conventional tool of public finance that is usually applied to education in the search for efficiency in policy making is that of benefit/cost analysis. Invariably, it yields estimates of the rates of returns from education that are then compared with returns from competing (noneducation) investments. Since the early 1960s much information has been generated by economists on both "private" and "social" rates for different periods. "Private" rates are usually defined approximately as the difference between after-tax income differentials and private resource costs. Social returns allude to the difference between before-tax income differentials and total resource costs. Invariably, private real rates of return are found to exceed social rates. The predominant reason offered is that the social resource costs (usually via government subsidies and grants) are so much larger than are private resource costs.[1]

Empirical Measures of Returns to Education

The social rates of return for investments in four years of college education in the United States are usually found to be lower than that for elementary and secondary education. Thus, in a survey of estimates from 1950 to 1970, Cohn reports social returns averaging 11.33 in college education and 13.1 in secondary schooling.[2] The social rates for elementary schooling are usually predicted to be higher than that for university training because the private costs, especially in the form of forgone earnings, are virtually nonexistent. Private costs in secondary schooling are higher than are those in the elementary level because the cost of forgone earnings begin to appear. But such costs are highest in the case of postsecondary education. Researchers, however, have varying attitudes about the proposition that a student in college forgoes income equal to 100 percent of the earnings of the average high school leaver. Some analysts estimate that the cost is two-thirds of this figure, and others assume 75 percent, and so on.

Vaillancourt and Henriques (hereafter referred to as V&H) provide estimates of the social rates of return concerning Canadians aged eighteen in 1981 faced with the choice of either attending university for three or four years or entering the labor force.[3] Since there are no adequate data to conduct a longitudinal analysis, they calculated an age earnings profile at a point in time, using cross-sectional data for that year and then assumed that the profile would remain stable in real terms through time. They found their earnings profiles to be well behaved, with individual earnings first increasing, then reaching a peak between ages forty-four and forty-eight, and finally decreasing until age sixty-five. The analysis was based on individual microdata from the Survey of Consumer Finance carried out by Statistics Canada for 1981.

V&H's results are reported in Table 5.1. The private rate of return is the rate that equates the discounted net (after income taxes) earnings income differential, associated with attending university, to the cost of obtaining it. The public rate (or what others call the social rate) of return is the rate that equates the discounted gross (before income taxes) earnings income differential, associated with attending university, to the cost to society of a university degree. The differences in the returns to three and four years of university schooling are solely due to differences in cost, since the same earning profiles are used. One of the chief focuses of the V&H study was the comparison of experience across provinces. And the figures revealed the rather striking find-

TABLE 5.1
Private and Public Rates of Return, Three or Four Years of University Studies
For Men in Canada, 1981

	Private returns	Public returns
Atlantic		
3 years	14	9
4 years	12	8
Quebec		
3 years	14	10
4 years	13	9
Ontario		
3 years	11	8
4 Years	9	7
Prairies		
3 years	9	7
4 years	7	6
British Columbia		
3 years	10	7
4 years	8	6

Source: Vaillancourt & Henriques, 1986, Table 4.

ing that the social returns are significantly higher in Eastern and Central Canada than in Western Canada.

But what is also clear from Table 5.1 is that the real after-tax private rate of return to a university education, whatever the province, is significantly higher than most alternative investment avenues for individuals, avenues such as long-term government bonds that usually yield between 3 and 5 percent in real terms. Since investment in university education is so attractive to individuals, it is not surprising that full-time enrollment has been continually increasing since the 1970s despite the slowing down of the rate of growth of the eighteen to twenty-four age group. For example, between 1975 and 1979 this age group grew 8.4 percent, while enrollment at post-secondary institutions rose 5 percent. By contrast, between 1979 and 1983 that age group grew only 3.2 percent, while enrollment jumped as much as 23 percent over this four year period. It is interesting too that enrollments have been increasing more strongly in Quebec and the Atlantic regions, where the private rates of return are seen to be the highest (see Table 5.1).

V&H observe that their results are in agreement with the findings of Dooley, who concludes that for males there was a reduction of between 5 and 10 percentage points in the relative earnings differential, between 1971 and 1981, between university graduates and those with a secondary school education.[4] Despite such a decline, the private rates of return remain outstandingly attractive to individuals. This being so, V&H argue, tuition fees could be increased in all regions of Canada without much effect on the demand for university enrollment. They estimate that a doubling of tuition fees would reduce private rates of return by no more than 3 percentage points for a three-year degree. At present, fees contribute on average about 15 percent of total operating costs.

With respect to social (public) returns V&H emphasize that these are at best equal to and often lower than the rate of return on physical capital. The policy implication of this observation is that provincial governments could reduce their subsidies to universities. For the rate of return on physical capital V&H rely on the work of Jenkins (1977), who reported a figure of 10 percent.[5] I shall comment further on this reference subsequently.

Qualifications

It will be convenient now to compare the estimates of V&H with my own calculations using a different source of Canadian data, namely the 1981 Census. Opportunity will also be taken to include qualifications that were omitted in the V&H study. The first of these relates to the part played by "ability" in earnings differentials. Many writers argue that it is extreme to assume that *all* income is attributable to education. In view of this some analysts assume that a given percentage of income differential is due to ability and practice ranges from zero percent to 60 percent.[6] In my analysis I will experiment with income percent differentials due to ability ranging from zero to 35 percent. (V&H recognize the point about ability but do not include any of their own estimates.)

A second qualification, and one that V&H also recognize, concerns that part of the costs of attending university that consists of forgone earnings. As mentioned previously, researchers have varying attitudes on this variable. In the extreme case, some writers will assume that a student in university forgoes income equal to 100 percent of the earnings of the average high school leaver. Analysts such as V&H assume that this cost is two-thirds of this figure. I will employ a proportion of 75 percent.

A third qualification concerns the source of the estimate for a social return on physical capital with which to compare the social return on education. I will argue that the reference to Jenkins, relied on by V&H, is inappropriate.

To come now to the fourth qualification, all previous estimates of returns to education seem to have neglected one important item: the marginal cost of public funds. Such cost is attributable to the fact that, because a perfect tax system (employing, say, lump sum taxes) is not available, certain unavoidable deadweight welfare losses are associated with tax collection. Recent retrospective estimates for the early 1970s turn out to be far from trivial. Economic theory suggests that such costs rise exponentially with the rise in government's share of G.N.P., and that share has of course been rising significantly over the last two decades.

The significance of deadweight losses from taxation is becoming well recognized in the literature.[7] The latest estimates for the U.S. are reported in Ballard, Shoven, and Whalley.[8] Using data for 1972 and applying general equilibrium analysis, these authors report that the marginal cost of raising one dollar extra revenue ranges between 17¢ and 56¢, depending on different assumptions of elasticities of savings and labor supply. If we wish to use the Ballard study for an indication of the welfare cost of taxation in Canada in 1981, however, we require further broad adjustments.

As shown by Browning and Browning, deadweight loss increases more than proportionately to the increase of government's share in G.N.P.[9] Another way of stating this is to observe that the excess burden of taxes increases exponentially with the direct burden. Since Canadian government's share of G.N.P. in 1981 (about 0.5) was greater than the U.S. government's share of G.N.P. in 1972, I predict higher deadweight losses than those reported in Ballard, Shoven, and Whalley. I believe that a figure approaching the higher end of the estimates of Ballard et al. is probably appropriate. Accordingly, 50¢ will be assumed to be the marginal deadweight cost of raising one additional dollar in revenue.

Usher argues, meanwhile, that the conventional deadweight loss analysis (adopted by writers such as Ballard et al.) underestimates the cost of public funds.[10] The reason for this is that it ignores the welfare cost of tax evasion (which also increases more than proportionately with government's share of G.N.P.). Incorporating tax evasion costs, Usher calculates that, with a government share of G.N.P. of 50 percent and tax evasion of 10 percent, the total cost of public funds is such that it costs 80¢ to raise $1 of tax revenue (i.e., the total burden on taxpayers when one extra dollar of revenue is raised amounts to $1.80).

Table 5.2 applies the (adjusted) estimates of Ballard et al, assumed here to be 50¢, and the latest estimate by Usher of 80¢, to our calculation of the social rate of return to Canadian university education under different assumptions about the proportion of the income differential that is attributable to ability.

My estimates in Table 5.2 refer to the social returns from a four-year university degree, using 1981 Census data. It is interesting, first of all, to compare them with those reported for 1980 by V&H. Using different data, and concentrating on provincial returns, V&H's findings suggest an across-province social average of about 7.5 percent. Their estimates, to repeat, were not

TABLE 5.2
Social Rates Of Return From University Degrees, 1980

Income Percent Differentials Due to Ability				
Marginal Cost of Public Funds	0	0.1	0.15	0.2	0.35
0	9.27	8.67	8.35	8.03	6.95
0.5	8.24	7.68	7.38	7.07	6.04
0.8	7.73	7.18	6.89	6.60	5.59

Data Source: The 1981 Census

adjusted for ability or for deadweight losses from taxation. Their figures were also confined to male students, whereas mine refer to males and females.

Analysis of Overall Canadian Findings

The most severe of my adjustments of the social rates from elementary education (see Table 5.2) consist of the combined assumption of 35 percent of earnings differentials deriving from ability plus a marginal cost of public funds estimate of 0.8. The result for university education is the dramatic decrease in the estimated rate, from 9.27 to 5.59. Even on the more moderate assumption that ability accounts for 0.15 of the income differential and that the cost of funds amounts to 50¢, the social rate is reduced significantly, to 7.38. One method of determining whether university training pays off socially, and the method chosen by V&H, is to compare the social rate of return from such investment in human capital with the rate of return on physical capital. Their reference to Jenkins suggests that the latter rate is 10 percent. In my opinion, however, this reference is not appropriate since circumstances had changed by 1980.

Boadway, Bruce, and Mints report an estimate of the real (gross) rate on aggregate capital 197-81 of 6.3 percent.[11] Since the trend seems to have been upwards at the end of this period, the figure of 6.5 percent seems to be a reasonable conjecture for 1980.[12]

Consider now the findings of Table 5.2 in the context of the conclusion by V&H that government subsidies to universities should be reduced. If we are to base our judgment exclusively on Table 2, concurrence with their conclusion is indicated only if we assume that ability accounts for 35 percent of income differentials and that the marginal cost of public funds is 0.5 or above. But there are several other factors still to discuss, factors that are not incorporated into Table 5.2. The three most obvious appear to be (1) externalities, (2) the use of education as a job market signal, and (3) higher education as a means of occupational licensure.

Externalities

Some observers argue that the typical private and social rates of return approach underestimates the benefits of additional schooling because it neglects the nonlabor market effects of that schooling. Such effects are commonly included under the term "externalities." In some quarters, indeed, this is the most crucial issue, when deciding on the merits of public intervention. According, for instance, to the leading U.S. textbook on the subject of the economics of education the rationale for public support of higher education rests mainly on the market failure argument concerning externalities.[13]

If higher education provides social benefits to society that individual students cannot capture, then the private demand for education will be less than the social demand, and underproduction of education will result.

An economic externality is said to exist when the self-interested action of one person or group in society indirectly affects the utility of another person or group. In other words, when individual X educates himself, he benefits not only himself but others in society. The content of the external benefits has not always been made clear, but the following examples have been suggested: increased economic growth for the nation, a more informed electorate, greater political participation, improved and extended research, reductions in crime and other antisocial activities.

With respect to economic growth, it should be noticed that the argument reduces to the proposition that increased human capital is beneficial in causing economic expansion generally. But, as the Friedmans have argued, the same proposition could be made about physical capital such as machines and factory buildings.[14] To be consistent with the externality argument justifying subsidies for postsecondary education, therefore, one should argue that, because of the consequences for growth, tax money should also be used to subsidize the capital investment, say, of General Motors of Canada or of G.E.C.

The main difficulty with the argument concerning external benefits is that they have still not been satisfactorily measured empirically. A conspicuous problem is that those who decide how much to consume from private motives may, depending on the price, generate external benefits that are entirely inframarginal to the decision concerning the efficient output. In other words, those who produce and consume education may do so at an efficient level even though others may benefit from their decisions (i.e., obtain external benefits free of charge). But, even if marginally relevant external benefits are revealed, some critics point out that the investigator should also look for negative externalities. An instance of the latter is the case of social unrest among a highly educated, yet significantly unemployed, intelligentsia. But, the main point remains that if there are no attempts to measure external benefits, even if only crudely, the case for subsidies to higher education on these grounds remains weak.

But suppose, for the sake of argument, that evidence has been produced showing that marginally significant externalities from higher education do exist. The success of a government program for internalizing them will be measured by the increase in enrollment that it accomplishes. Suppose that, typically, the authorities operate a college that provides X units of education. Prior to any government intervention, some families were purchasing zero amounts, others were buying from private universities something less than X, while a third group were purchasing from other private institutions more than X. After intervention the subsidized public college would obviously attract population from the first two groups so that, to this extent, total expenditure on education would increase. Consider, however, members of the third group, who are used to privately purchasing more than X education units. Economic theory predicts that some of them will desert their private college and will settle for the lesser X units at the public institutions since they will be more than compensated by their escape from between 75 and 85 percent of the per capita operating costs. *Their* action will have a *downward* influence on total educational expenditure. The final outcome thus depends on the numerical size of the different populations mentioned.

After his empirical study of the U.S., Peltzman estimated that if public colleges were eliminated college enrollment would fall by only 25 percent, while total expenditure on higher education would fall by something between zero and 25 percent.[15] This result implies fewer students in college but with each receiving, on the average, more education. On further reflection, however, Peltzman appears to have overestimated the fall in college population. The main reason for this is that in his calculations he omitted the fact (outlined above) of deadweight loss from taxation, the fact that it takes more than one dollar to raise a dollar tax revenue. Intervention, therefore, involves considerable negative income effects. Conversely, the withdrawal of government would involve a decrease in both taxation and in the deadweight losses. As a result there would be positive income effects. The latter would raise the demand for higher education because it is a normal good. For this reason the decline in higher education following government withdrawal would have been less than Peltzman's 25 percent.

When we allow for the increased costs of tax collection and evasion (see above), a conjecture that it now costs about $2 to raise an extra $1 tax revenue in the U.S. would appear to be quite realistic. The final implication is that U.S. government intervention is maintaining the quantity of education at levels not much different from what would occur without it. This conclusion is strengthened when we take into account the change in market structure after government institutions have crowded out private colleges. This phenomenon refers to the tendency for higher cost public monopoly establishments to replace the lower cost services of a private and more competitive college system.

Having reached this position, we must conclude that, even if positive marginal external benefits from higher education were demonstrated by collected evidence, it is not obvious that government intervention is very capable of capturing them. Government failure seems to be at least as strong as market failure. Alternatively, one may entertain doubts about whether external benefits are relevant at the margin. Judging from Peltzman's findings (even before our own adjustments to them), most college students in the U.S. would go to college even without subsidies, and they would receive better educations.

Education and Job Market Signaling

The information contained in Table 5.2, by itself, suggests that government subsidies in Canada should be reduced only on certain assumptions concerning (1) the effects on rates of return of "ability" and (2) the prevailing magnitude of the deadweight cost of public funds. The preceding discussion on externalities has not led to any substantial revision of this conclusion.

Consider next the fairly new specialist area of economic analysis that has now entered the advanced textbooks and that is known as "job-market signaling."[16] Since this type of analysis suggests that much education can be socially wasteful, there may be a case here for some downward revision of our estimated social rates of return. The waste from education is potentially present in those cases where there are differences in the productivities of workers that are not immediately observable to the employer but are known to the employees. The "best" workers may, in these circumstances, obtain education certificates if these are taken as a proxy for higher productivity by the employer, who can then be expected to pay them more than the other, lower productivity, workers. Used this way education simply redistributes income. It also causes net output to fall because of the diversion of resources into the education in question.

The more formal analysis is associated with four assumptions and one corollary (below).[17] Suppose there are two groups of workers—A and B. Type A consists of workers who have an intrinsic productivity per year (P_A) that exceeds that of workers in B $(= P_B)$ (i.e. $P_A > P_B$). If the employer sees no differentiating characteristics, he will pay each worker the same, regardless of group. In this case each worker receives per year:

$$W = P_A \frac{A}{A+B} + P_B \frac{B}{A+B} = \bar{P}$$

where P is the weighted average annual productivity.

Consider now the four assumptions necessary for a competitive signaling equilibrium to emerge wherein members of the A group have differentiated themselves by having acquired a signal of superiority in productivity, the signal being, say, an education diploma.

A_1) Symbolizing the cost of one year's schooling for group A members as A_{sc} and B_{sc} for B group members, the first assumption is: $A_{sc} < B_{sc}$.

A_2) It is not privately worthwhile for a B group individual to become educated. This implies that $P_A - P_B < B_{sc}$.

A_3) It is privately worthwhile for each A group member to become educated. This implies that $P_A - P_B > A_{sc}$.

A_4) For the equilibrium to be self-sustaining employers must ultimately and repeatedly find that the productivity of educated workers is, in fact, P_A and that the productivity of uneducated individuals is, in fact, P_B.

Corollary: The welfare losses from such a signaling equilibrium derive from the fact that education is assumed to have no human capital value but merely acts as a screening device. All that such education does is to (1) raise the wage of the A group members by separating them out from the others, a process that automatically lowers the wage earned by members of the B group and (2) lower net national output to the extent of the resources diverted to the (wasteful) education associated with the job signaling.

Some economists are now making policy recommendations on the basis of such argument. The work of Lang, for instance, indicates a policy that will indirectly curtail education and so achieve a welfare gain because wasteful job signaling will be reduced.[18] Insofar as there is truth in this kind of argument, we will be obliged to revise (downwards) our rates of return from education as reported in Table 5.2. Unfortunately, however, no empirical estimates are available to indicate the magnitude of the required adjustment.

Education Unionism and Occupational Licensure

Another challenge to conventionally measured "high" rates of return to education comes from those who maintain that much of the crude earnings differentials used are attributable to the use of education to restrict job entry. Surveys by H. Gregg Lewis in 1986 have estimated that unions in the U.S. increase wages above market levels on average by 15 to 20 percent.[19] One means of doing so is the imposition of "artificial" restrictions on entry.

Where closed shops exist the unions can effectively ration entry by demanding education requirements that are considerably higher than those of incumbent workers.

Trade unions, however, are by no means the only effective labor cartels. Professional associations, like the American Medical Association, are frequently charged with cartel-like behavior. And, in general, loosely organized resource-supply cartels find it easier to achieve their objectives of higher incomes by restricting entry to the trade than they do by trying to gain agreement on prices.

Such restriction activity shades into the process of occupational licensing since members of the professional association frequently have positions on the relevant boards. In Canada occupations in the medical and dental fields, law, engineering, architecture, accounting, and actuarial science have, for a long time, been regulated by licensing bodies operating under provincial statute. In some provinces, moreover, many of the skilled trades are regulated by autonomous or semiautonomous boards or agencies granted statutory licensing power.

The main aim of licensing is usually officially stated to be that of ensuring the rendering of services that society feels ought to be rendered because it is a better judge of what is good for the individual consumer than he himself is. But, as Dodge observes, such an argument appears suspect, because, in general, it has been members of the professions and trades themselves who have sought to have their professions regulated: "Governments have not forced self-regulation upon protesting professions but rather have yielded to the importuning of members of the professions and trades to establish by statute licensing agencies."[20]

In 1950 entry to dental, law, and medical schools in Ontario could be gained with no formal postsecondary training. Since then the *de facto* standard for admission to all three professional programs now appears to have become a university degree. The same is true of those accepted for articles in Chartered Accountancy. Meanwhile, the evidence shows an increase in the queue of applicants meeting the stated requirements.[21]

Insofar as education is thus used by unions and professional associations to act primarily as a restriction on job entry, there is obviously no guarantee that it contributes to social output in the usual human capital investment sense. But again, unfortunately, there is no reliable method of calculating the precise magnitude of the required downward adjustments to the estimates of rates of return contained in Table 5.2.

This discussion on the measures of efficient budget allocation to education reaches the following conclusion. When we consider the possibilities of the use of education in both job market signaling and occupational licensure, the findings of rates of return in Table 5.2 must be revised downwards, but precisely by how much it is difficult to say. But since, in any case, the rates reported in that table are, at best, not far above the returns available from government investment in physical (as distinct from human) capital, it seems strongly arguable, at least, that there is little case for an increase in Canadian government expenditure on university education. And this conclusion appears valid despite the tide of opinion that Canadian universities have been suffering from under-funding for several years. One new ingredient of reasoning in this essay, of course, has been the incorporation into the benefit/cost analysis of the marginal costs of public funds, a factor which, although far from trivial (as demonstrated above), has hitherto been unfortunately, and improperly, neglected.

It will be useful, finally, to examine the policy suggestion of V&H that tuition fees could be increased in all regions of Canada without the ensuing reduction in the (high) private rates of return affecting significantly the demand for university schooling.[22] Although my research has been concerned with social rates of return, it contains nothing to refute the V&H conclusions that private rates are well above alternative returns available to families and students. The implied prediction of this finding is that enrollment will be on the increase so long as the high private rate persists. I have produced evidence showing that continuous enrollment expansion is indeed the case despite the drop in the share of the eighteen to twenty-four age group in the total population.

V&H, however, add the proviso that their proposed tuition fee increase be accompanied by "appropriate changes in the Canadian student loan plan." Because they do not specify the particular changes they have in mind, and since the argument for a government loan system is, in any case, another aspect of the search for efficiency in the public finance of education, the next section will be devoted to this whole subject.

Efficiency in Educational Loan Markets

Efficiency in the public finance of higher education relates to the original purpose of intervention. One major purpose is normally assumed to be the removal of "barriers to access." The most widely quoted examples of such barriers are financial. Higher education would, of course, occur without intervention but at substantial prices. But millions of other goods and services are also sold at significant positive prices. Should we speak of financial barriers here too?

Obviously, the case for intervention must be linked, not merely to the existence of prices, but to an argument that in higher education they are so "artificial" or arbitrary as to constitute what can truly be called *unusual* financial barriers. Governmental removal of these is therefore urged. This policy is sometimes regarded as an efficiency operation, and sometimes as an interstudent equity move. Where special subsidies are thought to be required for interstudent equity, the advocates argue a need for a trade-off between equity and efficiency, implying that the two objectives are competitive rather than complementary. Since this area of debate appears confused, I shall attempt a further and deeper analysis of "financial barriers" as a necessary preliminary to later arguments.

There seems a consensus among economists, that the main reason for the specially "artificial" barriers and the consequent lack of interstudent equity, or equality of opportunity, is the prevalence of excessive interest charges facing qualified but low-income students.[23] The problem, it is argued, is not that education involves prices but that these prices are too high. The unusually high price of finance is, in turn, often construed as stemming from a capital market imperfection.

No rigorous empirical demonstration of such a proposition has yet been made, however. A crucial issue is the distinction between the student borrower's rate and the lender's realized rate.[24] When we deduct transaction costs, the lender's realized rate may be no different from that realized on physical capital. With educational loans, transaction costs such as the costs of information, screening, collection, and defaulting, are likely to be appreciable. If they are high enough, the allocation of capital could be efficient; that is, no artificial financial barrier need exist. The precise extent of transaction costs is an empirical question, and I must reemphasize that it has, so far, not been answered adequately; but clearly it has much to do with risk and default rates. Meanwhile, absence of evidence of abundant use of private loans for education does not necessarily mean that a capital market is imperfect or does not potentially exist.

In Figure 5.1 the supply curve for loans is so high that it fails to intersect with any point on the demand curve. This is not an imperfect, but an *inoperative* market. The question of the "true" height of the supply curve is obviously a key issue.

The direct way of stating the meaning of an imperfect market is of course to begin with an examination of common definitions of a perfect one. Confidence in the adequacy of markets exists where certain well-known assumptions are satisfied. These include the absence of monopoly, no transaction costs, and the existence of abundant knowledge. When some elementary transaction costs are introduced, costs such as invoicing, communication, and transport, we reach intermediate cases where we are still reasonably confident that markets can operate at least as practically as any alternative. With higher transaction costs, however, we have less confidence in market outcomes. This is especially so when there is considerable risk and imperfect or inadequate information. This is not to say that governments have better sources of information or risk-facing facilities, for in this area we must be especially cautious.

The market for human capital is one where we are confronted by both risk and information complexities. Many writers emphasize that human capital is not available on terms comparable to physical capital; with conventional loans, like a house mortgage, a physical asset can be repossessed in case of default. Without further discussion this argument could be semantic. Repossession cannot occur in the case of an educational loan because the law does not allow investors to hold equity stakes in other human beings. Such an argument does not constitute a direct proof that the capital market is "imperfect." Markets work only with a given legal framework. Here the framework is "restricted." This is so because the property rights of the worker (to pledge future income against a loan) are curtailed. It may be that we should avoid equating this constraint with "market imperfection"; given the legal framework, "very high" rates of interest *may* be compatible with a capital market that is adjusting to the circumstances with perfect efficiency.[25]

It is interesting, nevertheless, to probe deeper and ask why it was first necessary to so constrain the law. A market blockage may have been established deliberately, and this because of previous inadequacies in markets. It is unlikely that there was a complete or perfect set of risk markets. In such circumstances there are no prices to guide decision makers in a context of uncertainty. If there *was* a complete set of risk markets these would include a market for contingency lending so that individuals even from the poorest of families could borrow to finance their higher education. In such a market borrowers would pledge a percentage of future income differentials, and lenders would charge average borrowers a rate that, on average, paid for or covered the risk that others will not succeed in earning a sufficient differential. The latter individuals would thus be insured against complete destitution or worsening of incomes.

In the absence of a market in contingency loans, say because of severe information or policing costs, some individuals will be tempted to borrow on a noncontingent basis. This could, in some cases, have results that are socially repugnant. (Allowing others to have an equity stake in oneself *on a noncontingent basis* could lead to forms of slavery.) To prevent such consequences, governments would be prompted to protect individuals with bankruptcy or usury laws; and they might deliberately establish the market blockages previously mentioned. Much of this reasoning, however, is still conjecture. What we need next is some hard evidence.

In practice some private markets for human capital do exist even within the legal constraints (or blockages). How efficient are these? The problem of coping with high variance is basically one of adequate risk-pooling. There is no clear evidence that large finance houses and insurance companies do not al-

FIGURE 5.1

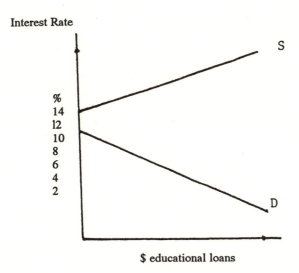

ready enjoy economies of large scale of such pooling of risk. Today multinational finance corporations frequently have pooling facilities that are bigger than those available to some governments, especially provincial or state governments. Moreover, as Friedman points out, there is no clear reason finance and insurance corporations cannot devise means to select from among the potential human capital investors and charge rates that differ according to individual prospects.[26] One method of implementing this policy would be to organize special company examinations and to have candidates independently assessed. Individuals who are the better prospects would then be more likely to invest because their rates would be lower than others; in this way selected individuals will be less called upon to subsidize the interest rates charged to poorer prospects—although some probability of failure will remain even among the screened prospects.

A perfect market requires free entry and also requires that traders have access to optimal information about bids, offers, and conditions. In the sense of freedom of entry the market for capital happens to be highly competitive.[27] In the sense of the need for full information among buyers and sellers there is much less confidence. Information, however, is expensive. It is especially so to lenders in human capital markets, whether they be private individuals or government officials. In such circumstances efficiency demands not *complete* but *optimum* information. The latter is found at the point where marginal costs and expected marginal returns from search are equal. If it is not remunerative to acquire "complete" knowledge, a market possessing incomplete knowledge is not necessarily imperfect.

If a government has no better methods than having private agencies for reducing transaction costs, it will create a misallocation of capital, not eliminate one, if it intervenes to lower interest rates to one common level. But now we reach a crucial part of the analysis. It can be argued that governments *are* in a position to reduce transaction costs. This relates to their access (1) to superior information and (2) to administrative economies. Governments have already invested large resources in establishing machinery for income tax assessment and collection. The marginal costs of using this machinery for educational loans collection should be relatively small. This advantage applies to noncontingent as well as to contingent loans. With contingent loans, however, there is an added advantage. Contingency systems depend upon the supply of accurate income statements long after the production of human capital has been completed. Governments have this knowledge automatically and cheaply through income tax statements. Government sponsored loans, therefore, could carry reduced interest rates, not because of subsidies from nonusers, but from genuine cost reductions in lending.

This argument needs some qualification however. First, full information about lifetime earnings is *not* available from government income tax files. Second, it is arguable that the screening of candidates for loans is better done by educational authorities. Universities, for instance, have better information concerning the progress of students and their worthiness to receive loans. What is strongly indicated, however, is the need for a division of labor; educational institutions can concentrate upon screening and government can accept responsibility for administration and collection. The reason that government authorities are at present so involved in the screening process is that loans are issued partly on the criterion of *parental* incomes. In a full contingency plan this would be irrelevant. Only the future income prospects of the student would count.

Much discussion suggests that the key advantage enjoyed by governments is their ability to mutualize risks. Because of the large variance in outcomes from human capital investments, it is argued, an individual will be reluctant to borrow in the form of a fixed money repayment loan. He may, however, be more likely to borrow in the form of a government loan that is contingent upon income (i.e., a fixed percentage of future income over a given period) and where, if his lifetime income is low, repayments are small. Since governments will obtain more revenue from the more successful, they will be able to cover the costs of financing the less successful. Thus: "The Educational Opportunity Bank mutualizes the risks of investment in education on the same way that fire insurance mutualizes the risks of investment in housing."[28]

One cannot deny that governments do possess such an advantage. But it is not necessarily absolute. When the private sector makes loans, it also mutualizes risks. Incorporated into the rate charged by the lender is an allowance for default; and this allowance is, in an accounting sense, paid for by the successful investors. This is the equivalent to the "extra" tax upon the successful in the Educational Opportunity Bank scheme. One cannot assume, therefore, that private markets are inefficient because they cannot mutualize risk. When asking what governments can do that the private sector cannot do better, the central focus should be upon the possibility of the previously mentioned administrative conveniences—but especially that of interest collection. One of the most demanding requirements of any educational loan system is an efficiently policed system of repayments and interest collection. It is in this area more than in any other that the private market is likely to confront the severest costs. With respect to a borrower's repayment and interest charges, Friedman argues: "payment could easily be combined with payment of income tax and so involve a minimum of additional administrative expense."[29]

This is a crucial point; but it is the *quality* of this government collecting channel more than the quantity of conventional administrative expenses that is the governing factor. The argument has to do with incentives to default. It is realistic to assume that there is a significant margin of people who will have no compunction in evading repayment if they believe the chances of escape without cost are good. Because the borrower does not pledge physical collateral he is more tempted to skip. It is strongly arguable that these chances would be better if the collecting agency is a bank rather than the income tax authorities. If the bank is guaranteed the loan repayment on default, it will have negligible incentive to pursue the debtor. If, however, the loan is registered in the income tax files, the only way to default is to become a vagrant and to forego lifetime social security benefits. This is the fundamental (deterrent) advantage that governments have over private markets: the costs imposed on defaulters are automatic and extremely large.

This point has not been clearly brought out in the literature. This point does not prove private market *imperfection*. It shows only that government has monopoly access to machinery unavailable to the private sector. Nevertheless, the possibility of using this key advantage strongly argues for government intervention—provided that government makes full use of it. If instead, governments concentrate, as they do now in Canada and in the U.S., upon guaranteeing educational loans to private banks, it is probable that defaults could rise to such a point that the true costs of lending to students eventually exceeds those in the market. Moreover, the new economic theory of bureau-

cracy predicts still worse.[30] The theory initially postulates that bureau personnel are no more and no less self-interested than are other individuals. While
such interest can often be channeled in such a way as to benefit society, the
incentives in bureaucracies are frequently to society's disadvantage. Self-interest here often finds simple expression in pressure by the bureau, not to
attain social efficiency, but simply to expand its own budget. Suppose a government "gets off on the wrong foot" with its student loan system and does not
use the income tax agency for collections; and suppose, indeed, that the possibility is completely lost sight of. The larger number of student defaults that
ensue will give the bureau an additional argument for expanding its own department. It will call for special personnel to investigate, monitor, and research the growing default problem. In addition to the costs of defaults there
will now be the costs of an expanding civil service, at first on an ad hoc or
temporary basis, but eventually on a permanent one. But, here we fringe upon
the study of public choice, which is the subject for a later section.

Statistics on Defaults

There appears to be considerable confusion and misinformation in the statistics reporting defaults on educational loans from government. Consider the
following simple example. A program that makes twelve-month loans lends
$100 in year one and $1000 in year two. Suppose all the year one loans defaulted in year two. What, at that time, is the rate of default? Surely it is the
ratio of the number (or value) of defaults to the number or value of the loans
that have become due. In our example the default rate is 100 percent. Year
two's loans do not become due until year three, so they are not related in any
way to the loans outstanding (loans that have become due).

In Canada the method used by the chartered banks is unsatisfactory because it does not follow the above logic. It calculates the loan losses for the
year as a percentage of the loans outstanding at year end. Thus, in our example the banks would report a loss of zero for the first year and of 10 percent
for year two.

The Canadian Public Accounts uses "percentage of net claims to outstanding guarantees," a method that in our above example would produce the erro-
neous loss rate of 16.7 percent. Various government departments, meanwhile,
calculate the loss for the year as a percentage of the mean of the opening and
closing balances in a program. Thus, in our example, they would report a loss
of zero for year one and 18.2 percent for year two, based on an average outstanding of $550 (i.e., *$100 + $1000*) and a loss of $100 in year two.

What then is the appropriate estimate of prevailing default rates connected
with Canada student loans if we use the correct method outlined above of

relating the defaults to the loans that have become due? From the annual reports of Canada Student Loans we observe that between the start of the program in 1964–65 and 1984–85 the cumulative total of loans discharged (loans that had become due) was approximately $1,600 million. Of this total, government paid to the participating banks $377.7 million or 23.6 percent. This government payment was required partly because of death ($6 million), partly following permanent disability ($0.8 million), but mainly for the reason of defaults ($370.9 million).

The figure of 23.6 percent, however, measures only the gross default rate. To obtain the net rate we need further adjustments. When the government pays off a loan to the banks in response to guarantee claims it is automatically considered to become a direct loan between government and student borrower. Some of these direct loans are subsequently collected by collection agents. To this extent, therefore, costs are reduced. Costs are increased, however, by commissions paid to collection agents and by administrative fees paid to the provincial governments.

The cumulative net loss rate after recoveries, less collection fees, came to 14.8 percent of the $1,600 million of accumulated guaranteed loans discharged down to 1984–85. Over the twenty-year period this ratio has averaged around 14 percent.

To place this finding in the perspective of the previous discussion of private capital market "failures," recall that the "proof" of such diagnoses was the claim that private market rates were too high. To simulate the private market, governments would have to internalize all costs and charge students loan rates that covered the costs of defaults as well as normal interest rates. Under Canada Student Loans the latter have been based on the average yield to maturity on government bonds during the six months prior to the start of the program year. On average such interest rates have been around 13.5 percent over the last five years.[31] The gross rate that governments would have needed to charge students, therefore, would be 13.5+14 percent or about 27.5 percent. The claim that private capital markets fail because their rates are too high obviously demands some statement as to what level is too high. If the benchmark is 20 percent then we must conclude from the above figure of 27.5 percent that governments fail also. If the average private rate of interest on an educational loan is, say, 21 percent then the case for a government loan system of the present type would collapse. This would immediately imply an obligation upon government to consider alternative loan structures and especially of the type that use the income tax machinery for purposes of control or collection (as originally recommended by Friedman). If government is not prepared to do this there is no case for its continued presence in the student loan business.

The above findings have relevance to the figures of social rates of return in Table 5.2. Since the figures of cost from which those rates were calculated excluded the annual costs of defaulting on student loans just examined, we have here still another reason for concluding that the net social rates in Table 5.2 were overestimated. The default costs have not been trivial. They amounted to about $149 in every $1000 lent over the last five years.

There are additional costs of the loan system that have hitherto been neglected. These arise especially from the government payment of interest on the educational loans of students while they are in college and for six months after they leave. In the last five years (1982–87) these costs have amounted to $296 for every $1000 loaned. Add to this the $149 per $1000 lent accounted for by defaults, $7 for provincial service fees, and $33 for the service of collection agents, and the net direct (extra) cost per $1000 guaranteed comes to $485. Furthermore, insofar as this cost is covered by taxation, we must add the associated deadweight losses. If we use the estimates based on Ballard et al. we increase the cost of $485 by 0.5, to $727.5. If we use Usher's method we increase by 0.8 to obtain a cost of $873 per $1000 loaned.

All of these findings are clearly pertinent to the proposal by V&H that tuition be increased provided that appropriate charges be made in the Canadian student loan plan. Obviously my analysis points urgently to the need to explore the feasibility of employing the income tax machinery as a means of collection. But it also suggests the possibility that, especially if the latter proposal is shown to be unfeasible, government move out of student loans altogether.

Equality of Opportunity

Before leaving the subject of public finance we should briefly examine another frequently stated motive of government intervention in higher education, that of providing more "equality of opportunity," equality, or equity. This obviously takes us into the area of public finance that is concerned with normative analysis.

If additional education is required in order to obtain more income, then allowing poorer individuals to obtain higher education is one means by which future income distributions will become more equal. One must observe, nevertheless, that even if governments pursue this line of thought, the allocation of subsidies directly to universities is only one possible instrument available; an alternative is to direct the money to students so as to maximize their choice and to encourage competition among institutions.

However, the case for intervention on equity grounds needs further scrutiny. First, it is necessary to make a distinction between two broad types of equity in the context of educational finance. Equity (Type 1) will refer to equity within the college-ability group. Equity (Type 2) will relate to equity between the college-ability and noncollege, typically lower ability, groups (or between users and nonusers of the education system). The emphasis here will be upon equity Type 2.

It will be interesting to examine the position of John Rawls, who has argued that any change or intervention should be allowed so long as those lowest on the income scale are not made any worse off.[32] By income scale Rawls means a lifetime scale. The avoidance of injury to the poorest has its corollary in the fact that the taxes they pay will be used in the most efficient manner and not to the disproportionate benefit of more fortunate classes. Now, "the less fortunate class" overlaps considerably with the group in society that does not receive postsecondary education. The fact that there are millions within these groups who do not receive the benefits, together with the fact that the same individuals are obliged to contribute via taxes to the finance of the higher education of the more fortunate, brings the present system into serious question on the very criterion of equity that is supposed to justify the intervention.

The percentage of the U.S. high school class of 1980 participating in full-time postsecondary education two years later was 34.46 percent. For the lowest quartile socioeconomic status it was only 18.84 percent. It should be remembered, moreover, that (1) not all students complete high school; and (2) of those who proceed to postsecondary education less than a quarter attend universities. More important, even if we did find that all socioeconomic groups were equally represented in postsecondary schooling, this does not deny that millions of nonusers of higher education at the bottom of the income scale would be forced to pay for the postsecondary education of others, whose lifetime income expectations are considerably higher than their own. Equity Type 2 would be sacrificed for Equity Type 1. The argument that higher education should be supported because, in the long run, graduates will pay back the subsidy in the form of higher taxes over their lifetimes is not convincing either because the repayment should strictly consist of subsidy money *together with accumulated interest.*

The Theory of Economic Organization

So far I have been discussing issues in the public finance of education. Now it is time to consider the public *provision* of education via state government enterprises. More precisely, we must consider, from the efficiency point of view, public over private operation and we must also examine and assess the different varieties of each that are available. In other words, it is now time to employ our second subdiscipline in economics: the theory of organization.

Private Nonprofit Universities

There is a temptation to think that because most private universities are legally nonprofit institutions, there is not much difference between them and public universities. Yet, because a firm is described by law as being a non-profit undertaking, this does not mean that something like profit is not operative in reality just beneath the surface. At private institutions students pay high fees that very often cover most of the cost of their schooling. The money spent by the student is either his own or comes from a loan or a scholarship. For this reason such students have a strong "profit motive" to see that they get value for money. If they do not, they can go elsewhere. Administrators, in other words, are not the only actors in the process of responding to incentives. If private students are able to shop around aggressively, which is the case if their fees cover most of the cost, administrators have to respond to their needs by producing at the lowest posssible cost as well as by providing the appropriate pattern (mix) of services. Moreover, the student himself will be a more efficient learner. It has been observed, for instance, that one graduate at Dartmouth College once remarked, "When you see each lecture costing $35 and you think of the other things you can be doing with $35, you are making very sure that you are going to go to that lecture."[33]

Another illustration of the argument that private colleges usually follow market incentives to the full, is the recent contention by the Friedmans that, besides teaching services, private colleges and universities also produce and sell monuments and research. Buildings, professorships, and scholarships are often financed by a benefactor who receives in return a memorial for his services. In the process, students become, in effect, like shareholding employees in the joint educational process. "The combination of the selling of schooling and monuments exemplifies the much under-appreciated ingenuity of voluntary cooperation through the market in harnessing self-interest to broader social objectives."[34]

It is prudent to keep in mind, however, a whole spectrum of educational institutions, from the pure public (state) university at the one polar extreme to the complete market or private enterprise university at the other. It is interesting that in his *Wealth of Nations* we find Smith attacking, not *all* universities in the eighteenth century, but some kinds in contrast to others. The most grotesque deteriorations in efficiency occurred, Smith insisted, where the whole of the incomes of the university personnel came directly from private (bequests) endowments, regardless of efforts: "In every profession, the exertion of the greater part of those who exercise it is always in proportion to the necessity they are under of making that exertion.... The endowments of schools and colleges have necessarily diminished more or less the necessity of application in the teachers."[35]

In other universities, the administrators and professors had to rely also on the fees from their students. Smith observed that the necessity of application, though more or less diminished wherever there was any element of private endowment finance, was not in this case entirely taken away from the teacher:

> Reputation in his profession is still of some importance to him, and he still has some dependency upon the affection, gratitude, and favourable report of those who have attended upon his instructions; and these favourable sentiments he is likely to gain in no way so well as by deserving them, that is by the abilities and diligence by which he discharges every part of his duty.[36]

Smith asks us to contrast this kind of university, which was like the one at which he taught in Glasgow, with those whose teachers were prohibited from receiving any fee from pupils. In this case a teacher's endowment-financed salary constituted the whole of his revenues from office. Smith contends, "His interest is, in this case, set as directly in opposition to his duty as it is possible to set it."[37]

Although Smith was referring to endowments made directly to a university, the same consequences arose from the custom of tying certain scholarships to a particular college. In this case the student had no redress when finding inefficient teaching since he could not transfer the scholarship elsewhere. Adam Smith, himself, seems to have been caught in this same trap. In 1740 he was appointed as a student to one of the Snell Exhibitions at Balliol College, Oxford.[38] It would have been much more in keeping with his system of efficiency had his scholarship been transferable between universities just as in the modern proposal for the education voucher. Had such choice been available it is very probable that Smith would have chosen one of the Scottish universities because he had a much better opinion of them than he did of those below the border. Unlike them, most Scottish universities charged student fees that covered a considerable proportion of total costs.

Private Endowments

In the nineteenth century the practice of endowing universities with bequests received further scrutiny by the political economists. John Stuart Mill, for instance, acknowledged that the right of bequest was an extension of the right of property. As such, endowments for education were to be accepted as a fact of life. If, however, they were held to cause serious imperfections in the private market for education, then economists had the duty to devise newer methods of allowing public endowment financing to operate.

The main trouble with endowments arose, Mill argued, when they were made in perpetuity. The wishes of the original donor often became impractical with a change of conditions centuries later. The trustees, meanwhile, often became so corrupted that they eventually began to think of the funds as their own property. The need was for some impartial body to interpret the appropriate use of the funds with the passage of time. Those who wanted to abolish endowments because of the problems were too extreme. To prevent misuse, endowments made in the distant past, Mill contended, ought, at least ultimately, to be under the complete control of the government.[39] The nineteenth century disciple of Adam Smith, Sir Robert Lowe, agreed with Mill but endeavored to be more specific in devising conditions.[40] Agreeing with Smith, he thought it was important to try to work into endowments "the merits of the free system." This could be done by incorporating bequests into a system of "payments by results." An educational institution should be rewarded with a flow of funds from endowments according to its proficiency and according to the number of students taught. Clearly, Lowe's system approached that of the modern voucher scheme proposal.

It is useful to keep Lowe's position in mind when considering the history of university education. In the nineteenth century especially the endowment was typically administered so as to end up serving the interests of the faculty and administration rather than of the student. Stanford University, for example, which, although established to provide undergraduate education, seems to have quickly deviated from the ideas of the benefactors to become like other institutions. Similarly disturbing was the attempt by the Rockefeller Foundation to shape higher education into a comprehensive *system* and to discourage unnecessary duplication and waste. In fact it is usually untrue that "duplication and overlapping" means waste; for competition to exist there must, in most cases, be at least two suppliers who "overlap" each other.

Subscribing to a consistent view of property rights, it is arguable that benefactors should be allowed to make their own conditions on the endowments they leave. Nevertheless, it is difficult not to be disturbed by the practice of the Carnegie Foundation in discriminating against church colleges from the beginning of the twentieth century. It may be contended that, so long as there is free entry, different benefactors will cancel out the idiosyncrasies of others. This contention, however, could not have been so reassuring in the 1930s when the trusts set up by Carnegie and Rockefeller contained over three-fourths of the known assets of foundations.

If the proposals of Sir Robert Lowe had been implemented from the mid-nineteenth century, a free and more competitive system would have emerged, even though Carnegie and Rockefeller had dominated the endowment "market." Lowe recommended that foundations and wealthy individuals have their endowments channeled through a special central agency (such as, in Britain, the Charity Commissioners) to educational institutions *simply according to their enrollments*. Although this does not constitute a voucher system in the direct sense, the result is the same. The student or his family triggers off an incremental portion of the grant that goes to the school or university by his decision to choose one particular institution in preference to others. Subsidies follow the student, therefore, just as they do with the conventional voucher. In this way the system embraces all the advantages of competition, free choice, and efficiency that are associated with voucher plans. It is reasonable to conjecture that if Lowe's mechanism had been adopted there would have been less chance for universities and other institutions to manipulate endowment funds for the purposes of the administrators and faculty. Whether the Carnegie Foundation could have discriminated against church colleges would have depended on the design of the constitutional body that was to have had the responsibility of allocating all the funds to universities. Compromise arrangements could have been introduced of course whereby, for instance, for every endowment dollar going to particular universities for such items as buildings and research, two dollars would have to be devoted to the common pool of voucher funds. The latter would have to be allocated in proportion to enrollments at the college of the student's choosing and would therefore be spent according to teaching efficiency as perceived by students and their families.

Private Universities Versus Public Monopoly

The effect of tenure systems is probably more pernicious in public than in private universities. Because of stronger union representation in public institutions there is less variance in rewards to faculty members since, in effect, the less productive members redistribute from their more efficient colleagues toward themselves.[41] What needs to be cautioned against, however, is the temptation to believe that, because private universities exist, their presence will provide all the necessary correctives to the shortcomings of the public sector. One necessary condition must be fulfilled for this view to be valid: a reasonably sized private sector must be maintained at present and in the future. The trouble is, as we have shown, that the presence of a strong and growing public undertaking is a continuous threat to the number of its competitors.

One is reminded here of the contrasting views of the classical economists on this question. In the early nineteenth century some of them were beginning to be attracted to the idea of government-as-enterprise, that is, to the idea that the government should be allowed to enter at any level of a market-provided service and "compete" with existing private establishments. The position in the early days was treated as fairly innocuous since the proposed interventions were seen merely as marginal experiments.

Of all the advocates, the name of John Stuart Mill stands out. In his *Principles of Political Economy*, published in 1848, he distinguished what he called undesirable or *authoritative* interference that controlled the free agency of individuals, from the nonauthoritative intervention designed to promote the general interest. An example of the latter would be intervention that, while leaving individuals free to use their own means of pursuing any objects of general interest, "the government, not meddling with them, but not trusting the objects solely to their care, establishes, side by side with their arrangements, an agency of its own for a like purpose."[42]

Under this rubric, Mill attempted to justify governments participating both in education and in business generally. With respect to education he argued: "though a government, therefore, may, and in many cases ought to, establish schools and colleges, it must neither compell or bribe any person to come to them."[43] A public (government) college should exist: "as one among many competing experiments, carried on for the purpose and stimulus, to keep the others up to a certain standard of excellence."[44] The argument that the public institutions would always be superior pace-makers was of course entirely a priori. No substantial evidence on the matter was yet available.

Since Mill's time, experience has shown that when a government agent enters a profession or industry there are automatic or unavoidable restrictions placed on the private competitors. For one thing, the public enterprise has the extra advantage of reliance on government tax revenue and on loans that rest on the public credit. Individuals connected with the public supply, moreover, often become a disproportionate political constituency in their own right and are able to press successfully for further degrees of protection and intervention.

Proprietary Academies

The point has already emerged that efficiency of academic institutions depends crucially on the structure of property rights surrounding them. So far we have examined (1) public colleges where most, if not all, of the costs are provided by government and (2) independent colleges that are privately endowed. We have also emphasized that, before the state-run higher educational institutions, the universities, such as Oxford and Cambridge, which operated without government support throughout the eighteenth century and well into the nineteenth century, were certainly not monumental successes. It is reported by Winstanley, for example, that by the mid-nineteenth century there was in Cambridge a growing resort by students to the services of private tutors (at a fee) as an escape from the inefficient teaching provided by the university and colleges.[45] Luminaries such as Edward Gibbon and Jeremy Bentham, as well as Adam Smith, were all highly critical of the privately endowed universities.

And again it was Adam Smith who diagnosed the source of the problem—inappropriate property rights specifications:

> If the authority to which the teacher is subject resides in the body corporate, the college, or university, of which he himself is a member, and in which the greater part of the other members are, like himself, persons who either are, or ought to be, teachers; they are likely to make a common cause, to be all very indulgent to one another, and every man to consent that his neighbour may neglect his duty, provided he himself is allowed to neglect his own. In the University of Oxford, the greater part of the public professors have, for these many years, given up altogether even the pretence of teaching.[46]

The argument appears to suggest that the only ultimate cure of the U.S. university's "cost disease" today is the gradual but planned withdrawal of government, but not necessarily government finance, from the academic industry. Without this event the crowding out effect will always make it difficult for new *proprietary* academic establishments to prosper. In Britain it is probably true to say that the unique case of the sole independent university at Buckingham is maintaining a threshold mainly because of the recent retrenchment of public spending on the "conventional universities." And it is remarkable that the Buckingham institution is the only one hitherto to have introduced such innovations as two-year degree courses, the substitution of two-to-five year contracts for the old tenure system, and academic years consisting of four ten-week terms.

Conclusion on Organization Aspects

The debilitation of typical universities in today's environment stems from years of over-supply of public funds. The argument by some economists that government intervention has been justified by the existence of public (external) benefits has been based on assertion rather than evidence. One part of the argument contains the *implicit* assumption that intervention will significantly expand educational output. Having applied the analysis of Peltzman (with our own modifications), we have reached the conclusion that significant educational output expansion following intervention has never been demonstrated. What we have been witnessing is a substantial expansion in the costs of an increasingly monopolistic public establishment and the slow demise or crowding out of competitive alternatives.

This is not to say that *any* form of privately funded education institutions will do much better. The authority of Adam Smith and others provides testimony to this. Private subsidies can be just as disruptive or enervating as are public subsidies. The main requirements are proprietary enterprises whose main source of revenue derives directly from the market and its system of payment by results. Such institutions only will experience the salutary feedback mechanism of the stock market, a mechanism that will constantly keep proprietary establishments progressively up to standard. Administrators' and professors' sovereignty should go. The consumer should be reenthroned.

The Theory of Public Choice

In the previous exploration of public finance (welfare economics) aspects of our subject in the first part of the chapter, the question of optimal subsidies was examined. It was shown that the literature frequently recommends intervention to internalize externalities from education. My own conclusion about whether externalities were empirically relevant at the margin was agnostic. But, to those who are convinced that they are relevant, the further question must immediately be addressed as to whether public officials enjoy the right kind of information and face the kind of incentive structures that are conducive to the "correct" public policy response.

Externality advocates often appear to assume implicitly that our democracy is one in which the preferences of an undifferentiated electorate are respected via an electoral process and then by subsequent executive, bureaucratic, and judicial actions. Yet such a scenario is inaccurate. The electorate is not undifferentiated. Typically, it is represented by special interests whose preferences dominate those of the general public. When citizens are brought together into a group, as for instance at their place of occupation, the political office holder has an interest in transacting with its leaders. Representation of dispersed individual citizens, in contrast, is much more costly. The office holder himself will receive more direct rewards by behaving in this way, and the result is a political process that produces private benefits to special interest groups at collective costs.

Expressed in other terms, there is no assurance that representative democracies can easily deliver optimum subsidies to internalize external benefits from education, as the usual welfare-regarding models of the public sector assume. Instead, the real world political process can be more confidently expected to produce particularized rather than generalized benefits. Subsets of the population (including office holders), therefore, stand to benefit at the expense of the general public.

Such argument predicts that educational subsidies will indeed emerge but that they will be directed more to the interests of the suppliers of education than to the general public. The supply interests here will be the organized teaching profession, the members of education bureaucracies, politicians, and politically articulate student groups. The result is that we start with a proposition about externalities that has been described as an instance of market failure, and we finish our analysis with the realization that, if political action is instigated as a "corrective," we soon run into at least equally serious problems of government failure.

Even if evidence of marginally relevant externalities of net positive value does emerge, this would still not constitute an argument for the present system of government financing. Ideally, government intervention has to be designed to increase educational output beyond what the market would achieve. If this is at all possible the most effective way to do it is to direct the subsidies to students in the form of scholarships or vouchers. Because students would then have the freest of choices among universities, the resultant competition would keep costs down to a minimum and/or would maximize output per dollar of expenditure. The fact that the supply interests have managed to persuade governments to avoid vouchers and instead to finance the universities directly is testimony to the asymmetric political power to which we previously referred.

Typical public universities have conventional bureaucracies that are interested in expanding their own budgets and in enhancing the welfare of administrators and others involved on the supply side. The inefficiency of such bureaus stems largely from their monopoly position. It is true that there exist some private institutions of higher education side-by-side with the public ones. Numerically, however, the private sector is small and is relatively shrinking. One must reiterate that this situation occurs largely because of the tendency of the public system to crowd out the private. The circumstances that make this possible include the obvious fact that tuition fees in private establishments are higher than those in public institutions, where the subsidy element tends to dominate. In 1986 average tuition and other fees in U.S. private universities amounted to $5,120, whereas the public equivalent was only $1,040.23.

The crowding out phenomenon is not new. In his *Wealth of Nations*, published in 1776, Adam Smith not only observed the tendency but also offered the crucial diagnosis: "Unsubsidized private education institutions in his day were a declining minority, he argued, because the salaries of the teachers in the public or subsidized establishments...put the private teachers who pretend to come into competition with them, in the same state as the merchant who intends to trade without a bounty [subsidy] in competition with those who trade with a considerable one...."[47]

It is not surprising therefore that the proportion of private to public higher education institutions in the U.S. has fallen from 35.7 percent in 1963 to 22.3 percent in 1983.[48,49] What is more, this decline is officially predicted to continue. Thus, it is estimated that by 1990 the proportion of private to public will have fallen to 20.5 percent.[50]

Insofar as bureaucracy increases the costs and reduces the efficiency of education, the freedom and encouragement of the genuine scholar is seriously impaired. His working environment is likely to become the subject of tight routine and regulation. Furthermore, the administrative hierarchy with which he is saddled will attempt to direct his energies toward obtaining the maximum financial return from government to pay the salaries of all participants, including those of the administrators and of the least efficient academics.

Some relevant evidence has recently been produced by William Orzechowski.[51] He tested the hypothesis that staff inputs in public institutions are used in greater proportion than than they are in private firms supplying the same service. His empirical analysis covered thirty-one states for the year 1968. He found that, for the same relative price of labor to capital by state, the public colleges in a state employed roughly 40 percent more labor than did private colleges for the same sized capital stock. He concluded that such a labor bias of public colleges and universities was due to behavioral reasons associated with difference in ownership. The public institutions were operated by administrators who were utility maximizers, and the fiscal residuum generated by these organizations was used to a considerable extent for overstaffing.

In another piece of research, David Sisk has argued that, because tuition is held below the market clearing price in public universities, market evaluation of the product mix is prevented, and the public authority is forced to monitor product attributes. The main attribute is enrollment.[52]

Consequently, because the public funding is directly linked to the number of students, university managers divert resources toward enrollment and away from instruction. The result is larger classes, lower admission standards, and less preparation for the classroom by instructors.

Public Choice and Equity

As previously mentioned, another leading argument urging government intervention is that income distribution can be improved by providing educational facilities, especially to the poor. I have pointed out that there are two dimensions to the equity question: Equity (Type 1) within the college-ability group and Equity (Type 2) between the users and nonusers of higher education. I emphasized that the latter version was the prior consideration if we are to adopt widely accepted notions of justice. In fact it is this same version that, in politics, seems to be deliberately neglected or submerged. Rational politicians will predictably choose to talk in terms of the particularized needs of the student group since it is more organized politically and can offer measurable benefits, in turn, to their party. The politician's prospects will be pursued more effectively in this way than by attempting to champion the interest of a widely diffused, unorganized, and less educated population that is made to contribute via taxes (especially indirect taxes) to a higher education system from which its members are personally disqualified. Higher education students, education bureaucracies, and politicians will all comfort themselves, meanwhile, with statements that they are supporters of "equity" simply by arguing for more money to reduce tuition in the interests of accessibility. What is concealed is the fact that most higher education students are middle class and would receive higher education anyway, even in the absence of any government intervention (see the previous discussion of Petzman's 1973 analysis). It is these students who benefit predominantly from the system; it is they who enjoy the "accessibility" to the incomes of poorer families who, partly because they typically receive the worst offerings of the public school system (kindergarten through high school), will have children who are not usually acceptable entrants to universities.

Public Choice and the Government Loan System

The way to stop middle-class students from drawing upon the incomes of poor nonusers of higher education is to implement an income contingent loan system. With this arrangement students would be called upon to repay their loans only if they reached high enough income positions in the future. The successful students, meanwhile, would be obliged to pay some surcharge to cover the costs of the less successful. In this way the middle class will be obliged to look after its own "poor" without having to depend on those who are unambiguously poor.

Despite the logic behind this argument it is a striking fact that, a quarter of a century after Friedman proposed it, the principal of a contingent loan system has still not been introduced by the public sector in America or in Canada. Equally arresting is the continuance of a bureaucracy, with its own special constituency, persisting with an inefficient method of loan policing and collection. For, the loan system still does not employ the income tax machinery, the method that Friedman originally advocated. Meanwhile, in Canada, as previously explained, for every $1000 lent government is involved in extra costs of at least $700.

In the U.S. the largest financial intervention continues to be, not the loan system, but the Basic Educational Opportunity Grant (BEOG) program. In the 1980s total outlays on BEOGs are exceeding $3 billion. Such subsidies to college students, to repeat, have the consequence of making individuals with higher expected incomes in the future even wealthier, and this at the expense of the less fortunate. The comment of the Friedmans in 1980 is still apposite: "In this area those of us who are middle-and upper-income classes have conned the poor into subsidizing us on a grand scale—yet we not only have no decent shame, we boast to the treetops of our selflessness and public spiritedness."[53]

But, despite such protest, the fact remains that the political process as we know it, and populated as it is with self-interested politicians, administrators, and interest groups, is apparently so constructed as to continue the Friedmans' "confidence tricks" in perpetuity.

Conclusions

The public finance approach to the issue of higher education recommends, among other things, the use of benefit/cost techniques to determine how far public investment in postsecondary schooling is socially worthwhile. My own research on these lines has challenged the tide of opinion in Canada that the public universities are underfunded. This conclusion has followed from new adjustments that I have introduced to the traditional benefit/cost formula, the two most important being (1) an addition on the cost side to allow for dead-weight losses from taxation and (2) a further addition corresponding to the enormous, but previously neglected, incidental costs associated with an inefficient public loan system. Beyond this I have drawn attention to the need for a downward revision to benefit/cost analyses (whether in Canada or elsewhere) because of the potential use of education in the socially wasteful practices of job-market signaling and occupational licensure. The finding of very high private rates of return, meanwhile, indicates that tuition could be raised significantly without large effects on enrollment.

With respect to the case for intervention on "equality" grounds, I have shown that the present system aggravates rather than ameliorates reasonable notions of equity.

Applications of the theory of market structure and organization have indicated the inevitability of the crowding out of private by public academic institutions and the increase of the monopoly power and social inefficiency of the latter. But it has also been shown that subsidies of any kind, whether public or private, tend to have potentially detrimental consequences for efficiency, and especially if they are directed straight to institutions rather than to students.

Finally, considerations of public choice remind us that the political process that advocates rely upon to pursue external benefits, equity, and so on, does not, in practice, respect the preferences of a wide and undifferentiated electorate but tends to allow particular interest groups (including politicians, bureaucrats, teachers, and middle-class students) to exploit asymmetric political power. The "pure" recommendations of traditional welfare economics (public finance) thus appear to be associated with some vision of perfect democracy and benevolent government. And it is in this way primarily that a conflict among economic approaches has been illustrated.

Notes

1. Elchanan Cohn, *The Economics of Education*, (New York: Ballinger, 1979).
2. Ibid.
3. Francois Vaillancourt and Irene Henriques, "The Returns to University Schooling in Canada," *Canadian Public Policy*, VI: 4, (1986).
4. Martin D. Dooley, "The Overeducated Canadians: Changes in the Relationships Among Earnings, Education and Age for Canadian Men: 1971-81," *Canadian Journal of Economics* (February, 1986).
5. Glenn P. Jenkins, "Capital in Canada, Its Social and Private Performance, 1965-1974," Discussion paper, *Economic Council of Canada* no. 98, 1977.
6. Cohn, op. cit., p. 46.
7. H.F. Campbell, *A Benefit/Cost Rule for an Additional Public Project in Canada*, Ph.D. dissertation (Queen's University, 1972); Edgar K. Browning, "The Marginal Cost of Public Funds," *Journal of Political Economy*, (1976), pp. 283-98; C. Stuart, "Swedish Tax Rates, Lab or Supply and Tax Revenues," *Journal of Political Economy*, (1981), pp. 1020-38; and A.B. Atkinson and N. Stern, "Pigou, Taxation and Public Goods," *Review of Economic Studies* (1974), pp. 119-28.
8. C.L. Ballard, J.B. Shoven and J. Whalley, "General Equilibrium Computations on the Marginal Welfare Costs of Taxation," *American Economic Review*, 75: 1 (March 1985).
9. Edgar K. Browning and Jacquelene M. Browning, *Public Finance and the Price System*, 3rd ed., (New York: Macmillan, 1987).
10. Dan Usher, "Tax Evasion and the Marginal Cost of Public Funds," *Economic Inquiry*, vol. XXIV, October 1986.
11. R. Boadway, N. Bruce and J. Mints, *Capital Income Taxes in Canada: Analysis and Policy*, (Canadian Tax Foundation, 1986).
12. Determined in private conversation with Jack Mints, one of the authors of the Boadway, Bruce, and Mints study, 1986.
13. Cohn, op. cit.
14. Milton and Rose Friedman, *Free to Choose: A Personal Statement* (New York: Harcourt Brace Jovanovich, 1980).
15. Sam Peltsmann, "The Effect of Government Subsidies in Kind of Private Expenditures: The Case of Higher Education," *Journal of Political Economy* 81: 1 (Jan. 1973).
16. See P.R.G. Layard and A.A. Walters, *Microeconomic Theory*, (New York: McGraw Hill, 1978).
17. A. Michael Spence, "Job Market Signaling," *Quarterly Journal of Economics*, (August, 1973).
18. Kevin Lang, "Pareto Improving Minimum Wage Laws," *Economy Inquiry*, vol. m (January 1987).
19. H. Gregg Lewis, *Union Relative Wage Effects: A Survey, 1986* (Chicago: Chicago University Press, 1986).
20. David Dodge, "Education and Occupational Licensure," in *Education for the Seventies*, (Economic Council of Canada, 1973).
21. Ibid.
22. Vaillancourt and Henriques, op. cit.
23. See E. L. Hansen and B.A. Weisbrod, *Benefits, Costs and Finances of Public Higher Education*, (Chicago: Markham Publishing Company, 1969).

24. George J. Stigler, "Imperfections in the Capital Market," *Journal of Political Economy*, vol. 75 (1967).
25. Stigler, op. cit., argues that the legal limitation on the worker's bargaining rights should be called an imperfection-of-the-labor-market. The term "imperfection," however, cannot directly be switched to the labor market. What is certainly happening is a market "blockage," constraint or restriction. A market that the government does not allow to exist can be neither imperfect nor perfect. Similarly, where only a part of a market is forbidden the resultant "inadequacies" are not necessarily inherent in the market system itself.
26. This appears in Friedman's version of his argument in *Capitalism and Freedom* (Chicago: University of Chicago Press, 1962), p. 105.
27. Stigler, op. cit.
28. Karl Shell et al., "The Educational Opportunity Bank," *National Tax Journal*, March 1968.
29. Friedman, *Capitalism*, p. 105.
30. See William A. Niskanen, *Bureaucracy and Representative Government* (Cambridge, MA: Harvard University Press, 1971).
31. Myles B. Foster, *A Study of the Government of Canada's Loan Guarantee and Direct Lending Programs*, (Ottawa, Canada: Department of Finance, 1986).
32. John Rawls, *A Theory of Justice* (Cambridge, MA.: Harvard University Press, 1971).
33. Friedman and Friedman, op. cit.
34. Ibid., p. 177.
35. Adam Smith, *The Wealth of Nations*, Book V (New York: The Modern Library, Edwin Cannan Edition, 1950), p. 283.
36. Ibid., p. 284.
37. Ibid.
38. E.G. West, *Adam Smith, The Man and His Works* (Indianapolis, IN: Liberty Press, 1976), p. 44.
39. J.S. Mill, "Endowments," *The Jurist*, 1833.
40. Sir Robert Lowe, *Middle Class Education: Endowment or Free Trade?* (1868).
41. Richard Freeman, "Unionism and the Dispersion of Wages," Harvard University Discussion Paper No. 629, June 1978.
42. J.S. Mill, *Principles of Political Economy* (reprint ed., :Augustus Kelley, 1969), p. 942.
43. Ibid., p. 956.
44. J.S. Mill, *On Liberty* (New York: F.S. Crofts and Company, 1947; reprint ed., London: 1972), p. 240.
45. D.A. Winstanley, *The University of Cambridge—in the Eighteenth Century* (London: Cambridge University Press, 1922).
46. Smith, *Wealth of Nations*, Book V, Chap. 1, Part III, Art. II.
47. Smith, op. cit. V, p. 265.
48. *Digest of Education Statistics 1985—86*, (Washington, D.C.: National Center for Educational Statistics, Table 139).
49. *Digest of Education Statistics 1986*, (Washington, D.C.: National Center for Educational Statistics, Table 87).
50. Projections of Education Statistics to 1990-91 by Martin M. Frankel and Deborah E. Gerald, National Center for Education Statistics, U.S. Department of Education 1982. Table 20.

51. William Orsechowski, "Economic Models of Bureaucracy: Survey, Extensions and Evidence," in *Budgets and Bureaucrats* ed. Tom Borcherding (Durham, NC: Duke University Press, 1977).
52. D. Sisk, "A Theory of Government Enterprise: University PhD Production," *Public Choice*, vol. 37, no. 2, 1981, pp. 357–63.
53. Friedman and Friedman, *Free to Choose*, p. 172.

6

The Economics of Fundamental Research

Stephen P. Dresch

This paper was initially undertaken in 1976 at the request of Bruce L. R. Smith as part of a larger study of the state of academic science, supported by the National Science Foundation. At the request of John W. Sommer, it was resuscitated for presentation at the meetings of the Association for Public Policy Analysis and Management (Austin, Texas; October 1986) and for inclusion in the present volume. I would note the contributions, direct and indirect, of the late Derek J. de Solla Price and of W. Lewis Hyde, Adair L Waldenberg, Merton J. Peck, Kenneth R. Janson, and (especially) Karol I. Pelc, none of whom, of course, can be deemed responsible for the conclusions reached.

Introduction

Discussions of the "economics" of fundamental research have two distinctive characteristics. First, they are almost invariably cast from a "statist" perspective, with the nation-state constituting not only the unit of observation but also the ultimately responsible actor. Second, they generally involve the pursuit of two parallel, nonintersecting lines of discussion, focusing, on the one hand, on the issue of the nation's need for research (culminating in an indefinitely long list of specific needs for or contributions of research, e.g., national defense, conquest of disease, economic growth, environmental quality...) and, on the other hand, on the issue of how much research the nation can "afford" (culminating in another, also indefinitely long, list of those compelling social needs that can be viewed as competing with research for scarce national resources, e.g., military preparedness, medical care, capital investment, and so on). While appearing to recognize that the essential issue concerns the relative benefits associated with alternative uses of resources, the nonquantified, virtually sacerdotal nature of the items appearing in each list (with many items appearing in both) effectively insures that the discussion will not contribute to informed and enlightened action on the part either of the state or of other agencies (public or private) within it.

171

The premise of this essay is that the fundamental inadequacy of the prevailing economics of fundamental research is the failure to identify what it is that research contributes to society. When this issue is clarified a more operational, decentralized, although perhaps no less difficult, approach to the issue of the allocation of resources to fundamental research becomes possible.

Social Warrants For Fundamental Research:
Ideational vs. Instrumental

Two essentially different views of the social functions of (or warrants for) fundamental research predominate in public and scholarly discussions of these issues. One conceives of research as having inherent social utility, while the other conceives of research as an investment in stock of useful knowledge. Because neither, it will be argued, provides an adequate basis for informed action, it is necessary to formulate a third perspective, one that conceives of research as an investment, not in knowledge in general, but in the capabilities of individuals, when those capabilities are in demand for purposes quite unrelated to research per se.

The Classical View: "Ideational" Science

Historically, the predominant conception is of fundamental research as an activity having social utility in and of itself, not unlike, e.g., pyramids or great works of art, music or literature. The value of science, in this "classical" view, is entirely in the eye of the beholder; the benefits of science are purely ideational, although no less real on that account. This ideational science might well have external objective ramifications, for example, it might influence behavior as a result of the impact of science on the way in which individuals view the world, but these ramifications would be indistinguishable from those of other classes of ideas (philosophical, religious, and so on). In this view, science itself has no direct application, and research, as the active, dynamic face of science, is not justified on grounds of its potential value in application. The value of research resides, simply, in the presence of scientists doing science, a mode of social consumption comparable to the building of public monuments or the commissioning of symphonies or other works of art. The presence of science simply constitutes one of the many expressions of a civilized society.

As discussed by Habermas,[1] central to this classical view of science was the perception of a virtually unbridgeable chasm between "theory" (including science) and "practice" (including technology). The concern of theory was with the "immutable essence of things," while the conduct of practical affairs was "pragmatically practiced according to traditional patterns of skill." In fact, this chasm was bridged, but only indirectly; theory "obtain[ed] practical validity only by molding the manner of life of men engaged in theory." Thus, the capacity to comprehend (and engage in) theory, to perceive the "immutable essence of things," provided an ethical orientation to action and thus represented a sociocultural qualification required of those whose practical actions would have consequences for others. Knowledge of theory provided the moral sanction for practical action, while practical action itself required only pragmatic, instrumental, technical qualifications that were quite unrelated to theory.

The Contemporary View: "Instrumental" Science

The preceding, historically descriptive relationship between theoretical and practical knowledge contrasts sharply with the contemporary perception that there exists a unidirectional flow from science to technology to practice. As reflected in the currently popular cliché concerning the progressively more pervasive impacts of science on virtually all aspects of human existence, theoretical, scientific knowledge does have the potential of direct, practical application: knowledge as the prerequisite for the ethical exercise of practical power has been superceded by knowledge itself as practical power.

From this perspective fundamental research is viewed as an investment in a stock of useful, directly applicable knowledge. Thus, through research, chemistry contributes knowledge directly employed in the chemical industry, physics contributes the knowledge necessary for nuclear weapons and high-temperature superconductors, and so on. This view of science as a body of knowledge, augmented through research, the applications of which are of direct benefit to society, underlies the conventional differentiation between basic research, applied research, and development. Research results in an augmentation or net addition to the stock of knowledge: basic research provides the superstructure of these net additions, while applied research fills in the crevices of direct relevance to particular applications. Development contributes the last engineering details. The essential point is that there is perceived to be a unidirectional flow from basic research to applied research to development, and the value at each stage derives from the stream of benefits flowing from the practical actions made possible by the advance of knowledge.[2]

Resource Allocation: Ideational vs. Instrumental Science

Clearly, these two contrasting perceptions of research are not mutually exclusive. On the one hand, science has, at least historically, been supported as a form of pure social (and individual) consumption, without regard to any possible practical benefits. On the other, certainly there does exist something that might be characterized as a stock of knowledge, augmentations of which, obtained through research, can be viewed as giving rise to a flow of future (albeit unpredictable) benefits. However, the fundamental issue is this: Which model, or perception of the role of research, is relevant to decisions at the margin concerning the level and composition of support for research? Stated differently, which model provides the most effective conceptual and operational basis for determining the (social) demand for and optimal allocation of resources to research?

In principle, either the intrinsic-utility or the investment-in-knowledge conceptions can be utilized, at least conceptually, to derive a social demand for and optimal allocation of resources to fundamental research:

1. If intrinsic utility is the justification, then the social demand is for a pure public (consumption) good, which can be represented as the vertical summation of individual demands. Equating the marginal social benefit represented by this demand function with marginal cost, the socially optimal allocation of resources to research is determined.
2. If fundamental research is justified by the benefits flowing from future applications of new knowledge, then it is conceptually meaningful to conceive of the present value of the flow of benefits to prospective extensions (investments) in the stock of knowledge, with equation of marginal benefits and costs again determining the optimal allocation of resources to research.[3] The only complexity is that, in contrast to stocks of conventional capital, the stock of knowledge is itself a pure public (capital) good, one the benefits of which it is undesirable, if not impossible, to fully appropriate privately.

While the investment-in-knowledge conception has progressively displaced the intrinsic-utility or ideational conception of research as the dogma of science, the intrinsic-utility conception retains substantial force with reference especially to fundamental research. This is attributable largely to the limited *ex ante* operational usefulness of the investment-in-knowledge conception to fundamental research. *Ex post*, it may indeed be possible to trace specific practical applications of science to particular advances in knowledge attributable to specific research undertakings. *Ex ante*, however, it is effectively impossible to identify those future applications that are contingent upon current research, necessitating that the existence of these future applications be accepted on faith. However, faith in the future applicability of prospective new knowledge is, fundamentally, only a doctrinal variant of the more general ideational or intrinsic-utility justification for research. Thus, ironically, the intrinsic-utility model not only provides a more operational approach to the determination of the social demand for research than does the investment-in-knowledge model, but it, indeed, subsumes the latter.

Thus, it is not surprising that appeals for support for science as an investment in prospectively useful knowledge commonly degenerate into appeals for support of science as an end in itself. Because it is impossible to anticipate what benefits will flow from fundamental research, it is inappropriate to ask the scientist to justify social subvention of his research; that research becomes its own justification.

Entirely apart from the issue of operational usefulness, a serious difficulty associated with both of the dominant conceptions of fundamental research (social-consumption and investment-in-knowledge) is that they call into serious question the rationality of the observed rate at which resources are allocated to research.

Ideational Science Versus Art. If research is supported as a form of pure social consumption, the benefits can be only ideational. However, the great mass of society's members can have, at best, only a vague awareness of the existence of scientists engaged in fundamental research, and even an attenuated understanding of the substance of that research will be accessible only to a vanishingly small minority of nonscientists. In this context, it is difficult to believe that society would be prepared to devote 1 percent of GNP to science (the approximate current allocation to basic and applied research) on the grounds of purely ideational social utility.

Whatever the level of utility derived by the "representative" member of society from the existence of scientists engaged in science, that utility would not be expected to be greater than the utility associated with, for example, the arts. Knowledge of and appreciation for the arts must be universal, but popular awareness of the arts must be substantially greater than is popular awareness and appreciation of science. People actually have first-hand exposure to symphony orchestras and operas, while virtually no nonscientist observes or is even aware of (much less obtains utility simply from the conduct of) scientific research. And, while institutions such as the Smithsonian, the Chicago Museum of Science and Industry, and Munich's Deutsches Museum offer popular entree to the wonders of science to significant numbers of people (although their emphases, and the interests of their visitors, focus primarily on technology rather than on science), the number visiting art museums must be substantially greater. Yet, the social resources devoted to science dramatically exceed the resources devoted to the arts (on the order of 15:1).

It might be said that the supply of inputs (especially of capable personnel) to social-utility-generating art is substantially less elastic than it is to social-utility-generating science. Specifically, it would be argued, social utility, whether of art or of science, flows not simply from artists or scientists engaged in art or science; rather, social utility is a function of the quality of artistic and scientific endeavor, while quality, in either art or science, is the consequence of the artistic or scientific talents of the practitioners, talents that are not uniformly distributed over the population. Thus, as the allocation of resources to either art or science is increased, the talents of marginal personnel (the last added to the cadre of practitioners) must decline, implying diminishing marginal social utility.

To explain the disproportionate allocation of resources to science relative to art on grounds of inelasticity of supply of talent, however, requires that the distribution of artistic talent be substantially more highly skewed than the distribution of scientific talent. In light of substantial evidence of an extremely skewed distribution of scientific talent (as discussed further below), this seems highly unlikely.[4] At the least, it is difficult to believe that differences in the distributions of artistic and scientific talents can explain the observed order-of-magnitude difference in social resource allocation.

Instrumental Science Versus Physical Capital. As an investment in knowledge motivated by anticipated future returns it might well be argued that the observed allocation of resources to fundamental research is not obviously irrational. With "advances in knowledge and n.e.c [not elsewhere classified]" estimated to have contributed 0.92 percentage points to the growth rate of national "income over the period 1929 to 1969, in contrast to an estimated contribution of only 0.5 percentage points attributable to growth in the physical capital stock, an investment in research (basic and applied) only one-fifteenth as great as gross investment in physical capital might seem, if anything, to be irrationally low."[5]

However, of the contribution of "advances in knowledge and n.e.c." to economic growth, much of that (unknown) component attributable to R&D must be assigned to development, and together research and development expenditure is almost one-fifth as great as gross physical investment. In light of such considerations as (1) the non-R&D related n.e.c. component of this "unassignable" contribution to growth and (2) the underestimation of expenditures on research resulting from inclusion of significant research support in other accounts (e.g., ostensibly instructional expenditures of the higher education sector), the apparent disproportion between investments in physical capital and investments in knowledge narrows further.

Also relevant here is the issue of the relative elasticities of supply of physical capital goods and of scientific talent. While capital goods sectors may exhibit relative inelasticity of supply in the short run, there is no reason to believe that this elasticity is not quite high in the intermediate and in the long run, when industry capacities can be adapted. In contrast, as suggested in the discussion of the relative elasticities of supply of scientific versus artistic talents, the distribution of scientific ability or competence is highly skewed, while this ability or competence is the primary determinant of the contribution of research to new knowledge. Thus, available evidence suggests that the marginal researcher, the last one admitted to the ranks of the active scientific community, contributes little or nothing to the stock of scientific knowledge.

Specifically, the distribution of scientific productivities is such that, in virtually all fields at all times, the greatest share of scientific output is produced by a very small fraction of all active scientists. Consider, for example, the cohort of young scientists publishing in the scientific literature for the first time in a given year, examined by Price and Gursey:[6] "Over the 30- to 40-year professional lifetime of members of the cohort, 25 percent of the cohort's members will contribute more than 5 percent of the scientific papers attributable to the cohort, and the most productive 5 percent will account for more than half of the cohort's published output. Two-thirds of the cohort will in fact vanish after their first appearance in the scientific literature. If any sort of quality adjustment were applied to these publications, the skewness of the distribution of scientific productivity would almost inevitably be found to be even more extreme.

The general conclusion must be that a very small proportion of ever-active scientists and scholars must be credited with the greatest bulk of contributions to scientific and scholarly knowledge, even allowing for a substantial margin of error in the computations and for possibly significant variations over fields. Thus, at the margin, resources devoted to research produce very little of ultimate scientific value. Assuming even a highly imperfect mechanism of selection (and, most importantly, of self-selection) of scientists, i.e., for predicting an individual's future scientific productivity (contingent on his pursuit of a scientific career), for all practical purposes it can be reasonably concluded that the scientific world (and the national economy) would lose little in terms of scientific knowledge as a result of, for example, *ex ante* abortion of 50 percent of a cohort that would otherwise reach the stage of active participant in fundamental scientific work at the research front. Whatever the reduction in support for scientific work, the reduction in the level of scientific output (additions to knowledge) would certainly be much less than proportionate.

Thus, for example, in a stylized model of fundamental science Dresch and Janson find that a roughly twofold (94 percent) increase in the size of the cadre of fundamental scientists, from 0.47 to 0.91 percent of the underlying population, would result in only a 50 percent increase in the quantity of scientific output (e.g., publications) and only a 36 percent increase in the scientific value of these contributions; while a further 225 percent increase in the science cadre, to 3 percent of the population, would increase the quantity of output by less than 100 percent and its scientific value by only 40 percent.[7]

In short, because scientific productivities are not uniformly distributed over the population, employment of a greater fraction of the labor force in the scientific enterprise would be expected to result in rapid diminishing returns as measured by contributions to knowledge. Even if the long-run returns to new knowledge were predictable, substantial, and nondiminishing, the stream of returns to small, scientific contributions of the marginal, or last hired scientist, engaged in either basic or applied research or in development would eventually be less than the benefit that would derive from alternate employment. At that point, funding of research (as an investment in knowledge or in its applications) should cease. Thus, the skewed distribution of scientific ability results in a highly inelastic supply of scientific knowledge, placing a severe brake on the flow of resources to investments in knowledge, while no similar brake is imposed on investments in physical capital.

From the foregoing considerations, it can be concluded that either the current level of support for scientific research must be of questionable rationality, or, at the margin, that support must be motivated by considerations other than intrinsic social utility or the augmentation of the global stock of knowledge. In the search for a third, alternative, conception of the social functions of and warrants for fundamental research, it is reasonable to begin by examining further the transition from the classical ideational view of science to the contemporary instrumental conception.

If there was any relationship historically between theory/science and practice/technology, it was the reverse of that conventionally posited currently: Advances in science were driven by advances in technology. Modern astronomy developed from the practice of astrology and from improvements in lenses, chemistry from the evolution of the dye and related chemical industries, classical thermodynamics from the development of the steam engine. In essence, practical action, experience, provided numerous uncontrolled experiments through which instrumental knowledge (technology) was augmented, and these augmentations of instrumental knowledge made possible advances in theoretical knowledge as well.[8]

The transition from the classical intrinsic-utility conception of the role of science to the current instrumental-investment conception can be argued to have been driven by a fundamental change in this historically descriptive relationship between science and technology. However, the characterization of the newly emerging relationship between science and technology as involving a unidirectional flow from the former to the latter is, at best, a seriously misleading caricature.

Perhaps the most misleading aspect of the conventional, unidirectional view of the science-technology relationship is the implicit attribution of purposiveness to scientific development. Scientific advances, supposedly, are motivated by their prospective practical uses or applications. In fact, when the consequences of scientific work can be predicted with any degree of certainty, the effort is inevitably primarily of an engineering nature. Fundamental knowledge may be augmented in the process, but this is essentially a byproduct, even an unintended byproduct, of technological work. Stated somewhat differently, science may have become susceptible to direct application, but specific prospective applications do not motivate or induce specific augmentations of scientific knowledge.

A more descriptive characterization of the evolving relationship between science and technology would emphasize reciprocity, multidirectional influences, and flows. Augmentations of scientific knowledge may not be motivated by specific practical consequences, but effective practical action necessitates, is dependent upon, scientific knowledge; scientific developments do have practical, technological implications. The technologist or engineer of several centuries ago would have benefited little from a theoretical knowledge of Newtonian physics; in contrast, the contemporary technologist is doomed to failure or, at the least, inferiority or inefficiency in the absence of fundamental scientific knowledge.[9]

Although the eventual feasibility of nuclear weapons cannot be argued to have provided the motivation for the development of nuclear physics, the effective realization of the objectives of the Manhattan Project would have been impossible in the absence of research-front knowledge of nuclear physics. Historically, effective contributions to science required the scientists' grasp of engineering, but not vice versa. Today, the engineer is comparably dependent on a research-front knowledge of science. For example, the key personnel on the Manhattan Project were scientists functioning as engineers, because only scientists possessed the fundamental knowledge necessary for the engineering effort. The relationship between science and engineering, between theory and practice, truly has become reciprocal.

At this point a third perception of the social role of fundamental research begins to emerge; in fact, knowledge does "advance," albeit in a manner that is unpredictable and with uncertain practical consequences. And, in a variety of pursuits a firm command over the margin of knowledge is a prerequisite of effective performance. Finally, research scientists do perform social functions other than research, and their effectiveness in these other functions is affected by, indeed is dependent upon, their participation in research.

From this third conception of the social functions of and warrants for fundamental research, very different from the intrinsic-utility and investment-in-knowledge conceptions, the purely scientific output of the research performer is irrelevant, no more than a fortunately accidental (and generally inframarginal) byproduct. The key issue concerns the effectiveness of the performer in some other dimension. Thus, for example, the value of the research of the academic scientist resides not in the articles he publishes, which are, in any event, read only by other (primarily academic) scientists (the most intensely interested of whom will have seen the article in draft or preprint form long before its formal publication[10]), but in the quality of his students, the value of his advice as a consultant to government or industry, and so on. More generally, the value of research is reflected not in the "new knowledge" (if any) that is produced and not in the (possibly nonexistent) "applications" of these (also possibly nonexistent) augmentations of knowledge, but in the capability of the researcher to produce on contract something that it is possible for a customer to order on the basis of knowledge at hand, whether a neutron bomb, an explanation for acquired immune deficiency syndrome, an adequately educated student.... Thus, as characterized by Price, "...society,

> somehow manifested, decides that some new understanding or new data is needed for a job (for example to locate a new airport, inoculate a population against some disease, advise on the building of various alternative energy plants, etc.) [T]he research function [is] clear. It is a question of knowledge that society needs and must provide...either through contract or through an agency charged with such a mission. In either case the customers know what they want and can later decide whether their wants have been satisfactorily provided in relation to the costs and competences. The service provided is then in the nature of an investment good and can be evaluated as technological research in terms of whether the outcome measures up to the service specified or contracted for."[11]

More generally stated, these directly valued functions involve (1) technological applications of expertise, not for the purpose of augmenting knowledge but rather for the purpose of achieving what is perceived (by the customer as well as by the supplier) to be a practical, attainable objective, and/or (2) the development of students possessing research-front knowledge and capable of providing these technological applications of expertise.

The Manhattan Project, the space program, the Strategic Defense Initiative, and the searches for causes and cures of specific diseases constitute particularly visible technological applications of research-front expertise. In practice, it may be difficult to distinguish these directly valued "engineering" services of research-front scientists from their fundamental research, and the distinction is certainly not well captured by the concepts of either development or applied research in the usual R&D trilogy. For present purposes it is not necessary to develop a fully operational definition of this activity. The essential points are that it is possible (1) for the customer (perhaps with expert assistance) to identify the objective or product, (2) for a suitaby trained individual or group to produce and deliver something approximating the desired objective or product, and (3) for the effectiveness of the producing individual or group (or, for the quality of the product) to be enhanced through knowledge of research-front developments. Knowledge in a more general sense can be augmented in the process, or the technological product so produced may, in addition to its primary objective, create the opportunity to acquire more fundamental knowledge hitherto unavailable, but these byproducts will not have provided the underlying rationale for the endeavor.

Viewed in these terms, the basic valuational question relevant to the support of research has the form: How much more effective as a producer of students, of vaccines for heretofore unknown diseases, and of sophisticated military hardware is a person who has been engaged in research than is one who has not been engaged in fundamental research? Increments in effectiveness can then be contrasted with increments in research activity, providing the basis for identifying the socially optimal allocation of resources to research. In this context, research has value precisely because knowledge does, indeed, advance. A casual nonparticipant observer can claim a command over any new knowledge only after an active participant in its development takes time to "popularize" the achievement. If we assume arbitrarily, but not unreasonably, that it takes ten years to fully establish and work out any significant change in the state of science to the point that it can be put forth (even to professionally interested nonparticipants in its development, as the net orthodoxy), and if, over the period of a decade knowledge in a given field doubles, as indicated by the rate of growth of scientific literature, then a "mere observer," even one professionally trained, will be operating, on average, on the basis of knowledge that is 50 percent obsolete. A parallel argument is developed by Price,[12] who notes that the investment required to bring an individual to the research front has roughly four years of postbaccalaureate training. With a growth rate of knowledge (scientific literature) of 7 percent per year (equivalent to the ten-year doubling period indicted above), in the absence of further investment in the maintenance of research-front capabilities, the Ph.D. scientist would obsolesce at an annual rate of 7 percent. Considering that, as a means of obtaining access to research-front knowledge, the alternate to further investment in an established scientist is the training of new Ph.D.'s at an annual rate of investment in the maintenance of research-front capabilities equal to 28 percent of the scientist's time (i.e., 7 percent of four years of graduate education). Because this quantification assumes, most importantly, that an established scientist is, on average, no more efficient than the average graduate student in the development and maintenance of research-front capabilities, when selection and self-selection of those scientists whose research-front capabilities are sustained would be expected to leave only the more efficient in this group (with others diverted into occupations not requiring research-front knowledge, e.g., management and administration), it would appear to offer an upper bound of the necessary rate of investment in the maintenance of research-front knowledge.

In light of the uncertainties associated with new knowledge, e.g., the unanticipated side-effects that may accompany a new drug, the as yet unrecognized environmental consequences of a new source of energy, or the adverse strategic responses of a potential adversary to installation of a newly feasible weapons system, in many applications a substantial obsolescence may actually be desirable. But, for most purposes this degree of obsolescence would entail serious costs, as for example, in failing to consider the implications of current research-front developments in decisions regarding substantial investments in a particular energy or weapons system that might be doomed to obsolescence before it would even reach the stage of operation.

Especially in the domain of advanced education and training, obsolescence of the indicated magnitude would imply probably fatal inefficiency. Imagine a graduate faculty whose active participation at the research-front had ended ten or more years earlier and who would, in consequence, be operating with 50 percent obsolete knowledge, capable of bringing graduate students only to the research front as it had existed ten years earlier. If it is assumed, reasonably, that the cost of bringing a graduate student to any research-front is independent of whether that front is current or obsolete, then the only cost of bringing the student to the current front rather than to the decade earlier front is the faculty research necessary to stave off obsolescence.

The issue with respect to that faculty research, then, is this: Is the value of a nonobsolete new Ph.D. greater than that of an obsolete new Ph.D. by an amount sufficient to justify support of that faculty research necessary to produce the former rather than the latter? That is, we must compare current value of the new Ph.D., who has been kept on ice (placed in suspended animation) for a decade with that of a new Ph.D. whose training has brought him into the current research front. Such a comparison, obviously, is difficult to make, since the world provides no obvious natural experiments on which to base the calculations.

One possible index of the relative value of a nonobsolete to an obsolete new Ph.D. might be provided by lifetime earnings differentials of Ph.D.'s related to the quality of graduate program, on the assumption that the "quality" index reflects differences in obsolescence of faculty. However, even if that assumption is justified, as it probably is, the better schools are more selective, suggesting that a significant fraction of the differential may be related to differences in innate talent, ability, and prior achievement. On the other hand, differences in the postschooling employments of Ph.D.'s from different quality classes of graduate schools suggests that graduates of the better schools tend to select employment with relatively lesser pecuniary income and greater nonpecuniary perquisites (interesting and challenging colleagues, prestige, and so forth). Thus, even the direction of bias would be uncertain.

In any event, if the difference in value could be determined, this would indicate the level of faculty research that would be justified solely on grounds of the implied benefit of less obsolete graduate students. If the (discounted) lifetime value of a 50 percent obsolete new Ph.D. V would be enhanced by ΔV as a result of an additional decade of knowledge, i.e., if he were rendered nonobsolete, and if the annual ratio of Ph.D. production to graduate faculty were y, then the level of research support per faculty member that would be fully compensated by the augmented value of new Ph.D.'s would be $\Delta V \cdot y$. More generally, the value of students (V) probably increases at a decreasing rate with increases in faculty research (R), reflecting a corresponding change in faculty obsolescence (Z), decreasing at a decreasing rate with increases in the level of research effort. The "optimal" degree of faculty obsolescence, then, would be that level of (Z) for which $(dV/dZ)(dZ/dR) - 1/y$, measuring R in monetary terms.[13]

The general point of the foregoing, to reiterate, is that (for purposes of decisions concerning the allocation of resources to fundamental research) research itself, or the products of that research, cannot be viewed as the essential output. Rather, research must be viewed as an activity essential for performance of other, directly valued, functions. Specifically, research represents the process by which the capabilities of researchers, and hence their effectiveness in education and production are maintained over time, in the face of what would otherwise constitute an inexorable process of obsolescence.

Institutionalization And Financing Of Fundamental Research In An International/Interorganizational Context

Any conception of the social warrants for fundamental research must address the issue of the motivations for the allocation of resources to science (as distinct from the socially optimal allocation), recognizing that these resources may be allocated by society at large (through the instrumentality of the state) or by its component parts, e.g., firms/enterprises, foundations, scientists individually, or in collectivities such as universities). This issue of motivation and the related issues of institutionalization and financing of fundamental research are particularly critical in light of the "free-good" character of the augmentations of scientific knowledge flowing from fundamental research and in light of the nonmonolithic nature of the global science enterprise. And, with reference to these issues, the three alternative conceptions developed above lead to radically different answers to the question of why societies and their constituent parts choose to devote resources to science.

Ideational Science

If fundamental research has only noninstrumental, intrinsic utility, then several distinctly different motivations can be identified for devoting resources to science. First, an individual or organization might allocate resources to research simply for the direct satisfaction derived by the individual or by the organization's members. If the satisfaction derives from the process of research per se, i.e., from participation in research (or its underwriting), then the optimal allocation will be that which will be implied by maximization of private utility. If, alternatively, that satisfaction derives from the ideational results of research (new knowledge), then the source of satisfaction is a pure public good; i.e., the pleasure I derive from research does not reduce the pleasure that you derive from that research. Because of this public goods character of research, either (1) individuals will attempt to obtain a free ride, implying an underallocation of resources to research, or (2) research will be supported by some overarching entity (or entities), for example, clubs or governments capable of achieving an appropriate consolidation (vertical summation) of individual demands.[14]

Second, the intrinsic utility may derive in part from the recognition by others of the research accomplished or supported by an individual or group. In this case, the support of research is deemed to confer prestige on the supporter, and research is undertaken as a form of conspicuous individual or social consumption. Historically, such considerations (as well as intrinsic private utility) can be argued to have motivated the support of science by the nobility,[15] by those of great mercantile or industrial wealth,[16] and by organizations such as the church. In the twentieth century, one might argue that national prestige has motivated governmental support of fundamental science,[17] with the status of a country determined in part by, for example, its share of Nobel laureates. The resultant prestige may be of value not only in its own right but also because of the influence it confers in other domains (e.g., diplomatic) or because of social as well as scientific emulation (e.g., of the political or economic system capable of achieving such prestige in science). This type of motivation is one of several possible sources of what might be characterized as "international competition" in science, a phenomenon that might also be observed on the part of other (sub- or supranational) entities (e.g., corporations) as well.[18] The critical point, however, is that science is of value not in its own right but because of its influence on the perceptions others have of the research-sponsoring entity, which will determine its level of support for science accordingly.

Finally, engagement in and/or support of research may be deemed necessary for the evidence it provides of the noninstrumental (e.g., social or cultural) qualifications for performance in other domains. Thus, as discussed above, the distinguishing character of the professions, historically, has been the possession by their members of appropriate (socially sanctioned) moral qualifications for the performance of functions having consequences for the welfare of others, with the capacity to comprehend and engage in science deemed to provide an ethical orientation to practical action. In this case, the level of scientific activity will reflect the level of demand for those personnel for whom science is deemed to provide necessary noninstrumental qualifications for performance and on the effectiveness of which the noninstrumental qualifications of these personnel can be regulated, either by the market or by governmental fiat.

Instrumental Science

Turning to the second, more contemporary, perception of research as an investment in a stock of instrumentally useful knowledge, serious problems are confronted. As has been discussed, knowledge as a stock of productive capital is distinguished by its public goods character. Once knowledge exists it may not be possible and, if possible, it will not be desirable (from a broader social perspective) to restrict access to and utilization of it.

To the degree to which access by others can be precluded, an entity may have some incentive to engage in research. However, the level of research that will be supported will be less than would be the case were the benefits of maximal exploitation to be recognized. The resultant underinvestment by private (socially subordinate) units and their motivations for precluding access by others are argued to provide the justification for governmental subvention of research, with provision of free access to the knowledge thus produced.

However, short of a global governmental subvention, governmental underwriting does not resolve the problem. Even if access by other countries to the results of any country's research can be prevented, global investment in research will remain nonoptimal. Although there may be international competition in science, much of the work supported in any country will be duplicative of that supported in others, and the progress of science in all countries will be retarded by comparison to a global regime under which access to each country's scientific accomplishments is freely available to all other countries.

In fact, in fundamental science it will be extremely difficult, if not impossible, to foreclose access, simply by the nature of the work involved. Within any system, e.g., country, science will have value only if it is relatively freely available to all. However, given the form in which fundamental science is disseminated, through publications and, even more importantly, through collaboration by scientists in "invisible colleges," free access within any domain will virtually foreclose prohibitions of access to external parties. Thus, it will be effectively impossible for any country both to insure free internal access and to foreclose external access.

Even in the case of the United States, a major source of fundamental research, these considerations have devastating consequences for the rationalization of the allocation of resources to research. If the U.S. contribution to total world investment in knowledge is measured, using for purposes of argument, the U.S. share of the world scientific literature, then it would appear that at least 60 percent of new knowledge generated by research would be available to the U.S. even if it invested nothing in research. Such a free-rider policy might be considered ethically wrong, and, more fundamentally, if it were pursued by all countries, a free-rider policy would obviously lead to zero global investment in knowledge. Nonetheless, at the margin it would appear that the U.S. would lose little in terms of the general stock of available knowledge as a result of even a significant reduction in the level of research support. Viewed differently, the access of the U.S. to global scientific production provides a further basis for anticipating an elasticity of supply of knowledge substantially less than that of physical capital.[19]

Antiobsolescent Science

An important implication of the third conception of research as the primary determinant of the capabilities of the researcher in other, directly valued, pursuits is that it effectively responds to the vexing "free-rider" conundrum encountered by the instrumental, "investment" conception of fundamental research, especially in international and interorganizational contexts: Indeed, much of the advance of the world stock of knowledge, perhaps 60 percent, would occur even if the U.S. invested nothing in research. However, that knowledge would advance even in the absence of U.S. contributions does not imply that this advance would be available to the U.S. without its active participation in the international scientific enterprise. To be in a position to draw upon the margin of knowledge requires scientific capabilities that can be acquired only through active work at the margin; to track the advance at a distance necessarily implies that the "front" that is observed falls significantly short of the active front. Thus, whether to contribute to the advance of knowledge or to attempt to obtain a free ride from the efforts of others is ultimately not an ethical but a pragmatic issue; to exploit knowledge one must contribute to the creation of knowledge. While developed with reference to countries (nations), this argument applies with equal weight to subnational enterprises, e.g., enterprises and firms.

The implication of this argument, however, is that there exists a necessary interdependence between the efficient level of scientific activity in any one country (or enterprise firm) and the level of scientific activity in others, and vice versa. The greater the level of scientific activity elsewhere, the greater the incentive to engage in research in order to monitor and to be in a position to exploit scientific achievements elsewhere. However, the effort required to monitor scientific development elsewhere must be less than that required to achieve those developments, especially in light of the skewed distribution of scientific talent, which will imply rapidly diminishing augmentations of knowledge as the scale of research-front activity is increased. By implication, an increase in scientific activity elsewhere will generate a less than equiproportionate increase in the rate of augmentation of knowledge and hence will motivate a less than equiproportionate increase in the desirable level of "own" research effort. Thus, there presumably exists a stable, "equilibrium" relationship between research in any given country (enterprise/firm) and research in the rest of the world.

This relationship is represented stylistically in Figure 6.1, in which the desirable scale of fundamental research in country "A," denoted R_i and measured either in (real) monetary terms or in full-time-equivalent employment of persons engaged in fundamental research, is represented as a function of fundamental research in country "B," R and vice versa. The positive slopes of the curves indicate the increase in scale of scientific activity in each country motivated by additional research in the other country. However, because the slopes are increasing at, respectively, increasing/decreasing rates, there is a point of intersection beyond which neither party finds it desirable to devote additional resources to research. These slopes reflect both diminishing scientific returns to research in each country (attributable largely to the skewed distribution of scientific talent) and the fact that monitoring scientific activity elsewhere is less than a full-time occupation, i.e., that research front developments attributable to one full-time-equivalent scientist can be monitored by a scientist devoting less than full time to work at the front.

It should be emphasized that these positive reaction functions do not represent the operation of an "international (or interfirm)" competition in science. The objective is not to outproduce the other country (firm) but to be in a position to exploit the other country's (firm's) scientific achievements. Thus, ironically, the desire to appropriate the knowledge of others provides the motivation to contribute to the aggregate stock of knowledge, a rather interesting reversal of the free-rider position.

While the general characteristics of these research reaction functions are unambiguous, their precise positions (vertical/horizontal placements) are less determinate. In light of the preceding discussion of the role of research, it can be anticipated that the level of research effort is ultimately determined by the domestic (or intraorganizational) extraresearch functions of scientists. The demand for technological applications of expertise determines, directly or in-

FIGURE 6.1

Fundamental Research Reaction Functions

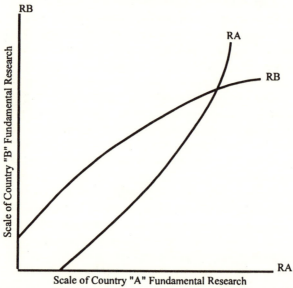

directly, the efficient allocation of resources to research, where the issue of the efficient allocation of resources to research is essentially one of the number of persons for whom knowledge of research front developments is a key determinant of effectiveness in other pursuits. Thus, for example, a change in the composition of economic activity in country "A" toward "meditation" would shift its research reaction function to the left (assuming that "meditation" is not a technologically sophisticated activity), while a military confrontation would move the function to the right.

This analysis has profound implications for the institutionalization and financing of fundamental research. While it is not possible to fully explore these implications within the confines of this discussion, the following provides at least a suggestive sketch.

The principal conclusion of the foregoing discussion is that fundamental research serves primarily as the mechanism by which the capabilities of scientific personnel are maintained over time. These capabilities have value, however, only to the degree to which they contribute to the effectiveness of research personnel in other pursuits. If there were to be no future demand for scientific/technological capabilities obtained and sustained through participation in fundamental research, then there would be no justification for maintaining the capabilities of scientific personnel, and research support could fall to zero (or to that level that would be justified by the intrinsic social utility of science).

In this context, the party with the most direct and immediate incentive to bear the costs of research is the researcher himself, who can anticipate higher earnings (prices for his services) in the future if he is less scientifically obsolete. Thus, in a pure market system the costs of research would be borne, in the first instance, by the scientist, who would recover these costs through subsequent earnings differentials attributable to research-maintained scientific knowledge and capabilities. Individual scientists would invest in their own capabilities (through research) up to the point that the return to that investment equaled the returns to other comparably risky investment alternatives. If there were an excess supply of nonobsolescent scientific capabilities at any point, the prices that could be commanded by research-front capabilities would be less than sufficient to compensate scientists for the costs of that research necessary to sustain these research-front capabilities, with the result that fewer individuals would invest in the maintenance of their capabilities; i.e., some persons would make career changes for which obsolescent capabilities would be adequate, while others would reduce the rate of investment, permitting their capabilities to degrade slowly over time. Conversely, an excess demand for nonobsolescent scientific capabilities would imply service prices more than sufficient to compensate for the costs of research, motivating higher proportions of suitably positioned individuals to acquire and maintain knowledge of research-front developments.

At a superficial level this model appears to be ludicrously at variance with reality. Clearly, researchers do not finance their research. Implicitly, however, this model may well be at least partially descriptive. If researchers did finance their research, their earnings, as consultants, contractors, faculty, and so on, would necessarily be significantly higher than actually observed earnings. Thus, it is possible to interpret the costs of research as an implicit component of gross compensation, a component that the scientist elects to reinvest in the maintenance of his research-front knowledge and capabilities.

This implicit model of scientists' self-financing of research may be highly descriptive in the case of those sciences, e.g., mathematics and theoretical physics, in which the dominant input into research is the scientist's own time. Consider a scientist for whom it is rational to devote 20 percent of his time to research (an investment that maximizes the present value of his lifetime earnings as a faculty member, consultant, and so forth). He is remunerated (in the form of salary or commissions) for the other 80 percent of this time, which he devotes to some other activity (teaching, consulting). Interpretively, had he desisted from research and devoted full time to the provision of income-producing services, his earnings (in the short run) would have been 25 percent greater, a differential that he elected, instead, to invest in the maintenance of his capabilities.

Notwithstanding its stylized form, this model suggests interpretations of several observations drawn from reality. Notably, it explains the apparent decline with age in the proportion of time devoted to research. *Ceteris paribus*, any time devoted to research will generate higher returns for a younger scientist than it does for his older colleague, simply because of the longer period over which he can expect to provide services; thus, at least beyond some age it will be rational for the scientist to shift the allocation of his time from research to service provision. Under plausible circumstances, this reduction in time devoted to research with advancing age will also be reflected in increased observed earnings. On the one hand, the older scientist, having rationally reduced his investment in obsolescence-offsetting research will experience a decline in earnings as a result of his progressively greater obsolescence; however, over some period (immediately following the reduction in his time devoted to research) this may be more than fully compensated by the higher proportion of his time devoted to service provision.

Consider, for example, Price's (upper-bound) estimate of the proportion of a scientist's time that should be devoted to maintaining his competence: 28 percent. Were he to reduce the proportion of his time devoted to research to zero, time devoted to service provision would increase by 38.9 percent $100/(1-0.28)$. Under Price's assumptions he would become obsolete at a rate of 7 percent per year; plausibly, this would reduce his earnings capability by 7 percent per year. However, the effect of the increase in time devoted to service provision would outweigh the effect of increasing obsolescence for the first 4.86 years $[-\ln 1.389/\ln 1.07]$ after his cessation of research. Thus, maximization of lifetime earnings (net of the costs of research) would dictate cessation of research approximately five years before the expected termination of the working lifetime (and even earlier if the real discount rate is greater than zero).

A second phenomenon explained by this analysis concerns the budgets of solicited grant and contract research. Here the sponsor essentially is contracting for a specific (anticipatable) product, and the service provided by the contractor is *not* fundamental research. However, budgets for such research are commonly, indeed notoriously, inflated; because these contracts typically provide only for cost reimbursement, this budgetary inflation is accomplished by exaggerating the time of the scientist required for the contracted project. The contracting agency is prepared to pay the higher price because only thus can it obtain the services of a research-front scientist. The scientist devotes the excess of budgeted over required time to the maintenance of his capabilities, i.e., to fundamental research. Thus, grant and contract support is frequently acknowledged in the fundamental scientific literature, not because augmentations of fundamental scientific knowledge were the intentions of the sponsors but because fundamental research is a "pirate activity" carried out in association with the provision of other services, when effective service provision requires fundamental knowledge. Only in the event of an excess supply of particular research-front capabilities will it be possible for the contracting agency to acquire such services at a price that does not provide for the maintenance of research-front capabilities.

The important implication of the alternatives of explicit versus implicit inclusion of research support in the gross earnings of research-font personnel concerns the locus of risk bearing and, hence, the role of institutions. If support for research is explicitly incorporated in the earnings of the scientist, then the scientist is ultimately responsible for decisions concerning the appropriate rate of investment in the maintenance of his capabilities through research. Thus, his anticipations of the future earnings differentials associated with greater versus lesser allocations of resources to current research will determine the level of his investment in research. Obviously, however, this decision must be made in the face of significant uncertainty concerning future demands for knowledge and expertise. To the degree to which he is risk averse, his investment will be reduced by comparison to the socially optimal rate of investment in research-front capabilities, i.e., to the rate of investment that would be observed if *ex post* moral hazard and *ex ante* adverse selection did not serve to constrain opportunities to insure against adverse market developments.

Institutionalization of research support, with the employing institution (1) compensating the scientist at a rate net of support for research, (2) underwriting the scientist's research, and (3) recovering the costs of research through its charges for the scientist's services to clients (students, agencies contracting for specific services, etc.), provides a mechanism by which it may be possible to effectively pool the risks associated with investments in research-front capabilities. The employing institution, maintaining a balanced portfolio of research-front capabilities, thus can utilize the unanticipatedly high returns to certain types of capabilities to compensate for lower than anticipated returns to others.

A serious constraint on the capacity of the employing institution to pool the risks associated with individual decisions to engage in obsolescence-offsetting investments in scientific capabilities derives from the capacity of individuals whose capabilities are in unanticipatedly high demand to expropriate the excess of actual over-expected payments for services. Risk pooling essentially means that future net earnings of the individual scientist will be dependent only on the previously anticipated (expected) state of demand, not on the state of demand actually confronted. Thus, the institution will incur losses on those whose expertise is in less than anticipated demand, recovering these through the higher than anticipated prices that can be commanded for the services of those whose capabilities are in unexpectedly strong demand. If, however, the scientist whose capabilities are in strong demand is free to exit the institution, either directly marketing his capabilities or associating himself with another institution, then the employing institution will not be able to retain title to these higher than anticipated earnings. Thus, provisions such as constitutional prohibitions of involuntary servitude, which preclude even the voluntary waiver of the right to sever an employment contract with an institution, serve to severely constrain the risk-pooling functions of employing institutions.

Although an institution may be precluded from utilizing legally binding agreements to insure that those whose research is supported by the institution will not expropriate unexpectedly high returns to that investment, certain classes of institutions may be able to utilize moral suasion to achieve the same end. Canons of professional ethics and collective ideologies and values, for example, those associated with the academic professions, can be viewed as providing, *inter alia*, for extralegal enforcement of voluntary agreements involving the waiver of the right of the individual scientist to expropriate the surpluses associated with unanticipatedly strong demands for his expertise. To the degree to which these are successful, the employing institution can serve a risk-pooling or insuring function. In actuality, however, success in restricting exit rights of employees is more likely to be attributable to collusion between collectively monopsonistic employing institutions than to the strength of the imposed extralegal constraints on individual mobility stemming from collective ideologies and values.

Even if employing institutions are incapable of performing a risk-pooling function, there may well be motivations for scientists to affiliate themselves with institutions. For example, the institution may perform an informational function for the market, providing a certification of the capabilities of the individual scientist, especially in the face of serious constraints on the capacities of those purchasing scientific services to effectively evaluate the capabilities of individual providers. Moreover, the conferring institution may be able to impose an effective charge on the scientist for this informational imprimatur, providing a potential source of funds to compensate for its self-insurance losses.

This entire system breaks down, however, if the scientist and his employing institution are precluded from incorporating in the charge for his services the costs of that fundamental research necessary for the maintenance of the research-front capabilities of the scientist, even when the market would permit recovery of these costs (i.e., even if there were no excess supply of research-front capabilities and, thus, no lower bidder could be found). As suggested above, grant and contracts for specific services generally (i.e., in equilibrium or excess-demand situations) do include budgetary slack necessary to cover associated capability-sustaining fundamental research.

However, in the case of one of the largest direct and indirect purchasers of the services of research-front scientists, government cost-accounting standards are intended to preclude this incorporation of an implicit charge for fundamental research in contracts for specific technological services. On the other hand, it has been impossible for the government not to recognize the necessity for research-front capabilities. Thus, to the degree to which prohibition of implicit funding of fundamental research has been successful, it has been necessary for government to introduce direct funding for this capability-sustaining research. Especially in light of the constraints faced by institutions in performing the risk-pooling function for which they are uniquely qualified, they have been prepared to accept constraints on the prices that can be charged for scientific services in exchange for direct governmental funding of fundamental research, thus explaining the emergence of fundamental-research-supporting agencies such as the National Science Foundation.

The adverse consequence of this creation of governmental agencies sponsoring fundamental research is that it breaks the connection between fundamental research and its justification, the maintenance of research-front capabilities for which there is an extraresearch function or requirement. Thus, it becomes possible, for example, for individuals performing no useful nonresearch functions to be supported only for purposes of their fundamental research. As a result, the supply of scientific talent to other activities (whether these do or do not require research-front capabilities) may be seriously reduced.

Moreover, this allocation to government of the responsibility for financing fundamental research centralizes judgments concerning expected future requirements for research-front capabilities. While an individual may under- or overestimate the future demand for his particular research-front capabilities, these individual errors are likely to be less than perfectly correlated across individuals, thus partially averaging out. In contrast, with a centralized determination, there will be no compensating under- and overestimations of future demands, since only one estimate (drawn from the distribution) will be made. Also, given lags between the various phases of the process of determining levels of governmental support, for example, between the assessment of need, the authorization of funding, and the actual awards of support, this governmentally managed system is likely to be seriously out of phase with actual market developments, even if these developments were accurately anticipated in the first instance. It is for this reason that a centralized system is likely to be characterized by successive boom and bust markets, recurrent expansions and contractions of supply of research-front capabilities.

Conclusion

The existing system of research support, especially governmental support, rests upon a fundamental misconception of the nature of fundamental research and of the contributions of fundamental researchers to society. Ironically, this "ideology of science," portraying the scientific products of research as having value in and of themselves, serves, ultimately, to devalue the competencies of scientists who possess a command over developments at the research front. Recognition of the very real value of research-front knowledge in the provision of directly valued goods and services, including advanced education, would serve to depoliticize science and would stimulate a more rational allocation of human talent to scientific and nonscientific pursuits.

Notes

1. Jurgen Habermas, *Toward a Rational Society* (New York: Basic Books, 1968).
2. While not of direct relevance here, it is interesting to note that the transition from the classical, intrinsic utility perception to the contemporary instrumental-utility, investment-in-knowledge perception involves a fundamental change in the perceived nature of theory and science as well as in the relationship of theory/science to practice/technology. From insight, albeit partial, into the "immutable essence of things," theoretical knowledge itself becomes transitory. While individual observations may (but need not) be "immutable," the meaning or interpretation of these observations becomes provisional, tentative, and subject to radical reformulation on the basis of future observations. While such radical reformulations occurred in the past, as in the revolutionary displacement of Ptolomeic by Copernican astronomy, these reformulations were the exception rather than the rule: most importantly, they did not undermine the subjective perception that scientific knowledge was concerned with immutabie essences. In contrast, among adherents of instrumentally utilitarian science, it would be difficult to find anyone who seriously believes in any immutable essence: contemporary theory is validated not by the insight it provides into the immutable but by its perceived usefulness, a usefulness that is at best temporary as new observations undermine existing theory.
3. Operationally, given any level of basic and applied research, the optimal level of development could be determined the principle of marginal cost equal to (discounted) marginal benefit. Maintaining the optimal rate of development as a function of the rates of basic and applied research, the optimal rate of applied research, given the rate of basic research, could be determined by the same principle. The same procedure would then be employed to determine the optimal rate of basic research, conditional on contingently optimal rates of applied research and development.
4. Jacques Barzun, "A Surfeit of Art," On the relative elasticity of artist's talent, see *Harper's* (July, 1987).
5. This decomposition of economic growth into components attributable to specfic sources of growth is taken from the "growth-accounting" analysis of B. F. Denison, *Accounting for United States Economic Growth 1929–1969* (Washington, D.C.: Brookings Institution, 1974).

6. See D. de S. Price and S. Gürsey, "Studies in Scientometrics, Part I: Transience and Continuance in Scientific Authorship," *International Forum on Information and Documentation* (Moscow, 1976) 1(2): 17-24; reprinted in D. de S. Price, *Little Science, Big Science...and Beyond* (New York: Columbia University Press. 1986), see also Chap. 2.

7. See S. P. Dresch and K. R. Janson, "Giants, Pygmies and the Social Costs of Fundamental Research, or Price Revisited" Technological Forecasting and Social Change, 32(4), 323-340 (1987).

8. For a discussion of technological advance as the driving force of scientific development, see D. de S. Price, *Science Since Babylon* (New Haven: Yale University Press, 1961).

9. Parenthetically, it might be noted that scientific developments may have one of two fundamentally different engineering effects. First, they might permit the scientifically knowledgeable engineer to accomplish something previously considered impossible. Second, they might permit something already possible to be accomplished more knowledgeably and efficiently. Consider the second: In the absence of scientific knowledge, the engineer is forced to rely on experience. Thus, experience in a prior situation guides action in a current situation. However, different situations are rarely identical in all relevant respects, with the consequence that prior experience never provides a certain guide to current action. As a result, the engineer who must rely on experience is forced to take a fundamentally conservative stance. For example, in the absence of precise knowledge concerning the properties of materials to be used in construction of a bridge, the cautious engineer "overbuilds" simply because he cannot anticipate the magnitude of the stresses that his materials will tolerate. In contrast, as noted by K. I. Pelc (seminar discussion), the scientifically knowledgeable engineer can "optimize," e.g., "precisely," tailor the construction of a bridge to the stresses to which it is anticipated to be subjected. However, because the engineer's knowledge (of the situation, of future stresses, etc.) is never complete, to optimize rather than overbuild also implies an increase in the risk of failure. Thus, Roman aquaducts survive while contemporary bridges unexpectedly collapse. With reference to the first effect of scientific knowledge—the capacity to accomplish something previously impossible—risks are inevitably encountered because of unanticipated concomitants of the intended outcome. On both counts, the scientization of engineering (the replacement of the conservative engineer by the scientific engineer) raises engineering risks. Of course, this increase in engineering risk is conjoined with, and can be considered part of the price of, the concomitant increase in engineering "power."

10. Thus, Derek Price, argues that the primary objective (and function) of scientific publication is not to disseminate new knowledge but rather to claim credit for discovery (*Little Science, Big Science*, p. 65-70).

11. D. de S. Price, "An Extrinsic Value Theory for Basic and 'Applied' Research," in *Science and Technology Policy*, ed. J. Haberer (Lexington, Mass.:Lexington Books. 1977).

12. Derek de Solla Price, "A Theoretical Basis for Input-Output Analysis of National R&D Policies" in Devendra Sahal, ed., *Research, Developmemt, and Technological Innovation*, ed. Devendra Sahal (Lexington, Mass.: Lexington Books, 1980).

13. This more general formulation assumes that any given degree of faculty obsolescence can be sustained over time with a constant rate of research activity and that greater research activity is required to sustain a lesser degree of obsolescence,

i.e., that it is easier (involves less research effort) to remain consistently further from the frontier.

14. If a corporation were to support fundamental research on purely ideational grounds, this would reflect the utility of its managers and would necessitate (a) the corporation's command of monopoly profits and/or (b) the insulation of the managers from the owners.

15. The Kaiser Wilhelm Gesellschaft, now renamed the Max Planck Gesellschaft (Society), provides an excellent example.

16. Thus, the Institute for Advanced Study was endowed by the mercantile wealth of Louis Bamberger and his sister, Mrs. Felix Fuld, while Rockefeller University was endowed by the industrial wealth of John D. Rockefeller. A more recent example is provided by Howard Hughes's endowment of the Howard Hughes Medical Institute.

17. Prestige-oriented national scientific institutions such as the Max Planck Gesellschaft, the Soviet Academy of Sciences, and the National Science Foundation come readily to mind.

18. Here a corporation might legitimately allocate resources to fundamental research on grounds of the "good will" generated thereby. Consider, for example, the good will derived by American Telephone and Telegraph Company from the prestige of Bell Labs.

19. For example, because the U.S. accounts for 40 percent of scientific "production," a doubling of U.S. output would increase the total scientific knowledge available in the U.S. by only 40 percent, implying an arc elasticity of at most 0.4. Further, this assumes that a doubling of inputs would result in a doubling of U.S. output, which, for reasons discussed, is probably unrealistic; thus, Dresh and Janson ("Giants, Pygmies") suggest an elasticity of scientific contributions (e.g., articles) with respect to resources (the size of the scientific cadre) of about 0.5, suggesting an elasticity of world output with respect to U.S. input of only about 0.2, i.e., a doubling of U.S. input would increase global output by only 20 percent. Focusing not on contributions but the scientific value of the contributions, Dresh and Janson indicate an elasticity with respect to resources of less than 0.4, suggesting at most a 10 percent increase in world scientific value as a result of a doubling of U.S. inputs.

7

Property Rights in Academe

Roger E. Meiners and Robert J. Staaf

Introduction

A number of commentators and scholars have criticized higher education for being inefficient and misdirected. Former Secretary Bennett of the U.S. Department of Education has chastised major universities for teaching the wrong things and for lobbying like big businesses. The Carnegie Foundation report, published in 1987, argues for a return to the liberal arts tradition in undergraduate education and a shift away from vocationalism. Others express concern about government intrusion on academic freedom. With a few exceptions, the criticism is void of a positive framework.[1]

This chapter explores higher education from a property rights perspective. Most of the criticisms directed at higher education are implicit normative arguments for changing property rights. Accordingly, it is useful to examine explicitly the property rights structure in higher education to explain the distributional and allocative consequences of higher education decision making.

The Coase theorem is central to the property rights approach. The theorem states that property rights ultimately will go to their highest valued use, or liability ultimately will be assumed by the least cost avoider provided: (1) property rights or liability rules are well defined and enforced, (2) there are no transaction costs, and (3) there are no income effects.[2] Property rights in the Coase context usually mean individually exclusive and transferable rights. But transaction costs or enforcement costs may be so high as to prefer nonexclusive (common) rights on efficiency grounds.[3] A classic example of this is the allocation of parking spaces at shopping center parking lots.

In this chapter we examine the wide range of property rights that exist in higher education from the perspective of the benchmark of individually exclusive and transferable rights. As Harold Demsetz pointed out, it is useful to examine markets as an exchange of rights rather than as commodities.[4] This would seem to be especially true of exchanges that occur in higher education. To talk of the university as providing, or the students as demanding, education is nebulous. What the university provides students with is a set of rights to resources subject to conditions and obligations. It helps to distinguish the major functions of universities—governance, education, and research—because of the different right structures. This chapter is organized into three major parts. The first part deals with the administrative function, the second part with the education function, and the third with research.

Administrative Or Managerial Functions

The "property rights" approach extends the theory of the firm and of consumer choice to explain behavior that emerges given alternative organizational arrangements. Information, transaction costs, and the structure of property rights have been shown to be important factors in understanding different organizational arrangements.

The focus here is on the consequences of the nonprofit nature of higher education institutions. A nonprofit organization can be broadly defined as one whose "owners" or directors (trustees) cannot fully appropriate the residual claim defined as the difference between revenues and costs. This constraint applies to both private and public universities. The lack of profit motive is compounded by the absence of a market for the control of individual colleges and universities. Unlike corporations owned by stockholders, exclusive and transferable rights in the residual do not exist in universities. University trustees and administrators do not face the vigilant evaluation of outsiders, who would have the incentive and a market mechanism to allow a takeover of the organization if it were being mismanaged. Hence, not only are trustees and administrators relieved or deprived of certain market pressures but, as will be seen, the absence of property rights and market measures induces them to behave differently than they would if property rights were fully defined and allocated.

Because profits cannot guide the decisions of university trustees or managers, the rules and monitoring procedures they use differ from what would exist under a profit motive. Trustees do not face the threat of a takeover, as do directors of publicly held proprietary firms. Hence, one would expect them to be more lax in their duties than they would be if there were rights to the residual claim that could be capitalized and transferred. Even if we assume that most colleges' trustees are capable, dedicated people, the lack of rights to a profit provides different incentives in terms of being informed as well as of behavior. The absence of a profit constraint permits trustees and managers the opportunity to pursue other goals.

What do the trustees maximize? Trustees and administrators have an incentive to be informed about university finances that are measurable. Like other nonprofit institutions and public bureaucracies, trustees and administrators are concerned with increasing the revenues of the university. Whatever nonpecuniary benefits are associated with the position of trustee or administrator, these benefits are likely to increase with an increase in revenues. Trustees will evaluate the success of university administrators by studying revenues (and expenses) relative to those of competing universities. Donations by foundations and alumni, government grants, and tuition revenues can be examined for growth patterns as a way of evaluating the performance of the top administrators. The revenues that finance the university must increase for the school to remain solvent and to increase its reputation over time, so that current and projected budgets should be the main financial concern of university leaders. Increases in revenues can be used to purchase distinction for the institution. Trustees have an incentive to keep the budget in balance since a deficit will create more demands on their time and will lead to diminished individual reputations similar to those of a bankrupt corporation.

Evaluation by Trustees

Trustees have a difficult time assessing the long-run consequences of their decisions and those of the university administrators. There is no stock market to reflect the collective present or discounted evaluation of the prospects of the organization. The lack of a market evaluation of the expected prospects of a university discourages administrators from investing in revenues (since it is risky) or in innovative projects that have long-term horizons. The costs will be borne now with no market evaluation of the expected future benefits. Administrators will, therefore, be less entrepreneurial with respect to educational innovations than they would be if there were property rights in risky ventures from which they could reap large rewards.[5]

College administrators are normally not fired for incompetence related to financial performance. Lack of performance is hard to discern, and, if it is understood, who will profit by acting upon the information? On what basis should trustees hire and retain a president? On what basis should a president hire and retain deans? Different approaches are tried; proven business ability, academic publications, reputation, and other criteria have been used to choose college administrators. No one has been able to demonstrate that any particular set of characteristics will produce the best college administrator. In academia certain managerial techniques are undoubtedly more successful than are others, but with poorly measurable goals, administrative success will be hard to evaluate.

The absence of a profit measure or motive makes it particularly difficult for trustees to evaluate the performance of candidates for university president. Credentials serve as the next best alternative, providing a measure of performance in previous positions. Since positive accomplishments are difficult to measure, credentials and the absence of negative information, such as of a scandal or controversy, will be the primary data used in reviewing and selecting top administrators.[6]

Negative feedback about candidates is difficult to evaluate since it is costly to determine the validity of such information and since there is little objective information regarding performance against which such information could be compared. Negative information will tend to have more effect in hiring and promotion decisions at universities than it does in for-profit institutions that have market measures.

Positive financial information in the case of nonprofit colleges is difficult to evaluate since one cannot tell if, for instance, budget increases are the result of the administrator's efforts, demographic trends, external political decisions, or decisions made despite the administrator's objection. Negative feedback, such as a resolution by the faculty senate to condemn the administration, will be information without offsetting standards against which to judge its merits. In any event, problems and controversy impose costs on trustees with few, if any, returns from the time invested in resolving such matters. Hence, administrators have incentives to minimize possible controversy that could generate negative feedback about their administration; this further reduces potential returns to innovative risk taking.[7]

Trustees at schools with strong church affiliations can help make sure the organization does not stray too far from some doctrinal requirements, but otherwise they can only look at subjective rankings of departments and of colleges and programs (which are more a reflection of the past than of the estimated value of future developments) to try to assess how their college is doing. Most trustees will assume that if their college imitates the behavior of others it will not be exposed to the risk of an unfavorable outcome or of an attack by other institutions.

College trustees will be more passive than they would otherwise be because there is no personal profit motive to be active and no profit measure on which to base decisions. Their passivity does not mean that they do no work or that they fail to devote their expertise to certain functions, but rather that they are likely to be less active in structuring the educational functions of the university than they would be if there were a market for university control. Were they to be active in monitoring the educational functions, no matter how well informed and well intentioned, they are likely to bear the costs of public criticisms for encroaching upon the "rights" of others.

Responding to the Market

Throughout history college administrators have responded to monetary incentives to produce certain types of education. In the nineteenth century the demand was for religious training. In the early twentieth century foundation money caused substantial changes in the "doctrinal orientation" of private colleges and universities and promoted excellence (whether achieved or not) in teacher training and the social sciences. More recently, substantial federal subsidies for agriculture, defense-related programs, and social science programs have all generated responses and new directions. Now many universities are searching for ways to attract corporate dollars, including the construction of technical research centers that can respond to business contracts.

Colleges and universities can be expected to respond slowly to changes that would force a shift of resources within the institution. The primary force comes from changes in demands by consumers. For example, in recent years a greater proportion of the students have sought programs in business and engineering and fewer have sought a liberal arts education. Some trustees and administrators respond to such changes in demands faster than do others (although more slowly than they would under a profit motive), so that their colleges will attract more and/or better students. This interinstitution competition gradually forces intrainstitution changes in programs.[8] Some schools fail to respond to such pressures and decline.[9] In this sense the market is at work. This does not mean that there is an efficient competitive process at work, but there is competition for resources at the margin that generates a product not completely unlike the product that would emerge from a for-profit system of colleges. There is more education because its production is subsidized, and it costs more to produce because the producers are not subject to the rigors of a profit motive, but the form of the product is still likely to be similar to what would be demanded if there were for-profit institutions.

Private versus Public

Trustees govern public and private universities. If both are nonprofit institutions, what differences exist? The lack of the public purse may mean that private universities will operate somewhat more efficiently. Private colleges are not subject to the state laws governing purchasing and employment practices that affect state institutions. In private universities one would expect to find more price discrimination (via scholarships) than one would in public universities; they can be expected to spend more on student recruitment, to offer more general student services, and, across institutions, to offer more diversity in satisfying particular student demands.[10] Private colleges also offer greater variance in employee compensation packages. That is, private universities should have a greater dispersion of faculty compensation rates within and across departments than one would find at public colleges. They are not bound by state laws regarding teaching requirements and implicit (for political reasons) or explicit restrictions on the upper range of professors' salaries.

Because public universities must appeal to the state government, legislators, and voters for most of their support, they can be expected to promote public service by faculty members and administrators as a criterion of employment. Public universities, in making themselves attractive to state governments, can be expected to avoid programs regarded as extreme by most people; private universities may offer such programs to attract a certain group of students. Public universities can also be expected to attempt to maximize enrollment so as to broaden their budgets and bases of political support, while private universities, unless in financial trouble, will discriminate more carefully on quality and type of student admitted in order to maintain reputation.

Within a university, fewer restrictions on faculty compensation arrangements will enhance the ability of administrators to attract and to keep superior faculty. Given identical budgets, an administrator at a private university should be able to attract more "stars" than can his public university counterpart. Whether that means that a superior education product will result is unknown, but "stars" attract research money, good graduate students, and better junior faculty.

Like trustees, college administrators do not have a profit motive for decision making. They face assorted criteria—prestige, "quality" of students, "quality" of faculty, amount of external support raised, and so forth. Internal decision making is faculty-dominated and in some respects is similar to the worker-managed firm. The primary reason for this is the absence of rights to the residual. But the absence of the right to a residual may in part be associated with the jointness of inputs, especially as between students and faculty, that creates an extreme monitoring problem and the difficulties of defining outputs that will be discussed later in more detail. Accordingly, there are problems of measuring effectiveness in terms of costs.

Internal Administration

Specialization of disciplines requires administrators to rely upon the faculty for providing expert judgment regarding the likely ability of prospective and current colleagues. Moreover, the rights of faculty, under the term academic freedom, often prevents administrators from imposing severe sanctions (monitoring) on faculty other than for moral transgressions. Mechanical publication requirements, measures of hours spent in the office, and teacher evaluations will not produce a quality faculty. Such rules would dispose of the few geniuses who do not publish much but who are valuable to their colleagues and perhaps to their discipline. There is no reason to believe that administrators will understand or value nonorthodox work or work habits more highly than will the faculty.

Another implication of the property rights approach is that more decisions will be made by committee. As Manne has noted, there is a lack of individual responsibility and nothing like a profit center to allow accountability. Committee decisions mask individual preferences and allow administrators to dodge responsibility for results. Some faculty members devote time to committees because that is where rights to certain resources can be established and allocated. The politicking surrounding such committees may be a relatively nonproductive use of time, but it is not clear that an autocratic decision maker would do better in evaluating research and teaching.

Numerous well-known departments appear to be ruled by a few outstanding scholars. As will be discussed, these departments typically rely on joint inputs in the research production process whereby the established scholar has an incentive to monitor the behavior of other members of the team, and the junior members of the team benefit from such monitoring in terms of increased job opportunities.

Institutions and departments that are more democratically controlled will produce some sort of "median faculty" result, which will have less variance relative to autocratic decision making. This reduces the quantity of innovative developments in academics, both good and bad. The tendency to a median faculty result should be evident in a number of ways. Insofar as all faculty participate in the process, they will prefer a reward package with little variance. That is, if the average pay raise one year is to be 5 percent, a median faculty result would limit the range from, maybe, 3 to 7 percent, while an administrator may prefer a range of zero to 15 percent. Faculty preference for such results is evidenced by the pay packages bargained for at unionized universities.

Median faculty preference with respect to resource distribution is also observed. In most schools such things as long-distance telephones, secretarial help, travel, library, etc. are treated as free goods—with expected results. This produces a requirement for some allocation of such resources, usually resulting in their being shared "equally." There is little incentive for a distribution based on faculty performance, but one would expect to find greater variance at private universities that can vary compensation schemes more than can public universities. Proprietary organizations treat some inputs as free goods too, but managers have less incentive to ration inputs on an equity basis.

Median faculty (committee) decisions and the incentive of administrators to shy away from risky activities may explain why tenure tends to be treated as an absolute when there is no legal requirement for that to be the case. Firing incompetent faculty members does not produce a gain that can be appropriated by other faculty (or administrators) except for the value placed on the new colleague. The practice of firing incompetents does generate a risk that one will later fall into that category. Further, because academia does offer considerable job security, it presumably has attracted people who are risk averse. To abolish tenure would result in an increase in faculty salaries or a decline in the quality of faculty members in response to the decreased expected value of the job. It would be difficult for any administrator to do that and expensive for a university, even if the trustees desired it.

In summary, trustees and administrators have incentives to monitor the financial condition of the university. As with any bureaucracy, administrators have incentives to increase budgets, a measurable input that reflects positively on their performance. But they do not have incentives or the ability to monitor many aspects of the internal production process or inputs. In this sense, the university is organized like the worker-managed firm. To understand the consequences of a worker-managed firm it is necessary to understand the rights and obligations associated with the teaching and research function.

Education Function

Despite the rhetoric of equal access and equal opportunity, no one argues that everyone has the right to be admitted to, or to receive a degree from, Harvard University or Clinch Valley Community College. Conditions are imposed by all institutions, such as a high school diploma or its equivalent and other satisfactory performance defined by the college; just as the right to purchase a Ford automobile is conditioned on the ability to pay the price, so it is with higher education, except that there are conditions beyond those of explicit prices.

The additional discrimination mechanism is not simply due to the fact that the monetary price is regulated or subsidized. For example, a for-profit flight school will not give an unconditional warranty that a student will receive a private pilot's certificate for a fixed price. Learning to fly an airplane requires the joint inputs of the fixed-priced based operator and the input of the student pilot. An unconditional guarantee would expose the firm to opportunistic behavior by the student, who would shirk his duties by substituting his own effort for that of the firm even though he may have a comparative advantage in certain activities that lead to competency in flying. There are no absolute warranties, and all are conditioned by expressed or implied terms. Of course, if private pilot certificates were subsidized and fixed-based operators were not able to claim the residual, then it is likely they would ration their services in a manner so as to shift more of the burden onto students and thus shirk duties in which they may have a comparative advantage over students. One can argue that this is inefficient in terms of the Coase theorem that does *not* include as one of its assumptions that the activity is subsidized or that the good or service is provided by a nonprofit organization. This is not simply a "transaction costs" argument. Rather it is an argument that the property rights are different than that, according to the Coase assumption, rights are exclusive and transferable.

Joint Production in Learning

Learning requires joint inputs of student and teacher. Moreover, each of the joint inputs cannot be easily measured or monitored in their productivity. This jointness, and the absence of the right of the teacher to claim the student's residual, such as increased earnings, creates incentive effects. For example, the cohort of university students who choose engineering as a major continually diminishes from the freshman to the senior year. On the other hand, the cohort of university students who choose education or the liberal arts continually increases from the freshman to the senior year as they proceed through the undergraduate program. That is, there is an asymmetry within programs of students switching majors that occurs on average more than once during their college careers.[11]

The faculty of engineering departments generally have high opportunity costs in the market and obtain significant research grants that are reflected in their compensation packages. On the other hand, the opportunity costs of teachers in the colleges of education and liberal arts are often considerably above what they can make in the market. These differentials mean that engineering faculty will tolerate less student shirking as the faculty have alternatives to teaching, whereas education professors have much to lose if student enrollments decline. Engineering professors are also able to extract more residual claims from engineering students (usually in the form of student effort and research assistance) simply because their research is more likely to have market value and measurable results. Finally, an engineering professor's salary is in large part determined by his opportunity cost in the markets, which is based on performance, including that of his students. This value is more measurable in the market compared to that of other disciplines that service the public and nonprofit sectors. Unprepared students entering the market will lower the value of the professor's market reputation and thus his opportunity costs. Education professors are in a market in which there are continuous debates as to how to define educational outcomes. As a result, education professors will place emphasis on inputs, including their own.

Students admitted to a university may have equal rights to access to faculty, but they do not have equal rights to degrees. There are market phenomena that influence the choice (demand) of majors (e.g., relative wage rates) and the supply of students who successfully satisfy the requirements of various degrees. While nonprofit organizations may not exactly emulate what would be the behavior of for-profit institutions, they may approximate such behavior.

The jointness problem in learning may be the primary reason many private colleges advertise small enrollments and class size.[12] There is no reason to expect that faculty are, by their nature, better teachers at private colleges than they are when they teach in public colleges of comparable stature. However, small class size makes it less costly for the instructor to monitor the performance of each student, makes it more costly (due to embarrassment if nothing else) for students to shirk in class by falling asleep or staring out the window, makes it less costly to assign and grade term papers, and (given that the private school advertises quality teaching) gives students a greater incentive to complain about shirking by the faculty. Students who choose small private colleges may recognize the need for faculty to monitor their behavior as well as that of the faculty, in a way similar to workers in Yugoslavian worker-managed firms.[13]

At public colleges, with larger average class sizes, students can shirk more easily, and it is more difficult to monitor students. The incentives to give writing assignments drop. Fewer students are likely to complain about "bad" teaching because they have lower expectations about the services they are purchasing relative to those who purchase higher-priced teaching at private colleges.

Administrators at private colleges have some incentive to monitor teaching, and such monitoring is more likely to occur when the faculty is relatively small because they advertise teaching quality, personal attention, and the like. A small decline in enrollment is very costly to a small private college. However, there is little reason to expect monitoring by faculty at private or public colleges since there is no way to capture any gains from teaching excellence by colleagues.

Caveat Emptor in the Academic Market

It is a mistake to equate education with any other commodity. As Israel Kirzner has pointed out, one does not have a demand for information since there is a presupposition one knows what he is demanding.[14] So it is with education. If students *knew* what they were demanding, there would be no demand. Traditional demand analysis that assumes perfect information must be qualified.[15] Education in Nelson's terms is an *extreme* experience good where students do not fully appreciate the good[16] or cost without considerable investments of time and, quite frequently, the passage of time.[17]

The problems that arise in the market for higher education, due to lack of knowledge and the experience nature of learning, are compounded by the absence of a contract or warranty whereby the student could sue for a breach.[18] Moreover, faculty, unlike other professions, are not liable in tort or contract such as a cause of action for malpractice.[19] In large part this is attributable to the jointness of inputs, prohibitions on slavery or involuntary servitude, and generally accepted measures of outputs. The latter is the result of an emphasis on First Amendment rights in higher education as exemplified by the terms "academic freedom" or "competition of ideas."

The academic market is one of the few areas in the law that recognizes caveat emptor (i.e., let the student beware). It is not likely that academic freedom would disappear if higher education were to suddenly become organized for profit. A shift toward caveat venditor (let the professor or university beware) would be more disastrous in higher education than it would be for other markets primarily because of the Coase theorem. To the extent that it is possible to contract around liability in product markets, liability will be assigned to the least-cost avoider. But, given the extreme jointness problem in learning and the problem Kirzner poses, how can students enter into contracts involving mutual assent?

Moreover, there is a moral hazard problem (opportunistic behavior) in that learning is not externally observable and can only be revealed by the student. What would prevent the student from claiming a breach of contract or malpractice by simply deliberately failing whatever output measure exams were given? The continual discussions about finding outcome measures for higher education are in essence an argument for regulating higher education, with the consequences of changing property rights from academic freedom and the competition of ideas to some notion of monopoly truth as defined by some reasonable-man standard or collectivity that in turn would permit caveat venditor.[20]

Capturing the Residual

The jointness problem associated with learning or teaching creates the problem of defining a teacher's output. Is a Harvard education more valuable than an education from Clinch Valley Community College because of its professors' skills and efforts or because of the students' skills and efforts? There is little market at universities for so-called good teachers.[21] That is, whatever investments a professor makes in being a good teacher is specific to the university and cannot be exported or capitalized in the market.[22] Moreover, the professor is not able to capture any of the residual that accrues to the students in the form of increased earnings.[23] There is an analogy with the theory of the firm in that the owners are the ones who monitor the inputs because they own the specific capital that is at risk if there is shirking or a diminished brand-name. A research professor, on the other hand, invests in capital that is more general and can be exported in the market. That is, if a university experiences a decline in its reputation and financial base, research professors can still maintain a return on their capital by moving to another university.

This specificity in human capital explains why professors who specialize in teaching devote considerably more time to internal governance (e.g., committees and faculty senates) than do professors who invest in research capital that is marketable and capturable. But the analogy with the firm cannot be carried too far. While those professors who invest in capital specific to the university have an incentive to monitor inputs, unlike the private sector, the returns to monitoring joint inputs cannot be capitalized or transferred. Investments made in obtaining tenure may require trading off the monitoring of inputs where the individual is not able to capture all of the gain versus investments in tenure that he is able to capture exclusively.[24] Because tenure is obtained via a political process, there are payoffs to being on committees that decide rules and allocation of certain resources, as well as being in a position to logroll for one's own tenure.

This does not mean that faculty with specialized capital have no incentive to hire faculty who do research. A department or college comprised of only faculty with specialized capital will be at a comparative disadvantage in salary negotiations with the administration because of the absence of market-forces. Hiring research professors who command market prices will tend to raise the average salary, permitting specialized professors to make arguments for a salary increase. Moreover, to the extent that the overall prestige of the department or university is increased, as perceived externally to the university, increased overall funding may result from increased enrollments or from the ability to be more selective in admitting students, thereby benefiting specialized faculty whose fate is tied to the prestige of the university.

The incentives of administrators are mixed in terms of hiring teaching and service versus research faculty. Specialized faculty are less likely to create an embarrassment to the university that research faculty can create with controversial research. In addition, administrators have more discretion in allocating funds within a university when there are no market signals. Finally, the administration can avoid responsibility for internal governance by giving the function to specialized faculty who have incentives to be very active.

On the other hand, a university with specialized faculty is not likely to be able to increase its budget, at least from foundation and federal sources, at the same rate as could a research university. Administrators of specialized faculty also become specialized and have fewer job alternatives. Administrators who desire to increase job opportunities are likely to invest in more general capital. These investments will take the form of contacts with foundations and the developing of lobbying skills. To be successful in fund-raising it is beneficial to have products to sell (like research) other than teaching. Thus, administrators are able to capture a portion of the gain from increased prestige that, for the most part, can only come from an increased emphasis on research.

Common Property Rights

Now consider the students' property rights in the campus, buildings, and facilities. For the most part the rights in the physical capital are common within a class as opposed to individual exclusive rights. There are several exceptions, such as a student's right to his dorm room or, on rare occasions, when the university rents assigned parking spaces. But even here the rights of exclusivity and transferability are limited. For example, the right to lease a dorm room is conditioned on admission and satisfactory performance at the university. The lease is generally not assignable. It is interesting to note that universities do not price discriminate between residents and nonresidents in terms of room and board. This is because the private market exists at the margin for these services. Indeed, the provision of room and board is the least subsidized of university services. The university might be able to capture some locational rents, but this ability is limited by the market.

For the most part, student rights to university resources are common rights. In part, this may simply be the result of high transaction or of enforcement costs. For example, it would be possible to allocate the resources of the library on the basis of price, such as by rental agreements. But transaction and enforcement costs are likely to exceed the revenues derived from such exclusivity based on market prices. Similarly, it is possible to price or auction off certain professors who are in demand instead of rationing their services on the basis of queuing. But, if the professor has no claim to the residual, he has no incentive to favor price allocation, and his colleagues will certainly oppose it.

Perhaps the principal reason for the absence of the price system in academe is to instill loyalty or a sense of belonging to a private club, a sense that might not be realized if all transactions are at arm's length.[25] Most private clubs also do not extensively use the price system to allocate resources.[26] Common experiences are not necessarily created by a market that responds to individuals at the margin. Because of information costs, most employers' response to a student's degree, besides class rank and major, reflects a general impression of the particular university. Employers do not engage in a detailed examination of the student's transcript or to the qualifications of the faculty. Thus, the image, reputation, or trademark of the university as a whole is a means to economize on information. In a sense, the system of common property rights leads to more standardization than might be the case if university resources were allocated on the basis of a price system. Moreover, given imperfect human capital markets, good teachers or library resources would not necessarily be better allocated (i.e., to their highest-valued use) under a price system.[27]

Related to the reputation or collective image of a university is the aversion, with several exceptions, for universities to directly advertise, compared to private firms who sell trademark goods.[28]

Many universities have marketing departments that teach marketing, but the marketing faculty are seldom called upon to use that knowledge in promoting the university. Recent economic literature has explained how investments in brand names and trademarks creates specific capital that is at risk if quality should be deceptive.[29] Specific capital serves as a performance bond to consumers that is forfeited if quality claims prove to be deceptive since then consumers will not make repeat purchases. That is, the specific capital (advertising investments) serves as a market enforcement mechanism, as opposed to legal enforcement, of explicit or implicit contracts regarding quality.[30] Investments in quality assurance in academe should be especially important in light of the previous discussion of students' rights or of the university or faculty's liability. That is, there is no legal recourse for a student receiving a defective product. Yet administrators, and especially faculty, are adamant in their criticisms of advertising.[31] In public institutions there are sometimes statutory prohibitions against certain types of direct advertising expenditures.[32] But even notable private institutions, such as Harvard, do not directly advertise.

A partial explanation lies in the absence, again, of a claim to the residual from advertising. Perhaps a more plausible explanation is that both public and private universities are subsidized, thereby creating an excess demand. That excess demand serves as a signal of quality relative to price. Most academics, even those who espouse equal opportunity, deride those institutions that truly have open admission policies. It is the same reaction one gets from public announcements regarding the rights of the unemployed to sign up for unemployment compensation. Queuing, even with a market system, is often used as a sign of quality. Similarly, or especially, with faculty who do not have market information on their services, queuing is a signal of their quality or value. Advertising, as long as nonprice rationing mechanisms are used (admission standards), might simply increase costs without benefits.

Research Function

While there is considerable jointness of inputs in the teaching function, as between professor and students, the jointness of inputs in the research function primarily exists among faculty members.[33] A faculty member would consider another faculty member's evaluation of his teaching skills as an encroachment on his rights. That same faculty member might actively seek his colleague's comments and criticisms of his research. This difference in behavior can be explained by the joint input relationships. First, the external professor has no incentive to be concerned about his colleague's teaching productivity since he also has no claim to the residual. Second, for reasons discussed, it is difficult to measure the relative performance of students and professors due to teaching quality.

But research productivity can be appropriated. The research market is evaluated by peers. Critical review of research by departmental colleagues can result in considerable advantage in getting things published, if for no other reason than reducing the time frame from submission to publication. Colleagues can offer criticisms that anticipate the referees. In addition, there are gains from trade from specialized knowledge in coauthorship. Each partner can claim the residual from publication. Team teaching a class offers no reward and, if anything, an incentive for team members to shirk since there is no claim to a residual.[34] Faculty can capture some residual from colleagues' publications in journals; as value in being associated with that department rises, internal salaries rise and opportunities increase elsewhere. That is, even tenured faculty without publications can benefit from an increase in the research output of their colleagues. Textbooks are not highly valued because the residual (royalties) are collected exclusively by the author and are not a signal of research quality to the profession.

Research, unlike teaching, often has capturable residuals that can be immediately realized. Many grants provide release time from teaching, summer salary support, travel funds, support for graduate assistants, and other discretionary funds of direct benefit to faculty members.[35] University administrators often capture some of the residual. At many schools, grant overhead is shared on some formula basis by faculty, departments, and administrators. Administrators then have off-budget dollars available, thereby providing added incentives to support researchers. Since compensation packages are essentially fixed for a faculty member or administrator at a given university, the best opportunity for income supplements from internal sources (nonconsulting or local real estate market) comes from grant monies.

Jointness in research inputs among faculty creates more of a team approach between faculty and students as well, especially in graduate education. The time investment for natural science and engineering graduate students to receive their Ph.D.'s is considerably less than it is for a doctoral candidate in the liberal arts. Graduate students in the sciences are used by faculty as inputs in conducting research, which is largely measurable and specialized capital where substitutes are not costlessly available. In return for the students' research assistance, the faculty enter into implicit contracts with students to devote efforts to ensure obtaining degrees. Thus students receive a return from their efforts. The possibility of continuous dealings with other students helps ensure the enforcement of the contract.

On the other hand, the English professor uses research assistants for things like library research, which is largely substituted by any number of students. The research output is often of a type that does not provide a benefit to the graduate student in completing degree requirements, and there is no jointness in production to form the basis of an implicit contract.

Summary

The application of property rights theory to the structure of higher education is insightful, even if tentative, toward understanding the workings of universities and the result of our nonprofit system of higher education. To propose that this or that should be done in higher education may be entertaining and satisfying, but it does little in moving us closer to a better understanding of the incentives at work in the institutional structure in which we operate.

Notes

1. Some exceptions include Henry Manne, "The Political Economy of Modern Universities" in *Education in a Free Society*, ed. Anne Burleigh (Indianapolis: Liberty Press, 1973); Armen Alchian, "The Economic and Social Impact of Free Tuition," *New Individualist Review*, Winter 1968, p.42; and Armen Alchian, "Private Property and the Relative Cost of Tenure," in *Economic Forces at Work* (Indianapolis: Liberty Press, 1977); and Robert McCormick and Roger Meiners, "University Governance: A Property Rights Perspective," Center for Policy Studies, Clemson University, Sept., 1986.
2. Ronald Coase, "The Problem of Social Cost," 3 *Journal of Law & Economics* 1 (1960b).
3. See Steven Cheung, "The Structure of a Contract and the Theory of a Non-exclusive Resource," *Journal of Law & Economics* 49 (1970b).
4. Harold Demsetz, "Toward a Theory of Property Rights," *American Economic Review, Proceedings* 347 (1967).
5. Evidence of this may be gleaned from the explosion of continuing education programs that originated for the most part outside the universities. After the size and profitability of this market was demonstrated by independent entrepreneurs, universities moved to compete in this market but still only command a fraction of the revenues.
6. This was found to be the case in nonprofit hospitals (See Kenneth Clarkson, "Some Implications of Property Rights in Hospital Management," *Journal of Law & Economics* 363 [1972]).
7. This would seem to be especially true at public universities. For example, the president at most public universities is the principal lobbyist. Controversy sur-

rounding the president's administration will hamper the university's ability to increase appropriations vis-à-vis competing universities.

8. Many states have a central organization to which individual universities must appeal to obtain approval for new programs or colleges. Often these organizations use the argument that it would be a waste of state resources to have duplicate programs and thereby deny approval. Thus, there may be little interinstitutional competition among state institutions, with most interinstitutional competition coming from private institutions who benefit from the cartelization of public universities within a state.

9. From 1963 to 1983 an average of six private four-year colleges ceased operations per year (*Education Statistics,* Table 110, U.S. Dept. of Education, 1986).

10. In the case of electric utilities, Peltzman found greater price discrimination in privately owned firms than in public firms (See Sam Peltzman, "Pricing in Public and Private Enterprises: Electric Utilities in the United States 14 *Journal of Law & Economics* 109 [1971]). We do observe that state universities practice discrimination on the basis of a student's residency status. Consistent with Peltzman's finding that utilities may price discriminate against nonvoters, in higher education we observe students of eligible voters offered education at a lower price than children of nonvoters. In addition, there is generally a two-tier admission standard in state universities that discriminates against nonresidents. At the margin, the absence of political discrimination results in private universities being able to be more selective because of a larger pool of potential students.

11. See Richard McKenzie and Robert Staaf, *Academic Freedom and Student Sovereignty* (Blacksburg, Va.: Public Choice Monograph Series, 1975).

12. In 1983 only 36 public four-year colleges and universities (6% of the total) had enrollments under 1,000, but 797 private colleges (55% of the total) had enrollments under 1,000. Twenty-one percent of all public colleges had enrollments under 2,500, while 83 percent of all private colleges had enrollments under 2,500. The average enrollment at private four-year colleges was 1,740; whereas public four-year colleges had average enrollments of 9,245 in 1983 *Digest of Education Statistics 1985–86*, Table 104, 1986).

13. Barry Newman, "Yugoslavia's Workers Find Self-Management Doesn't Make Paradise," *Wall Street Journal,* 25 March 1987, p. 1.

14. Israel Kirzner, "Information and Knowledge," mimeographed, (New York: New York University, 1976).

15. A notable exception to the traditional analysis of information is the property rights approach taken by B. Klein and K. Leffler, where they argue consumers do not do some cost-benefit calculation in obtaining information on product quality, but rather look at the seller's specific capital at risk if quality should be deceptive. That is, there are many cases where the costs of enforcing contracts exceed the benefits of enforcement so that it is not obtaining information claimed by the seller that leads one to purchase, but rather the costs imposed on the seller if it is deceptive. Similarly, the student is not likely to be specifically informed about the faculty or what the university offers, or claims to offer, but rather relies on the reputation of the institution. The alumni, administration, and faculty have a stake in maintaining the reputation. While there may not be strong incentives to monitor, compared to for-profit firms, for reasons discussed, there is some incentive. That is, the student has little incentive to become specifically informed about quality, for reasons that Kirzner points out, but in addition the student has no

rights to enforce if quality should be deceptive ("The Role of Market Forces in Assuring Contractual Performance," 89 *Journal of Political Economy* 615 [1981]).

16. In the early 1970s both authors were at Virginia Tech, where future Nobel prize winner James Buchanan was teaching. One semester he decided to teach the undergraduate public finance course. One of us sat in the course and observed that the students behaved no differently than had one of us taught the course. They were unaware, or did not care, that this should have been one of the most memorable courses in their undergraduate career, as Buchanan is an excellent teacher as well as researcher. Perhaps students attending more elite institutions are able to discriminate better among faculty, but at Virginia Tech there seemed little additional interest in the opportunity afforded them by this learning experience.

17. Nelson categorizes goods as either search goods, whereby the consumer can determine quality prior to purchase (e.g., lettuce or dresses) or experience goods, where quality can only be determined after purchase by experience (e.g., canned goods or software). Experience goods are associated with investments in brand names and trademarks that are at risk if quality claims should prove to be deceptive (Philip Nelson, "Advertising as Information," 81 *Journal of Political Economy* 729 [1974]).

18. It is interesting to note that computer software only warrants the material disc and not its function. An attorney at the FTC wanted to start an inquiry into this warranty problem. The absence of a warranty, similar to learning, is because of the jointness problem of the software and user, as well as the absence of control over use.

19. It should be noted that a good surgeon is able to capture some of the future gains from a life-saving operation by patients' continued business and references, whereas the good teacher is able to capture very little of the students' future earnings. Thus, liability for teacher malpractice would likely lead faculty to become much more risk averse in teaching unconventional or unpopular ideas. Moreover, teaching would likely become more theoretical and abstract by avoiding applications where liability could attach. The faculty incentive problems that would arise with teaching malpractice liability are similar to those that face administrators of the Food and Drug Administration in approving a new drug application.

20. The consequences of the search for outcome measures in higher education is discussed in general terms in Ronald Coase's article ("The Market for Goods and the Market for Ideas," 64[2] *American Economic Review* 384 [1974]).

21. The only market that seems to exist are for those professors that have experience in successfully teaching very large introductory service classes. The demand exists because of the reduction in teaching loads or smaller classes available to other members of the faculty.

22. Because there is an absence of a return from teaching, this does not necessarily mean there will be no investments in good teaching or good teachers. Many academics, similar to those other professions, earn rents in what they do because salaries or wages are determined at the margin. For example, our personal experiences with James Buchanan and Gordon Tullock suggests they earn rents even though their salaries would seem to be below the opportunity cost they could earn in consulting. That is, there are a number of teachers who simply enjoy teaching (students and faculty) and accept incomes below their opportunity costs in return for the nonpecuniary benefits of teaching. Our concern is that, at the

margin, an increase in investment in being good teachers requires a change in property rights that affects those teachers at the margin who do not have nonpecuniary benefits from teaching, or affects those teachers where nonpecuniary benefits are eliminate at the margin. For obvious reasons, it is difficult to discriminate between teachers who earn rents and those who do not. It is not in the interest of teaching professors to claim they earn rents, especially in light of the absence of a market for good teachers. Researchers, on the other hand, will receive their opportunity costs, regardless of revelations of the rents they receive, because there is a market that works at the margin.

23. As noted above, there are relative differences across disciplines.

24. While tenure rights are not transferable or cannot be capitalized, they do represent rights to a stream of income similar to an annuity. Thus, tenured faculty will have an incentive to be concerned with the long-run consequences and finances of a university. (This may explain why some high-quality private universities give, as a fringe benefit, "free tuition" to faculty children. This gives the faculty-parents more reason to be concerned about quality of teaching and overall institutional quality.) These concerns, of course, will be discounted because of the absence of the right to transfer (sell) tenure and therefore to capitalize its value. Moreover, similar to trustees and administrators, professors do not have market information to guide them in evaluating long-run consequences. Tenured professors, however, have more at risk than do trustees and are likely to be more conservative in proposing or accepting new projects or ventures.

25. See James M. Buchanan, "An Economic Theory of Clubs," *Economica* 1 (1965).

26. Harvard does not maximize tuition revenues because it would, in the long run, reduce the club value of Harvard to alumni, faculty, and various donors. The value of a Harvard degree would depreciate, forcing tuition down.

27. There are, of course, limitations to this reasoning, as Adam Smith warned us of in the *Wealth of Nations,* but information costs and specialization (including knowledge) were surely not as great in 1776 as they are in 1987.

28. Schools do send out expensive brochures and catalogs to prospective students. In addition, regional and national televised sports events will usually have a professional advertisement about the school. As Robert McCormick and M. Tinsley have pointed out, investments in the athletic programs have positive returns that spill over to academics ("Athletics versus Academics," Center for Policy Studies, Clemson University, No. 20, July 1986).

29. See n. 14.

30. The amount of specific capital required to serve as an indirect performance bond will be related to factors such as how frequently the good is purchased or durability, and the costs of legal enforcement and consequential damages if the good should turn out to be defective. For example, despite state legislation encouraging the sale of "generic" drugs, there have been few inroads into the trademark pharmaceuticals market. It is possible to produce some generics in one's basement or garage. Someone injured by a defective generic drug may successfully sue the manufacturer, but the judgment is likely to be of little value. On the other hand, Squibb will lose its trademark value if it produces a defective product.

31. The principal investment in specific capital that private firms engage in is brand advertising that has an extended pay-off period and thus depends on market survival (repeat purchases). However, there are some firms, such as Neiman Marcus, that make investments in thick rugs, ornate furnishings, and buildings that are likely to have a low opportunity cost. Similarly, some universities also invest in

ornate exteriors of buildings and stadiums that can be interpreted as specific capital that has a low opportunity cost in alternative employments. These investments serve as quality assurance expenditures to prospective students by creating an impression of permanence and not of a fly-by-night operation The huge capital investments in athletics is not only a means of regional and national advertising that can increase the reputation of lesser-known schools by directly competing with more established schools, but a signal to the students that the university is committed to remaining a university. It is also likely to help create a sense of loyalty.

32. Private institutions, of course, are not in a position to advertise on the basis of price given public institutions, but presumably they can engage in catchy brand-name advertising.

33. It is beyond the scope of this paper to examine whether teaching and research are substitutes or complements. If there is complementarity, it is likely that research has indirect spillovers to teaching rather than vice versa. Professors who teach and do research simply have less opportunity cost in investments to remain current.

34. Despite the rhetoric of interdisciplinary programs, these programs have generally turned out to be "interdysentery." The only successful programs have been those in which one discipline dominates the other, such as law and economics and public choice.

35. Support in the form of state or federal grants almost always must be channeled through the university, even though the researcher may work independently and without the use of university resources. A principal reason for this arrangement is to avoid embarrassment to the funding agency in the event funds are misused. Again, agency bureaucrats have no claim to the residual of the research, with little incentive to monitor, but an incentive to avoid the embarrassment of publicity of fraud, misuse of funds, or controversial research. Institutional sponsorship will mean that the university will bear a large part of the responsibility. Similarly, a nonprofit foundation has incentives like bureaucracies but is not likely to be as concerned with controversial research and more likely to be concerned with satisfying its own interests.

III

The Political Economy of
Scientific Research

Introduction to Part III

John W. Sommer

Each of the three chapters that follow are concerned with scientific research, an important domain of higher learning. The majority of this research is funded by the state (federal and state governments), and the most fundamental research is conducted in the institutional setting of the university. This allocation arrangement is a phenomenon of our time; over the past half century the federal government has replaced philanthropy and the universities as the chief provider of resources for fundamental research. Meanwhile, the universities have replaced industry as the chief place of conduct of this research. As these changes have been effected the state has developed into the most influential agent in the establishment of the basic research agendas of American scientists, arguably affecting the course of this form of intellectual life (and the institutions with which scientists are affiliated) much more profoundly than it has influenced either the arts or the humanities.

Where direct interference by government in government-supported arts (the Mapplethorpe affair of 1989 for example) has received much attention and has provoked great protest in the arts community, it is rare, although not unknown, to find such blatant government interference in scientific pursuits. Nor do individuals in the scientific community react with the intense outrage characteristic of those in the arts. Could it be that the scientists have, to a much greater extent, accepted both the largesse of the state and, tacitly, its guidance? Has government influence become so pervasive and its role in establishing the very categories of thought within which scientists conduct their research so accepted that scientists are reduced to complaining about the "red tape" of grant acquisition instead of voicing concern on more fundamental issues? The answer to these questions seems to be "yes," although one might hear the chief beneficiaries of the system protest that they are totally free to pursue their research programs. And, why not?

Science policy is directed at influencing what scientists choose as problems. Science policy identifies what fields of thought will and will not be supported. Science policy directs which fields will be favored with fellowships and traineeships to encourage students to choose them as careers. Such strategic and influential funding agents of the state signal the institutions as to

219

what is "right thinking" and, over time, such support influences who remains, indeed who the leaders are in the colleges and universities. By 1994 science policy in the Clinton Administration had taken a further step toward government control by announcing "output" categories toward which federal research support would be directed. These steps were taken in the name of "competitiveness" and they have been interpreted by the science community as an assault on basic research. In truth, they are little more than the inexorable working out of the endless tension between the scientist's context of discovery and the politician's context of justification.

Aranson describes the working out of this arrangement, elaborating on how various institutions emerge, such as disciplinary lobby groups, to participate in federal resource use. Lindsay reviews the role of government influence, direct and indirect, on the supply of scientists and engineers. Both authors raise questions about the efficiency of government policy compared to market solutions, and their conclusions will not raise the hopes of those who yearn for an efficient government. Martino also traces this theme carefully in his contribution on the economic goals of science and technology policy.

Aranson lays out a fundamental basis for consideration of "knowledge creation," offering first a welfare economics approach that disregards political institutions and then a public choice approach that examines, both theoretically and empirically, the workings of a representative democracy in the realm of science and technology decision making. He begins by pointing out that any resources allocated to scientific and technological activities have opportunity costs relative to foregone opportunities to use them otherwise. There are other opportunity costs in allocating resources to the management of these activities, which brings one to a consideration of industrial or academic organization, private versus public allocation, particular public policies, jurisdiction, and other matters that impact choice.

In his treatment of welfare economics Aranson points out that its perfectly competitive market assumption is violated in three ways: (1) allocations occur with the use of imperfect information to connect the specific allocations of resources to the results; (2) the results of the allocations may become "public goods" and lack appropriability; and, (3) the body of "unknown knowledge" is a common pool available to any who would try to appropriate from it, and because the system of its exploitation rewards those who make the first discovery, there may be greater than optimal allocation to research by competing scientists.

Aranson then addresses the solutions to these problems, touching first on the patent system and its propensity to create monopolistic conditions. Government production of knowledge, or subsidy of production, the next solution, is shown to be fraught with the difficulty of a centralized decision maker trying to cope with fragmented, decentralized, and centrally incoherent information. The third solution he poses is the scientific community itself and its characteristic propensity to evoke a spontaneous order among the aggregate of activities called scientific research.

In the second part of his chapter Aranson turns to the ways in which political and governmental institutions create, or fail to create, public choices out of citizen preferences. He does so by constructing a general model of the electoral process and then introduces three familiar problems: rational ignorance, rent-seeking, and disequilibrium. Of the first, rational ignorance, he cites data revealing that citizens remain largely ignorant, and rationally so, about scientific issues. But this same ignorance does not extend to those whose livelihood is derived from scientific and technological pursuits; indeed, it is in their interest to make use of the informational asymmetry to influence the legislators. He writes: "[T]hese people might understand in highly specialized ways the benefits of government subsidies to research, but they will have no way to register the opportunity costs of those subsidies for others." Rent-seeking flows directly from this situation of rational ignorance, as well-organized interest groups, including government agencies themselves, pursue the public supply of private goods whose costs are spread across the electorate. This gives rise to the situation in which the lobbyists appear to be more interested in the payrolls, equipment budgets, and facilities than they are in knowledge creation. Third, Aranson analyzes the general problem of disequilibrium, which emerges in processes that employ majority voting and that are characterized by strategic voting and log-rolling.

No institutions of government, legislatures, bureaus, or courts escape the problems Aranson outlines, although they may impact particular institutions in different ways. For example, legislatures may be more interested in applied technological developments rather than in basic research because the former facilitate rent-seeking, whereas administrative agencies may exhibit the opposite preference because basic research imposes less accountability than does applied technological development.

His serious critique notwithstanding, Aranson concludes that because knowledge creation is so evidently a public good, the problems associated with private interest may not be problems we should solve in isolation from other, more egregious, rent-seeking in other policy arenas, e.g., tobacco subsidies, "lest reform eliminate partially redeemable categories of public activity while leaving unredeemable categories with larger shares of the national product."

Martino picks up this theme when he observes that most people consider science and technology to be important sources of economic growth, even though a search of the literature reveals that the exact relationship cannot be specified. He points out that in study after study of the effects of research and development on individual firms in an industry, on specific industries, and on industry groups the results show that the more research and development performed, the more productive and profitable the firm. The only exception is that government purchased research and development usually does not contribute to productivity or profitability of the industry conducting it, although it may contribute to some other industry. That said, Martino notes the generally inadequate methods for the global assessment of payoffs for investment in basic research.

Government policies toward scientific and technological activities, both positive and negative, are examined to determine whether they stimulate innovation. He concludes that patent policies were achieving this objective, whereas antitrust policy has had the opposite effect. R & D tax credits have been very ineffective in stimulating increased research and development. One result of such policies may be the emergence of a product or of a process that cannot exist without continued government subsidy but that displaces others with established market niches. An example of this kind of event might be the extension of rural electrification under government fiat and the demise of a promising wind technology in the 1930s.

Studies show that no satisfactory criteria have been developed to determine how much support should be given to science and technology, nor which projects should be selected to receive support, let alone which institutional setting is best able to make use of the support, but this has not slowed the pace of government distribution of funds for R & D. Economic criteria have foundered on the problem of identifying the prospective return of specific projects. Martino points out that "technical" criteria, even in the few cases where they can be applied with relative objectivity, cannot justify funding of science and technology over art, literature, or other "humanistic" pursuits. This absence of clear justification has not, in Martino's estimation, prevented the scientific community from developing a belief that public support for their chosen careers is an entitlement. This widespread belief requires extensive public debate.

Martino cites a wide range of studies that have shown that for the government to try to "pick winners" is a recipe for disaster. Government support of "generic" R & D for an industry has been effective in some cases. However, to be effective, the initiative for projects must come from the industry, and industry participation is crucial to the success of the activity. In a related issue Martino examines the extent to which the increasingly applied character of academic research has affected the communication among scientists and concludes that there have been too few efforts at serious research in this area to render a conclusion.

In effect, Martino concludes that not enough is understood about the effects of public funding of science and technology to permit answers to fundamental questions of "how much" and "which," and until such answers can be devised it is truly impossible to distinguish between support of science and support of painting, sculpture, music, literature, and the other arts. One may expect a wave of protest from those committed to a materialist development program allegedly dependent on the sciences, but we should not hold our breath awaiting a reasoned justification.

Lindsay turns our attention to one particular area of science policy, the question of scientific and engineering manpower and whether there exists a "shortage" that will do harm to the "competitiveness" of the United States. This is an arena of popular debate these days and one in which clarity has been lacking. In developing that needed clarity Lindsay is first concerned with the question of "how much is enough?"

Lindsay observes that there are several different meanings of shortage, even within the technical purview of economics, and he discusses the necessary distinctions between them, pointing out how these alternative methodologies give rise to different meanings of shortages.

Although we hear much these days about shortages of science and engineering personnel, a critical evaluation of the rhetoric requires a baseline upon which to gauge the extent of such a shortfall, and it is insufficient merely to point to yesterday's requirements and to project these into the future. Having enough is meaningful only in terms of the achievement of some goal, and while such a goal can be helpful for those who want an answer to the question of whether jobs will be filled in the future, Lindsay feels that the methods employed to determine the supply of personnel are inadequate.

Beyond these debates over shortages, the question of whether or not the government should take an active role in the enhancement of this specialized labor supply is also reviewed. Lindsay then asks the question of whether, in the face of the clear inappropriability of the knowledge, why any particular government, among many, would wish to invest in the development of specialized personnel when scientific knowledge produced abroad can be substituted for home developed knowledge either by information flows or by its embodiment in immigrant scientists and engineers. He suggests that there is good reason to rely on international neighbors to fund research and the development of scientific and engineering personnel, not just to shift the cost to others, but to avoid the tax burden: "By levying additional taxes to fund scientific research, we therefore not only confer the benefits of that research to other countries free of charge, but to impose additional tax distortions on our own economy and to impair our ability to compete." Lindsay's previous work on the medical profession suggests the wisdom of what is likely to be an equally unpopular conclusion among both the science establishment and U.S. chauvinists.

Taken together, these three chapters tell us much about the role of the state in higher learning, suggesting that most of what passes for policy is weakly undergirded by analysis and evaluation. The authors also point out why it is unlikely that we can expect otherwise.

8

Normative and Positive Theories of Science and Technology Policy

Peter H. Aranson

Modern governments face difficult choices concerning the funding of scientific research and applied technological development. Should American taxpayers, for example, spend over $12 billion for a superconducting super collider, $35 to $40 billion for a space station, or $3 to $5 billion to map the human genome? Would we spend an additional dollar more productively to support basic research or applied technological development? Does "large" or "small" science represent a better investment choice? And, will it make more sense for private-sector firms to pay for their own research or to receive government subsidies.

Economic analysis offers two theories to explain and predict how public officials make choices concerning nearly all forms of public expenditures. This chapter reviews some specific applications of these two theories for science and technology policy. The first theory is based on welfare economics. It provides a *normative* framework for deciding on the nature and extent of public support for basic scientific research and applied technological development, although measurement problems make it unlikely that it can offer more than very general rules for decision making. This theory also fails to be *explanatory* or *predictive* of most public-sector decisions. The second theory is based on public-choice economics, and while it does explain and predict actual decisions, it enjoys no obvious normative content.

Each theory forms the core of an orthodox approach to discerning the nature of democratic choice. But specific models growing out of each theory utter sometimes conflicting predictions, whose implications for public policy toward science and for the design of the institutions that fund and conduct research go beyond the concerns that motivated their development.

Science and Technology in the Theory of Welfare

Scholars interpret the findings of the economic theory of welfare as sometimes predicting (explaining) actual political decisions, but more often as normative: these findings tell us what government officials *should* do but they
seldom predict their actual decisions. If public officials face incentives that
reward them for the adoption of welfare-regarding policies, of course, and
provided that these officials have adequate information, then these findings
predict that they will choose policies that improve citizens' welfare, however
defined.[1] But as we shall discover when we consider public-choice theory,
government officials seldom face the incentives or enjoy the information that
would allow them to "do the right thing."

Welfare Theory and Competitive Markets

In the economic theory of welfare, the value of research occurs in the discovery of knowledge that makes possible new products or processes, the improvement of existing ones, or the lowering of costs of production. The
measurement of value grows out of the preferences of individual human beings, and not those of some omniscient observer. People best reveal their valuations in markets, by the prices they are willing to pay for new or improved
products and by the savings they achieve from less costly or newly discovered
processes. The value of research, therefore, finds its ultimate manifestation in
the products and processes that research makes possible, as that value is revealed in market relations.[2]

As there are markets for goods, services, and productive processes, so there
are also markets for research and the new knowledge that it creates. Welfare
theory concerning research ordinarily begins with models of competitive markets. These incorporate several defining assumptions. There are many buyers
and sellers, so that no agent's decisions alone can affect price. There are no
coalitions of buyers or sellers and no barriers to entry or exit.[3] The goods that
trade in a competitive market are homogeneous, meaning that they are perfect
substitutes and there is no brand-name identification. All agents enjoy perfect
information about the availability of prices, quantities, and productive technologies. The goods and services produced and exchanged also must be
appropriable and divisible. They are appropriable if a full span of control exists over the positive and negative incidents of ownership, production, and
consumption. That is, each unit of a good or service is owned, and all benefits
and costs are borne by those who own them. They are divisible if two or more
persons, households, or firms cannot own or consume the same unit of a good
or service.

These assumptions insure that a good or service trades at a single price, each productive resource flows to its highest valued use, zero economic profit prevails,[4] and the final allocation is Pareto optimal—we cannot change it without making at least one person worse off.[5] Markets may be fairly robust in their efficiency properties to significant departures from these assumptions. But a failure to satisfy one or more of these assumptions also may signal a potential source of "market failure." This means that we could improve upon the allocations of resources that occur in the market, leaving at least one person better off and no one else worse off, with some theoretically achievable, alternative allocation. As we shall discover, welfare theory often calls upon government to adopt policies that make such alternative allocations possible.

Science, Technology, and Perfect Competition

Appropriability and divisibility. Both basic research and applied technological development[6] create the economic good of new knowledge. But the market for that good may violate the assumptions of perfect competition concerning appropriability and divisibility.[7] Absent a method for protecting property rights to it, the beneficial use of new knowledge remains nonappropriable: its discoverers or owners cannot enjoy the full benefits flowing from its use, because others simply can mimic their actions, to benefit from the new knowledge that they have not paid to discover. Nor is the beneficial use of new knowledge necessarily divisible. The ability of existing users to employ a quantum of new knowledge does not decline if we add one more user to the previous pool of users.

Nonappropriability may make research effort, and therefore the supply of new knowledge, suboptimal. For example, one firm in an industry of many firms making the same good may invest in discovering a new manufacturing process that improves the product or allows its production at a lower average cost. Suppose, however, that the firm's competitors effortlessly can observe and adopt this new process, because the discovering firm enjoys no protection in its use. The researching firm then could not recapture any of its investment in discovering the new knowledge. The price of the good quickly converges to a competitive level, not reflecting the cost of knowledge creation, because other firms will not have paid research costs and can set price at their marginal cost.[8] No competitive firm should undertake knowledge-creating activities under these conditions.

Suppose that government then tries to overcome this problem by giving the investing firm property rights in the beneficial use of this new knowledge, perhaps through a patent system. Our difficulties will not end there. The patent system makes the new knowledge appropriable, but the same knowledge is in essence potentially nondivisible. If public policy allows the discovering firm alone to enjoy exclusive benefits from its use, other firms cannot use the same knowledge, which they could in the absence of patent protection without diminishing the available stock of knowledge, once the knowledge has been discovered. While unrestricted use leads to pricing at marginal cost, restricted use may create some level of market power, a monopoly problem, thereby violating an assumption of perfect competition, which results in a price above marginal cost, and therefore inefficiency.

The policy maker, in sum, faces a dilemma. If patents protect the beneficial use of new knowledge, then we expect more investment in research, and therefore more new knowledge to be discovered; but we also expect the protected firm to price monopolistically, leaving the new knowledge unexploited by other firms. If public policy allows other firms to use this knowledge, however, then we expect less of it to be discovered.

These observations identify the production of new knowledge as the possible production of a public good,[9] and it does not differ from the production of other public goods, such as national defense and public peace. Because the market production of such goods may be suboptimal, government might correct the "market failure" by enacting subsidies or ownership of benefits, as with patents.

Public officials also might wish to supply some other public goods, such as national defense and public health, which in turn may require knowledge that has not yet been discovered. In such cases government action "solves" a different public-goods or external-benefit problem. Public officials then might act as demanders of research and development from private-sector firms (or from government laboratories), which act as ordinary factor suppliers.[10]

Risk and uncertainty. A second market failure is claimed to exist in private choices about scientific and technological research. It grows out of the absence of perfect information, certainty about the future. Imperfections in information take many forms, so it is useful to distinguish among the kinds that may prevail.

The assumptions of perfectly competitive markets initially require complete certainty, a condition under which buyers and sellers have known sets of alternatives that exhaustively and mutually exclusively denote their possible actions. Each action leads invariably to a known outcome among a set of possible outcomes, over which the decision maker has a well defined preference ordering. The decision maker then chooses the alternative with which he associates the outcome that stands highest in his preference ordering.

The assumption of perfect information seems appropriate for static models of consumer choice and for producer choice when the decision maker selects from among known technologies and mixes of productive factors in well-defined markets with stable, predictable prices. The assumption seems strained for decisions involving intertemporal choice, including most capital investments. Such investments incorporate a temporal separation between the time of the decision to acquire the capital good or make the capital investment and the resulting flow of income from it. Where such a temporal separation exists, the connection between action (investment) and the outcome of the choice to invest (profit or loss) may not be transparent. A decision to invest directly or indirectly in research—the production of new knowledge—*is* a decision to invest in a capital good.

Interpreting knowledge as a capital good whose instrumentalities are scientific research and technological development, however, does not identify the kind of more general informational connection between investment choices and possible outcomes that might prevail. The traditional literature about decision making identifies three possible connections.[11] The first is certainty, where the choice of an action leads invariably to a specific outcome or set of outcomes. Second, research-investment decisions may occur under conditions of risk. Such choices include completely and perfectly known sets of alternatives (investment choices) and outcomes (returns). But for each alternative chosen, an outcome occurs with a known (or orderable) probability. Risky choice thus is like a lottery.

Third, the decision may occur under conditions of uncertainty, in which the alternatives (in this case called strategies) and outcomes are fully known, but the probabilities that various states of nature occur, connecting alternatives contingently with outcomes, are unknowable or meaningless. These situations describe cases of duopolistic or oligopolistic interaction, involving the conjectural variations of games of strategy and the like. The intellectual roots for studying them lie in the theory games and in the works of Knight[12] and others.

To these three connections we might add a fourth. The decision may occur under conditions of radical uncertainty, because *ex ante*, some possible outcomes may remain unknown or unknowable. Radical uncertainty is associated with the Austrian School of economics, and with Shackle[13] in particular.

In the study of public policy toward science and technology, we can ignore the first of these conditions, certainty, because it provokes no necessary governmental actions to address its effects. The remaining informational conditions, however, correspond to different forms of research, each with a different public-policy prescription. Risky choice arises in ordinary product-development decisions, where the alternatives are to invest or not in a particular project, and the outcomes remain well-specified (the product will or will not be marketable at different levels of profit or the process will or will not produce cheaper or better products); but the probabilities associated with these outcomes are only subject to estimation. Uncertain choice arises in decisions to engage in races between or among firms to develop products or processes or to patent first.[14] And radically uncertain choice corresponds most closely to decisions to invest or engage in basic research, where at least some of the outcomes that might result cannot be specified.

The perceived market failure that accompanies each of these kinds of imperfect information varies with the particular condition. Under risky choice, risk-averse decision makers might forego investment in risky projects, when less risky alternatives, even with lower expected returns, are available.[15] For example, suppose that we measure the comparative returns to research against a benchmark of the return on riskless government bonds paying ten percent interest per year. A risk-neutral decision maker would require a return of just slightly greater than twenty percent from an investment in research with a success probability of fifty percent, to allocate resources to that research and not to government bonds. But to invest in the same research project, a risk-averse decision maker would require an even higher return, a greater success probability, or both. Risk-aversion thus may lead to a suboptimal allocation of resources to research, as compared with risk-neutral choice.[16]

Market failure is said to emerge under uncertain choice for a different set of reasons. If legal provisions—a patent system, for example—create a "right of first possession" in new knowledge, then two uncoordinated firms engaged in a research race may duplicate effort or cost, thereby reducing the total net return to research.[17] The same effect may occur if first discovery and entry into a market create other barriers for subsequent entrants. But if its discoverer *cannot* appropriate the beneficial use of new knowledge—if, for example, there is no patent protection—then no research may happen because of the free-rider problems associated with public goods and external benefits.

Finally, market failure seems most noticeable in the case of radical uncertainty associated with basic research. Sometimes, as with experimentation, the researcher first formulates an hypothesis in terms of the predictable outcomes an experiment is designed to test. Even in those situations, however, the economic "usefulness" of the findings can be wholly obscure. But in much theoretical work involving pure mentation and no experimentation, *ex ante* the outcomes may seem unknown or unknowable. Consequently, while the researcher might find even great intrinsic reward in his activity, he remains far less informed about the benefits to others that he associates with its unspecifiable outcomes. Under these circumstances a suboptimal level of research activity, and therefore output of new knowledge, may occur.[18] Stated differently, there may be no market for the results of basic research, so public officials may be called upon to supply the missing market.

Scale problems. A problem of scale sometimes emerges if the optimal size of a research facility may be too great for several separate research institutions combined to afford. The capital market, too, may exhibit imperfections concerning risk-preferences involving large scale investments, although that is unlikely. Once such a facility is supplied, furthermore, each subsequent use lowers its average total cost per use. The new generation of particle-accelerator devices is an example of this phenomenon. And with globally declining average total costs per additional use, the facility (more accurately, its owner) constitutes a natural monopoly. This condition violates an assumption of perfect competition, that of many sellers. But the public-goods aspect of the facility also might lead to suboptimal private supply, suggesting the appropriateness of government subsidy for large-scale science, provided that benefits exceed costs.

Limitations on the Welfare Model of Knowledge-Creation

The normative aspects of welfare theory are so fully accepted, that its many limitations find little consideration in discussions of public policy toward scientific and technological research. The structure and conclusions of the theory, nevertheless, have become the subject of recent debate, making apparent its several internal and external limitations.

Internal Limitations: Problems within the Economic Theory of Welfare

Internal limitations consist of findings *within* the structure of welfare theory that provide counterclaims to the argument, "the market fails, therefore government." Three internal limitations of the model include the weighing of costs and benefits, inframarginality, and problems of imperfect information.

Costs and benefits. A "publicness" of a good does not alone compel its public production, subsidy, or other collective action. Government should not subsidize the production of many public goods or goods that are at least partially public, because the cost of public action exceeds the benefit. For example, while the public sector reasonably might subsidize basic research on heart disease, cancer, and stroke, it probably should not do so to find a cure for adolescent acne. The costs of inefficient allocations include those of opportunities foregone to do other things with the misallocated funds, in either the private or the public sector.

Inframarginality. A good also may be only partially public, in that it creates private benefits for its producer or consumer but with beneficial external "spillover effects" for others. The degree of a good's publicness, as well as its price and demand characteristics, may form a configuration that makes the external benefits entirely "inframarginal" to a decision concerning efficient output. Some forms of education may exhibit such properties.[19] Those who produce and consume education may do so at an efficient level, even though others may benefit from their decisions. In such cases the public sector has no welfare-increasing alternative.

Information. Finally, the supposition that government officials can discern the correct level for producing a public good, in this case new knowledge, implies certain assumptions about their information that place several of the prescriptions of welfare theory in doubt. The information problem goes in two directions, either of which can affect the ability of public officials to forge appropriate policies.

First, several firms may make up a competitive industry, and each might prefer to have *someone* engage in creating the public good of new knowledge, to improve a product or lower its average cost of production. But as we note earlier, if any firm undertakes this research, then all others may benefit, even if they contributed nothing to discovering the new knowledge. That is, they will free-ride on another firm's research investment.

All of these firms might agree to let government tax each of them, to solve the free-rider problem. But how will public officials set the correct tax? They might do so by asking each firm what the research would be worth to it. But then the free-rider problem reappears, because each firm, in revealing its preferences, will report a valuation of zero, hoping that all other firms honestly will reveal their respective valuations and be taxed accordingly to provide the public good. Because the value of research cannot exist apart from these individual valuations, the resulting preference-revelation problem may create a suboptimal public allocation to knowledge creation. And if public officials then try to guess the correct tax, they are likely to be mistaken.

The second aspect of the information problem grows out of the subjectivist and Austrian critiques of central economic planning. Knowledge falls into two categories: knowledge that already has been discovered and knowledge that has not yet been discovered. Firms have incentives to assimilate and efficiently to deploy pre-existing knowledge, according to its usefulness. Knowledge that has not yet been discovered and which it is the goal of research to reveal, by contrast, has not yet been deployed: its value remains unknown. Nor can a central authority collect the kind of decentralized and sometimes unanticipated information required to discern the unknown value of undiscovered knowledge.

As Hayek[20] suggests, the totality of such information is given to no one single person. Even if it were to exist, It would remain widely and radically decentralized throughout the economy. Its importance at any moment may be apparent to no one. Hence, the notion of a single authority collecting, processing, and acting on this information—especially to provide an aggregate valuation of knowledge not yet discovered—remains a chimera. The opportunity costs of public action, chosen under public officials' own form of ignorance, might then increase beyond those of inaction, merely because of faithfully executed error.

Both the preference-revelation problem and the decentralized-information problem afflict government policies aimed at encouraging knowledge creation, at each and every stage, from pure basic research to applied technological development. But the Austrian critique goes further, to distinguish qualitatively between the nature of uncertainty at these two poles of the research continuum. The Austrian critique does weaken belief in the robustness of public-sector interventions in applied technological development. Accurate judgments about valuations and related information remain radically decentralized even in these processes, although many or even most of the possible outcomes of research may be anticipated. But with respect to pure basic research, information about or predictions of possible outcomes often remains not merely radically decentralized, but also beyond the powers of human anticipation.

External Limitations: Market and Nonmarket Alternatives to Government Subsidy

The theory of external benefits and public goods, however afflicted with internal limitations, does provide a necessary but not sufficient justification for government subsidy of particular varieties of knowledge creation. That subsidy may take the form of direct government production of research or of payments to proprietary and nonproprietary institutions and persons to engage in knowledge creation. But the theory suffers under additional limitations with respect to a policy prescription of subsidy or direct governmental production: there exist alternative, less intrusive and arguably superior governmental policies and responses of nongovernmental institutions. These alternatives deserve exploration.

Patent systems. The development of a patent system is the most important of these alternatives. Patents create property rights in the beneficial use of knowledge for its discoverers or their assignees. They thereby allow investors to capture at least some of the benefit their investments in knowledge creation generate, leading to a greater amount of research, and therefore new knowledge, than otherwise might occur. But the appropriateness of patent protection depends crucially on whether the underlying new knowledge is gained from applied technological development or from basic scientific research. We first consider patent protection for the results of applied development. Devising a globally optimal patent system to protect these results may be impossible. For example, competing firms without patent rights may try to "invent around" a patent. This strategy may provoke overinvestment in research while simultaneously reducing the returns to the original patent holder. The definition of what is and what is not a patentable product or process also may remain obscure at any borderline drawn. This problem invites costly litigation and generates further uncertainty, which partly may defeat the purpose of a patent system.

The period of patent protection is similarly an important policy variable. The problem of choosing an appropriate period mirrors that of deciding whether to have a patent system. Because a patent gives its owner a temporary monopoly, if the period is "too long," the accompanying costs of monopoly may outweigh the benefits that the new knowledge provides. If the period is too long, a superoptimal amount of research also may occur. If it is "too short," the amount of research, and therefore new knowledge, may be suboptimal.

In response to this problem, government officials might adopt an *ex post* reward structure designed to adjust the time period, patent by patent, according to the usefulness of the knowledge created, expected economic returns from it, *ex ante* risk, and the firm's original investment in research. But such a system encounters all of the problems associated with any kind of policy requiring the central collection and processing of information about matters that may remain inherently unknowable. It also invites lawsuits from competitors concerned about the length of the award, and the costs of that litigation may exceed the net value of the knowledge gained.

In spite of its unavoidable errors, a patent system with a fixed period of protection avoids these kinds of lawsuits and is relatively simple to operate. Beyond internalizing external benefits to the discovering firm, a patent system also performs a "prospect" function, enabling the fullest use of the knowledge discovered under it.[21] Under patent protection beneficial owners of new knowledge can search for marketing and development opportunities and complementary products and processes, to increase the value of the knowledge in use. Without patent protection they must act in secrecy or forego such explorations entirely.

U.S. patent law also encourages early patenting, which reduces costly but duplicative research efforts through an "announcement effect." Early patenting gains added importance in an environment of radically decentralized information about opportunities to discover new knowledge and about the importance of that knowledge. "Races to patent" in such cases may be few, because only a single firm may discern a particular research opportunity. But early patenting informs all other firms both that a particular opportunity has been foreclosed and that a complementary product or processes now may be available for commercial exploitation.

While patent protection may prove beneficial for applied research and development, it would be too costly to give the same protection to the results of basic scientific research. Present patent law appears to recognize this distinction. Ideas by themselves remain unpatentable, and basic research, unlike applied technological development, ordinarily results in new ideas, not new products and processes subject to commercial exploitation. The presentation of ideas, of course, remains subject to copyright protection.

Why is this difference in the treatment of basic research and applied technological development appropriate? To the extent that it has no apparent commercial use, knowledge gained through basic research has no problems of appropriability *in rem*, because there are no immediate economic returns to appropriate from the sale of products or processes.[22] No advantage lies in conferring a proprietary interest in sole use on a scholar who computes the next unknown prime number, discovers another black hole in space, or discerns the existence of yet another elementary particle.

Imagine, for example, the retarding effect on subsequent research if those who discovered the structure of DNA and RNA had patents to protect their results. Either they would be the only ones who could conduct further research in this area, or the use of their discoveries would be limited to those who had paid them for permission to do further research.

Just the opposite result seems desirable: the fullest possible use of new scientific knowledge. But there must be incentives to foster basic research. Not surprisingly, therefore, the incentive structure that has evolved in the basic-research community rewards discoverers whose findings, through subsequent research uses, lead to other breakthroughs. The reward to discoverers takes the form of research grants and academic promotion. Copyright laws and professional standards to prevent plagiarism protect the "ownership" of knowledge that researchers discover. But once the knowledge is published, it is available to other scientists for replication and extension.[23]

Risk, uncertainty, and economic organization. If a patent system can resolve appropriability problems with respect to applied technological development, what responses might resolve problems of risk or uncertainty? In the economic theory of welfare, the model of the firm under conditions of perfect competition is one of atomistic, unintegrated producers acting as if they are owned by single individuals.[24] Firms nevertheless enjoy a variety of potential organizational responses to risk and uncertainty, which become evident when we enrich this basic model.

First, for simple risky choice, the owner of a closely held firm, because his investment represents such a large proportion of his wealth, cannot easily diversify into a host of other investments that would reduce the potential future variance in his portfolio's value. As a result, the single owner may not invest in risky (high variance) ventures, such as research.

In response to this problem of concentrated risk, the firm can go to capital markets, to sell ownership shares to other stockholders who are able to diversify their holdings.

The resulting "separation of ownership and control," however, may lead to problems if the interests of shareholders (owners) and managers (those who control) do not coincide.[25] In particular, a manager who owns but a few shares in the firm might prefer less research and greater managerial compensation than would shareholders, but the capital market itself, through the parallel market for corporate control in the form of takeovers and mergers, provides a corrective for this problem. If managers do not invest in the appropriate level and quality of research, then the publicly traded firm will earn lower profits and provide a good takeover target for raiders, who will replace incumbent managers with superior management teams.[26]

Second, the firm might create its own internal diversification by integrating several different research projects under its own ownership and control. By thus extending the scope of its research operations, the firm can reach a point where *ex ante* expectations of success converge with actual experience, thereby reducing substantially the variance of its returns from research. Venture capitalists and technology-oriented mutual funds provide the same diversification function for firms that specialize in research and development, but they do so external to the firm's organization.

These responses assume that patents protect the beneficial use of any knowledge discovered. But even where they do not, or where some secret research and development is required before patents issue, the firm enjoys the possibility of vertically integrating production and management teams with research teams, to protect trade secrets that research teams might develop, and to reduce the costs of postcontractual opportunism by either party to a contract between unintegrated (separately owned) research and production teams.[27] This solution should emerge in areas of imperfect patent protection or prolonged research and development activities.

As distinct from risky choice, the problems of uncertain choice, including conjectural variation about other firms' research or development strategies, can occur both with and without patent protection. Contemplating the reward of patent protection, as we note earlier, firms may engage in wasteful, duplicative efforts in the race to patent, spending too much money in the aggregate devoted to research and development. With no patent protection, however, conjectural variation can lead to a suboptimal level of research and development. Without patent protection, firms similarly may overinvest in research that they can protect as trade secrets and engage in superoptimal degrees of vertical integration between research and production teams. But with patent protection they may test the boundaries of patent law by sometimes wastefully inventing similar products and processes.[28]

Property rights in basic research. These alternatives to government subsidy or production occur within the framework of applied technological development, where risk or uncertainty applies to the research-investment decision. But in basic research, as we note earlier, the information problem often becomes one of radical uncertainty, where the results of the investment may remain unpredictable and far from any expectations of commercial exploitation. Similarly, we would want to promote the widest possible dissemination and use of basic-research findings, subject to cost considerations. So in this area of knowledge creation we uniquely prefer to *avoid* of some forms of appropriability and divisibility of beneficial use.

But these observations fail to identify methods for rewarding investments in basic research. Patents do not protect beneficial use of its results, and there remains a substantially opaque connection between those results and commercial exploitation. How, then, might people gain incentives to invest directly or indirectly in the basic-research enterprise?

It is here that some form of government subsidy may appear desirable, provided that current levels of basic research seem suboptimal. But we must temper even this conclusion. First, if basic research outcomes remain unpredictable, and if their commercial use seems equally unforeseeable, then it is not apparent how we might assess returns to different investment levels or patterns. That is, the same information problems that afflict applied technological development afflict the subsidizer of basic research, and certainly more so.[29]

Second, if we bifurcate the subsidy decision, so that one person decides which research to propose to conduct and how to do it, while another, a public official, decides how much to spend on which areas of research, then neither person alone has enough information to reach an optimal decision. The researcher knows most (although perhaps not much) about potential benefits, and the bureaucrat or legislator should know much about the opportunity cost of the expenditure (although for reasons that we explore in the next section, he will know very little). Under this distribution of information, the "correct" decision is unlikely to emerge.

Reflecting on this nonproprietary structure of bifurcated benefits and costs with no apparent "bottom line," we nevertheless should recognize that institutional responses do emerge in basic research, especially at the university level. As we note earlier, these responses tend to establish a kind of property right in some returns to research success, although not those rights associated with a fully proprietary system.

The basic researcher operates in an environment whose formal and informal rules enhance the likelihood that he will receive "credit" for his knowledge creation. Reputational returns to creating new knowledge seem partly appropriable, through a system that punishes academic dishonesty and fraudulent appropriation of credit for others' works. Promotion and tenure rules also encourage publication in the most widely read professional journals, increasing the (rate of) dissemination of new knowledge. But these rules also sanction premature claims, through the requirement that one's results be replicable and by fostering replication by others.

While tenure may protect academic freedom to do research and publish results, that is not its principal function in science. (Indeed, tenure provides little protection to untenured faculty members, who are most likely to need it; it protects instead those who have complied with prevailing orthodoxy before the award of tenure.) Tenure in science is more a means for allocating the right to take the greatest research risks to those who best can use that right.

Suppose that a new, untenured researcher engages in a single, radically uncertain project, which, even with the most diligent effort on his part, has a high probability of failure. If failure does occur, then at the end of the traditional six years, those who award tenure will have learned little about his capabilities, because of the inherent radical uncertainty of the project that he chose. Hence, they may decide to "waste" his knowledge-creating resources. The tenure system thus gives the untenured researcher an incentive to attend to smaller, more risk-free projects within the common body of knowledge, where, incidentally, he seems more likely to find error than do his tenured colleagues.

With the award of tenure goes a substantial diminution of restraints on taking large research risks. But the "right" to take such risks belongs to those who have proved themselves, concerning their technical competence, productivity, their full familiarity with the prevailing core of knowledge (preventing duplication), their diligence, and to a lesser extent, their originality.

Stated differently, because of radical uncertainty, we cannot discern *ex ante* what results are likely to flow from a given basic research project. We can only judge the past success that a researcher has enjoyed. We could not make such a judgment on the basis of a six-year career if the researcher had undertaken a single, radically uncertain project and failed. Thus, it is not surprising that the biggest subsidies in most fields go to the most established senior researchers with the best records of success. But reflecting the inherent radical uncertainty under which the subsidy-granting officials choose, the criteria for awards in basic research commonly exhibit a diminished regard for the "importance" of research to be funded, and a greater concern for the likelihood that there will be any results at all.

This description of the basic-research community does not imply that its members' work is uncoordinated or haphazard or unproductive. Quite to the contrary. A system that rewards young researchers for becoming familiar with, correcting, and extending the common core of knowledge provides ample incentives for most researchers to learn that core, recognize its anomalies, and push out the frontiers of knowledge in an orderly manner. If the right to take great risk flows to proven, responsible scholars, the probability of wasteful error or outright fraud will decline. The members of the basic research community are highly entrepreneurial in their research pursuits, and there appears to be little formal organization or coordination of their efforts. But the "spontaneous order" that characterizes their activities resembles the order of the market for goods and services itself.[30] And this order has evolved without the intervention of government officials.

Science and Technology in Public Choice

The preceding discussion of welfare theory, as applied to policy making toward scientific research and applied technological development, suggests these rules for government action. First, at the level of basic research, a policy of subsidy or direct government knowledge creation may be appropriate, provided that the costs outweigh the benefits.[31] Second, at the level of applied technological development, some form of patent protection instead of government subsidy recommends itself.[32] Third, where public officials choose to provide some public good other than knowledge creation, they may have to purchase knowledge-creating activities from the nongovernmental sectors.

In each of these policy areas, of course, welfare theory supposes that information is sufficient to do the kind of cost-benefit analysis to choose the appropriate structure of property rights in patents or to select the correct research projects to fund. But do public officials enjoy the kind of information and face the sorts of incentives that lead to the adoption of these policies within and among categories of research? Public-choice theory argues that they do not.

Simple Voting Models: The Problem of Rational Ignorance

We want to understand the nature of information about public-policy alternatives found in the political system and the character of incentives concerning the demand for and supply of public policy toward science. So we begin with the simplest model of a democratic election. In this model citizens either vote directly on public-policy alternatives or choose representatives who make public policies for them. Citizens judge candidates for office according to sincerely and faithfully constructed platforms containing the underlying public-policy proposals. But even this simplest model requires further structure to yield predictions. For example, the contest might be over a single issue, such as the funds to be allocated to basic research, or over several issues, including the structure of taxation. The rules of voting may or may not allow abstention, and the contest may be in a plurality-rule, winner-take-all system or in a proportional-representation system.

If the contest occurs in a single-issue, plurality-rule election system with two motions or candidates, and if several technical conditions are satisfied,[33] then an equilibrium motion or platform results, one that defeats or ties all other motions or platforms, located ordinarily at the median voter's most preferred position.[34] The resulting allocation may or may not be efficient, depending upon the distribution of citizens' most preferred positions along the issue dimension.[35]

But a more careful inquiry into the voter's choice leads to a different result, one that undermines the notion that voters evaluate candidates according to a common dimension measuring the level at which government produces some public good, such as funding for research or development. This result also undermines the notion that candidates or officeholders can or do make public-policy decisions according to the criterion of allocative efficiency, as welfare theory would contemplate.

Consider the citizen's decision problem in voting. Most generally, the citizen votes (does not abstain) if

$$PB - C + D > 0,$$

where P is the probability that his vote makes or breaks a tie in favor of his preferred motion or candidate; B is the difference in utility he would experience from the victory of his preferred candidate or motion, minus the utility he would receive from that of his less preferred one; C is his cost of voting; and D is the "consumption utility" he associates with voting, including the satisfaction from complying with the ethic of participation.[36]

With reasonable values of P, B, and C, and supposing that D equals zero, P in a large electorate is so small that it seems most unlikely that anyone would vote. The addition of the D-term adds to the predicted amount of voting but at the expense of making the theory tautological (the citizen votes because he wants to vote). Even so, the *instrumental* value of voting, PB, appears to be small, compared with the *consumption* value of voting, D.

Now consider the voter's incentive to gain additional information about the issues and the candidates' positions on them. Suppose there is some "objectifiable" B-term for the voter (for example, the difference in the wealth levels he would experience from the enactment of each candidate's proposal), which he presently does not fully know. Then, the B-term's discounting by P, the probability of his being the pivotal voter, would make the entire term, PB, very small. The voter might invest in acquiring more information, to help him make a "correct" voting choice, meaning that he would pay to learn more about the candidates' actual positions and how the enactment of each position might affect his welfare. But if the instrumental value of the vote is very small, the voter will not invest additional resources to improve his chances of making a more accurate decision about how to vote, a decision that is practically worthless to him. He will rely solely on his present stock of knowledge to make his voting choice.[37]

The term "rational ignorance," which is associated with this reasoning, is at least partly misleading. The voter does have *some* information. But that information is biased in particular ways. The consumer, for example, buys thousands of products on whose prices or other attributes government policy might have some effect. Concerning these effects the voter rationally may purchase no additional information. But the voter *has* paid a "sunk cost" to acquire information about the single product of which he is a direct or factor supplier, and which represents the largest source of his income. For example, producers will know much more about the effects of specific government policies on their industries than consumers will know about those effects on the thousands of different goods and services they purchase.

The occasional exception to this hypothesis tends to prove the rule. Sometimes a good or service becomes overwhelmingly important to particular groups of consumers. It may reflect a significant part of their budgets or have some other inordinate impact on their lives. Therefore, specialized groups of consumers, like producers, will have paid the sunk costs for acquiring a disproportionately greater level of information about associated public-policy alternatives. Victims of particular diseases and the members of their families, once they have become politically organized, provide appropriate examples of this phenomenon.[38]

Rational ignorance leads voters to assess policies and the candidates who adopt them on *distributive* margins: "How much better or worse off will this policy make me in my role as a producer or specialized consumer?" But voters do not and cannot calculate the full *allocative* consequences of these policies, including opportunity costs, although information about allocative consequences inevitably must inform optimal public-policy creation.

There is ample evidence of rational ignorance about science and technology, and about government policies toward science and technology in particular. Miller, for example, reports the results of extensive surveys of the adult population (in 1979) concerning levels of scientific knowledge.[39] He finds that in an elementary way, nine percent of those polled understand the scientific approach, fifty percent understand basic scientific concepts, 41 percent understand science public-policy issues, but only seven percent enjoy "scientific literacy."

These numbers alone are not sufficient to categorize the *entire* population as "ignorant." But Miller then reports some indirect evidence about how market and political environments differently affect the information of consumers and voters, respectively. Recall that only 41 percent of those polled understand science public-policy issues. Much of this information doubtless reflects the population's sunk costs of education (sixteen percent of those without high-school degrees are so informed, but 81 percent of those with graduate degrees understand science-policy questions). Nevertheless, fully 74 percent of the entire sample report a change in eating habits, pursuant to published accounts of the carcinogenic effects of chemical additives. The difference between 41 percent with science public-policy information and 74 percent with a changed consumption pattern more than likely reflects that political choice about science policy has its value discounted by the P-term, while market choice about the safety of food does not. Stated differently, the citizen ordinarily gets what she buys in the supermarket, but she does not necessarily get what she votes for in the polling booth.

If rational ignorance characterizes many political choices about science and technology, those who *will* enjoy information will be producers (scientists and science bureaucrats) and specialized consumers (sufferers of particular diseases and managers in industries that use the results of research as indirect factors of production or as appropriable capital goods). These people might understand in highly specialized ways the benefits of government subsidies to research. But they will have no way to register the opportunity costs of those subsidies for others, even if they wished to do so. Hence, voting and related political-demand activities take the form of highly fragmented claims on the treasury but not of claims to assess the opportunity costs of satisfying these demands. So allocative consequences related to efficiency inform few of voters' public choices about science and technology policies.

Interest-Group Decision Making

Do decisions made on distributive and allocative margins coincide? Probably not. Public-choice theory predicts from the distributive motives of political actors the adoption of nonoptimal public policies. Public-choice models underlying this prediction begin with interest groups, whose leaders decide how to allocate resources in the political process. One set of models presents those leaders with two choices. First, they can lobby public officials for an allocatively efficient government supply of public goods. Second, they can lobby these officials to secure the allocatively inefficient public supply of private goods for the members of the particular group. The theory of rational ignorance predicts that such leaders and their group members would not have the information to lobby for the first. But even if they did, game-theoretic models of the political process predict that they will lobby for private benefits.[40]

Interest groups in these models would find that using their private political resources to demand the governmental production of public goods would be tantamount to supplying such goods. In essence, then, the public sector "fails" to supply public goods for precisely the same reason that, in the structure of welfare theory, the private sector does so: there is no easy way to price, reward, or make a market in the public-sector production of public goods.[41]

A second set of models posits a pre-existing political market in private goods, in which private suppliers of goods and services lobby public officials for regulations and subsidies that will increase their wealth. They may seek regulated price increases, for example, or restrictions on competitive entry. Four results follow from successful political actions of this sort. First, there is a deadweight loss because the output of the protected industry is too small relative to the efficient level.[42] Second, because prices rise, part of the remaining consumer surplus (the excess of what consumers would be willing to pay, over what they actually pay for units of the good or service) is redistributed to producers. Third, real resources are used up in political competition to secure these private benefits for the industry. Fourth, suppliers must "pay" politicians for their political gains, which payments perform no useful economic function. The "rent-seeking" process thus described ordinarily is wholly inefficient.[43]

Legislative Decision Making

In representative political systems, several institutions intermediate between citizens' and interest groups' political preferences and demands (sometimes aggregated through political parties) and the public policies eventually chosen. These include the legislature and its internal committee structures, the executive branch, the bureaucracy, and the courts. Those who populate these institutions hold their own public-policy preferences and private interests, face institutionally determined rules and incentives, and share characteristic methods and limitations in collecting information about citizens' welfare and demands, all of which may affect the policies they eventually enact and enforce.

Studies of the legislative process concentrate on a description of the legislator's strategy set, under the assumption that the strategy chosen affects his probability of reelection. Representatives who adjust their strategies to maximize this probability tend to remain in office longer than those who do not. This tendency gives the legislature's public-policy choices their essential character.

Legislators' strategy sets include the possibilities of engaging in advertising, position taking, and credit claiming.[44] Advertising, the activity least related to particular public-policy decisions, includes attempts to gain favorable name recognition. Advertising skills may vary, but they have only muted significance for most legislators' eventual public-policy decisions. Position taking, which refers to the representative's publicly announced stands on issues and to his votes on roll-call ballots, is only mildly connected to electoral success. Before final votes on passage, each representative enjoys ample opportunities to shape legislation in the committee process, away from public scrutiny. Similarly, constituents understand that each legislator is but one of many, so individual legislators' votes, while discoverable if the roll is called, have only minor probative value.

Credit claiming forms the core of the legislative process insofar as reelection is concerned. A legislator might claim credit for three sorts of laws. The first creates general statutes from which flow a stream of public goods: benefits and costs that affect nearly everyone, because they *do* produce public goods. The second creates private, divisible benefits for identifiable groups and constituencies in the electorate, at collective cost to everyone else: the traditional rent-seeking configuration. The third may produce public goods, such as national defense or knowledge creation, but the actual physical production or supply of factors occurs in identifiable legislative districts or among particular national but cohesive groups.

The first kind of legislation provides few credible opportunities for credit claiming. A legislator cannot believably argue that he alone has reduced the national rates of unemployment or inflation or added to national defense or knowledge creation. Most voters understand that such legislation is the product of the executive branch and 535 members of Congress, not that of a single legislator. The second kind of legislation, however, provides full opportunities for credit claiming. A legislator *can* claim credit for bringing a new hydroelectric dam, post office, highway, army base, or national laboratory to his district, because voters understand that each other member of the legislature, *ceteris paribus*, would have preferred to have had the facility in his district. The third kind of legislation often supplies the instrumentality for the second, in the form of the porkbarrel.

In sum, the strategic imperative of creating private, divisible benefits for identifiable constituencies and groups drives the legislative process. The legislator, accordingly, works on distributive margins by creating private benefits at collective cost. The resulting legislation may be explicitly redistributional (the second kind) or incidentally may produce public goods, at a level and cost that reflect no efficiency considerations, but that also creates an omnibus opportunity for porkbarrel laws (the third kind).

When confronted with a decision to pass a public-goods program or one that creates private benefits at collective cost (mirroring the choice problem discussed earlier concerning interest groups), the legislator ordinarily prefers the second strategy to the first.[45] The legislature, then, is a market for private benefits supplied at public cost. Indeed, the legislature's committee organization facilitates this process by fragmenting decision making among interested groups of lawmakers, each of whom knows the positive, distributive, political, and narrowly economic effects of his actions but has little or no information about the allocatively inefficient incidents of the resulting resource extraction that supports the process.

The Executive Office

Most contemporary representative democracies concentrate many public scientific and technological choices within the offices of the chief executive, who also serves as the "chief legislator." He and his agents might be able to collect information on costs and balance demands, to the end of diminishing the effects of interest-group rent-seeking and legislative rent-provision. But we have no theoretical reason to expect that such a result actually occurs.

First, the executive office is divided into public-policy categories, either along cabinet or ministry lines or in special offices fragmented among public-policy subject-matter jurisdictions. Leadership and staff to fill these offices generally are recruited from the affected groups and constituencies, and such persons have no transparent sources of information about globally efficient policies and opportunity costs, except, say, the opportunity costs of trading off monetary increments in one category of science or defense or education spending against another.

Second, the executive's concerns about reelection and legislative support for his programs shape expenditure policies. Models of this process discern a pattern very much like that found in the legislature. In particular, if the chief executive engages in an incremental decision process, deciding on programs and spending levels one or a few at a time, and if rational ignorance prevails in the electorate, then a net accretion of private-benefit programs occurs over time. Even if citizens become sensitive to increased taxes, attempts to introduce a rationalized, zero-base budgeting process or some other form of global choice process will lead to redistributions among program categories, but not from considerations of efficiency. Instead, considerations of the political productivity of spending will govern, with no necessary connection to efficiency.[46]

In sum, even in the presence of budgetary constraints, both the legislators and the chief executive allocate resources to various programs not according to efficiency criteria, but by the political productivity of additional dollars spent on each program. This calculation involves an opportunity cost of plurality foregone from any alternative expenditure pattern, which is a decision made on distributive margins, not a calculation of the external benefit foregone, which is a decision made on allocative margins. Some public goods may be produced, but the policy debate tends to reflect wholly pecuniary, distributive concerns.

The Bureaucracy

Three views of bureaucracy appear in public-choice analysis. The first depicts bureaus as independent entities under diminished legislative or executive control, which fashion policies to serve the interests of bureaucrats.[47] Such models parallel an earlier concern with the "separation of ownership and control" in large corporations[48] but they remove that concern from the private to the public sector. These models often cite legislators' information problems and the agency's monopoly on information as reinforcing a bureau's overall monopoly on public production.

The second view depicts bureaus as more or less perfect agents of their respective legislative oversight committees.[49] This view marshals evidence from various agencies, showing that changes in the political makeup of a congressional oversight committee precede changes in agency policies, of the sort that changes in the committee's membership would imply. Committees need not exercise day-to-day control over, or establish informational parity with the agencies, because agencies anticipate committee members' preferences and act to serve their (constituents') interests.

The third view posits that an agency's legislative oversight committee can monitor only imperfectly the effects of agency decisions.[50] For example, quality of output, especially where the bureau provides a service to the public, may be very difficult to monitor. The legislative committee cannot compare its bureau's quality of service with that of other suppliers, particularly where government pricing of the service below an efficient level has eliminated market competition. In these situations legislative committees tend to monitor the quantity of bureau output. And if quantity remains impossible to monitor, legislators fall back on measures of agency inputs (factor employments) and activity. Such agencies enjoy some discretion, but they maximize returns on distributional margins (perhaps among suppliers of factors to them, which are found in various congressional districts), and legislators *can* monitor those margins.

Which of the three views of bureaucracy best predicts actual practice is difficult to say. Depending on their missions, different agencies may conform better or worse to the predictions of different models. But none of these views provides evidence for the kinds of policy choices by bureaus that welfare theory would contemplate. The "monopoly-bureau" hypothesis adds the agency as yet another interest group, competing for resources on distributional margins, which may or may not reflect the interests of affected groups and constituencies. The "perfect-agent" hypothesis casts bureaus as reinforcing the rent-seeking and rent-providing tendencies of the legislative market in public policy. And the "asymmetric-monitoring" interpretation demonstrates that the pecuniary benefits associated with activity-level variations, reflecting private benefits provided to factor suppliers, dominate the policy process. Under none of these hypotheses are informational or incentive properties consistent with welfare-theoretic concerns.

Science, Technology, and the Character of Public Choice

The preceding discussion is neither detailed nor complete, and more questions remain than a brief expository development can answer. Nevertheless, a review of some science-related examples of how citizens and public officials in public-choice environments depart from the prescriptions of welfare theory may prove helpful. Equally important, a delineation of the claims of public-choice theory may be appropriate, because the theory is often interpreted as claiming "too much."

Some Examples of Rent-Seeking in Science and Technology Policy-Making

Consider first the limited claim of welfare theory that government subsidy may have a role in basic research, but not in applied technological development, except where government is a demander of new knowledge as a complement to its production of other public goods such as national defense. Now consider the political decision to allocate an additional dollar to basic research or to applied technological development.

If the dollar goes to basic research, the chance of adding to the stock of new knowledge might increase, but because of radical uncertainty, the marginal product of the dollar remains impossible to specify. The new knowledge might find some future, commercially exploitable use. The ultimate beneficiaries will be so diffuse, numerous, and unorganized, however, that, given rational ignorance, they cannot easily organize in the political market place. Hence, the only "payoff" that the politician could receive would be campaign contributions, endorsements, or other sorts of political coinage, coming from a share of a research grant itself. Stated differently, the politician might respond to the demands of potential grant recipients, who merely want more money. But there is no lobby for the *output* of a research project that is wholly unpredictable.

Consider, by contrast, the political decision to allocate an additional dollar to applied technological development. The subsidy goes to the development of a readily marketable product, so the politician can collect payoffs from the firm, as a function of an enhanced expected income stream. Because the results of basic research tend to be nonappropriable, and because of the relatively longer time horizon to payoffs attached to the basic research dollar, public officials, at the margin, should prefer to allocate federal research dollars to applied technological development, not to basic research.

The history of state and federal science spending tends to confirm this prediction. Nearly all of pre-World War Two spending was on applied research or development. And though writers such as Bush affirm a simple faith in basic research,[51] federal allocations increasingly have gone to applied technological development. Today even the National Science Foundation's redirected thrust has become the explicit linking of industry with university scientists in cross-disciplinary centers spread throughout the United States. Most of the work in these centers is of an applied or developmental nature. While we can discern no apparent welfare-related justifications for this development, we certainly can discern ample political incentives for it within the rent-seeking models of public-choice theory.

This development has changed the nature of the basic-research community's appeal for funds. University presidents, development officers, and researchers themselves seldom argue today about the desirability of funding knowledge creation for its own sake. Instead, they conform their appeals and proposals to the political market place. Science leaders speak of the "relevance" of research to the fulfillment of "national needs." Diseases are to be cured, slums turned into residential gardens, and energy produced cleanly and cheaply.

Beyond the inefficiencies involved, the basic allocational problem associated with this development is that the stock of new knowledge itself, as an output of basic research, is not increasing as fast as it could under a welfare-regarding allocation of federal funds. Surely that stock is increasing, but slower than it might. Therefore, *applications* of basic research results in technological developments are drawing on a supply of basic knowledge that is expanding too slowly. If, indeed, the stock of basic knowledge becomes relatively fixed, then spending more and more federal (and private) dollars on applied research, against a fixed capital stock of basic scientific knowledge adds fewer and fewer increments of usable applied-development output. Such expected declines in the marginal productivity of applied-research dollars merely represent a prediction based on the law of diminishing marginal returns.[52]

A second implication of the contrast between welfare and public-choice theories lies in decision making in science bureaus. Lindsay, as reported earlier, shows that certain aspects of bureau output are monitorable while others are not.[53] In general, output quantity is monitorable, but output quality is not: because government subsidizes output, users exercise a diminished amount of "consumer sovereignty"; indeed, there may be little or no competition in the subsidized service, so there are no benchmarks for comparisons of quality. Sometimes output quantity itself remains unmonitorable, in which case bureaus and legislators resort to activity-level measures (factor employments). Both bureaus and legislators, then, maximize on monitorable margins, which means that they maximize either output or factor use, but pay little attention to quality.

Safety is one dimension of output quality. NASA, for example, apparently maximized the output of shuttle flights (taking staff levels, the number of launch facilities, and the number of orbiters as constraints) but did not seek to enforce an acceptable level of risk to crews and equipment.[54] The Chernobyl explosion may have occurred because of similar calculations aimed at maximizing output. But developments other than disasters also give evidence of these effects. Today additional federal dollars to science find justification in such pecuniary externalities as the number of laboratories or centers constructed in specific congressional districts, degrees awarded in various states, and grants flowing to particular areas of research complementary to target industries, with little regard for output *quality* or value.

Indeed, one finds the same forces at work in the awarding of grants to basic research. The more radical uncertainty there is in a proposal, the less likely it is that its results will be predictable, or that one can predict any results at all. The tendency, therefore, is for grant makers to award support to research whose results are most predictable, which often means research that the applicant in large measure already has completed.

Third, the assumptions of perfect competition include markets with many buyers and sellers (consumers and producers). The model works well where a price system prevails, with appropriability and divisibility of the goods and services produced, bought, and sold. But government subsidy or direct production suppresses the informing function of price: to signal buyers and sellers of new or foreclosed opportunities. Centralized political or bureaucratic decision making, unlike decentralized markets, requires some informational alternative to market prices, to calculate opportunity costs of different investment portfolios.

Public officials may be unable to make such calculations, even though the administrative process actually might require a costing of various alternatives. Making such calculations and enforcing their policy implications also would supplant the political process with a planning process. The ultimate decision makers would remain political actors, however, with all of their informational constraints and incentives. Hence, their legislative actions in turn would suppress the planning process. In the construction of science bureaus and policies, politicians would carry out the logic of these incentives by fragmenting bureaus and allowing "end runs" around formal science-bureau decisions. Two recent examples of these tendencies include "porkbarrel" allocations outside of established peer-review channels and the ever increasing balkanization of the National Institutes of Health.[55]

Delineating the Theory in Scientific and Technological Applications

Because the preceding discussion may seem unduly pessimistic and not a little unrealistic, some of its claims may require further delineation. First, public-choice theory does not imply that firms, scientists, and science bureaucrats are "evil" persons engaged in feeding at the public trough to further their own ends. Instead, the theory's claim is the more limited one, that even public-spirited firms, scientists, and science bureaucrats enjoy the best information about the benefits of their activities to themselves and their institutions. They enjoy much less information about the benefits that their work makes possible for others. And they enjoy almost no information about the opportunity costs of their subsidies or about the allocative inefficiencies that those subsidies might produce.

Second, science policy choices are no worse than others made in the public sector. All policy areas suffer from the same problems, and science policy actually might suffer less than do other areas. To the extent that public officials are drawn from the science community, optimal choices seem more likely to emerge *within* narrowly defined expenditure categories than is true, say, of spending on national defense or highways, in which industry-provided decision makers would become advocates for their firms. The scientific method itself imposes some discipline on choosers in terms of the productivity of alternative allocations. And no science-bureau program officer would prefer to support allocations that might subject him to ridicule in the science community, to which he someday might wish to return.

Third, rent-seeking and the associated public provision of private benefits do afflict every category of governmental expenditure and regulation, and neither the private nor the public sector may have a straightforward way to make a market in public goods. So if people prefer some level of *public* public-goods production, they must create a private incentive system to achieve it. Therefore, rent-seeking may form a necessary though lamentable cost of producing public goods.

Because knowledge creation, especially with respect to basic research, so evidently may be a public good, the private-interest problem is not one that allows partial solution. For example, institutional redesign might have the goal of suppressing the private-interest nexus of legislation concerning the support of research. But if the problem of rent-seeking is not addressed in other policy areas, in which public goods seem wholly absent (tobacco subsidies and tariffs provide good examples), the overall quality of legislation might decline, and with it the likelihood of an adequate level of funding for basic research. Any solution to rent-seeking, therefore, must be fully systemic, covering all policy areas, lest reform eliminate partially redeemable categories of public activity, because they cannot compete politically in a public-choice environment, while leaving unredeemable ones with larger shares of the national product.

Notes

1. Economists identify welfare-increasing policies in two ways. The first relies on Pareto optimality. For a policy to be Pareto-optimal, there cannot be another policy that improves at least one person's welfare without making someone else worse off. The second way is a form of utilitarianism. A wealth-maximizing policy is one that maximizes aggregate wealth, although it might impose losses on some while conferring offsetting gains on others. Wealth-maximizing policies that create at least one loser are not Pareto optimal. But the two concepts of welfare-increasing policies *may* converge if the identities of winners and losers remain unknown when the policy is chosen. This construct is the so-called "veil of ignorance," behind which people would choose a wealth-maximizing policy even if some of them might be worse off after its adoption, provided that they expect to be better off in the aggregate. See James M. Buchanan and Gordon Tullock, *The Calculus of Consent: Logical Foundations of Constitutional Democracy* (Ann Arbor, MI: University of Michigan Press, 1962); John Rawls, *A Theory of Justice* (Cambridge, MA: Belknap Press of Harvard University, 1975). The two concepts also may converge if the winners must compensate the losers, to gain their consent to the change. Buchanan argues that only with compensation leading to unanimity could an observer claim that a policy change is desirable. James M. Buchanan, "Positive Economics, Welfare Economics, and Political Economy," *Journal of Law and Economics* 2 (October 1959), pp. 124–138.
2. This accounting of the value of science does not include its intrinsic value to researchers or to charitable donors. To the extent that doing or supporting research has such value, the amount of government support required to offset a possibly suboptimal amount of research resulting from market decisions actually declines.
3. A barrier to entry is a cost that a firm must pay to enter an industry that is higher than that paid by incumbent firms in the industry. High capital costs alone are not barriers to entry, *ceteris paribus*, unless they are systematically higher than incumbents paid. See, e.g., George J. Stigler, *The Organization of Industry* (Irwin: Homewood, IL: 1968).
4. "Zero economic profit" means that the producer or seller earns a market rate of return from an investment in the capital goods that produce the good or service. This return makes up (part of) accounting profit.
5. Similarly, for each good traded, price equals average total cost, marginal cost, minimum long-run average total cost (each firm is at efficient scale), and marginal revenue.
6. Many scientists and science policy makers reject a basic research-applied technological development dichotomy. University scientists engaged in basic research, especially when called upon to explain the "social utility" of their government grants, sometimes protest that they also engage in technological development or basic research with applied spin-offs; industry researchers engaged in applied technological development, when challenged to explain the public benefits (flow-

ing beyond the firm) of their government subsidies, explain that they must do "some" basic research, whose beneficial use extends to other firms. Policy makers support these claims, to the extent that they act as agents of one research community or the other. This chapter incorporates the notion of a difference between basic and applied research because of its power within a the normative welfare model and its implications for predictions growing out of public-choice theory. Denials of a distinction appear to generate more from motives of advocacy than from theoretical impossibilities. See generally Charles V. Kidd, "Basic Research—Description versus Definition," *Science* 129 (13 February 1959), pp. 368-71.

7. Kenneth J. Arrow, *Essays in the Theory of Risk-Bearing* (Chicago: Markham, 1971).

8. Technically, we say that these other firms are "free-riding" on the researching firm's investment.

9. Richard R. Nelson, "The Simple Economics of Basic Scientific Research," *Journal of Political Economy* 67 (June 1959), pp. 297-306.

10. There remain some questions about whether these factor suppliers should enjoy continuing proprietary interests (for example, patent rights) in the beneficial use of any new knowledge they might discover, but such problems are not concerns of this chapter.

11. This enumeration of decision making under conditions of imperfect information is suggested in R. Duncan Luce and Howard Raiffa, *Games and Decisions: Introduction and Critical Survey* (New York: Wiley, 1957).

12. Frank H. Knight, *Risk, Uncertainty, and Profit* (Chicago: University of Chicago Press, 1971).

13. G.L.S. Shackle, *Epistemics and Economics* (Cambridge: Cambridge University Press, 1972).

14. Yoram Barzel, "Optimal Timing and Innovations," *Review of Economics and Statistics* 50 (August 1968), pp. 348-55.

15. Arrow, *op. cit.*

16. This discussion greatly oversimplifies the calculations. Its significance lies in the observation that government is the "perfect insurer," meaning that its portfolio of investments is so large, and therefore so well diversified, that "it" is risk-neutral.

17. Barzel, *op. cit.*; David D. Haddock, "First Possession *versus* Optimal Timing: Limiting the Dissipation of Economic Value," *Washington University Law Quarterly* 64 (Fall 1986), pp. 775-92.

18. The problem remains of defining optimality under conditions of radical uncertainty. Government officials and private grant-making panels can try to estimate the effects of various public policies or rewards on the overall rate of inventive activity. But such information does not prove useful for discerning the comparative merits of particular policies or grants within or among individual categories of allocations.

19. Edwin G. West, "The Political Economy of American Public School Legislation," *Journal of Law and Economics* 10 (October 1967), pp. 765-800.

20. Friedrich A. Hayek, "The Use of Knowledge in Society," *American Economic Review* 35 (September 1945), pp. 519-30.

21. Edmund W. Kitch, "The Nature and Function of the Patent System," *Journal of Law and Economics* 20 (October 1977), pp. 265-90. But see Douglas A. Smith and Donald G. McFetridge, "Patents, Prospects, and Economic Surplus: A Com-

ment," *Journal of Law and Economics* 23 (April 1980), pp. 197–203, and Kitch, "Patents, Prospects, and Economic Surplus: A Reply," *id.*, pp. 205–207.

22. On those occasions when basic research does result in commercially exploitable products or processes, beyond simple "ideas," patent protection would be appropriate.

23. There is an additional difference between basic research and applied development, which implies that public policy should treat them differently. The results of applied technological development seem corrigible in the market. If a result is "incorrect," then it has little or no commercial value, giving all future investors in related knowledge creation an appropriate set of signals concerning their future choices. But basic-research results often seem incorrigible within a (narrowly-defined) market relation. Accordingly, such results—knowledge gained—should be fully usable by others, to insure corrigibility, extension, and the suppression of research duplication (as distinguished from replication).

24. If markets are not competitive, meaning that some firm has market power, then that firm may capture most of the benefits from research and development. Public utilities, such as electric companies, for example, may be regional natural monopolies of sufficient size to internalize and gain substantial benefits from research. But then the problem of monopoly arises.

25. Adolph A. Berle and Gardner Means, *The Modern Corporation and Private Property* (New York: Commerce Clearing House, 1932); Arrow, *op. cit.*

26. Henry G. Manne, "Mergers and the Market for Corporate Control," *Journal of Political Economy* 73 (April 1965), pp. 110–120; Nicholas Wolfson, "A Critique of Corporate Law," *University of Miami Law Review* 34 (July 1990), pp. 959–94.

27. Benjamin Klein, Robert G. Crawford, and Armen A. Alchian, "Vertical Integration, Appropriable Rents, and the Competitive Contracting Process," *Journal of Law and Economics* 21 (October 1978), pp. 397–426. Postcontractual opportunism occurs when two agents have made joint investments specific to each other's activities, and one of them tries to gain the surplus that the agreement generates, in a manner that breach-of-contract law may or may not address. The researching firm, for example, may develop new knowledge that it then tries to sell to a firm that is willing to pay a higher price than its contracting partner had agreed to.

28. The idea of "inventing around" existing patents, to develop close substitutes does not have clear implications for public policy. Some virtue may attach to allowing a competitor of the patent holder to improve upon the patented good or process. Little virtue would attach to allowing a "knock-off" to enter the market at a lower price, merely because its manufacturer had not paid the cost of development.

29. The evidence suggests that research in general, and applied research in particular, leads to net increases in national product, with evident external effects (spillovers). See generally, Peter H. Aranson, "Theoretical Considerations in the Analysis of Returns to Basic Research," Paper prepared for a Workshop on An Agenda for Science Policy Research, Division of Policy Analysis and Research, National Science Foundation, Washington, D.C., September 17–18, 1987; Zvi Griliches, *R&D, Patents, and Productivity* (Chicago: University of Chicago Press, 1984); Adam B. Jaffe. "Technological Opportunity and Spillovers of *R&D*: Evidence from Firms' Patents, Profits, and Market Value," *American Economic Review* 76 (December 1986), pp. 984–1001; Jaffe, "Real Effects of Academic Research," *American Economic Review* 79 (December 1989), pp. 957–970.

30. Gordon Tullock, *The Organization of Inquiry* (Durham: Duke University Press, 1966).

31. The "costs" included in this calculation are not simply the denomination of the level of subsidy or the dollars spent directly on producing new knowledge. Instead they are "opportunity costs," the costs of not spending funds and the human or physical capital involved on other alternatives foregone. For example, the money might better be "spent" in the form of tax reductions, or for other government programs. Even if we designate a certain level of funding for a "science budget," there remains the problem of setting priorities among different projects for support within that budget. Stating the matter in terms of opportunity costs, of course, does not resolve the problems of assembling the requisite information to make such choices.

32. For an application of these prescriptions for research on HIV, arguing that government should fund basic research but not the development of specific therapies (which pharmaceutical companies should undertake with the promise of patent protection), see Richard A. Posner and Thomas J. Philipson, *Private Choices and Public Health: The AIDS Epidemic in an Economic Perspective* (Cambridge, MA: Harvard University Press, 1993).

33. For example, the voter's payoffs must be "single-peaked," meaning that these payoffs, defined over the issue dimension (government spending on basic research, say) have at most one peak, or maximum; there exist no local maxima.

34. The basic setup of the election model assumes that there is some underlying dimension of public policy alternatives, such as the percentage of the science budget to be spent on basic research. This dimension is a straight line, and each citizen has a most-preferred position on that line. Candidates for office then choose positions on this dimension as their platforms. If both candidates choose the position of the median voter, provided that we satisfy some technical assumptions, then they tie. If one is at that position while the other is not, then the candidate at that position wins the election.

35. Distributional symmetry of voters' most preferred positions is a sufficient condition for the existence and uniqueness of an equilibrium. See William H. Riker and Peter C. Ordeshook, *An Introduction to Positive Political Theory* (Englewood Cliffs, New Jersey: Prentice Hall, 1973). If the condition of distributional symmetry is violated for an election with more than one issue, we cannot guarantee the existence of an unique equilibrium (winning) motion. Nor can it be guaranteed in single-issue elections if preferences are not single-peaked. These problems may lead to intransitive political choice. For example, with three motions—A, B, and C—the voters may reveal a "collective preference," wherein A defeats B, B defeats C, but C defeats A. See generally Kenneth J. Arrow, *Social Choice and Individual Values*, 2nd ed. (New York: Wiley, 1963); William H. Riker, *Liberalism against Populism: A Confrontation between the Theory of Democracy and the Theory of Social Choice* (San Francisco: W. H. Freeman, 1982). While this problem remains a central concern of public-choice theory, and although it has important ramifications for science and technology policy-making, I do not discuss it here. But see Giles W. Mellon, *An Approach to a General Theory of Priorities: An Outline of Problems and Methods*, Princeton University Econometric Research Program, Research Memorandum no. 42 (July 1962).

36. William H. Riker and Peter C. Ordeshook, "A Theory of the Calculus of Voting," *American Political Science Review* 62 (March 1968), pp. 25–42.

37. Anthony Downs, *An Economic Theory of Democracy* (New York: Harper and Row, 1957); Peter H. Aranson, "Rational Ignorance in Politics, Economics, and Law," *Journal des Economistes et des Etudes Humaines* 1 (Winter 1989/1990), pp. 25–42.
38. Political organizations—interest groups—often achieve significant scale economies in the collection, assembly, evaluation, and dissemination of public policy information for their members. They thereby substantially reduce the cost of acquiring political information. But the resulting bias in this information should be apparent, as our subsequent discussion of interest groups makes clear. See Peter H. Aranson and Peter C. Ordeshook, "Public Interest, Private Interest, and the Democratic Polity," in Roger Benjamin and Stephen L. Elkins, eds., *The Democratic State* (Lawrence: The University Press of Kansas, 1985).
39. Jon D. Miller, "Scientific Literacy: A Conceptual and Empirical Review," *Daedalus* 112 (Spring 1983), pp. 29–47.
40. Aranson and Ordeshook, *op. cit.*
41. This model may appear to predict that lobbyists and government officials never support or supply the governmental production of public goods. But that conclusion is unwarranted. The supply of most public goods requires significant purchases from the private sector. The supply of national defense, for example, relies on significant private industrial sectors for weapons systems, food, clothing, and other goods and services, including research and the new knowledge it makes possible. The actual level of national defense produced doubtless reflects the political demands by such factor suppliers for government contracts, not the allocatively efficient level at which national defense should be produced. See Peter H. Aranson and Peter C. Ordeshook, "Regulation, Redistribution, and Public Choice," *Public Choice* 37 (1981), pp. 69–100. The same forces characterize most private sector demands for support of research and development.
42. That is, consumers would be willing to pay suppliers more than it would cost them to provide additional units of the good or service.
43. James M. Buchanan, Robert D. Tollison, and Gordon Tullock, eds., *The Theory of the Rent-Seeking Society* (College Station: Texas A and M University Press, 1980). A rent is a payment to a factor of production or to the producer of an end product or service greater than that necessary to bring it into existence. Rents may be economically inefficient if there is wasteful competition in pursuit of them, a process called "rent-seeking," which occurs regularly in politics.
44. This enumeration of legislators' strategies is from David R. Mayhew, *Congress: The Electoral Connection* (New Haven: Yale University Press, 1974).
45. Aranson and Ordeshook, "Public Interest, Private Interest, and the Democratic Polity," *op. cit.*; Barry R. Weingast, Kenneth A. Shepsle, and Christopher Johnsen, "The Political Economy of Benefits and Costs: A Neoclassical Approach to Distributive Politics," *Journal of Political Economy* 89 (August 1981), pp. 642–64.
46. Aranson and Ordeshook, "Public Interest, Private Interest, and the Democratic Polity," *op. cit.*
47. William A. Niskanen, Jr., *Bureaucracy and Representative Government* (Chicago: Aldine Atherton, 1971).
48. Berle and Means, *op. cit.* Because politicians work on distributive margins, it is not apparent to them how to restructure the bureaucracy to achieve allocatively efficient ends. Stated differently, public officials do not enjoy the kinds of market responses (takeovers, for example) that have emerged in the private sector to

reduce problems associated with the separation of ownership and control. Different political parties may compete for control over the bureaucracy, but the goal of each party remains merely to use the bureaucracy to create another pattern of redistributions to private interests, at collective cost.

49. Barry R. Weingast and Mark J. Moran, "Bureaucratic Discretion or Congressional Control? Regulatory Policymaking by the Federal Trade Commission," *Journal of Political Economy* 91 (October 1983), pp. 765–800.

50. Cotton Mather Lindsay, "A Theory of Government Enterprise," *Journal of Political Economy* 84 (October 1976), pp. 1061–77.

51. Vannevar Bush, *Science: The Endless Frontier* (Washington, D.C.: National Science Foundation, 1980).

52. The law of diminishing marginal returns says that as more and more variable factors of production are applied to a fixed factor of production, the returns to these additions eventually will decline, and may even become negative. For example, suppose the fixed factor is a plot of agricultural land. We may apply more and more variable factors to it—labor and fertilizer, say—but the added output will grow smaller and smaller. The application here analogizes basic knowledge to the fixed factor, or capital asset, and applied technological development to the variable factor(s).

53. Lindsay, *op. cit.*

54. Linda R. Cohen and Roger G. Noll, "Government *R&D* Programs for Commercializing Space," *American Economic Review: Papers and Proceedings* 76 (May 1986), pp. 269–73. See also Cohen and Noll, *The Technology Pork Barrel* (Washington, D.C.: The Brookings Institution, 1991).

55. These tendencies may not be wholly undesirable. First, the agencies presently using peer-review processes already are part of a science porkbarrel process. They merely have formalized the process, giving established researchers control over the allocation of funds. Some competition from the legislature may not be entirely unhealthy. Second, with increasing decentralization (of NIH divisions, say) comes an increasing ability to collect and process decentralized information, at least within the limited purview of the grant-making division. But increasing decentralization also entails a diminished ability to assess opportunity costs more globally. So some optimal level of decentralization (or centralization) may prevail in the administrative model, but legislators neither enjoy the information nor face the incentives to discover it.

An additional institutional variation not considered here concerns decentralizing science and technology policy through a federal arrangement. While this variation has problems, it may partly resolve the problem of gaining information about the comparative benefits and costs of various science and technology policies. Decentralization allows that information to emerge as the result of multiple experiments, one conducted in each jurisdiction. A decentralized process might thereby facilitate opportunity-cost calculations by (decentralized) public agencies. Such a process will also limit the extent of damage or waste caused by public policy error, while simultaneously making that error more apparent.

9

Science and Technology for Economic Ends

Joseph P. Martino

Introduction

Issues involving the relationship between science, technology, and the growth of the economy are central to the current policy debate. This paper identifies some important issues and describes what is currently known about them. The following issues are examined:

1. What is known about the extent to which science and technology foster public and private economic objectives?
2. What methods have been proposed for assessing the payoffs from both publicly and privately supported basic and applied research?
3. What is known about the effects of government policies, both positive and negative, on both targeted and untargeted scientific and technological activities?
4. What criteria have been suggested for public support of general science and technology activities?
5. What is known about public sector support of technology for commercial development?
6. To what extent has public support of science and technology come to be seen as an entitlement?
7. What has been the structure of private and public support for science and technology in the U.S., and what changes have taken place over time?

Science And Technology For Economic Objectives

Government officials and businessmen, as well as academic scientists, have increasingly identified science and technology as critical elements in the growth of the economy and in the production of goods and services.

To some extent this identification has resulted from the erosion of America's share of world exports by high-technology products from Japan, Germany, and England. Over the past several years, numerous research projects have investigated the relationship between advances in foreign technological capability and increased U.S. imports of high-technology products. In general, these research projects have supported the hypothesis that improvements in foreign technology precede greater imports of technologically advanced goods.

However, the idea that science and technology boost the economy is much older than the current concern about "Japan, Inc." In the late 1960s a labor government in Great Britain established a Ministry of Technology with the specific purpose of supporting technology, in the hope that new technology would revive British industry. Before that, French fears of being overwhelmed by American technology were captured in Servan-Schreiber's *American Challenge*.[1]

Scientists and technologists have encouraged the belief that their work contributes to economic growth. Vannevar Bush and the other contributors to *Science, The Endless Frontier,* for instance, argued strongly that science was fundamental to continued American prosperity:

> Progress in the war against disease depends upon a flow of new scientific knowledge. New products, new industries, and more jobs require continuous additions to the knowledge of the laws of nature and the application of that knowledge to practical purposes. Similarly, our defense against aggression demands new knowledge so that we can develop new and improved weapons. This essential, new knowledge can be obtained only through basic scientific research.[2]

They further contend:

> The Government should accept new responsibilities for promoting the flow of new scientific knowledge and the development of scientific talent in our youth. These responsibilities are the proper concern of the Government, for they vitally affect our health, our jobs, and our national security.[3]

This view on the part of scientists and technologists, that science and technology are needed for economic growth and productivity improvement, need not be seen as purely self-serving. Many scientists and engineers have been directly involved with new technology that produced entirely new markets and industries.

Despite the fact that "everyone knows" science and technology are good for economic growth, both government and business policies toward science and technology must be guided by actual facts rather than by fond hopes. Therefore, it is necessary to ask what is actually known about the extent to which science and technology can be used to achieve desired public and private economic objectives.

Over the past two decades there have been numerous studies of the relationships between economic growth and scientific and technological activity. Several of these studies are discussed below.

The Evidence From Patents

Jacob Schmookler pioneered studies in the use of patent statistics to analyze the relationship between technological activity and the economy.[4] Schmookler showed that invention, as measured by patent statistics, was correlated with economic demand for reduced cost or increased performance.

That is, invention occurred when there was an economic payoff expected from it, leading people to invest resources in producing innovations. He also made the distinction that, while an invention may be made *in* an industry or may draw upon a particular branch of science, it is made *for* an industry in which it is expected to pay off. There is no necessary connection between the industry in which it is made and the industry for which it is made. Likewise, there is no necessary connection between the science underlying the industry in"which it is made and that underlying the industry for which it is made. Science may make possible a particular solution to a problem, but it is the existence of economic demand for the solution that drives the innovation.

Schmookler's conclusions are strengthened by some results obtained by Scherer. In 1974 the Federal Trade Commission conducted a line of business survey, for which 443 corporations reported domestic sales, R&D costs, and other variables, in 276 stamdardized industry categories. Scherer matched this data against data on patents obtained roughly two years later.[5] These 443 corporations accounted for 73 percent of the total company-financed R&D reported to the National Science Foundation and received 61 percent of the patents issued to industrial corporations.

The evidence that patents are linked to innovation, and that innovation in turn is linked to economic activity, allows us to draw the conclusion that innovation makes economic growth possible but does not force it. The demand for an innovation must first exist. Without that demand, no amount of additional science or technology will push the innovation into existence. Without the science or technology, however, the economic demand will remain unfilled, and the economy may stagnate.

The Chemical Industry

Jora R. Minasian argued that conventional economics was unable to explain the growth in wealth in the United States: "Real income per capita in the United States roughly quadrupled from 1869-78 to 1944-53. Per capita inputs of labor and capital weighted by their relative contribution in the base period (the nineteen twenties) increased only by some 14 percent. This suggests that there has been a substantial increase in the net national product that can not be explained by the increases in inputs, conventionally measured."[6]

He then extended the conventional production function to include changes in technology. He tested the hypothesis that the greater the R&D expenditures of a firm, the greater its growth in productivity, using a sample of firms in the chemical and pharmaceutical industries. His results were quite straightforward: the greater the R&D expenditures of a firm, the greater its growth in productivity.

Multiindustry Effects

Nestor E. Terleckyj studied the effects of R&D on productivity in the set of thirty-three manufacturing and nonmanufacturing industries for which Hendrick had already developed data on productivity growth, labor, and capital for the period 1948–66.[7] The classical Cobb-Douglas analysis of production had utilized two factors: labor and capital. Kendrick had extended this analysis to include "disembodied" technological change. Terleckyj extended this treatment to include accumulated R&D capital stock.

Terleckyj also attempted to separate the effects of R&D on the industry that performed it from its effects on those industries that bought the improved products resulting from R&D. These latter industries obtained the results of R&D *embodied* in what they bought from the R&D-performing industry, even if they conducted no R&D themselves.

Terleckyj notes that the immediate observation from his data is that there is no correlation between productivity growth and R&D. The airline industry, for instance, had the highest annual productivity growth rate of the thirty-three industries examined (8 percent), yet it conducts essentially no R&D whatsoever. Transportation equipment and ordnance had the highest intensity of R&D of all industries (25.5 percent of value added), yet only a moderate rate of productivity growth (3.2 percent). However, when his data are converted to show R&D embodied in purchased goods, whether these are intermediate goods or capital goods, the range of variation among industries is reduced greatly. Many industries buy a large number of R&D intensive products, even though they may conduct little R&D themselves.

Terleckyj then correlated his data on R&D, whether performed or purchased in embodied form, with productivity growth, after accounting for the effects of non-R&D variables. He found that R&D was a significant explanatory variable for growth in productivity for the manufacturing industries and large but not statistically significant for the nonmanufacturing industries. Of particular interest is the fact that the coefficients for R&D embodied in purchased goods were positive and statistically significant for both manufacturing and nonmanufacturing industries.

Basic Research and Productivity

Edwin Mansfield examined total factor productivity growth in twenty industries. The result was that basic research expenditures by an industry had a strong and statistically significant effect on increasing total factor productivity in that industry, even when applied research expenditures are held constant.[8] Mansfield also examined interfirm differences within an industry.[9] The results were similar to those at the industry level. Basic research conducted by individual firms had a strong and statistically significant effect on the firm's growth in productivity, even when applied research expenditures were held constant.

The Airline Industry

The work of Ralph C. Lenz et al. was based on the prior work of Terleckyj.[10] It was specifically intended to examine the effects of R&D on productivity in the airline industry. Lenz et al. estimated returns from R&D by three different methods. One was the growth in labor productivity of airline employees. The second was the effectiveness of disembodied technology. The third was obtained by estimating the size and cost of the "phantom fleet" of 1927-technology aircraft that would have been required to perform the actual passenger and cargo transportation the real airline fleet performed from 1928–76.

The labor productivity method revealed that labor cost per-seat-mile for U.S. domestic airlines decreased from about 30¢ in 1928 to slightly over 1¢ in 1980 (in constant 1967 dollars). The production function method found that when changes in labor and capital are accounted for, technology alone was responsible for productivity growth of at least 7 percent per year. The "phantom fleet" approach found that cumulative savings from 1927 to 1976 resulting from technology improvements in the airline fleet came to $262 billion (in constant 1970 dollars). This not only far exceeded the actual expenditures for aeronautical R&D, it far exceeded the cash flow that would have resulted from investing the R&D expenditures in commercial paper. However, it took nearly fourteen years for cumulated savings to exceed cumulated R&D. Thus, the savings from aeronautical R&D, while enormous, took time to achieve.

R&D and Telecommunications

Philip Abram and Kan-Hua Young undertook an econometric study of the effects of R&D in the U.S. telecommunications industry.[11] They found that spending $1.00 for R&D on telecommunications will, in the long run, increase telecommunications revenues by $3.49, and will decrease need for capital by $1.56 and decrease total wage bill by $3.28. However, there is a lag before these returns are realized. Abram and Young compute that at a discount rate of 10 percent (typical of the rate of return on capital in American industry), 99 percent of the returns on R&D expenditures are realized in seven years.

R&D and Economic Growth

These many studies report different aspects of the relationship between R&D and economic growth. However, their results have never been synthesized. Thus, while it is clear that science and technology do benefit the economy, there is still a great deal of research to be done before the science policy debate can be enlightened with reasonable knowledge of just how that benefit is achieved.

Moreover, the benefits of R&D are not unmixed. New technology can lead to the "creative destruction" described by Schumpeter, in which whole industries are wiped out, the owners lose the value of their capital, and workers see their skills become worthless. Clearly this aspect of the relationship between technological activity and economic growth also deserves study.

Assessing The Payoffs From Basic And Applied Research

In many cases the benefits from research have been significant. The benefits from publicly funded agricultural research are readily evident, for instance. Even so, attempts to assess those payoffs have provided mixed results. Even in retrospect, it is not always possible to reach agreement on the payoff from scientific and technological activity.

In 1966 the Defense Department undertook "Project Hindsight," to attempt to identify the source of technological innovations that had enhanced U.S. military capability. The study came to the conclusion that then recent basic research had made no contribution to military capability.[12] The National Science Foundation, reacting to the study, sponsored several studies, including TRACES (Technology in Retrospect and Critical Events in Science), which found important and then recent basic research contributions to several commercially significant technologies.[13] Other studies conducted by the defense basic research community reached similar conclusions.

Here were two studies addressing the same question, yet reaching differing conclusions. The studies raise two questions that are important from the standpoint of current policy concerns. First, what methods have been suggested for assessing the payoffs from both publicly and privately supported basic and applied research? Second, to what extent have these methods been validated, and how?

It is worth examining the Hindsight and TRACES studies of the payoff from basic research because they illustrate the problems that can arise when an attempt is made to evaluate even research that is already completed, let alone that which is only prospective. We will then examine some studies of the economic payoff from industrial innovations.

Basic Research

The Hindsight study approached the issue by looking backwards from technology. A set of military systems was selected for which a predecessor system could be identified. The improvement of the selected system over its predecessor was then estimated. The researchers then identified the specific technological advances that made the improved system possible.

The final step was to trace the circumstances under which these advances occurred. In many cases the Hindsight investigators were able to interview the people responsible for the innovations that made the new systems possible. In other cases they had to depend upon written records. Their conclusion that is of primary interest here was that R&D had a significant payoff in terms of lower cost for a given mission or improved performance at a given cost. A more controversial conclusion was that basic research had made no identifiable contribution to the systems they examined. None of the persons interviewed, nor any of the records, mentioned any specific basic research results that had been utilized in improving the technology that made the newer systems possible.

The National Science Foundation, disturbed by the Hindsight findings, sponsored the TRACES study to try to offset the adverse findings. The TRACES researchers began with a set of high technology products and identified the basic research findings, that is, the specific gains in understanding that made a rational development program for these products possible. The defense basic research community was also concerned by the Hindsight findings. One study, reported by Martino, reversed the procedure utilized by both Hindsight and TRACES.[14] Instead of asking what the origins were of specific technologies, it asked whether any uses had been made of specific results from defense-funded basic research. Several hundred specific instances were found in which research results, often less than ten years old, had been applied to improve the performance or to reduce the cost of some weapon or other military system.

Two conclusions can be drawn from these studies. First, basic research does have a payoff, and often pays very quickly. Second, a search for the payoff from basic research must be made carefully because the scientific roots of technological advances are often not obvious, even to those engineers who are responsible for making the advances.

Industrial Innovations

The case of industrial innovations should be easier to deal with than was the case of military innovations since industrial innovations are sold in a market. In principle, the benefit to users can be estimated from their willingness to pay.

Mansfield et al. studied the social and private rates of return from industrial innovations.[15] From cooperating firms, they obtained a sample of innovations introduced between 1950 and 1980. For each innovation they were able to estimate the rate of return to the firm introducing the innovation and also to users (each innovation provided savings to users). In computing social benefits, they took into account both the savings to the user and the profits of the innovator, as well as the reduction in profits to suppliers of whatever the innovation replaced. Their findings were that the private rate of return to the firms introducing the innovation ranged from below 10 percent to over 40 percent (before taxes), with a median rate of return of 25 percent. They found that, in general, the social rate of return was much higher than the private rate of return, with a median value of 56 percent. For about 30 percent of the innovations, the private rate of return was so low that, in retrospect, introduction was a mistake for the innovating firm, even though the social rate of return was quite high and, from the standpoint of society the innovation was worthwhile.

These results tend to support the common view that innovators cannot appropriate the full benefit of their inventions and, therefore, may tend to underinvest in innovation.

This approach to estimating the payoff from industrial research and development is at present the best available. It has not been used on a wide scale. However, it does appear to be valid. If anything, it probably underestimates the social return to innovation since it omits any benefits not represented by the consumers' surplus resulting from savings over whatever the innovation replaced.

Effects Of Government Policies

The intent of government policies regarding science and technology is to cause the development of science and technology to be different from what it would have been otherwise. But what is actually known about the effects of government policies on science and technology? Many aspects of the effects of government policies on science and technology have been studied and the conclusions presented in the literature. Research findings regarding the effects of government funding of research will be discussed later in the chapter. For now, discussion will focus on research findings regarding patent policies, antitrust policy, and R&D tax credits.

Patent Policies

One of the problems alleged to exist in a market economy is that people are faced with disincentives to conduct research to produce new knowledge. Research is risky; the sponsors may find they have nothing to show for their expenditure. Even if they do get some useful new knowledge, they may not be able to appropriate the benefits of that knowledge because others may imitate it. As Nordhaus puts it, "information is expensive to produce, cheap to reproduce, and difficult to profit from."[16] The purported result is that, in a market economy, there is likely to be a tendency to underinvest in the production of inappropriable new knowledge.

The patent system is an attempt to overcome the imitation problem. It creates property rights in new information, thus allowing the inventor to prosecute imitators. By granting the inventor a monopoly on the use of new but inappropriable information, a patent system provides an incentive to produce new knowledge. The limited life of a patent is intended to strike a balance between providing enough of a monopoly to reward the inventor and not allowing the inventor to gouge the public.

Patents and Economic Theory. Nordhaus employed conventional economic theory to demonstrate that the longer the life of a patent, the greater the amount of inventive effort that will be undertaken and the more important the inventions that will be realized.[17] He then derived the total welfare to the economy (gains from new knowledge minus losses because of monopoly) as a function of patent life. He concluded that the total welfare is remarkably insensitive to the life of a patent. Welfare reaches a maximum for a patent life somewhere between eight and twenty years and declines very slowly after that. In addition, for "run of the mill" inventions, the maximum welfare achieved under a patent system is about 98 percent of that which would be obtained if the same rate of inventive activity were to take place without the patent monopoly. However, for inventions that are very significant, or in cases where elasticity of demand is high, the maximum welfare obtained under a patent system is only 60 percent to 70 percent of that which would be achieved if the same rate of inventive activity could take place without a patent monopoly.

Nordhaus's theoretical conclusions are that, at least for small inventions, the patent system functions efficiently to produce new knowledge, and the public reaps almost all the benefits that are to be had from the new knowledge.

Empirical Studies of Imitation. Mansfield conducted a series of empirical studies to determine the extent to which the patent system actually encourages the production of new knowledge that would not have been produced otherwise. One of these examined the costs of imitating an invention in order to determine whether imitation was as costless as Nordhaus and others assumed.[18]

In the imitation study, Mansfield and his coworkers examined forty-eight innovations introduced by firms in the chemical, drug, electronics, and machinery industries. They obtained from the imitating firms the costs of developing and introducing the imitative product. The costs included "applied research, product specification, pilot plant or prototype construction, and manufacturing and marketing startup [If there was a patent on the innovation, the cost of inventing around it is included]."[19] Mansfield found that the average imitation cost was about 65 percent of the original innovator's cost, and the average imitation time was about 70 percent of the original innovator's time from start to marketing.

The conclusion of this study was that imitation costs are typically less than are innovation costs and that the research component of these costs, that is, the cost of reproducing knowledge, is often quite small. Empirically, patent protection does precisely what it is supposed to do—protect the innovator against someone who reproduces knowledge cheaply.

Antitrust Policy

The wisdom of antitrust policy as a means of maintaining competition has been debated at length (see, for instance, the arguments against antitrust by Armentano).[20] However, the focus here is the effect of antitrust policy on the advancement of science and technology.

In examining antitrust policy, we will consider the monopolists's incentive to innovate and the effect of antitrust policy on research joint ventures.

The Monopolist's Incentive to Innovate. It is argued that a monopolist will be unwilling to destroy his investment in existing technology, and therefore will not innovate as rapidly as would be socially desirable. Note that this argument contradicts the argument that in a competitive economy, individual firms will underinvest in innovation. According to this latter argument, a monopolist would have more incentive to invest in innovation than would competitive firms since the monopolist could come closer to appropriating all the benefits. Analyses relevant to this issue examine invention outside the using industry and innovation by a monopolist in the industry:

1. *Selling the innovation to the using industry.* Fixler examined the incentives to invent under the assumption that the inventor was not part of the industry using the invention.[21] He carried out the analysis for two sets of conditions, giving four possible combinations. One condition was whether the market for innovations was dominated by the inventor or by the buyer. The second condition was whether the payoff from the invention to the buyer was certain or uncertain. Fixler's conclusions are: "Regardless of the dominating agent in the transaction, neither the competitive industry nor the monopoly unambiguously provide the greatest incentive to invent. This is true under both certainty and uncertainty." He goes on to consider the effect of a possible merger between the inventor and the invention user, and

concludes: "Regardless of the market structure of the buyer and under both certainty and uncertainty, the incentive to invent is greater with a merger than without a merger." His analysis identifies conditions under which a monopolist will have greater incentive to innovate than will a competitive industry, and under which conditions the converse will be true.

2. *Innovation in the monopoly industry.* Donnenfeld examined the case in which the monopolist is himself the inventor and looked at whether the monopolist will tend to underinvest in research, as proposed by the argument given above.[22] His conclusion is: "Markets dominated by firms with monopoly power may create incentives to over-invest in R&D relative to the socially desirable levels. In addition, if these markets are characterized by fluctuations in product demand, the monopolist may react by further increasing his investment in R&D."

3. *Research Joint Ventures.* Ordover and Willig point out that antitrust policy is traditionally based on static analysis of the economy.[23] A merger is considered to be anticompetitive if the candidates for a merger are seen as competitors, especially if one or both already has significant "market power." They go on to note that the problem with this static analysis is that the American economy is dynamic, with rapid technological progress, where competition is driven by product and process innovation. They argue that traditional antitrust policy should be modified to take into account the possibility that research joint ventures (RJV's), and horizontal mergers between "competing" firms may increase the rate of technological advance, thereby enhancing competition rather than reducing it. Our fundamental conclusion concerning an RJV without restraints on product-market competition is that the RJV almost certainly speeds innovation and enhances product-market competition if the primary R&D competition the venture candidates face is from others rather than from each other.... Where the candidates possess power in the relevant product-markets before anticipated innovation, then the threats their unilateral advances pose to each other should be assessed on the basis of both preinnovation and postinnovation product lines.... Where the candidates have no preinnovation power in the relevant markets...the RJV almost certainly speeds innovation and enhances competition. They advocate similar conditions for judging the acceptability of a horizontal merger. The crucial consideration should be the increase, if any, in the pace of innovation resulting from the merger, as compared with the pace of innovation without the merger. Their argument is that, over the long run, society gains more from continuing innovation than it does from competitive pricing of technologically stagnant products. This is a drastic change from traditional views of proper antitrust policy.

4. *Conclusions regarding antitrust.* The results of the few studies of the effects of antitrust policy on innovation all sustain the same conclusions. First, antitrust action to accelerate innovation is in many cases not necessary since there are circumstances in which the monopolist has an incentive to make a greater investment in R&D than do the firms in a competitive market. Second, the way antitrust policy has been applied in the U.S. has been detrimental from the standpoint of encouraging innovation.

R&D Tax Credits

The idea behind R&D tax credits is the same as that behind most other forms of government intervention: in the absence of some government intervention, the private sector will underinvest in inappropriable R&D, primarily basic research. The R&D tax credit is intended to overcome this tendency.

An R&D tax credit was included in the 1981 Economic Recovery Tax Act. Mansfield conducted a survey of 110 firms responsible for 30 percent of all company-financed R&D in the U.S. to determine how much effect the R&D tax credit had on their research budgets.[24] His findings were: Without the credit, the R&D expenditures of the firms in the sample would have been about 0.4 percent lower in 1981, about 1.0 percent lower in 1982, and about 1.2 percent lower in 1983 than in fact was the case, according to the firms themselves. Further, based on the firms' estimates, the extra R&D stimulated by the tax credit seems to have been considerably less than was the revenue lost to the Treasury.

Mansfield also noted that Sweden and Canada had similar laws and had found them to be ineffective. He surveyed Swedish firms that accounted for 80 percent of company-financed R&D in Sweden and found that, without the tax credit, R&D expenditures would have been about 1 percent less than was actually the case.

Canada had implemented an R&D tax credit and a direct deduction of increased R&D from taxes. Mansfield surveyed firms that accounted for 30 percent of company-financed R&D in Canada. The survey results indicate that the tax credit increased R&D expenditures by about 2 percent, and the tax allowance by about 1 percent.

Robert Eisner et al. examined the perverse incentives built into the tax credit, showing that inflation would provide a tax credit even with no real increases in R&D spending and that shifting expenditures from "unqualified" to "qualified" categories can also produce a credit with no increase in R&D spending.[25] Conversely, however, an increase in R&D spending one year can decrease the credit for later years by increasing the "base" from which increases are computed.

The empirical evidence, then, not only in the U.S. but in Canada and Sweden, is that an R&D tax credit is not an effective means of increasing private R&D expenditures. The increase in R&D may actually be less than the loss in taxes.

Criteria For Public Support

Since World War II, it has been taken for granted that science and technology deserve public support. This acceptance of public support was rooted in two somewhat different considerations. The first consideration was that a broad definition of relevance was appropriate for basic research done in support of military technologies. The second consideration was that an improved solution to a military problem might be made possible by basic research which, at the time it is being done, appears to have no connection whatsoever with the military. Thus, on the basis of defense alone, there was seen to be a justification for public support of research, using a very broad definition of relevance.

However, the advocates of public support for research did not stop with military considerations alone. The authors of *Science, The Endless Frontier* argued that economic growth was also a justification for public support of research.[26]

Regardless of the justifications for government support of research, military or economic, there are two issues that must be examined.

First, how much total public support is appropriate, especially in view of other demands on public funds? Second, which scientific and technological activities will receive support and which will not? These two issues can to some degree be separated. Even if support were distributed by lottery, for instance, the question of total magnitude would still exist. Moreover, for any finite total magnitude, so long as the cost to obtain public support is less than the value of that support, demand will exceed supply. Hence, there must be some means of selecting those activities to be supported and rejecting those that will not be supported.

Governments face these problems in supporting any activity, whether it be defense, road-building, or garbage collection. Somehow decisions must be made regarding "how much" and "which." In making these decisions about science and technology, however, the criteria used should in some way involve the relationship between the scientific and technological activity to be supported and the objectives of the government in providing support.

Criteria have been suggested for resolving both questions—how much and which. We will look at each briefly.

How To Determine How Much

Kenneth J. Arrow has used conventional economic theory to argue that private support for basic research will be expanded only until private benefits equal private costs.[27] However, because it is impossible for the sponsors to exclude others from receiving the benefits of many basic research results, at this level of research support social benefits still exceed private costs. Mansfield showed that for the set of innovations he studied, the social benefits often vastly exceeded both the research costs of the innovation and the returns to the sponsors of the innovation.[28] Those who support this view, therefore, argue that society should supplement private support of basic research by an amount sufficient to equate social benefits with total private and social costs. Unfortunately, there is a serious problem with this proposed solution.

No measure of social benefits has yet been devised that would make it possible to apply this criterion. That is, some of the social benefits from research (e.g., reduced sickness, better national defense) are incommensurable with the costs (physical resources, researcher time, etc.) of that research. The economic solution of equating marginal costs with marginal benefits founders simply because the two cannot be measured on the same scale, not even in dollar terms. Moreover, it is unlikely that any measure of social benefits will ever be devised for this purpose since it would have to solve the problem of "interpersonal utility comparisons." It would require that we compare the value of the benefit accruing to one person from the research with the value of the benefit foregone by another person who was taxed to pay for conducting the research. The fundamental problem with this concept of equating marginal social benefit with marginal social cost is that it treats society as a unitary actor with a single, coherent value structure. Society is actually an abstraction. Attempting to equate marginal social costs and marginal social benefits commits the logical fallacy known as "misplaced concreteness."

How To Determine Which

Alvin Weinberg has pointed out that there is no escaping the necessity for choice among scientific areas for allocation of R&D resources.[29] He argues further that when choices are made by panels representing individual fields, they tend to allow their enthusiasm for their fields to carry them away. What is needed, he argues, is a set of criteria that allow both the scientific aspects and the nonscientific aspects of the choices to be made clear. He then presents what he calls internal and external criteria for choosing which sciences to support.

The internal criteria have to do with a scientific field itself:

1. Is the field ready for exploitation?
2. Are the scientists in the field really competent?

These questions can be answered only by people working in the field, hence they are "internal" criteria. As Weinberg points out, these are the criteria typically used when the participants in a field are urging that funds for it be expanded.

Even when the internal criteria might justify support of a scientific field, Weinberg asserts that these conditions are only necessary, not sufficient. External criteria must be applied as well, to determine which fields should be supported and to what extent, in competition with other fields. He suggests the following criteria:

1. Technological merit—the extent to which the technological ends that are supported by the science are themselves important.

2. Scientific merit—the extent to which other fields of science are depending on advances in the field in question. If the field is a "bottleneck" that is holding up advances elsewhere, it is more deserving of support than is a field that has little connection with the rest of science.

3. Social merit—the extent to which the field in question is relevant to human welfare and to the values of humanity.

While these criteria have some value in the abstract, they are very difficult to operationalize. Moreover, they depend upon data that may not be available, and hence it is not clear that they can actually be applied in concrete circumstances. Finally, they beg some important questions regarding the appropriate magnitude for public support of scientific and technological activity, not to mention who will render the judgments about each project to be considered.

Conclusion

The problem here is not that reasonable sounding criteria have not been suggested but that the suggested criteria cannot be made operational. This presents an apparently insoluble dilemma. There are no rational criteria available to utilize in making choices about public support of research, yet so long as government policy is to support research, choices must be made.

In the absence of criteria that sound reasonable and that can be made operational, decisions about public support of science and technology tend to be made using criteria that have little or nothing to do with the science involved but much to do with the relative political strengths of those who benefit and those who pay. In fact, it could hardly be otherwise. The notion that public funds can be expended in a way free of politics is a utopian dream.

Moreover, viewed from the perspective of the politicians, even scientifically sound criteria for selection of research projects appear to resemble the arguments presented by any other special interest. For the scientists involved to argue that a particular field is "ripe for exploitation" sounds like special pleading. For scientists in field A to argue that field B should be funded because they need the results to be obtained sounds like logrolling. Ultimately, to the nonscientist, any purportedly objective criteria for deciding "which" and "how much" will sound like "because we say so."

Therefore, it is no accident that in 1983 the total federal expenditures for basic research came to $6.97 billion, while the Commodity Credit Corporation alone spent $8.6 billion on farm subsidies. Farmers as a group have more political power than do basic researchers.

Probably the most that researchers can do is to keep the allocation of resources to research from becoming completely dominated by interest-group politics. The recent but growing practice of bypassing peer review by direct appropriations, for instance, may turn out to be a turning point in the history of the relationship between science and the federal government. If this practice continues to grow, ultimately any shred of scientific justification for deciding "how much" and "which" will disappear.

Government Support Of Research For Commercial Payoff

Some of the successes of government support for science and technology involve support of basic research. Many today, however, argue for government support of technology intended to be introduced commercially. In examining government support for commercial research, we will consider the need for government support, the effects of various kinds of government support, and the limited empirical evidence regarding the success of government support.

Need For Government Support

One of the first issues that needs to be addressed is whether government support is needed. Arrow and others have argued that firms in a competitive industry will underinvest in research because they will be unable to appropriate all the results of that research.[30] If private support of research were less than optimal, government support could be justified.

As pointed out in the preceding section, even if this were true, there are no criteria available to decide how much is enough. It is at present not possible to fine tune government support to the point where marginal social cost exactly equals marginal social benefit from the research being supported.

Another consideration, however, is whether it is even true that private firms will invest less than the socially optimum level of resources in research. Scherer reminds us of the obvious fact that rivalry among firms does lead to aggressive and vigorous R&D programs.[31] He then analyzes the incentives of rivalrous firms to innovate, considering both product improvements that improve the firm's competitive position in a fixed market and those that create new markets or that increase the size of the market.

His conclusions are essentially as follows. Under conditions of competition, firms will accelerate their development schedules for new technology in order to achieve it more rapidly than if they did not have to fear competition, even though this means lower profits. Consumers receive the benefits of new technology earlier than they would have otherwise, thus reaping a social benefit that more than offsets the reduced benefits to the rivalrous innovators. However, if the innovation does not increase total demand, but merely increases the amount of competition within a fixed market, the firms may actually spend *too much* money on research and development, in the sense that the private and social benefit is less than is the private cost.

Scherer's result is important since it contradicts the notion that under conditions of competition private firms will underinvest in R&D. However, Scherer's result does not specifically address the appropriability of the research results. It deals only with the situation in which the firm must meet its competition, whether or not the competitors can later utilize the results of its research without repeating that research. Other researchers have examined the issue of appropriability of results.

Alternative Forms of Support

Prafulla Joglekar and Morris Hamburg analyzed the effects of alternative forms of government support for commercial R&D.[32] They distinguished between effects on basic (inappropriable) research and applied (appropriable) research. They considered two types of government support. The first, matching subsidies, are all government expenditures that are proportional to expenditures by industry for R&D, including R&D tax credits and other forms of matching payments. The second, seed money, includes all government expenditures that are made without regard to industry matching. These include expenditures in government laboratories, government grants to universities, and direct contracts with private firms.

Joglekar and Hamburg develop a model in which inappropriable research benefits an industry as a whole, while appropriable research benefits the firm conducting the research. They further assume that each firm has a set of projects with appropriable payoffs in which it can invest as an alternative to R&D. They use their model to determine a Pareto-optimal level of research investment, which would be reached if the firms could avoid the "free rider" problem, with each investing in inappropriable research up to the point where its benefit from all the inappropriable research conducted in the industry is equal to its own investment.

Their first conclusion is that total investment in inappropriable research in the industry will be suboptimal. They then argue that government intervention could be justified in this case, and they examine the effects of both seed money and matching subsidies.

They conclude that provision of seed money is counterproductive. The more seed money the government provides, the less will be the total industry investment in inappropriable research. The only exception to this is when some minimum investment is required before any benefit is obtained at all. In such a case, the government can achieve its goal of increasing the industry expenditure by spending just the threshold amount but no more.

They also conclude that while the use of seed money is ineffective, the use of matching subsidies is effective but not very efficient. The amount of government expenditures will be "many times" the induced additional spending by the firms. In short, it is very difficult for the government to bring industry expenditures on inappropriable research up to the optimal level. This result is consistent with the empirical studies of R&D tax credits conducted by Mansfield and by Eisner et al. and reported earlier in the chapter.

When Joglekar and Hamburg examine appropriable research, their model shows that interfirm collaborative research can be very effective in increasing the amount of investment in R&D since each collaborating firm reduces the amount it has at stake on a risky outcome but gains benefits proportional to its contributions. Unfortunately, as they point out, such interfirm collaboration is generally held to be in violation of U.S. antitrust laws. Thus, the effect of current antitrust policy is to force suboptimal levels of R&D on appropriable but risky research.

Joglekar and Hamburg look at an alternative form of government support, namely joint industry-government consortia.[33] Again, if participants could gain in proportion to their contribution, the result would be an increase in the level of R&D. However, current U.S. government policy on such consortia is to claim ownership of any resulting patents for itself—"A private firm shouldn't be allowed to profit from a patent paid for with public money." In effect, this policy makes the results inappropriable since the government has the right to license the resulting patents to firms that did not participate in the consortium. The end result of this policy is to force a reduction in industry investment in risky but appropriable research.

Finally, Joglekar and Hamburg use their model to examine basic (inappropriable) research in a homogeneous industry (i.e., all firms are the same size and have identical characteristics).[34] They conclude that industries with one or more of the following characteristics will tend to underinvest in inappropriable research, thus increasing the need for government intervention:

1. Industries involving a large number of firms

2. Industries with intense interfirm competition (note that Scherer reached the opposite conclusion)

3. Industries with a lesser threat from other industries (e.g., of substitute products)

4. Industries with smaller amounts of investable resources

5. Industries with relatively fewer risk-averse firms

Evidence Regarding Government Support

Government attempts to foster the commercial development of technology seem to have had results quite different from those found in agricultural research or in basic aeronautical research. Not only has the research not been effective, its justification has been questionable.

Justification For Government Support. George Eads and Richard R. Nelson discuss the justifications given for government support of a breeder nuclear reactor and of a supersonic transport aircraft, both intended for commercial use.[35] In both instances the pressure to initiate development came from government agencies responsible for the technology, not from the firms that would use it. They also note that one of the reasons given for federal support of these programs is that industry would not undertake them or would not pursue them as rapidly as they would be pursued with federal support.

The arguments for government support were that the large size of the investment required (the development cost of the Supersonic Transport, for instance, exceeded the net worth of even the largest aircraft manufacturer), the long lead time before any return would be obtained, and uncertainty about total costs and returns, made it unlikely that private firms would pursue these technological opportunities as rapidly as their advocates desired.

Eads and Nelson note, regarding the cost argument, that IBM raised $5 billion in the early 1960s to develop and market the System 360, an amount that exceeded its net worth and that was more than the estimated cost to develop and deliver the first Supersonic Transport. Hence, the argument from size of funding is not compelling.

Instead, they note that the reason for low industry interest in the Supersonic Transport was the low expected rate of return compared with returns expected from alternative projects the firms could pursue instead. Even studies by advocates of the Supersonic Transport showed only modest increments of benefits over cost. The justification for government support of these projects was weak. The projects were pushed by agencies that had a vested interest in developing the technology, not by users who saw an economic benefit from the technology.

The Empirical Evidence. Several studies provide empirical evidence regarding the effectiveness of government action in commercializing new technology.

The Aircraft Industry:

Eads and Nelson contrast the Post World War II performance of the American and British commercial aircraft industries. The American aircraft industry was successful in dominating the world market. In 1970, some 80 percent of the world commercial airline fleet was built by U.S. manufacturers. This dominance resulted from the good economic performance of the aircraft. In all cases, these aircraft were developed at private expense, with the manufacturers risking their own money. By contrast, the British government paid up to 50 percent of the cost of developing and introducing new aircraft and required the nationalized British airlines to purchase the aircraft. The British aircraft industry did indeed produce some technologically advanced aircraft. However, none of the products of that industry were bought in large numbers by non-British airlines, simply because the aircraft could not compete with the low initial and operating costs of American products.

Breeder Reactors:

With regard to the breeder reactor, Eads and Nelson point out that most of the arguments for accelerating it were based on its "inevitability." When developed to its full potential it would be cheaper than other sources of power. However, that very fact made eventual commercial development inevitable. The issue, then, became one of accelerating the development through government subsidy. The sole question should have been whether the benefits from having the technology sooner outweighed the costs of accelerating the development. Unfortunately, the analyses by advocates of the breeder reactor compared the situation of having it sooner with the situation of never having it at all. The proper time-cost tradeoff was never made. Nor were the benefits of having it sooner compared with the benefits of projects that would have to be foregone or delayed because the breeder was accelerated.

Cross-Industry Studies:

Nelson and Langlois report the results of an extensive study of government attempts to foster the commercialization of technology.[36] They identify four kinds of government action: 1) procurement of R&D to carry out some government objective such as defense, 2) programs to support research in "generic" technologies of interest to an entire industry or groups of industries, 3) programs to support applied R&D in the service of well-defined users, and 4) programs to "pick winners" and to pay for their development. Their first category is not relevant to our concerns here.

In the second category, they find both successes and failures. Agricultural research and biomedical research have both been successful in getting results commercialized. The same was true of aeronautical research under the National Advisory Committee for Aeronautics, NASA's predecessor agency. However, two attempts under the Carter Administration, the Cooperative Automotive Research Program and the Cooperative Generic Technologies Program, were failures. In these two cases, the authors find that the initiatives for the programs came from the federal government and that there was little industry participation.

In the third category, Nelson and Langlois identified another aspect of agricultural research, the experiment stations, which were heavily clientele-oriented. These were highly successful. However, an attempt to conduct R&D for the commercial housing industry, although patterned after this type of agricultural R&D, was a failure, again because of centralized initiatives that overlooked the importance of local conditions such as building codes.

In the fourth category, Nelson and Langlois examine the Supersonic Transport and Operation Breakthrough (an attempt to apply modern technology to house construction). Both were commercial failures. The government simply is not competent to pick winners. Moreover, Nelson and Langlois point out that the problem is not uniquely American. The Anglo-French Concorde was also a commercial failure, as was the RB 211 jet engine (supported by the British government), the Soviet Tupolev TU-144 Supersonic Transport, and the U.S.S. *Savannah*, a nuclear-powered vessel.

Empirical Conclusions:

Eads and Nelson argue that the programs to develop the Supersonic Transport and the breeder reactor were a transfer to the commercial sector of the technology forcing efforts pioneered in the Manhattan Project and Project Apollo.[37] While these projects might have had some virtue in situations of wartime urgency or in pursuit of noneconomic national goals, there is no track record to indicate they can be successful in producing commercially viable products. On the contrary, the evidence in the U.S., as well as in other nations such as Britain, France, and Russia, is that governmental attempts to force the pace of technology result in economic white elephants.

Nelson and Langlois discuss the problems of government support for commercial R&D and conclude that there are important requirements to be met if the support is to be successful.[38] First, the industry to be helped must see the need for the research and must help guide it. Second, the researchers involved must be interested in the purely scientific disciplines underlying the technology, otherwise the research becomes scientifically sterile. Third, the program must be decentralized and closely involved with the people who must eventually adopt the technology. Fourth, the phenomenon of government "picking the winners" has a record of 100 percent failure and is to be avoided completely.

Reasons For Poor Performance. The problem with government support of commercial R&D is not one of poor choice of projects or one of poor choice of personnel to manage specific projects. The essence of the problem, as indicated by Public Choice theory, a relatively new branch of economics, is that government officials face incentive structures different from those faced by successful private entrepreneurs. To government officials the satisfaction of important constituencies is more important than commercial success.

Eads and Nelson note that U.S. dominance of the world-market for commercial aircraft was due, not to sheer technological performance, but to introduction of new technology only when it brought commercial benefits. In each case, the decision to introduce a new aircraft incorporating new technology was made by a firm that was risking its own funds. In such cases, great attention is paid to the commercial viability of the aircraft. Airlines, both U.S. and foreign, are much more concerned with the ability of aircraft to pay for themselves than they are about technological performance.

Summary

The analysis of government support for commercial development has led to mixed research results. Researchers cannot even agree whether firms, either competitors or monopolies, will overinvest or underinvest in research. Beyond this, there are many gaps in the study of specific forms of government intervention to cure the (possible) underinvestment. However, case studies show that many types of government intervention are definite failures, and even the successes cannot always be replicated in other situations. Public Choice theory has not yet been adequately brought to bear on the problem of incentives facing the government.

Government Support As An Entitlement

One issue that inevitably arises from large-scale federal support of science and technology is the extent to which the scientific community comes to see that support as an entitlement. When over half the scientists and engineers in the U.S. receive federal support either directly or indirectly, with the proportion in the academic community being even higher and in the medical research community even higher yet, it is entirely possible that the scientific community might come to look upon support as an entitlement.

This becomes important because of the possible conflict between the views of the scientific community and the rest of society. If society views support of science in terms of a *quid pro quo*, while researchers view it as an entitlement, a conflict is almost inevitable.

The Original Intention

Federal support as an entitlement was not the intent of those who laid the foundations for federal support after World War II. Vannevar Bush saw science and technology as the fountainhead of prosperity, health, and a strong defense.

Scientific and technological activity should be supported because such support would benefit the nation. As *Science* put it: "The postwar system was based implicitly on the importance of science to national security; the funding of basic research was justified by recollections of the decisive impact of radar, rockets, the atomic bomb, and other wartime developments on the outcome of the conflict."[39]

However, the original intention did not necessarily govern indefinitely. Those scientists who came well after World War II might have interpreted the system differently from those who helped establish it in 1945. There is some evidence that they did interpret federal support of science as an entitlement.

The Response to the Mansfield Amendment

In 1969, Congress passed a military research and procurement bill that had a "sleeper" clause in it. Section 203 was named after its author, Senate Majority Leader Mike Mansfield. It required that any basic research supported by the Defense Department must have a "direct and apparent relationship to a specific military function or operation." Senator Mansfield stated that his intention was to cut out of the defense budget approximately $400 million which, as he saw it, was being spent on research with no connection to the military.

In Fiscal Year 1970, the first year in which the Mansfield Amendment was in effect, the Defense Department interpreted it in such a way as to cut out programs totaling only about $10 million. However, the total soon mounted. Even though other mission agencies did not have Mansfield-type amendments in their budget authorizations, they took the hint and started to eliminate programs that were not clearly related to their missions, with most of the impact being felt by universities.

By April 1970 the Department of Defense, NASA, the Atomic Energy Commission, and the National Institutes of Health had selected research totaling $60 million to be terminated, and it was expected the total would increase as other agencies took the same approach.

The Defense Department naturally tried to have the Mansfield Amendment repealed in the Fiscal Year 1971 budget. The position of the universities was somewhat different. They did not lobby to have the Mansfield Amendment repealed, but instead to have the National Science Foundation's budget increased enough to offset the cuts in the mission agencies. In part, this reaction was due to the campus opposition to the Vietnam War, which had just passed the peak of U.S. participation.

The "statesmen of science" who did appear before Congress to testify for more funds spoke largely in terms of damage to the economy resulting from the reduction in funds. However, the lower-level scientists, particularly the recent graduates, looked at the matter from a different perspective. Their comments, made at scientific conferences, intimated that somehow they had been betrayed. They felt they had been led to expect support, and suddenly the support was withdrawn.

The reaction of the scientific community to the Mansfield Amendment suggests that many researchers looked upon federal funding as an entitlement, whereas Congress and the public looked upon it in terms of a *quid pro quo*.

Survey Results

A recent survey asked scientists about their opinions regarding certain aspects of federally supported research.[40] Some of the comments received from the survey respondents implied that researchers were deserving of support in a way that other people were not. The following comments, selected from those received in the survey, illustrate this point:

1. Managing under uncertainty. Some of the comments dealt with the problems faced by researchers, especially Principal Investigators, when grants were not renewed promptly. Respondents made comments such as this: "We are particularly concerned about the scientists engaged in our research efforts. Due to NIH's inability to formulate their final budget (Congress's delay with the budgeting process), we did not hear until September 9th that the grant had been renewed effective September 1st (for years 10, 11, and 12). The psychological anxiety of the people supported by the grant must be very great."

2. Continuity in funding. The solution uniformly suggested was longer grant periods: "We need more multi-year projects, not one year at a time. It's important to avoid gaps in funding." One has to ask—wouldn't any small-business owner like to have a certain level of business guaranteed for a fixed period? What makes researchers so special?

3. Attracting and retaining people. One of the reasons continuity of funding was considered important was the problem of attracting and retaining people to work on projects when renewals were late or follow-ons uncertain: "We need more three-year programs so that graduate students can count on support to complete Ph.D. research."

4. Long term support. Even more interesting were those survey responses that, in effect, said that once a researcher had demonstrated competence, he or she should be funded essentially forever: "If a competent researcher has demonstrated expertise and a good track record, then it is wasteful to subject him to the possibility of having to 'turn off' a project and wait for renewal funding. If the researcher loses space or personnel it can be very costly to restart."

5. Support all good researchers. Some respondents came even closer to considering research support as an entitlement. Consider the following response: "The government should fund good people, almost regardless of what they are doing."

Clearly one could not have expected the respondents to this survey to say that government funding should be reduced. On the contrary, a call for more funding might very well be expected of them. Nevertheless, while these respondents do not come right out and say that good researchers are entitled to funding, some sound as though they think that way.

Moreover, it is important to recognize that these respondents are not being selfish. Many of them undoubtedly feel they made a bargain with society. They would go through the effort of learning science and of gaining competence in research, in many cases postponing the establishment of a family and the achievement of a settled position in life. Once they completed that rigorous apprenticeship, they would undertake scientific research that would ultimately benefit society in a myriad of ways. In return, so long as they continued to demonstrate their competence, they expected support for their research, without having to justify the need for it.

Summary

An important aspect of the science policy debate is the extent to which researchers have come to look upon grants as an entitlement and how the research community has organized itself into an interest group to assure that research funding is continued. To the extent that researchers and the public differ in their views of the degree to which researchers are entitled to support, a conflict is inevitable.

Another important aspect of the science policy debate is the extent to which research support should be an entitlement. Are science and technology of such overriding importance to the economy that all "good" proposals by "good" researchers should be funded? If so, then criteria for "good" research and researchers are needed; if not, then criteria for "how much" and "which" are needed, as discussed earlier in the chapter.

The Structure Of Government And Private Support

Prior to World War II, support for science and technology in the U.S came largely from private sources. These included not only commercial organizations but private foundations and individual philanthropists. The scientific "entrepreneurs" who built the major astronomical observatories of the early part of this century—the big science of the day—obtained the bulk of their funds from individual philanthropists.

By contrast, in every year since World War II over half the support for basic research in the U.S. has come from the federal government. However, federal support has come from a variety of agencies, each with its own mission. Moreover, federal support has been marked by several major shifts in policy since 1945. As just one example, the Office of Naval Research was established by law shortly after World War II, to provide support for basic research of interest to the Navy. Science had helped win World War II; therefore, support of basic science was in the national interest, and support by a military organization was appropriate. Twenty years later, the situation had changed dramatically. The Mansfield Amendment to the Defense Appropriations Act provided that no agency of the Department of Defense could support research that did not have direct relevance to military needs. Several years later the policy was again reversed, and basic research agencies in the Department of Defense were given more latitude in their choice of research to support. Their research programs were still to be relevant to military needs, but relevance was interpreted more broadly.

The Mansfield Amendment, and its reversal, were not the only shifts in policy regarding federal support of science and technology. They simply illustrate the point that federal policy on support of science and technology has not pursued a continuous course in the fifty years since federal support became a major factor in American scientific and technological enterprise.

Private support for science and technology has likewise seen several changes of direction. The economic good times of the late 1950s and early 1960s saw significant industrial support of basic research. With the 1970s came a greater emphasis on applied research, with more concern for immediate profits and payoff.

The overall structure of support for basic research, applied research, and development shows some significant changes as well as some surprising constants. The total U.S. expenditures for R&D more than doubled from 1960 to 1985 (in constant dollars). However, the distribution among the components remained remarkably constant: about 13 percent for basic research, about 22 percent for applied, and about 65 percent for development. However, the sources of those funds changed fairly dramatically over the same period.

The proportion of basic research funds that came from industry dropped by almost a factor of two from 1960 to 1965 and since then has remained fairly static, between 15 percent and 20 percent. The federal government's share has varied between 65 percent and 70 percent. The proportion from universities has also increased, from about 10 percent to about 15 percent, remaining fairly constant since 1970.

The situation for applied research and for development are similar to each other but quite different from that for basic research. The proportion coming from universities has remained essentially constant, about 4 percent for each, while there has been a steady shift from government to industry funding for both components since 1970.

The constancy of the proportions for each component, despite the radical shifts in sources of funding, implies some kind of societal feedback at work. While there is not a "market" for R&D in the sense that there is a market for manufactured goods, some market-like process is at work to maintain the balance among components despite the change in source. Research is needed to identify the nature of this societal feedback.

Summary

The preceding sections have presented research findings on several important topics that have a bearing on the science policy debate. Despite their shortcomings, some conclusions can be drawn. First, science and technology are economic activities, pursued to achieve economic or other social goals. They are necessary but not sufficient conditions for growth in productivity and wealth. They reduce costs, create new markets, and make resources (capital, labor, materials) available for other uses by reducing the amount required for a given level of wealth production.

However, we need to know more about the linkages from basic research through development to economic and social impacts. More research is needed to identify the routes and mechanisms by which economic demands motivate researchers and inventors and the routes and mechanisms by which new knowledge is converted to economically valuable products or processes.

Second, we need better ways of assessing the payoffs from science and technology, for both market and nonmarket applications. Government agencies need to be able to evaluate the payoff from science and technology in carrying out their missions. Private firms need to be able to evaluate the payoff from science and technology in terms of reducing costs, increasing market share, creating new markets, and economizing on resources in short supply. While uncertainty cannot be eliminated completely, there is reason to believe that the current assessment capabilities can be improved.

Third, despite the proliferation of demands for "science policy" and for "industrial policy," and despite the proliferation of specific proposals under both rubrics, there are significant gaps in our knowledge of what the effects of those policies might be. We need to know more about the effects of such things as tax credits and antitrust policy on the advancement of science and technology. We need to know both the intended effects on the targeted fields of science and technology and the unintended effects on the untargeted ones. Finally, we need to be able to deal with the multiple and interacting effects of several policies at once. The effects of a particular policy may be totally different in one context from its effects in another.

Fourth, to the extent that public support for science and technology is justified, we need better criteria to answer the questions "how much" and "which." Under many of the criteria proposed for the support of science and technology, it would be equally possible to justify the support of painting, sculpture, music, literature, and the other arts. If support of science and technology is different from support of the arts, then that difference must be clearly articulated and incorporated in the criteria for "how much" and "which."

Fifth, we need a better understanding of when privately funded research will be too high or too low and, therefore, when government intervention might be justified to lower the level of private support or to raise or supplement it. Moreover, we need to include in our analyses of the effects of government support for science and technology, the effects on the economy of the taxes that are the source of the support. When these effects are taken into account, the level of privately funded support may turn out to be much closer to optimal than present models imply. When government support of commercial technology is justified, we need a better understanding of the incentive structures that would induce government officials to make decisions that parallel those that would be made by private entrepreneurs, instead of decisions that nullify the commercial intent of the project.

Sixth, we need to examine in greater depth the attitude of scientists and engineers toward government support of science and technology. To what extent have they come to think of such support as an entitlement? Do we want them to think of it as an entitlement? If not, then how should they think of it? What obligations should they recognize as incumbent upon them for accepting something that is not their due but that has a *quid pro quo* attached to it?

Seventh, we need to examine the social feedbacks that seem to be at work to maintain the structure of support for science and technology despite shifts in sources of support and shifts in attitudes on the relevance of basic research. Why have the ratios remained relatively constant despite shifts in sources of support? Do we want them to remain constant? If not, what structural changes are needed to shift them to where we want them to be? Do we even have any idea of where we should want them?

Notes

1. J.J. Servan-Schreiber, *The American Challenge*, (New York: Atheneum, 1968).
2. Vannevar Bush, *Science, the Endless Frontier*, (Office of Scientific Research and Development, 1945, reprinted July 1960 by NSF), p. 5.
3. Ibid., p. 10.
4. Jacob Schmookler, *Invention and Economic Growth*, (Cambridge, MA: Harvard University Press, 1966).
5. F.M. Scherer, "The Propensity to Patent," *International Journal of Industrial Organization*, 1 (1983), pp. 107–28.
6. Jora R. Minasian, "The Economics of Research and Development," in National Bureau of Economic Research, *The Rate and Direction of Inventive Activity*, (Princeton: Princeton University Press, 1962).
7. Nestor E. Terleckyj, "Effects of R&D on the Productivity Growth of Industries," (Washington, D.C.: National Planning Association, 1974).
8. Edwin Mansfield, "Basic Research and Productivity Increase in Manufacturing," *The American Economic Review*, 70: 3 (December 1980), pp. 863–73.
9. Edwin Mansfield, "Contribution of R&D to Economic Growth in the United States," *Science*, 175: 4021 (February 1972), pp. 477–486.
10. Ralph C. Lenz, John A. Machnic and Anthony W. Elkins, "The Influence of Aeronautical R&D Expenditures upon the Productivity of Air Transportation," (Dayton, OH: University of Dayton, 1981).

11. Philip Abram and Kan-Hua Young, "The Effects of R&D on the U.S. Telecommunications Industry," *Aeronautics & Astronautics* (May 1977), pp. 46-52.
12. *Interim Report on Project Hindsight*, (Washington, D.C.: Office of Defense Research and Engineering, 1966).
13. Illinois Institute of Technology Research Institute, *Technology in Retrospect and Critical Events in Science (TRACES)*, report to the National Science Foundation, 1969.
14. Joseph P. Martino, "Is Basic Research Relevant to Military Problem-Solving?" *Armed Forces Management* (November 1966).
15. Edwin Mansfield, John Rapoport, Anthony Romeo, Samuel Wagner and George Beardsley, "Social and Private Rates of Return from Industrial Innovations," *Quarterly Journal of Economics*, 91 (May 1977), pp. 221-40.
16. William D. Nordhaus, *Invention, Growth and Welfare*, (Boston: MIT Press, 1969), p. 10.
17. Ibid., p. 83.
18. Edwin Mansfield, Mark Schwartz and Samuel Wagner, "Imitation Costs and Patents," *The Economic Journal*, 91 (December 1981), pp. 907-18.
19. Ibid.
20. See, for instance, the arguments against antitrust by Dominick T. Armentano, *Antitrust and Monopoly: Anatomy of a Policy Failure*, 2nd ed., (New York: Holmes & Meier, 1990).
21. Dennis J. Fixler, "Uncertainty, Market Structure and the Incentive to Invent," *Economica* (November 1983), pp. 407-23.
22. Shabtai Donnenfeld "Monopoly and the Incentive to Innovate," *Southern Economic Journal*, 48: 3 (January 1982), pp. 778-84.
23. Janusz A. Ordover and Robert D. Willig, "Antitrust for High-Technology Industries: Assessing Research Joint Ventures and Mergers," *Journal of Law and Economics*, XXVIII (May 1983), pp. 311-33.
24. Edwin Mansfield, "How Effective is the R&D Tax Credit?," *Challenge*, (November/December 1984), pp. 57-61.
25. Robert Eisner, Steven H. Albert, and Martin A. Sullivan, "The New Incremental Tax Credit for R&D: Incentive or Disincentive?" *National Tax Journal*, (June 1984), pp. 171-79.
26. Bush, op. cit.
27. Kenneth J. Arrow, "Economic Welfare and the Allocation of Resources for Invention," in National Bureau of Economic Research, *The Rate and Direction of Inventive Activity*, (Princeton: Princeton University Press, 1962).
28. Edwin Mansfield, "Basic Research and Productivity Increase in Manufacturing", op. cit.
29. Alvin Weinberg, *Reflection on Big Science*, (Cambridge, MA: The Massachusetts Institute of Technology Press, 1967).
30. Arrow, op. cit.
31. F.M. Scherer, "Research and Development Resource Allocation Under Rivalry," *The Quarterly Journal of Economics*, LXXXI: 3 (August 1967).
32. Prafulla Joglekar and Morris Hamburg, "An Evaluation of Federal Policy Instruments to Stimulate Basic Research in Industry," *Management Science*, 29: 7 (September 1983), pp. 997-1015.
33. Prafulla Joglekar and Morris Hamburg, "An Evaluation of Federal Policies Concerning Joint Ventures for Applied Research," *Management Science*, 29: 7 (September 1983), pp. 1016-26.

34. Prafulla Joglekar and Morris Hamburg, "A Homogeneous Industry Model of Re-source Allocation to Basic Research and Its Policy Implications," *Management Science*, 32: 2 (February 1986), pp. 225-36.
35. George Eads and Richard R. Nelson, "Government Support of Advanced Civil-ian Technology: Power Reactors and Supersonic Transports," *Public Policy*, 19 (1971), pp. 405-27.
36. Richard R. Nelson and Richard N. Langlois, "Industrial Innovation Policy: Les-sons from American History," *Science*, 219 (February 18, 1983), pp. 814-18.
37. Eads and Nelson, op. cit.
38. Nelson and Langlois, op. cit.
39. *Science*, (May 15, 1970), p. 802.
40. Nicholas A. Engler and Joseph P. Martino, "Is Research Still Fun," (Dayton, OH: University of Dayton, 1986).

10

Universities and the Training of Scientists

Cotton M. Lindsay

A Committee on Undergraduate Science and Engineering Education of the National Science Board published a finding (March 1986) that declared:

> Unless education in mathematics, engineering, and the sciences is made more effective for all students and more attractive to potential faculty members, and especially to the presently under-represented (women, minorities, and the physically handicapped), both the quality and the number of newly-educated professionals in these important fields will fall well below the Nation's needs—with predictable harm to its economy and security.

No attempt was made in the findings of this report to identify the needs that would go unsatisfied or to specify the nature of the harm that was anticipated. On the contrary, this report, whose chief theme is a call for greater financial support for university science programs, seems to document only one fact—that the universities are doing an unsatisfactory job at present.[1]

This paper concerns itself with these issues posed but left unanswered by the report of the National Science Board. Is there a shortage of scientists and engineers in the United States today? What indeed is a shortage, and what, if any, are the implications of a such a shortage for government policy? Indeed, is there a role for government involvement in the education and training of scientists? The answers to these questions are not self-evident.

A Taxonomy of Shortages

Concerns over a so-called shortage of scientific and engineering personnel occur with frequency in the media, in industry forums, and on the floors of Congress. In 1980 this concern expressed itself in the formation of the Committee on Education and Utilization of the Engineer by the National Research Council to conduct a study of the state and the future of engineering education and practice in the United States. It also resulted in the organization of a symposium on labor market conditions for engineers by the Office of Scientific and Engineering Personnel in February 1984, and in the establishment of a biennial series of publications entitled *Science and Engineering Personnel: A National Overview* by the National Science Foundation.

As material of this sort grows increasingly refined, and thus necessarily more technical, it is important to understand precisely what is meant by the finding of a shortage or its opposite, a surplus. The designation of a shortage means not having enough. The presence or absence of a shortage must therefore turn on the definition of enough, and enough can be defined in a variety of ways. The latest NSF *National Overview* lists a number of margins in which scientists and engineers play major roles, including "efforts critical to promoting technological innovation and economic growth as well as improving industrial productivity, international competitiveness, and national security."[2]

It is rare when someone who alleges to have identified shortage or surplus actually makes an empirical connection between goals such as these and current labor market conditions. On the contrary, after paying lip service to the set of arenas that define having enough (or too many), including those mentioned above, the methodology typically veers off into a less demanding, if at the same time less informative, quest. For the purposes of the studies in question "enough" is thereafter defined in terms of labor market conditions in the present or some golden era of growth and innovation in the past. The question addressed in practice is whether we have or can expect to have enough scientific and engineering (s/e) personnel to fill positions that are expected to become vacant either through retirement or through growth in demand.

This is not a meaningless exercise. It can provide valuable guidance to educational planners, to those in authority who seek to know the effectiveness of existing or planned programs for the support of science and engineering, and finally to young scholars, who may be considering a career in one of these fields. However, although useful, these studies do not answer the questions they pose, and it is important to understand why they do not and thus to appreciate the shortcomings of these studies.

Contributing to this confusion is the fact that economists use the word "shortage" to mean at least three distinct things. The conditions giving rise to each of these shortages are quite different, hence their implications for policy differ radically. The place to start a critique of these studies is therefore to define each type of shortage and to describe the conditions in which it might emerge.

Shortage Meaning Price Is Too Low

To someone with a little economics training, the word shortage means only one thing, that the market price is too low. More is demanded than will be supplied at the existing wage. The difference in these two quantities is called a shortage. Under normal conditions, we give little concern to shortages of this type. Competition by employers can be expected to push the wage rate up to its equilibrium level. And, as the wage rate rises, the difference between the quantity demanded and supplied diminishes. Unless for some reason (like the imposition of wage controls) the wage rate is prevented from clearing the market, such a shortage will soon eliminate itself. The policy implications of the existence of such a shortage are clear: promote wage and price flexibility and foster labor mobility to admit rapid expansion of supply toward the equilibrium number. Nothing more is required.

Shortage Meaning Price Is Too High

Ironically, economists have also identified as a shortage conditions under which price is actually higher than its long-run equilibrium level. In the same vein a "surplus" is associated with conditions in which the current price is lower than the equilibrium price in the long run. Pronouncements concerning the presence of a shortage or its opposite must obviously be interpreted with care.

This interpretation of conditions is appropriate in labor markets like s/e manpower, where the "pipeline" from market signal to the output of a trained worker is substantial and where it is desirable to have an even age distribution of workers in the field. Full long-run equilibrium requires that the existing wage bring forth exactly the number of new workers required to replace those leaving plus any net increment required due to demand growth. A shift in demand that raises earnings of already trained workers in these fields significantly above their long-run equilibrium level will not under normal circumstances return immediately to equilibrium. In the interim a technical shortage exists: the wages of workers in this field are higher than at equilibrium, and fewer workers are supplying labor in this market than are required at equilibrium.

Depending on the magnitude of the shift in demand, it may take years for supply to expand to the extent necessary to restore equilibrium. Even if potential science and engineering students have unbiased information about current market conditions, it will take a considerable period of time after conditions become more favorable for supply to eliminate the implied shortage, defined in this case as the difference in the existing supply and the supply required to return the wage down to the equilibrium level. Students who recognize the more attractive market conditions must still be trained, and the rate at which increasing numbers may be turned out by science and engineering programs depends on the capacity of our training facilities. Qualified students may seek admission to these training institutions, in response to this perceived shortage, in larger numbers than there is the capacity to admit them.

Statistical Identification

One method of identifying the presence or absence of such a shortage is to estimate the system of structural equations that characterize this market. Such a system was estimated by Keith B. Leffler and Cotton M. Lindsay for physicians in the United States over the period 1947 to 1973, and the resulting system was used to forecast conditions in this market from 1978 to the year 2000.[3]

Estimation of such a structural model for s/e manpower would require separate estimates of the demand for these personnel, the demand for and the supply of university positions for the training of inflow of new scientists and engineers, as well as supply from other sources such as foreign-trained personnel. Once estimated, the position of short-run supply relative to the long-run equilibrium quantity in each year identifies the magnitude of the shortage, if any, in that year.

The success of this model in its application to the market for physicians suggests that conditions in the s/e manpower market can be reasonably simulated. Indeed, Richard B. Freeman's (1972) estimates, though now out of date, provide a good framework for the development of such a model. However, recent projections of shortages have eschewed this approach in favor of far less informative methodologies.[4]

Human Capital Returns

A widely used method requiring a far less extensive data base, though providing less guidance, is to estimate the profitability of investment by potential students in s/e training. The return stream over the expected career of the trainee is estimated using the difference in current wage earnings profiles between the occupation to be evaluated and an alternative career lacking this training. The cost of such an investment is estimated by imputing foregone earnings during the training period and a measure of the direct cost of tuition, books, and so on. The difference in the present values of the returns and cost streams measures the profitability of such investments by young scholars.

The presumption is that, given free entry, these profits will fall to zero when supply expands to the long-run equilibrium number of s/e personnel.[5] A finding of positive profits may be interpreted as indicating that wages in these occupations are higher than the long-run equilibrium level, that is, that a shortage of this type exists in this market. In similar fashion, a finding of losses indicates that wages are lower than might be expected in long-run equilibrium and that a surplus of these personnel exists currently.

Although indicative of current market conditions, this methodology is not without problems. The estimated profitability of investment in s/e training depends critically on the choice of the interest rates used to discount expected future earnings in the chosen careers. The correct rate is that at which young unsecured borrowers might obtain loans to finance their consumption while in school. Leffler and Lindsay (1981) have estimated such a rate for medical students, but there are good reasons to believe that the interest rate faced by science or engineering students is higher.[6] The rate of noncompletion of schooling among medical students is very low, and their expected earnings upon graduation considerably higher than those of s/e personnel. A lender is thus exposed to less risk of nonpayment of such loans among medical students and may, therefore, lend at lower rates.

Also of concern is the correct measurement of the return stream for such human capital investors. Conventional practice is to accept the premium in earnings received by graduates over the earnings of those with only a high school education as a measure of the return stream on these investments. Lindsay has pointed out that such estimates of these returns are biased downward, and that it will typically be necessary to correct for the expected longer hours worked in more human capital intensive occupations before the presence or absence of a shortage or surplus can be identified with confidence.[7] In technical terms, this bias emerges because a portion of the earnings differential between the career requiring training and that lacking the training reflects the substitution effect of the higher opportunity cost of leisure in the higher-wage occupation. Methods of correcting this bias are discussed in Lindsay (1971) and are implemented in Lindsay (1983).[8]

Because all occupations are not equally attractive, another source of bias enters these calculations. Implicitly, this methodology attributes any premium earned in engineering or in a scientific field over earnings requiring no college to the investment in college itself (ignoring the treatment of a work intensity differential discussed in the previous paragraph). However, some, and perhaps all, potential s/e personnel would be willing to give up some earnings to perform this work. It may be the case, in other words, that at the long-run equilibrium in this market suppliers of these services are willingly accepting losses on their human capital investments.

A single snapshot estimate of the profitability of investments in training for a single career can therefore give a deceptive message. One way to partially control for these nonpecuniary characteristics of alternative careers is to estimate returns in a widely separated range of years to attempt to determine whether excess or subnormal returns seem endemic to the occupation under consideration. Where this is found to be the case, a correction factor can be applied to determine the net profitability of the investment. This procedure is discussed in Lindsay.[9]

Assuming that the above mentioned difficulties have been taken into account, positive net profitability will indicate the presence of a shortage or surplus in a particular career. Unfortunately, this procedure will not indicate

the numerical magnitude of this shortage, as will the structural procedure outlined above. It will indicate, in other words, the extent to which earnings in
s/e careers exceed or fall short of the long-run equilibrium earnings in such
careers. However, it will not inform us concerning the number of additional
s/e workers that are required to reach that long-run equilibrium condition in
markets where shortages are identified. Some measure of long-run demand
and supply conditions in these markets is required to assess the quantitative
dimensions of these sorts of shortages and surpluses.

Policy Implications

The policy implications of these sorts of shortages are more complex than
are those of the simple static shortage or surplus associated with incomplete
price adjustment. The elimination of a shortage of this type can impose large
economic costs on society, and the gains from a rapid return to equilibrium
must be weighed against those costs. Expansion of the supply of s/e personnel
to close these gaps requires an extension of the nation's training capacity, and
the extension of this capacity comes at a substantial price.

Where expansion of training capacity is deemed necessary, this should be
done carefully with an eye toward a few common-sense observations. Much
of the investment in training facilities is not recoverable. A large increase to
meet perceived shortages will rapidly leave a substantial capacity redundant
in a few years. The sad result of over-rapid expansion of medical school capacity to relieve shortages produced by the introduction of Medicare and
Medicaid in the late 1960s is particularly instructive.

In the decade and a half following the enactment of that legislation medical
school capacity more than doubled. The capacity in 1965 provided an inflow
of students consistent with a steady-state stock of physicians of almost exactly the number practicing in that year (based on an expected forty-year career in medicine). Doubling the rate of output, of course, doubles the eventual
steady-state stock. Even allowing for the predicted population growth to 242
million in the U.S. by the year 2000, this suggests an eventual increase in the
physician population ratio by that year of roughly 60 percent.

The lesson of this experience should be clear. Small changes in the rate at
which people are trained can yield, after a sufficient period of time, large
changes in the number performing this work. As this investment is largely
irreversible, the cost of reaching equilibrium sooner may be a period of costly
surplus in subsequent years. Great care should therefore be taken to examine long-run future consequences of changes in the rates at which these long-
lived assets are produced before the "quick fix" to a perceived shortage is
applied. The cure, as in the case of U.S. physicians, might be worse than the

disease. Perhaps more important is the fact that shortages measured in terms of human capital profitability are themselves dependent on the level of support currently provided to training institutions. If, for example, the government were to suddenly double the support provided to all students of science and engineering, this training would become economically more attractive from a human capital investment point of view. The implications of these observations for the use of this standard of having enough are not encouraging to the policy analyst. A situation in which the market is in equilibrium by this definition can be transformed into a shortage by having the government increase its support of s/e students. Such a definition of a shortage has serious limitations.

An Economic Shortage

Up to this point we have considered two types of shortage, that associated with incomplete price adjustment and that associated with the extended pipeline time from market signal to emergence of the trained respondents to that signal. Neither of these measures relate the existing stock of trained manpower to the policy norms mentioned in the introduction. Efficiency is the standard by which achievement in these terms is measured, and neither of these shortages really informs us concerning this important standard. Unfortunately, there is no direct way to gauge the efficient number of trained personnel of a particular kind. We can define this standard in theory, and we can infer things about its satisfaction in different market settings, but economics simply does not offer a means of assessing efficiency directly. We can, however, muster indirect evidence that sheds light on the efficiency of present stocks of this manpower (see below). We will therefore consider what theory says about the economically efficient stock of s/e personnel, then consider some indirect evidence.

The economically efficient number of s/e manpower is that which equates social contributions and social costs of these resources at the margin. If social cost were fully borne by suppliers of these services in the market and social contribution were fully reflected in the earnings of these workers, we might presume that market and economic shortages were identical. In the complex world in which we live, however, neither condition is satisfied to permit us this easy a way out.

On the demand side, we have the appropriability problem. The product produced by s/e manpower is knowledge which, once produced, is difficult to market successfully to demanders. In some cases the protection of property rights in knowledge, through patents and secrecy, fail to guarantee sufficient rewards to make efficient investment in this good attractive. The allocative problem posed by the appropriability of a good may be summarized as follows: the supplier may not withhold his product in order to command payment from consumers. The appropriability problem is a feature of a class of goods referred to in economics as "collective consumption goods," or public goods. There is a presumption among economists that achievement of efficiency requires government involvement to overcome this and other problems. Though this literature is vast, formal demonstrations of a reduction in transaction costs with government involvement are lacking, and the arguments are typically poorly framed. Indeed, the appropriability problem is often offered as a justification for government involvement in scientific research as well as in the training of scientific personnel. In the absence of any other intervention in the market for s/e manpower, one might conclude that an economic shortage of these resources was present, the result of the appropriability problem on the demand side.

However, the appropriability problem is not observed in this sort of isolation. In the first place, one of the major demanders of the services of these personnel is the government. As shown in Table 10.1, nearly 14 percent of all scientists and 11.6 percent of all engineers are employed by government. More than one quarter of all scientists are employed by universities that also enjoy substantial government subsidies. This support adds to the demands that private users of this knowledge register in the market, increasing its value above marginal private contribution. On the supply side, the social costs of supplying these services are partially borne by the government as well. Large subsidies to the training of engineering and scientific manpower are provided, lowering the cost of acquiring these skills below their marginal social costs.

The net effect of this existing intervention by government on both sides of the market is to expand the long-run equilibrium number of scientists and engineers in this country. In the absence of any such programs, it seems plausible that the market equilibrium quantity would contain too few. In view of the extensiveness of these subsidy programs, however, any such conclusion is difficult to credit. We have no way of knowing the position of the optimum economic number relative to the market equilibrium to justify such a conclusion.

Importing Knowledge

Before moving to a discussion of recent studies that purport to identify shortages, as well as some preliminary estimates of my own, it is worthwhile to consider briefly the issue of appropriability from an international point of view. The argument is made that scientific knowledge may be underproduced by unregulated markets due to its public good characteristics. Where such knowledge in not appropriable, producers will find it difficult to capture its

TABLE 10.1
Employment Patterns, Scientists, and Engineers in the U.S., 1982

Type of Employer	Engineers	Reported	Pct. of Scientists	Pct. of Reported
Bus./Industry	360,045	51.5	843,952	83.2
Educ. Inst.	192,214	27.5	32,148	3.2
Government	96,836	13.9	117,685	11.6
Other Reported	49,416	7.1	20,258	2.0
Not Reported	9,961		36,829	
Total	708,472		1,050,872	
Total Reporting	698,511		1,014,043	

Source: National Science Foundation, *The 1982 Postcensal Survey of Scientists and Engineers,* 1984, Table B-19.

full market value through sale, hence less than the socially optimal amount will be produced.

A role for government can emerge from this discussion; in the absence of other government intervention, social welfare can be increased through government subsidies to appropriate types of scientific research and perhaps to the training of scientific manpower. There remains, however, one aspect of this issue that needs to be considered. Even if it were possible to determine that the extent of scientific research and training was insufficient, there is no implicit mandate that the *American* government finance the necessary subsidies.

There are many nations with the economic resources that permit them to invest in scientific research and the trained personnel capable of filling such a perceived gap. It might be argued that research of this type confers advantages on the country sponsoring such research, but there is no evidence that this is true. On the contrary, it is precisely where the production of such knowledge confers advantages that the role of government in its finance is vitiated. For, if inventions may be protected from competing users, including users overseas, then the knowledge is by definition appropriable, and private producers will produce it in efficient amounts. If, on the other hand, new knowledge is of a type that moves freely across international borders, then we need not fear a loss of international competitiveness in allowing other governments to share the cost of its discovery.

Importing Scientists

In a similar vein it can be argued that in providing ourselves with efficient numbers of trained s/e personnel we should also not turn our backs on the international labor market. Just as it can be argued that a country need not provide a home for those who make discoveries in order to enjoy the fruits of scientific research, the argument can be extended to scientists themselves. In order to increase the number of scientists and engineers, it is not necessary to train them. In the first case, one imports the technology or the already produced products, or both. In the second case, one imports the scientists and engineers already trained. Indeed, this result requires little active policy on the part of the government at all; an easing of immigration restrictions is all that is required to promote, rather than inhibit, a "brain drain," wherein the U.S. is the net beneficiary.

The example of the market for physicians in America provides a reasonable laboratory with which to examine this strategy at work. Doctors are even less mobile than are scientists and engineers, because the nature of medical practice is such that it is costly for physicians to leave established practices to settle elsewhere. Yet, during the late 1960s and early to mid-1970s when Medicare and Medicaid had dramatically expanded the demand for physician care, we imported large numbers of foreign-trained physicians. Indeed, at its peak in 1976 the proportion of newly licensed doctors in this country trained elsewhere amounted to more than one third.

The strategy implied by the foregoing arguments is to import already trained s/e personnel from foreign countries so as to avoid some of the costs of their education. U.S. policy here seems to be precisely the opposite of this model. We are devoting a large share of our s/e training resources to foreign nationals. For example, a study by the Labor Policies Studies Program, Oak Ridge Associated Universities, suggests that half of the engineering Ph.D.'s awarded in 1981 went to students possessing either temporary or permanent visas.[10] Approximately 20 percent of these foreign students possessed permanent visas. To be sure, a large number of these foreign nationals remained to be employed in the United States. For example, as many as 62 percent of these foreign national Ph.D. engineers trained in U.S. universities in 1980–81 and 56 percent of the foreign Ph.D. physical scientists and mathematicians trained here were employed here in 1982.

Still, even if we were to retain two out of every three of these students, this seems an unusually costly way to supplement our pool of s/e manpower. For every two foreign nationals we train and keep we have to bear the cost of training one who works elsewhere. Or put differently, one out of every five Ph.D. engineers and a larger proportion of the Ph.D. scientists trained in U.S. universities employ that training outside the United States. It is clear that all nations cannot simultaneously reduce the burden of scientific support by importing scientists and engineers from abroad. Everyone cannot be a net importer of s/e personnel. It would appear, however, that we are presently bearing a disproportionately large share of this worldwide burden.

Recent Projections

Concern over possible existing or future shortages, in engineering in particular, have led to an outpouring of research into this issue in recent years. The American Electronics Association has recently produced a survey-based projection of market conditions for eight categories of professional engineer and technician and for four categories of technical paraprofessional. A summary of this study is provided in Pat Hill Hubbard.[11] Attracting more concern, however, are the highly technical projections of the Bureau of Labor Statistics (BLS) on the one hand and the National Science Foundation projections on the other.[12]

Although the BLS study makes projections through 1995, while the NSF confines its projections to 1987, the procedures are quite similar, so that there is little reason to discuss them separately. Both conclude that, with the exception of certain areas such as computer specialists and aeronautical engineers, there is no evidence of an existing or predictable shortage. While providing some reassurance that conditions will not be remarkably different in the near future than they were in the past, these studies are of limited value in answering the question of whether there will be enough scientists and engineers in the sense that we have addressed here.

Both proceed by examining the net effect of inflows and outflows on the supply side of the market and by comparing it to the engineering and scientific manpower requirements forecast for the reference years. The potential inflows are represented by graduates of training programs, immigrants from abroad, and occupational mobility. The potential outflows are due to separations, retirements, and deaths. These flows are projected forward and compared with an estimate of total employment in these areas to determine the extent of imbalance, if any, between these two figures. No effort is made to relate the extent of impact any of these flows will have on the supply side to wages paid.

Interpretation

In addition, behavior on the demand side of the market is not modeled in a sensible way. So-called requirements are obtained by harnessing a massive input/output table to determine the number of engineers and scientists of each category required per dollar of output produced in each sector of the economy. Output of each sector is then forecast, and the requirements are simply added up. The model, therefore, relies on the grossly illogical assumption of a fixed production of technology compared to production in which industry demand for labor of a particular type depends solely on industry output. Wages in such an industry play no role in determining requirements.

Furthermore, these requirements themselves (i.e., the input/output ratios) are not themselves based on market equilibria, representing, therefore, in some sense conditions that prevailed when quantities demanded and supplied were in balance. Rather they reflect conditions that existed in some base year when the original input/output table was assembled. The basis for these projections may therefore be a reference requirement that itself represents severe shortage or surplus conditions.

It is precisely this sort of planning in terms of available resources on the one hand and ad hoc requirements on the other that is responsible for the gross market imbalances observed in Eastern Bloc countries, where shortages and surpluses are the rule. The long frustration of these countries with attempts to regulate production and distribution through a planning model that takes no account of market forces should warn us not to take too seriously results based on similar formulations. One hopes that the agencies that sponsored the development of these studies will in the future turn their efforts toward economic models that make better economic sense.

A Test of the Effects of S/E Support

Science and Output

We have raised the possibility that government support of science and international competitiveness are unrelated. We stated that an efficiency argument for government support of science holds only for scientific discoveries that are truly inappropriable, and to the extent to which this knowledge is appropriable it will flow freely across international boundaries, conferring its effect on all countries equally.

In this sense, there is real reason to restrain our support of scientific research in this country and to rely on our international neighbors to fund it. There is more to this argument than merely shifting a portion of this cost onto others. Subsidies to science and engineering provided by the government must be financed through taxation, and the greater the tax burden, the larger the social cost of the dislocations and inefficiencies produced by the tax structure itself. By levying additional taxes to fund scientific research, we therefore not only confer the benefits of that research to other countries free of charge, but we impose additional tax distortions on our own economy and impair our ability to compete.

Such a conjecture is difficult to test. International data on support for scientific research and s/e training are scanty and provide little more than anecdotal support at best. Yet they do support it. Japan and Germany, two countries that experienced rapid economic growth in the postwar period have historically devoted a share of

GNP to government-financed R&D of between a half and a third of that of the U.S.(Organization for Economic Cooperation and Development).[13]

A test of sorts may be performed on this hypothesis, however, using state data. Although no language barriers exist among states, the importance of a common language in the diffusion of knowledge is easy to exaggerate. It is far less costly to learn a language than it is to learn electrical engineering. Furthermore, if there are engineers and scientists in this country trained abroad, these personnel may acquire the knowledge developed elsewhere with ease and transmit it to their fellow workers.

We hypothesize that the rate of growth of individual states in the U.S. is unaffected by government support of science research or training in that state. Rather, we maintain that the knowledge produced in any one state flows across state boundaries. To the extent to which it contributes to measurable growth at all, we hypothesize that it does so uniformly in all states, regardless of the level of science support.

The Support Variables

The hypothesis was tested using multiple regression analysis. The dependent variable in the regression is the rate of increase in per capita income over the decade of the 1970s. This is our measure of economic growth. Two variables were used to capture the effect of scientific support by state. The first of these is the proportion of the population by state that are scientists or engineers, i.e., the per capita number of s/e personnel. These data were taken from the 1982 Postcensal Survey of Scientists and Engineers.[14] Though they relate to a year outside the period of study, the populations of engineers and people in general in a state change slowly, and there is every reason to believe that the 1982 proportion of scientists and engineers is an excellent proxy for that proportion during the 1970s.

The second regressor employed is the per capita federally funded research and development expenditures at universities and colleges for 1976. Data by state are unavailable for years before 1976, and expenditures after this date would logically have little time to affect growth during the decade in question. The distribution of these funds seems to exhibit a great deal of stability over the period, however, and it seems reasonable to assume that the 1976 distribution is representative of that spending over the entire decade.

Other Explanatory Variables

Other factors clearly contribute to the growth of states. It has been argued that the 1970s witnessed a so-called sunbelt effect as industry moved into states on the southern perimeter of the country due to a combination of low wages, lack of union strength, and favorable climate. In order to control for the possible effects of these factors three variables were added to the regression. Manufacturing wages rates for 1975 were included, as were the percent of workforce who were union members in 1976, and normal daily temperature in the month of February.

Another important factor in the growth of income in states during the 1970s was the effect of rapidly growing oil prices due to output restrictions by OPEC. States with substantial oil reserves during that decade could expect growth resulting from the exploitation of these mineral resources. A variable was therefore included measuring crude oil production in 1975.

Education is often claimed to be a stimulus for growth. Undoubtedly there is a correlation between the level of education attained and income as attested by hosts of studies of this effect by economists in the past two decades. These tests are typically framed in terms of years of schooling rather than in educational spending, however. It is less clear that increased government spending on education improves earnings. We nevertheless included a variable measuring per capita direct state and local expenditure for education, to test the hypothesis that high levels of expenditure affect state economic growth.

Finally, as pointed out earlier, economic theory suggests that taxes retard economic activity by distorting resource allocation and by reducing incentives to produce. Two variables were included to measure this effect. First, a high level of taxes will make economic expansion and development unattractive to local businesses as well as to potential developers from other states. A variable measuring the per capita tax burden for 1967 was included for this purpose. Secondly, an increasing tax burden will signal the possibility of even higher future taxes and will discourage long-range projects. We therefore included in the regression a measure of the increase in per capita taxes from 1970 to 1980.

Statistical Findings

Regression results are reported in Table 10.2. As is apparent from the results on the two science variables, our test failed to reject the null hypothesis that government support for science does not foster economic growth. Although in this regression the coefficients of these variables have positive signs, both have very low t-ratios and are thus insignificantly different from zero. Indeed, when some variables are omitted, the coefficient on R&D expenditure is negative and significant.

These findings are inconclusive concerning a sunbelt effect. Although union strength does seem to retard growth, the wage rate variable has the wrong

TABLE 10.2
Income Growth by State, 1970–1980

R² – .64 Variable	F – 7.96 Estimated	N – 50 Coefficient/(t-ratio)
Intercept	1.9876	(9.61)
Science Variables		
S/E per capita	1.8598	(0.22)
Fed. R&D per capita	0.1629	(0.12)
Sunbelt Variables		
Manu. Wages 1975	0.0011	(1.34)
Union Membership	-0.0037	(1.70)
February Temp.	-0.0011	(0.62)
Educ Spending per capita	0.0030	(0.36)
Taxation Variables		
Tax per capita 1967	-0.0011	(3.29)
Tax growth 70-80	-0.0947	(4.28)

sign; wages in manufacturing are positively related to growth at a very weak significance level, a finding inconsistent with the sunbelt effect story. Temperature, the variable with the clearest association with the sunbelt states themselves, did not predict growth at all. State and local expenditure on education was also unrelated to growth.

The tax variables both performed as predicted, however. The effects on growth of both these variables were negative and highly significant. Indeed, a $100 premium in taxes in 1967 was sufficient to reduce nominal growth over the decade by a full 10.6 percent. An increase in the rate of tax growth from the first to the third quartile among states was sufficient to reduce growth over the decade by another 9.5 percent.

Conclusions

This chapter has been about shortages of scientific and engineering manpower and whether the government is doing enough to support the training of these personnel in this country. A portion of the chapter was devoted to a discussion of the shortcomings of the methodology with which both the labor department and NSF assess these shortages. Although this methodology purports to identify and measure economic shortages, they in fact do little more than compare tomorrow with yesterday. The question of why yesterday is a benchmark for anything is never made clear.

An argument for some government to provide some support can be made. However, the present government already provides a rich menu of programs fostering both the development of new ideas and the training of personnel to discover them. Arguments about appropriability of knowledge cannot be used to justify an open-ended commitment to science. There is some point clearly beyond which the value of additional resources committed to science is less than its opportunity cost. Second, public good arguments such as these typically fail to come to grips with the fact that there are many nations and thus many governments. The very nature of the appropriability problem implies that scientific knowledge produced abroad can be substituted for home-produced knowledge with little loss.

It has been argued that scientific knowledge moves readily across borders and that countries that lag behind others in the production of knowledge can nevertheless enjoy its fruits at little cost in terms of economic growth and competitiveness. The last section of this chapter tests this hypothesis on U.S. data by state. The failure of the number of scientists or of the amount of government funding of research to affect income growth lends credence to this hypothesis.

Notes

1. It is revealing to note that of the 27 witnesses who testified before the committee at public hearings, 19 were representatives of universities or teacher groups. Four were high-tech industry representatives, and three were public employees.
2. National Science Foundation, *Science and Engineering Personnel: A National Overview*, (Washington, D.C., NSF, 1985, p. vi–viii).
3. Keith B. Leffler and Cotton M. Lindsay, "Markets for Medical Care and Medical Education: A Long-Run Structural Approach," *Journal of Human Resources,* 16 (Winter 1981), pp. 20–40.
4. Richard B. Freeman, *The Market for College Trained Manpower: A Study in the Economics of Career Choice*, (Cambridge, MA: Harvard University Press, 1971; and Richard B. Freeman, *The Overeducated American*, (New York: Academic Press, 1976).
5. See W. Lee Hansen, "Total and Private Rates of Return to Investment in Schooling," *Journal of Political Economy,* 71 (April 1963), pp. 128–40; and W. Lee Hansen, "Shortages and Investment in Health Manpower," *The Economics of Health and Medical Care*, (Ann Arbor, MI: University of Michigan Press, 1964) for early statements of this methodology. Hansen's use of the internal rate of return for this assessment can be misleading, however. This problem is discussed in Cotton M. Lindsay, "Measuring Human Capital Returns," *Journal of Political Economy,* 79 (November/December 1971), pp. 1195–215.
6. Keith B. Leffler and Cotton M. Lindsay, "Student Discount Rates, Consmuption Loans and Subsidies to Professional Education," *Journal of Human Resources* 16 (Summer 1981), pp. 468–76.
7. Lindsay, "Measuring Human Capital Returns," op. cit.

8. Ibid.; and Cotton M. Lindsay, "Real Returns to Medical Education," *Journal of Human Resources*, 8 (Summer 1983), pp. 331–48.

9. Lindsay, op. cit., (1983).

10. *Foreign National Scientists and Engineers in the U.S. Labor Force 1972–1982 1972–82*. (Oak Ridge, TN: Labor and Policy Studies Program, Manpower Education, Research and Training Division, Oak Ridge Associated Universities, 1985).

11. Pat Hill Hubbard, "Technical Employment Projections, 1983–1987: A Summary," *Labor-Market Conditions for Engineers: Is There a Shortage?* (Washington, D.C.: Office of Scientific and Engineering Personnel, National Research Council, 1984), pp 11–26.

12. Results of the BLS projections are described in Ronald Kutchner, "Future Labor-Market Conditions for Engineers," *Labor-Market Conditions for Engineers: Is There a Shortage?* (Washington, D.C.: Office of Scientific Engineering Personnel, National Research Council, 1984), pp. 27–38. The NSF projections are described by Jean E. Vanski, "Projected Labor-Market Balance in Engineering and Computer Speciality Occupations, 1982–1987," *Labor-Market Conditions for Engineers: Is There a Shortage?* (Washington, D.C.: Office of Scientific and Engineering Personnel, National Research Council, 1984), pp. 39–58; and in National Science Foundation 85–302 (1985, Chapter 1).

13. *Patterns of Resources Devoted to Research and Experimental Development in the OCED Area*, (Paris, France: Organization for Economic Cooperation and Development1975). See also Rachel McCulloch, *Research and Development as a Determinant of U.S. International Competitiveness*, (Washington, D.C.: Committee on Changing International Realities, National Planning Association, 1978).

14. *The 1982 Postcensal Survey of Scientists and Engineers*, (Washington, D.C.: National Science Foundation, 1984), NSF 84–330.

About the Contributors

John W. Sommer, the editor of this volume, is Knight Distinguished Professor at the University of North Carolina and research fellow at The Independent Institute in Oakland, California. He received his Ph.D. in geography and regional science from Boston University, has been senior policy analyst at the National Science Foundation and dean of the School of Social Sciences at the University of Texas at Dallas, and has taught at Dartmouth College.

Dr. Sommer is a member of the Standing Committee on Science and Society for Sigma Xi, the Scientific Research Society, and he has been a fellow of the National Academy of Sciences, director of the Foreign Service Officer African Training Program at the African Studies Center, Boston University, and director of the Peace Corps Training Program for Togo and Grenada. He has further been a consultant to the governments of Kenya, Trinidad and Tobago, the State of Louisiana Board of Regents, and numerous business firms.

Dr. Sommer is the author of *Dallas: The Dynamics of Public/Private Cooperation, Games by Design, Human Geography in a Shrinking World, Modal Cities, Multidisciplinary Research and Education, Pockets of Poverty in Southwestern Cities,* and *The Quest for Excellence.* A contributor to numerous scholarly volumes, his many articles and reviews have appeared in *African Historical Studies, Annals of Regional Science, Cato Journal, Environment and Planning, Environmental Ethics, Focus, Historical Geography, Issues in Science and Technology, Journal of Geography, Ontario Geography, Pan African Journal, Science, Simulation and Games, Texas Business Review,* and many other journals. His articles have also appeared in *American Scientist, Reason, The Wall Street Journal,* and other publications.

Peter H. Aranson is professor of economics at Emory University and co-editor of *Public Choice.* He received his Ph.D. in political science from the University of Rochester and Dr. Aranson has taught at Carnegie-Mellon University, Georgia Institute of Technology, University of Miami, University of Michigan and University of Minnesota. He is a contributor to fifteen volumes, a member of the Editorial Board for the *Journal of Politics* and the *Cato Journal,* and the author of the book, *American Government: Strategy and Choice.* His articles and reviews have appeared in the *Administrative Law Review, American Political Science Review, Cornell Law Review, Journal of Economic Literature, Supreme Court Law Review,* and other journals.

Stephen P. Dresch received his Ph.D. in economics from Yale University, and he been dean and professor of economics and business at the School of Business at Michigan Technological University, a member of the House of Representatives for the State of Michigan, research associate at the National Bureau of Economic Research, director of research in the economics of higher education at Yale University, chairman of the Institute for Demographic and Economic Studies, and research scholar at the International Institute for Applied Systems Analysis. A contributor to twenty scholarly volumes, Dr. Dresch is the author of *An Economic Perspective on the Evolution of Graduate Education, The Economics of Foreign Students, New Patterns for College Lending, Occupational Earnings 1967–81*, and *Substituting a Value-Added Tax for the Corporate Income Tax.*

Antony Flew is professor emeritus of philosophy at the University of Reading in England. He is a member of the Council of the Royal Institute of Philosophy, and he has taught at seventeen universities around the world. He is the author of over 175 articles and reviews in scholarly journals, and he is a contributor to the *Encyclopaedia Britannica, Collier's Encyclopaedia, Encyclopaedia of Bioethics* and the *Encyclopaedia of Philosophy*. Dr. Flew is the author or editor of thirty books, including *David Hume, Evolutionary Ethics, God and Philosophy, Hume's Philosophy of Belief, Thinking About Thinking, The Politics of Procrustes, A Rational Animal*, and *Sociology, Equality and Education.*

Nathan Glazer is professor of education and sociology at Harvard University, co-editor of *The Public Interest*, and a member of the Board of Advisors for The Independent Institute. He received his Ph.D. from Columbia University, and holds honorary doctoral degrees from Franklin and Marshall College, Colby College, Long Island University, and Hebrew Union College. Dr. Glazer has been appointed to various Presidential Task Forces on urban affairs and education as well as numerous committees for the National Academy of Sciences, and he is the author or editor of seventeen books, including *Affirmative Discrimination, Beyond the Melting Pot* (with D. Moynihan), *Ethnic Pluralism and Public Policy* (with K. Young), *The Limits of Social Policy, The Lonely Crowd* (with D. Riesman), and *The Urban Predicament* (with W. Gorham).

C. Ronald Kimberling is senior vice president and provost of Phillips Colleges, the largest private college system in the United States. Having graduated *summa cum laude* from the California State University at Northridge, he received masters degrees in American studies, mass communications, and English. Dr. Kimberling received his Ph.D. in English from the University of Southern California, and he is the recipient of five honorary doctoral degrees. Dr. Kimberling has served as director of enrollment at the University of Southern California, Assistant Secretary for Postsecondary Education in the U. S. Department of Education, and vice chairman and executive vice president of United Education and Software. He is a member of the Board of Trustees of West Coast University and the College of Oceaneering.

Cotton M. Lindsay is the J. Wilson Newman Professor of Managerial Economics at Clemson University. Having received his Ph.D. in economics from the University of Virginia, he has also taught at Arizona State University, Emory University and UCLA. Dr. Lindsay has been a member of the California Governor's Task Force on Regulation, member of the Health Policy Advisory Group for the 1980 Presidential Transition Team, and consultant to the U.S. General Accounting Office. He is the author or editor of the books, *Applied Price Theory*, *Contemporary Price Theory*, *Canadian National Health Insurance*, *National Health Issues*, *New Directions in Public Health Care*, *The Pharmaceutical Industry*, *Veteran Administration Hospitals*, and *Why the Draft?* His articles have appeared in numerous scholarly journals.

Joseph P. Martino is senior research scientist at the University of Dayton Research Institute. He received his Ph.D. in mathematics (statistics) from Ohio State University. He has been a fellow for the American Association for the Advancement of Science, associate editor of the journal *Technological Forecasting and Social Change*, director of engineering standardization at the Defense Electronics Supply Center, and chief of the Environmental Analysis Branch of the Air Force Office of Research Analyses. He is a contributor to the books, *Management of R&D and Engineering* (D. Kocaoglu, ed.), *Forecasting in the Social and Natural Sciences* (S. Schneider, ed.), and *Corporate Crisis Management* (S. Andriole, ed.), and the author of the books, *Technological Forecasting for Decision Making* and *The Use of Nuclear Weapons*.

Roger E. Meiners is professor of law and economics at the University of Texas at Arlington. Having received his Ph.D. in economics from Virginia Polytechnic Institute and State University, he has served as director of the Center for Policy Studies at Clemson University, director the Atlanta Regional Office of the Federal Trade Commission, associate director of the Law and Economics Center at Emory University, and member of the South Carolina Insurance Commission. A contributor to The Independent Institute's forthcoming book, *Hazardous to Your Health* (R. Hamowy, R. Stroup and D. Theroux, eds.), he is the author or editor of fourteen books including *Barriers to Corporate Growth* (with B. Baysinger and C. Zeithami), *Economic Consequences of Liability Rules* (with B. Yandle), *Federal Support of Higher Education* (with R. Amacher), *Managing in the Legal Environment* (with A. Ringleb and F. Edwards), *Taking the Environment Seriously* (with B. Yandle), *Victim Compensation*, and The Independent Institute's book, *Regulation and the Reagan Era* (with B. Yandle).

Joel H. Spring is professor of education at the State University of New York, College at Old Westbury, where his specialty is the history of educational policy in the twentieth century. A member of the Board of Advisors for The Independent Institute, he received his Ph.D. from the University of Wisconsin, and Dr. Spring is the author of *American Education, Conflict of Interests, Education and the Rise of the Corporate State, Educating the Worker-Citizen, A Primer of Libertarian Education,* and *The Sorting Machine Revisited.* His articles have appeared in *Educational Theory, History of Education Quarterly, School and Society, School Review,* and other journals.

Robert J. Staaf was professor of law and economics at Clemson University until his untimely death in 1991. He received his Ph.D. in economics from Temple University, and his J.D., *cum laude,* from the University of Miami. Dr. Staaf served as senior economist at the Federal Trade Commission, senior associate at the National Center of Higher Education Management, associate economist in the Division of Urban Affairs at the University of Delaware, and president of The Economic Associates. His books include *An Economic Theory of Learning, Externalities,* and *The Uses of Economics in Litigation* (with R. Miller), he was a contributor to fourteen volumes, and he authored thirty five articles in scholarly journals.

Edwin G. West is professor of economics at Carleton University, Ottawa, Canada. He received his Ph.D. from London University, and Dr. West has taught at Emory University, Oxford College of Technology, University of California at Berkeley, University of Chicago, University of Kent, University of Newcastle, and Virginia Polytechnic Institute and State University. He is the author or editor of *Adam Smith: The Man and His Works, Adam Smith and Modern Political Economy, Economics, Education and the Politician, Economics Today, Education and the Industrial Revolution, Education and the State, Non-Public School Aid, Student Loans,* and *Subsidizing the Performing Arts.* A contributor to numerous scholarly journals, his special areas of interest include public finance, the economics of education, and the history of economic thought.

Index